# THE
# WHISPERING
# GALLERY

*Beatrix, Rosamond, and John Lehmann*

# THE
# WHISPERING
# GALLERY

*Autobiography I*

---

## JOHN LEHMANN

HARCOURT, BRACE AND COMPANY
NEW YORK

# CONTENTS

*The frontispiece is reproduced from a photograph by
Howard Coster*

There is that whispering gallery where
A dark population of the air
Gives back to us those vocables
We dare not robe in syllables

I speak of the whispering gallery
Of all Dionysian poetry
Within whose precincts I have heard
An apotheosis of the word. . . .

GEORGE BARKER
(*Letter to a Young Poet*)

# INTRODUCTION

THERE are many reasons why one should wish to tell the story of one's life even at a time when one hopes that there is still a long stretch of it to come. Most of us have known people, of both sexes, who have been inspired to make a kind of manifesto for those who followed them out of a frank avowal of a path they have trod, in the manner of Rousseau; but I am certain I do not belong to their company. Others, defeated or maligned or suffering from one of the many forms of persecution mania, may feel the need to justify themselves in the face of their critics, real or imagined; being of a fairly sanguine temperament, I do not. Not that I 'lack gall to make oppression bitter'; rather, that I have never allowed myself to feel oppressed for very long, believing that one's life is full of unexpected twists and turns and that a new opportunity—as good as any one has met before—may be just round the next corner.

When I decided to write this book, I think my purpose was mixed from several quite different motives. I wanted, first of all, to tell a story I believed to be interesting to others besides myself, before the traces of it should be even more difficult to recover than they are already. I wanted, in that story, to re-create as far as possible the living forms of lovable and remarkable people I have known, who are now dead; and to give my own account of certain happenings and endeavours in which I was intimately involved, and which seem to me likely to be a matter of curiosity in the future—even if only for the studious explorers of the byways of literary history. Above all, I had come to the point where I wanted to understand myself by analysing my past, and perhaps in so doing help others who have followed the same bents to understand their own selves. In this age of accelerating hurry (nobody knows quite to what end) and distraction (for nobody knows quite what good), a sane man must surely want to possess his own past, pausing for a short while on the side of the track to reflect

and discriminate.   Perhaps in happier times people did so by
a kind of natural ease and instinct; nowadays it is scarcely
possible without putting it all down on paper.   And I count
myself lucky that a publisher's interest has helped to make the
pause longer than it could otherwise have been.

It would be absurd, of course, for me to try to tell the whole
story of my life.   For one thing, it would not be interesting to
more than a handful of people; for another, no one, I believe,
could endure to dig up and expose to public view the whole of
his past, with all its pains, its disappointments, its guilt—even
on the psychoanalyst's couch it resists the spade.   And if I
were put in the dock and had to swear that I had told ' the
truth, the whole truth, and nothing but the truth ', I should
have to tear the book up; memory not only falsifies innumerable details at different times in one's life—but is also, as
Proust was so well aware, a kind of sentry waiting for a password that one cannot possibly know beforehand.   To some
parts of my experience I discovered the passwords by lucky
chance; others I may never find.

In the face of these difficulties, what I decided to do was to
follow certain dominant themes through my life as far as I
could.   Poetry has always been an absorbing passion with
me: the reading of it, the study of the lives of the poets, and
the attempt to write it myself.   I do not think one needs to
estimate one's own contribution to a particular art very highly
to believe that the story of how one came to love it and practise
it, and to explore the secrets of its nature, may have some
significance and may even be stimulating to others who have
the capacity to do something very much better.   One theme,
therefore, that I have tried to follow through, is my education
in poetry.   And that will naturally lead to another theme: the
story of how my love for the spirit of poetry led me—by paths
already marked out by my ancestry, by impulses in the blood
and influences of early environment—to assume the role of
impresario to the creative work of others, both as editor and
publisher.

There is another theme which inevitably plays a large part
in this book, and that is the search for meaning.   Everyone
nowadays, except those lucky ones who never feel the need to

question or reject the religion of their fathers, is obliged to construct some working philosophy as a compass for his passage through the world, and if he remains spiritually alive is always changing and reconstructing it. I am the child of my generation; and if some parts of this story have a familiar ring, I can only plead that for truth's sake I cannot alter them and if that were all I had to tell I would not have written.

Some passages in the later books of this first volume inevitably overlap (though briefly) with certain chapters in two previous books of mine, *Down River* and *New Writing in Europe*; but as they are both long out of print, I hope I shall be forgiven by those who know them. I should also like to express my thanks to many who have helped me with advice and encouragement, in particular my sisters Rosamond and Beatrix, Mr. William Plomer, Mr. Victor Weybright of the *New American Library*, and Mr. John Guest of Messrs. Longmans, Green; to Mr. George Barker for allowing me to take the title of the book from the poem which I quote at the beginning of the Introduction; and my gratitude to my mother, to Mr. W. H. Auden, Mr. Quentin Bell, Mrs. Frances Cornford, Mr. E. M. Forster, Mr. Christopher Isherwood, Mrs. Orwell, Mr. V. S. Pritchett, Mr. Michael Redgrave, Mr. Stephen Spender, Frau Berthold Viertel, Mr. Leonard Woolf, Messrs. Jonathan Cape and The Hogarth Press, who have given me permission to quote from letters or other material in which they hold the copyright.

# I

## JEWELS IN A CAVE

*I was born to this house :*
*The joys, the terrors, groping thoughts and dreams,*
*Unconfined apprehensions of the world*
*That lie in childhood like jewels in a cave*
*Half in the light, half in unmeasured dark,*
*Had their scene here for me.*

# I

WHEN I try to remember where my education in poetry began, the first image that comes to mind is of my father's library at our old family home of Fieldhead, on the Thames. It is an autumn or winter evening after tea, for James the butler has been in to draw the blinds and close the curtains, and my father is reading under a green-shaded lamp. He is sitting in his big arm-chair, drawn up towards the fire blazing in the dark-tiled fireplace; and I am sitting opposite to him on a sofa, with a large red cushion on my lap. On the cushion is a heavy blue-bound volume of *Punch*—perhaps of 1871 or 1898 or 1907, the last having a special fascination for me as being the year of my birth, and therefore surely containing some mysterious presages of destiny—and I am completely absorbed in it, not for the first time nor probably for the second or third time, for a great part of my childhood seems to have been spent in looking through the long series of *Punch* volumes. We were all of us—Helen, Rosamond, Beatrix and myself—immensely proud of our father's connection with it. When he retired in 1919 he had been a member of the ' Table '—on which his initials are still to be seen, carved close to those of Thackeray—for just on thirty years, and nearly every week until his last illness some prose sketch or verses had appeared above the familiar initials of R.C.L. in its pages. Our pride stimulated our interest in the past of *Punch*, and I think I learnt more of the social and political history of England by going through the bound volumes over and over again as a child, than years of later schooling taught me. There was even a time when I believed I could go to the shelf and immediately draw out the right volume when any particularly famous cartoon or drawing was mentioned. I had my favourites among the artists: Tenniel frightened me a little, but his grim and powerful cartoons bit deep into my imagination; it was only later that I learnt to appreciate at its proper value the

3

delicate art of Charles Keene; but Du Maurier above all attracted me, and I knew some of his drawings so well that I could almost believe I had been present in those elegant music-rooms and conservatories myself when the so elaborately documented jokes had been made.

Let me try to describe the library. My father had had it built on to the house after his marriage, when he also built the children's wing in which we grew up, thus transforming a bachelor's establishment, designed for a life devoted to the pleasures of the river, into a roomy family home. It had a high ceiling like a college hall, which made it seem of vast proportions to a small boy coming down from his nursery for the enchanted hours before bed-time. The effect of height was enhanced by the row of windows running above the book-cases which covered the entire north wall. Up there, on the in-accessible sills, my father had put some of his athletic medals and cups and a bronze statue of a rather limp-looking youth in modest nineteenth-century rowing costume, which had been presented to him for coaching the *Berliner Ruder Klub* many years before I was born. I remember considering it with feelings of anxiety, tinged even with shame, during the first war, when it was bad enough for a boy in his first year at a private school to bear a German name, and being glad that it was out of reach—its inscription perhaps out of sight.

The south wall, broken by the big fireplace and the door, was also covered with book-cases, and above them, in ornate gilt frames, some large and rather lifeless portraits in oils by my great-uncle Rudolf: my father as a young man, my grand-father in a jaunty sombrero with folded arms, Wilkie Collins, and James Payn the witty and much-loved editor of *The Cornhill*. To me they were as awe-inspiring as they were remote; but more awe-inspiring and more remote was the portrait, also by my great-uncle, of a smartly-dressed, white-bearded Robert Browning, which was hung high up above the carved screen that opened on to the eastern window-embrasure. Appropriately facing the bard, who looked in his portrait more like the successful chairman of a city finance company, at the other end of the room and above the french windows that gave on to the garden, was an outsize picture of a genial French

Abbé sipping his wine and reading a book: a terrible picture, but it had been painted by Pen Browning, and my grandfather had bought it for 150 guineas in 1876, more I believe to please his friend, the artist's father, who wrote him an enthusiastic letter of thanks for the encouragement he had given Pen, than because he found any special merit in it. Another much-treasured Browning relic stood in its frame on the mantelpiece: a piece of notepaper from my grandfather's house at 15 Berkeley Square, on which Browning had written a few lines in 1886 in the most diminutive handwriting imaginable, to prove to an assembled dinner-party that his eyesight was still perfect. Even as a boy I found difficulty in deciphering the four lines in English, let alone the two exquisitely neat quotations from the Greek, without a magnifying glass.

The special atmosphere of the library, which I can recall to mind with the utmost vividness at any time, wherever I may be, came partly from the high beam-striped roof without ceiling, but chiefly from the books in all the darkly glowing colours of their gold-printed leather bindings. The main part of the collection had been bought and bound by my grandfather, and was almost entirely contemporary to his own day, except for some early nineteenth-century editions of the Elizabethan dramatists; my father had added some sets, old and new, of his favourite seventeenth- and eighteenth-century authors, and had very much increased the proportion of historical works—history being a taste that he shared with my mother. The accent of the collection, however, still seemed to lie on the Victorian novelists and poets; my grandparents had been the close friends of many of them, and glimpses of Dickens, George Eliot, Wilkie Collins, Bulwer Lytton and Browning were among my father's earliest boyhood memories. Out-topping all, Dickens was the hero of the library. There were at least three editions of the novels, two of them with the original illustrations, which rise as vividly to me out of my childhood as the pictures in *Punch*. Almost as soon as we could read a book at all we were started on Dickens, and if it was not a volume of *Punch* that lay on the red cushions in our laps during those still evenings of reading, it was *David Copperfield* or *Great Expectations* or *Nicholas Nickleby* or *Bleak House*: so that David's first visit to Peggotty's cabin on the seashore and Lady Dedlock's flight through the snow and Nicholas's arrival at Dotheboys Hall are among the earliest events I can remember, almost as if they had been part of my own experience. Indeed, the description of Dotheboys Hall caused a dread of the inevitable day when I should have to leave for boarding-school, which was only partly alleviated by my parents' assurance that things were no longer as bad as all that. After all, to judge from the *Magnet*, they *were*; and, my imagination played on by the sinister tales of older boys in the neighbourhood, I refused to be taken in by the farcical customs, taboos, striped caps and esoteric language that appeared to have invaded the world of school since Nicholas's day. The reality, when it came, was so strangely different, that in spite of the fact that I lay awake night after night for weeks in misery at being cast out from the paradise of home, I soon learnt to find happiness there, and to believe that, since schools had improved so miraculously since Dotheboys Hall, we must be living in an age of miraculous humane progress—that only the Kaiser had spoiled.

## 2

My father's desk was beside the french windows, and behind it, in the lowest shelves of the book-cases, only to be reached by crawling on all fours, were some of the books that fascinated me most: several very old volumes of natural history, astronomy and geology with engraved plates foxed at the edges, some large, heavy, illustrated books on Japan which my grandfather had brought back from a far-away tour to the East, and all the books associated with my great-grandfather, Robert Chambers. Every edition of the *Vestiges of Creation* (the immediate forerunner of Darwin's *Origin of Species*) was there, *The Traditions of Edinburgh*, *Chambers's Cyclopædia of Literature*, and the complete *Encyclopædia* itself in calf binding.

Scotland was very remote from the Thames Valley existence of my childhood, and it was only later that I gradually became aware how much I owed, how much we all owed, in our tastes and capacities, to the Scottish side of the family. If one's destiny lies in one's heredity as well as in one's environment, then my interest in editing and publishing as well as my impulse to be a writer are clearly derived from the Chambers. And how they came into the book world is a story in which chance played a surprisingly large part; to be precise, the behaviour of certain French prisoners of war in the little town of Peebles just before the Battle of Waterloo.

Even in such a distant part of Britain the French wars caused enough commotion. According to my great-grandfather's account there were militia regiments stationed in the town and in the surrounding country, and there was a constant demand for recruits to fill their ranks and those of the regular army. Soldiers marched to and fro with drums beating and colours flying to inspire the sleepy inhabitants with martial enthusiasm, rumours of defeats and victories were brought by excited travellers who galloped in from over the border, and illuminations were staged to celebrate the most famous feats of arms. Peebles, however, was sufficiently out of the way to be considered a suitable place by the Government for the residence of prisoners of war on parole. The first to come, a couple of dozen or so, were sailors caught off the coast of the Netherlands, simple folk who quickly learnt some handicraft to supplement the small official allowances they received. They settled into the life of the place without too much repining, hated by no one and with no malice in themselves towards the hosts they had never intended to visit. A few years later they were followed by a different class of prisoners, naval and military officers who had been captured in the Peninsula by Wellington's men.

The arrival of this second contingent made a deep impression, as a contemporary witness relates:

> There was speedily a vast sensation in the place. The local militia had been disbanded. Lodgings of all sorts were vacant. The new arrivals would on all hands be heartily welcomed. On Tuesday, the expected French prisoners in an unceremonious way began to drop in. . . . They came walking in twos and threes—a few of them lame. Their appearance was startling, for they were in military garb in which they had been captured in Spain. Some were in light blue hussar dresses, braided, with marks of

sabre wounds.   Others were in dark blue uniform.   Several wore large cocked hats, but the greater number had undress caps.   All had a gentlemanly air, notwithstanding their soiled boots, and their visible marks of fatigue.   Before night, they had all arrived; and through the activity of the agent of the Transport Board, they had been provided with lodgings suitable to their slender allowance.

How civilized it all sounds, compared with the state of prisoners in the improved European wars of our own age of progress, sexually segregated, herded behind barbed wire into wooden huts, with all their movements watched by machine-guns and searchlights.   None of these officers is known to have broken parole, and they soon became welcome guests in the households of the better-off citizens of Peebles.   They were, however, the cause of a serious calamity in the life of one of these citizens, who happened to be my great-great-grandfather.

James Chambers came of a family that had been living in Peebles for centuries.   The earliest ancestor of which there is record was one William de la Chambre, ' Bailif e Burgois de Peebles ' in the list of those who signed bonds of allegiance to Edward I at Berwick-on-Tweed in 1296.   James had inherited a small cotton-manufacturing concern which prospered reasonably; but being of an easy disposition, and much attracted to the society of the rare birds who had invaded his native town, he extended credit to them to purchase cloth from him far beyond the bounds of prudence and in spite of the frequent remonstrances of his canny wife, Jean Gibson.   The inevitable blow fell suddenly: one day the Government ordered the prisoners to be moved to Dumfries, and a few days later they were all gone.   Loud were their protestations that they would discharge their debts the moment they returned to their homes at the end of the war; but never a penny of his money did my great-great-grandfather see.

He was ruined.   And from that ruin came the family migration to Edinburgh.   His two young sons, William and Robert, set out ahead, without a sixpence in their pockets, to earn their living there in the humblest way that offered itself.   They began with copying and job-printing; a lucky break made it possible for them to start second-hand bookselling; and after years of struggle and cautious Scottish thrift, they had the idea of founding a magazine for popular education, afterwards to be known (as it still is known) as *Chambers's Journal*. An immediate success rewarded them, and they went on to the founding of the publishing firm of W. & R. Chambers, from which eventually issued the famous Encyclopædia. Soon Robert became well known as author as well as publisher, and his house the meeting-place of many of the most learned and gifted people in Edinburgh society of the time. Among these visitors happened to be two German brothers, whose father had been a portrait-painter in the Free City of Hamburg: Frederick and Rudolf Lehmann. Frederick had established himself as a merchant in Leith; Rudolf was an artist, destined to be a fashionable portrait-painter to whom ' everyone ' sat in the London of the 'eighties; and within a few years each of them had married one of the daughters of Robert Chambers.

Great-uncle Rudolf had had a particularly interesting life. His eldest brother, Henri, had been sent at the age of seventeen to study art in Paris, became a pupil of Ingres and apparently made a hit at the Salon of 1835 with his first picture. The rest of his life seems to have been a success story with only the rarest and briefest set-backs. It is true that he lived to see the mural decorations he painted for the Hotel de Ville and the Palais de Justice destroyed in the Commune; but when he died in 1882 he was an Officer of the Legion d'Honneur, a member of the Institute and Professor at the École des Beaux Arts. Rudolf had followed Henri to Paris soon after he was established there; and in 1838 the two brothers made their way to Munich, then in the noonday of its fame as an artistic capital. Next followed the traditional and inevitable Italian tour: they lingered for some years, with Rome as their headquarters, before returning to Paris. Rudolf had his first success in 1842, when he won a gold medal at the Salon with a picture that Henri had taken to Paris for him. It is easy, I suppose, to see an artist's life in Italy a hundred years ago in a falsely rosy light, but the account Rudolf gives of their early years there— particularly after the award of the gold medal, when commissions began to come in—the bohemian carousals and the famous parties among the international celebrities who made their homes in

Rome, the romantic brilliance of the ecclesiastical ceremonies and
processions—they witnessed the election of Pius IX and the
ebullient celebrations that followed this popular event—the
carefree roamings through the unspoilt Italian countryside with
long summer expeditions into the Volscan and Alban hills, the
sense of time unlimited and the good things of life for a song, are
enough to make anyone's mouth water in the Age of Anxiety
and NATO.   Painters appear to have been much courted,
indeed during the season their studios were scarcely ever free
from hordes of distinguished visitors, all of whom had to be
politely welcomed as possible clients.   In his book, *An Artist's
Reminiscences*, Rudolf wrote:

> The foreign visitors in Rome were at that remote epoch very
> different from those of today.   Lord Brougham had not dis-
> covered the Riviera, nor were there railways to allow of a flying
> visit.   People came for as many months as they come for days
> now (1894), and, strange as it may sound, Rome was considered
> the healthiest and pleasantest of winter resorts.   Those who
> usually came to spend the winter may roughly be divided into
> members of the English aristocracy, travelling with a numerous
> retinue in their own carriages; Legitimist, ultra-Catholic French
> families of the Faubourg St. Germain; German families of all
> classes and creeds, under the spell of Goethe's enthusiastic Roman
> letters; shoals of Russians, and American families and artists;
> professors and literary men of all creeds and nationalities in untold
> numbers.   The papal court would keep aloof from this yearly
> invasion of the barbarians.   But they were joyfully welcomed by
> the Romans, whose only source of income they were at that time.

Rudolf in his book speaks rather contemptuously of Rome's
reputation as an international art centre, but he and his brother,
installed in studios in the Palazzetto Borghese, seem to have
found prosperity, as well as happiness.   The move to Paris
a few years later plunged them into very different scenes and
a difficult struggle for existence:  for soon after they arrived
the Revolution of 1848 broke out.   During the February rising
Rudolf was ill in bed, but a letter from Henri survives, of which
the following is one of the most graphic passages:

> At the Pont Royal I met the triumphal procession conducting
> the Gouvernement Provisoire to the Hotel de Ville with cries of

' *Vive la République!* ' on my side of the Quai; on the other side, the mob was tossing everything out of the Tuileries windows and firing salvos into the air for joy. Meanwhile the faces of the bystanders wore an expression of horror, caused partly by the incredible rapidity with which this change of scene had taken place, and partly by the uncertainty in which they were plunged concerning everything, especially as many believed that the princes, general, and the army were still in the forts and would surprise Paris by night. In this state of mind the evening was passed. Next morning, our legion of the Garde Nationale assembled in the Mairie, and as there were no troops whatever left in the town we were distributed in all directions. From thence a sergeant and four men (of whom I was one) were sent to the École Militaire to prevent plundering there. We were the first to arrive on the scene. An incessant stream of drunken ruffians partly armed flowed now past us, now towards us, with banners and drums. They were in search of weapons. . . . I was orderly to the Minister of War that day, and Perthuis was his adjutant. I had an order to transmit to the General commanding the Garde Nationale, so I had access to the Tuileries Palace with a ' *Laissez-passer* '. What a sight and what a lesson! The fancy took me to pass through the state rooms in exactly the order one had to pass through them to pay one's homage to the king. A detailed description would lead me too far. Where the velvet canopy of the throne stood, was now bare wall with large chalk inscriptions of '*Vive la République! Vive la Suisse! Vive l'Italie! Vive la Liberté pour la troisième fois reconquise, le 22, 23, 24 Février! Respect aux objets d'art!* ' In fact, of all the life-size portraits of marshals, only those hated by the populace were shot at and torn.

By the time of the June rising, Rudolf had recovered, and describes how he was at work one day on a painting of St. Sebastian when he heard ' the ominous beating of the " Rappel ", two long strokes and one short one on the drum, calling the Garde Nationale to arms, the deep tolling of the Tocsin, the hurried closing of shop-shutters in quick succession, like *peloton* firing, and the deep boom of distant cannon ', which announced the outbreak of the rising in the Faubourg St. Antoine. As his brother was again under fire as a Garde National, and finding inaction intolerable, he himself volunteered, and was given a piece of cardboard to tie round his hat on which was printed ' *Garde National du 4ième Batt., 10ième Légion, 4ième Compagnie* '.  He recorded some horrifying details of the random slaughter and the agonies in the crowded, stinking, airless and waterless prisons; and also one extraordinary incident in the Place de la Bastille:

> Suddenly a tall girl, a well-known artists' model, who had recently sat to me for the Ste. Cécile, made her appearance.  ' Bonjour, M. Lehmann,' she said in the quietest of tones, as if she had met me in my studio.  ' Shall I take you over the battlefield? ' and as I readily accepted her offer, she added, ' You had better remove that piece of cardboard from your hat.  The Gardes Nationaux are no favourites hereabout.'  I did as she bade me, and followed her into the long, desolate Rue du Faubourg St. Antoine, which was intersected by numerous partly destroyed barricades, about fifty yards distant from each other.  She had some incident to relate about the taking of each one of them, after a desperate struggle, by the troops.  ' On this one Monseigneur Affre, the Bishop of Paris, was shot just as he held up the crucifix, endeavouring to stop the firing and bring about an armistice.  On that one my poor brother was shot, but he never relinquished his grasp on the red flag.  What can you do against cannon? ' she added with a sigh.  ' But never mind—our day will come!  We women always sat knitting on the barricade next to the one that was being fought for, retiring gradually as the troops advanced.'  I thought of the tricoteuses of 1793, of whom these were the grandchildren!

One odd memento of this period is still in my family's possession: a Sèvres vase, which was presented to Rudolf in lieu of a medal—because all the medals bore the effigy of Louis Philippe, and the newly born Republic refused to distribute them.

In 1867 Rudolf came back to settle in London for the rest of his life.  Meanwhile, Frederick had migrated with his wife, Nina Chambers, to Sheffield, where he had interests in steel; and there my father, the eldest of a family of four, was born in January, 1856.

# 3

THE most magical place in the house for me was the window-embrasure half-way up the front stairs, where they turned by the grandfather clock. The windows were of opaque coloured glass which shut out the view of the garden below, but allowed the hot afternoon sun of summer to stream through in wandering splashes of red and green and gold on to the banisters. On the ledge below the windows were some Chinese bowls and covered dishes, the bowls always filled with lavender, and the dishes, when one lifted the lids, giving forth the delicious aroma of dried rose-leaves.

These scents seemed to steam off the ledge on sunny days all through the summer, and I was drawn there to let the lavender sift through my fingers and to put my face into the rose-leaves and inhale, deep and long. And then I would open one of the windows to get my favourite glimpse of the garden: the paved circle in front of the french windows of the library, planted all through the year with the season's flowers, and to the right beyond it, festooned with climbing roses, the archway which divided the two bosky plantations of flowering trees and shrubs, lilac, laburnum, Japanese cherry and chestnut soaring above them, and to the left the old walnut-tree with the vista below its wide-spreading branches through the apple and cherry trees to the long herbaceous border that lay under the walls of the kitchen garden. Directly below, behind a high hedge, was the entrance to the boiler-room which always seemed to me, peering cautiously but not venturing into the forbidden darkness, a danger-fraught entrance to mysterious nether regions. As I watched one of the gardeners climbing down the iron ladder to stoke up the furnace, I often used to wonder whether he would ever come up again—perhaps he might steal through underground passages that emerged far away by the potting-shed; perhaps the floor would give way in the concentrated heat, and he would sink with all the heaps of coke into fathom-less crevices of the earth.

My memory of the earliest years of my life, before time was an adversary one was always conscious of, just behind one or just ahead in a race that was not of one's choosing, is cloudy, with erratic rifts in the clouds. As I try to imagine myself then, sitting in the window-embrasure over the garden, I can see certain pictures very clearly, and the rest scarcely at all. The pictures I see are nearly all of ritual events that took place year after year: tea under the walnut-tree, with James bringing out the tray with cucumber sandwiches and Fuller's cake and the silver urn over which my mother would preside, or the deck-chairs under the laburnum-tree in June with my father reading the newspapers and my mother a book, or the dogs sitting on the library steps under the red-and-white-striped sun-blinds and drowsily watching the birds hopping about the lawn. I can hear the calling of doves and chorus of blackbirds and thrushes in all the trees at sundown, and I can hear the mowing-machine as it makes its alternate strips of light and dark green over the grass in a massacre of daisies' heads. I can hear the murmur of talk as my parents take their guests slowly across the lawn down to the river: I am waiting for the coast to be clear, to slip down myself into the garden without getting involved, perhaps to look for my tortoise in the long grass of the lower orchard, perhaps to try to catch the orange-bellied newts in the lily-pool, lying on the edge with my sleeves rolled back, quite hidden, but knowing that I would answer when I heard my nurse Julia calling for me. I can even catch rare glimpses of particular happenings; my mother, for instance, lining us up with our American cousins, her nephews and nieces, to be photographed by the paved circle, or the Great Dane, Lufra, bounding up to me and nearly knocking me over. Little else swims out of the mist with any clarity, except one incident when I was three years old: the first glimpses of a strange machine I was told was an aeroplane, which had come down in a chalk-pit behind the Tennyson Downs in the Isle of Wight—of that more later. Even fading prints in the family photograph album, of myself, ridiculously chubby and curly-haired, looking aggressively out of my pram, or peering shame-lessly between the curtains of a stranger's bathing-tent at the sea-side, stir no response. The password is still to be found.

The window-embrasure on the stairs has other associations of childhood joys and fears for me.  I was put to sleep in my parents' bedroom, but even the moon-like glow of a night-light in its little white china cage could not allay the terrors that assailed me before they came up to bed themselves.  There were huge ornate wardrobes in the room, and soon after my nurse had left me, possessed by a spirit of active malevolence, they began to creak and crack.  I was convinced some monster would suddenly open one of the big doors and advance upon me, and very soon—almost every night—I was in tears.  I had made promises, of course, not to believe in these monsters, and not to forsake my bed in search of consolation; but they were all too often impossible to keep.  I would get up and creep to the top of the stairs, then a few steps down towards the embrasure, in the hope of hearing the echoes of conversation from the dining-room or drawing-room to reassure me.

These terrors did not cease for years; and then I found an antidote to them in—of all books—Black's *Medical Dictionary*. I had discovered it one night beside my mother's bed, and my eye, caught by the weird diagrams of internal organs, began to read the accompanying articles.  For a long while it was my nightly companion, much to the amusement of the rest of the family, and my parents when they came up would find it beside my bed as it had fallen from my hands as I sank into sleep. How much I understood of it, I do not know; but it did not make me morbid, nor, alas, did it make me an expert on human ills and their cures.  Even by the time I went to my preparatory school, I had forgotten nearly all of it.

But it was not only to escape the bogeys of the night that I used to creep down the stairs after going to bed.  There were the evenings when my parents gave dinner-parties, and my sister Beatrix and I would wait for the guests to cross the hall on the way to the dining-room when we heard the gong boom out down below.  As noiselessly as we could, we would hide behind the banisters and peer through, to catch a glimpse of the glittering brocaded dresses and the jewels, the fabulous world of grown-ups *en fête*.  Then, about half an hour later, Beatrix would creep down into the corridor behind the green baize door, and, hiding in the telephone-room, wait until Ernest the footman brought her the choicest left-over tit-bits, which she would bring back triumphantly in her soap-dish. And sometimes I would go down by myself, for a special treat: to hear my sister Rosamond playing the piano in the drawing-room. I revelled in a tune called 'Holy Night' which she had just mastered; she knew how it carried me away on wings of voluptuous bliss, and would even play it specially for me. Then I would go back to bed perfectly happy, and even Black's *Medical Dictionary* had no further charms that night.

# 4

An artist can have no greater luck than to be brought up in surroundings of natural beauty which he is free to explore at his own will: by the sea-coast away from the towns, in a mountain setting of lakes and forests, a lush river valley or a garden cunningly planned for surprise and pleasure at all seasons of the year. There he may learn to know, and assimilate into himself, the rhythms and mysterious harmonies of the year, the multitudinous everyday miracles of plant, insect, animal life, the unaccountable empathies, intertwinings and transformations in which he comes to feel that he himself takes part with powers that are not in his conscious direction; thus images are invisibly laid up in his mind rather as precious pictures are stored in mountain caves in wartime, out of which the secret agencies of the imagination can summon them as symbols and correspondences that never fail. What poverty an artist must feel who has never had this luck: for me it was the garden of Fieldhead and the reach of the Thames between Marlow and Cookham that flowed by its western edge.

The extraordinary thing about the garden was that no situation could have been more unpromising, less likely to reflect an image of romantic perfection in a child's mind. Originally, when my father bought it, it had been a big field leading down to an old ferry with an inn that stood beside the landing-place. To round it off, he had bought up some old cottages on the south side, and pulled them down: all that remained of them were the gnarled apple-trees of unknown age that grew on the lawn between the house and the kitchen garden. At the time when he first made his home in Bourne End the village scarcely existed. There were a couple of shops, a post-office in one of them, that served the few big houses along the river-side, and a boat-building establishment a little further up. Then the railway arrived, crossed the river exactly at the bottom of the garden, and built its station and shunting yard all along the north side. My father planted a long line of poplars to shut it out; but he could not shut out the smell of what the goods-trucks contained, nor the ricochetting clatter they made as they were being shunted about. And yet the presence of the railway at our back-gate provided an extra element of romance when I grew old enough to be interested in trains and engine-numbers; and before that I remember how comforting it was to me, sleepless in the inhuman vacancy of night, to hear the last train rumble over the bridge soon after midnight, and hiss as it drew up in the station, its mission accomplished with a firm daylight dependability, its human load safely delivered. It was my friend, that train; and my friend too was the goods-engine that began to shuffle and bang about the yard between four and five in the morning, with its message that night was not endless and that solid human beings were going about their regular tasks, defying the impalpable ghosts that peopled my own childish darkness.

The house itself, as I realized only later, in my teens, was badly sited in the grounds and awkwardly built; so that except for the library, my mother's drawing-room beside it and the three bedrooms directly above, the choice of views was either looking over the garden, cold and north, or south and warm but looking directly over the lane where a row of ugly workmen's cottages had been built, ineffectively screened by some dank shrubs, cypresses and a yew-hedge. To this day I cannot understand why the architect planned it in that way, or why my father agreed. My own nursery looked over the lane; and from my window I used to watch the antics of the children who abounded in the cottages, half-repelled but also half-fascinated by this close-up view of the incomprehensible lives of the poor. They seemed cheerful, noisy and vigorous enough in spite of their dishevelled clothes; and ready to shout gleefully rude remarks at us too, though my parents, declared radicals and full of kind works, were popular and respected in the village. The cottages were only one manifestation of the graceless, straggling village that had grown up round Fieldhead since my father had built it. It really had nothing to recommend it except the smiling Buckinghamshire faces of its inhabitants: everywhere ugly brick cottages scattered over what was once one of the prettiest parts of the valley below the line of the Chilterns, a new and hideous little church almost directly opposite our front-gate, an even worse Methodist chapel, and a row of featureless modern shops along a road on the other side of the railway, that had been absurdly and pompously named The Parade. It was given its *raison d'être* partly by the holiday attractions of the river as movement into and out of London became easier and faster, but much more by the paper-mills that lay just beyond it on the road to Woburn Green. The nearest unspoilt village was Little Marlow, a few miles up-river, where the church, the manor-house and the vicarage had remained the core of the community and in the same classic relationship to one another as for hundreds of years past. Further upstream Great Marlow, though it had become a busy little town with ugly slums on its outskirts, had still enough of its old character for it not to be hard to imagine its features when Shelley and Peacock lived there; and further downstream Cookham, set against the romantic dark cliff of Cliveden woods with the weir plunging just below the bridge, had much of the charm of Little Marlow, though it had grown bigger—a favourite riverside spot of an earlier generation. Only Bourne End disfigured the scene; and yet it was not till long after I had gone away to school that I became properly aware of its ugliness, so permeated was it for me with the overflow of Fieldhead's enchantments.

The garden had almost everything that a child could want to make him happy. Above all, it had the quality of making one feel one had never fully explored it. I always imagined that I would suddenly come upon some secret corner, hidden in the bushes or among the potting-sheds, or along one of the little overgrown paths: there, perhaps, I would discover a rusty old pump over a disused well, or a forgotten sundial long enveloped in undergrowth and overshadowed by the growth of poplars and chestnuts, or a storeroom of treasures from a time before I was born, or a rare shrub that I had never seen in flower, a fig-tree bearing fruit behind a brick archway I had never gone through. No formal garden, more elegantly and elaborately planned, could have given this impression. And the flowers: how could one ever know or remember them all? Roses, clematis, ceanothus and honeysuckle twined over every wall and pillar and trellis, the border was a raging fire of colour all the summer, wherever you went there were rose-beds, lavender walks and wild patches full of violets and daffodils in spring and briar roses later in the year, primroses and narcissi grew under the apple- and pear-trees in the orchards, and every part of the garden seemed to have a different and delicious perfume, lilac, syringa, honeysuckle, Mexican orange, mint and thyme, lavender and peony, and mingling with them everywhere all the various scents of roses, even where the bitter, pungent odour of walnut leaves hung on the sultry summer air.

The lily-pool, hidden in its cypresses and bamboos, with its teeming life of gold-fish, newts, water-beetles and tadpoles, all lurking under the reddish-green mats of the leaves, was one of the secret places of the garden for which I had a particular love; but there were others that drew me almost as strongly. Between the lower orchard and the railway line, hidden by pine-trees and branches of hazel-nut, was a little path that led down to the back-gate of the kitchen garden, with a dump of leaf-mould on one side under the pines and some gardeners' sheds and dog-kennels on the other. This was a favourite area of concealment in the games of hide-and-seek and clumps we were always playing, and to which the garden lent itself so well; when I heard the ' coo-ee! ' it was one of the first places I would make for, imagining I saw the corner of a jersey or skirt or a flattened hand behind every branch and pile of logs. The dog-kennels were the source of one of the bitterest, most terrible disappointments of my whole childhood. They had been constructed for great danes and St. Bernards, for which my father, a fanatical dog-lover, had a special liking. They were large, more than tall enough for a child to stand upright in and roomy enough to lie down in, and each had a long fenced yard in front of it. My sisters decided to make 'homes' of them—they had long been disused—and with my parents' amused encouragement each took over one of the three kennels, and filled it with articles of individual preciousness; Beatrix, inspired as she was at the time by Boy Scout dreams of adventure and camping on the veldt, installing herself with even greater enthusiasm and thoroughness than Helen or Rosamond. Three: but where was the fourth? What my sisters had, I had to have too. Envy, and the sense of being shut out from the enjoyments of others, to which as the baby of the family I was keenly sensitive, began to sour my days. Finally my mother promised that I should have something just as good for myself, and went into consultation with Mr. Goodman, the head-gardener. My spirits rose, as my mother told me that my own 'home' would be arriving any day. At last the great moment came: a bulky object, I was told, had been delivered by goods-train the night before. I rushed down the garden, to find Goodman hammering away at—a packing-case of moderate size, far, far smaller than any of the kennels. I was appalled: I stared at it incredulously, and then burst into tears of rage and disillusionment.

Not far off, at the edge of the lawn, stood the Pavilion, which my father had built out of the bricks of the cottages he had pulled down. It was really a good deal bigger than what a garden pavilion suggests, consisting of a large hall with various smaller rooms leading off it, and could quite easily have been made into a pleasant home for a moderate-sized family. For many years, while we were growing up, it was used as a school-room: my parents had had the idea of engaging two or three teachers for ourselves and proposing to friends that they should share them with us. The scheme turned out a success, and many years of my childhood were dominated by the presence of the day-school in the garden and the friends I made there when I eventually joined it myself. The boys stayed until they left for preparatory school, but the girls much longer; Helen and Rosamond, in fact, until they went to Cambridge. It was well fitted for this purpose, not only because of its size but also because of the big lawn that stretched in front of it, a lawn on which games of tennis, croquet, Tom Tiddler's ground, grandmother's steps and hide-and-seek could all be played at the same time. Another game, which we invented for ourselves, could be played on the high sloping roof, a mixture of fives and tennis for two players with racquets and a tennis ball. The ball spun and bounced on the tiles, and sometimes flew off at an unexpected angle when it hit the ' hazard '—the dormer window in the middle—whirling into the weeping beech-tree at the side or disappearing totally into the shrubbery. Inside the Pavilion, ranged all down one side, was a series of lockers which contained relics of my father's sporting past : old dumb-bells, weird Japanese fencing-masks and boxing-gloves with the stuffing bursting out of them. There always seemed to be something in those lockers I had not discovered before, something I often did not understand the use of. The Pavilion was lit by popping gas chandeliers which hung down between the rafters and provided a flickering illumination for the children's dances that were sometimes held there : I can remember very little of them, but I can still faintly hear, at the bottom of a deep well of my mind, the strains of a polka, and the lancers, and Sir Roger de Coverley.

Just behind the Pavilion, surrounded by a miniature box-hedge, were three little flower-beds which had been presented to my sisters as gardens of their own, where they could grow the flowers they chose for themselves out of penny packets. It seems odd that, in so vast a garden, with flowers of every sort abounding wherever one looked, we should have thought it necessary to have planting space of our own; but everything else except those rather obscure and overshadowed plots was under the Olympian control of the head-gardener, and was hardly ever to be touched without incurring his displeasure, and therefore they were prized beyond measure. A sweet-william or a canterbury bell that flowered there, after weeks of eager tending with one's own small green watering-can, was a joy and triumph quite eclipsing the great pageantry of the herbaceous border spread out in the full sun only a few yards away. Needless to say, as soon as I was old enough to be

moved by the same ambition, I demanded a plot too; and as
there was no more room alongside the other three, I was
allotted one on the other side in an angle of the Pavilion walls.
It was almost totally deprived of sun, but I suppose that Goodman had slyly advocated it because the disorder he expected
could not be seen from any main vantage point in the garden.
I felt slightly cheated, as I had over the kennel-houses, but
became—for a season or two—an ardent gardener, enrolling
all grown-ups who could be persuaded to aid me at any hour
of the day, though the coloured pictures on the seed-packets
were apt to remain much more satisfying to me than the flowers
when they came up (if they did).

My sisters' gardens were at the opening to the woodland path
that was known as the Lovers' walk.   And just inside, behind
the St. John's wort, and shadowed by the overhanging branches,
was the most hallowed spot in the whole garden: the dogs'
cemetery, a cluster of weather-stained tombstones standing over
sad little hummocks in the ground.   Engraved on the stones
were the names of dogs that had had their day before I was born,
known to me only by life-size paintings that were hung upstairs
or in back corridors, stiff photographs of week-end groups in
which they were clustered on the library steps or sprawled over
my father's feet, or by the legends that were sometimes told
when my father had old family or rowing friends to stay.
There was buried Ben, the black labrador of uncanny intelligence who guarded my mother whenever my father was away
for long periods, barking on the stair-landing every night at
10 p.m. until she came to bed, and in the middle of the night
with equal regularity putting his soft muzzle on to her bed to
make certain she was still there; and Rufus, most beloved of
all my father's dogs, a spaniel to whom he wrote some famous
and much-anthologized pieces.   These, the oldest stones, were
almost obliterated by rain and lichen; others, more clearly leg-
ible, had been wept over by my sisters when they were first put up,
and could stir an occasional fading memory for me out of my
perambulator days.   The first that I can myself at all clearly
remember being put up was for a pekinese called Tai-Tai,
really the property of E. V. Lucas, for whom we were keeping
her: she had been run over by a cart as she scampered across a

country lane while we were all out on a walk together. The
burial was performed by the gardeners, as it was unendurable
for any of us children to attend after having witnessed her death
agonies, and storms of tears flowed whenever we approached
the new grave. The deaths of animals were the raw, unassuageable sorrows of our childhood, and it seems impossible that I
shall ever weep again as much as I did over those earliest
tragedies.

I loved the great flower-beds in the garden; I loved the
rose-covered arbours, the lily-pool, the clumps of chestnut trees
with their pink-and-white candelabras of blossom; I loved the
grey stone ornamentation of sundial and bird-bath and flower
urns; I loved the smoothly striped expanses of lawn after
mowing and the unkempt lawn with its daisies and buttercups
and clover; but above all I think I loved the kitchen garden.
The feathery green forest of the uncut asparagus, hung with
orange bobbles at midsummer; the purple lines of beetroot,
the plumes of the carrots, the light green curly luxuriance of
the lettuces, the ribbed blue-green chinese boxes of the cabbages
where the white butterflies flopped and dallied, the arching
stakes that carried the twinings of the runner-beans with their
winged flowers; all spoke of the rich and infinitely varied
fruitfulness of the earth and appealed to taste as well as to sight
and smell. I would watch the hairy green globes of the goose-
berries turn golden-yellow and sticky, relishing the moment of
bursting between my teeth; I would creep under the raspberry
nets, more secure but scarcely less furtive than the starlings and
blackbirds, to pull the just ripe berries off their hard green
holders, or prowling on all fours among the straw that cosseted
the strawberries, turn up the leaves to discover an occasional
scarlet pitted monster lurking underneath. More wonderful
to me even than the netted rows of the berries, were the red-
brick walls just behind the greenhouses and the frames for the
violets, where the peaches, nectarines and figs grew. How
often I climbed up on to the wall, to discover a hidden fig that
had hitherto eluded picking, all purple and soft and juicy.
How many mornings and evenings I would slip down to see
whether a nectarine had ripened and would yield to a gently
pressing thumb, whether a peach had fallen, lawful booty, into

the grass below.   Over the wall, where the gardeners' wheel-barrows, spades, forks and rakes leaned in their sheds against the piled flower-pots, a bonfire was smouldering with sweet drifts of smoke that wandered towards me; I could hear the splashing of oars from the invisible river, or the hurdy-gurdy tune played on a steamer passing under the railway bridge, while shouts and laughter echoed from bathers among the reeds.

# 5

ALWAYS at Fieldhead, though it was nowhere visible from the house, one was conscious of the river.   This was partly the result of our upbringing as children of a father for whom water sports had been the passion of his life, and who had originally built the house in order to be able to indulge this passion with the friends of his bachelordom; but the river had an irresistible mysteriously indefinable attraction apart from that.   The garden was not a paradise in itself, but only in association with the river; its beauty was heightened and given meaning by the fact that the river ran at the bottom of it, and not merely because the presence of the river changed the quality of the air and the quality of the light.   The garden was a dallying place on the way to the river, and the river was the real purpose of the people who refreshed themselves there.   For the river not only provided the joys of punting, canoeing, scull-ing, rowing, picnicking and bathing, but more than that, was a magic highway of the great world, transfiguring the traffic that passed along it.   There were evenings of glittering, illusive light in summer and misty mornings of mirror-still reflections and mingled rainbow colours in early autumn, when the barges, the pleasure-boats, the racing craft that slid into view round the up-river bend beyond the sailing club, and passed, and dropped out of sight at the other end of the great sweeping S-curve the river's course described through Bourne End, seemed hardly real, but the symbols in some poem or song—for music certainly seemed to emanate from it.   All this, of course,

was not to be analysed or consciously apprehended by me at that
time, as I sat in my sailor suit by the bank and watched it all
as from a private garlanded box or balcony, but felt in the heart,
where it set in motion a tune, a dance of words for images that
all the years of adult life have failed completely to recapture
or translate.

As one walked down from the french windows of the library,
past the walnut tree and between the old apple-trees on the
lawn, one came to the gates into the kitchen garden, through
which a long tunnel of roses, honeysuckle, clematis and vines,
whose grapes never fully ripened, led to the dark laurel boskage
of the garden's end and another gate. The river-garden was
divided from the rest of the garden by a right-of-way; one
shook open another wooden gate on the other side of the path—
and immediately the play of light off water was in one's eyes,
the familiar faint smell of river-water and weeds was in one's
nostrils. Perhaps at that moment a string of barges was passing
under the dark-green bridge, the tug lowering its funnel as it
chugged through, or a motor-boat with silent, smartly dressed
occupants gazing royally to left and to right, or a skiff with
noisy country-folk getting into a tangle with their oars; and
immediately after, as the ripples reached the banks, one heard
the slapping of the water against the camp-shedding, and the
raft heaved, pulling at the ring that moored it to the creaking
post and scattering the shoals of sticklebacks I used to try to
catch with the old tin bailer.

The Boat-house, built to accommodate any eight, Leander,
Cambridge or Oxford that my father might be coaching, was of
noble proportions and contained all sorts of craft, some in
active use and some more ageing memorials of exploits in the
past. It had a curious musty river smell, delicious to me as
jonquils or ripe apples as I pushed back the heavy roller doors
after an absence from home, a smell compounded of water-
weeds drying on paddles, greased rowlocks, sheepskins, cobwebs and varnished timber. The punt always lay in the water,
except in flood time, ready for an expedition or a crossing of the
river at a moment's notice; but inside the Boat-house were a
canoe and a skiff which belonged to my mother and in which we
were all taught to scull, both boats well to the front and handy

for a quick launching; further back in the gloom, dappled with the quivering light reflected off the river, lay the more serious uncompromising craft of the sport, a light double-sculler, a racing four often used in local regattas when my father with some of his old companions of the oar competed under the colours of his own Club, and a neat single-sculler, with outriggers but rather too heavy for racing, known as the rum-tum. There was also a huge family boat, technically known as a ' randan ' and called ' The Water-baby ', complete with enormous picnic baskets, crockery and plate. My father rowed it down from Henley one summer's day with my mother and myself to steer him, an astonishing feat for a man of over fifty which made him feel, as he said at the time, as if he were harnessed to a motor-bus. It was the most memorable expedition of my childhood, lasting the whole afternoon till dinner-time : at every lock he was recognized and entered into long conversations with the lock-keepers as we slowly sank away from the neat little gardens of roses and geraniums on the falling water. Up above these giants, supported on cross-bar shelves, were the two most exotic denizens of the Boat-house. One was a catamaran, a genuine South Sea craft, which consisted of a very narrow punt balanced by a huge boom, reputed to be very fast but seldom risked—only perhaps by the intrepid Beatrix. It had been given to my father by an admirer, as had the even more singular racing sculler of antique design that lay on the opposite side. This had been built in Australia in the eighteen-sixties, and was entirely round, shaped like a cigar with murderous sharp points at either end, and had outriggers (of doubtful advantage), but a fixed seat. My father kept it, I think, really as a joke, a museum exhibit : some of us did try to go out in it—but only in a bathing-suit.

High up, on the topmost tier of the struts, near the nests of the swallows, lay a quantity of oars, some with the Fieldhead colours on them, some designed for an eight which was no longer there. These unused oars evoked as nothing else, not the old Leander caps, the medals in the library, the challenge cups that adorned our dining-table on festive occasions, or the innumerable photographs of eights and fours which my father had coached, or in which he had rowed himself—these **strong**

and slender oars called out of a legendary past for me my
father's rowing fame and a picture far more human and vital
than the 'Spy' cartoon that hung in the bedroom corridor,
of a man supple, athletic, radiant in the confidence of his
strength and the love that all who knew him bore towards him.
That man, alas, I scarcely knew: when the mists of childhood
clear he is already beyond the fullness of his powers and soon to
be afflicted with the illness that kept him an invalid for the
last ten years of his life.

Attached to the Boat-house were two other rooms, one which
had become a lumber-room and was turned by me into a place
for the construction of weird and useless steel objects with my
Meccano set, for my first experiments in carpentering and for
the sawing out of horrible arty flowered designs in wood with my
treadle fretwork machine—which I used to present with a glow
of triumph to my mother or one of my sisters.   The other was
a changing-room, also hung with pictures of famous rowing
events of ancient times, with an unpredictable shower-bath
behind a canvas curtain—it worked when one least expected it
and as soon as one had clothed oneself, but never when one was
naked and awaiting.   Dimly also I remember some pairs of old
white flannel rowing-shorts, so long out of use and untouched
that one day a robin was observed to fly out of one of them,
which revealed on inspection a nest with three eggs.   Here we
changed for our bathing on summer evenings before dinner
about six o'clock, when the falling sun lay on the reddening
Virginia creeper that covered the Boat-house walls, and our
parents sat in their deck-chairs in the shade of the chestnut tree
with the dogs beside them panting from the heat.   We were all
taught to swim at the earliest possible moment, one of our
parents supporting us with a belt suspended from a pole that
went round our middles, while we kicked and splashed and
swallowed a great deal of river-water alongside the raft.   Thus
we learnt to feel at home in water before our teens, and our
father could safely entrust us with any kind of boat.

Very often a dip off the raft came at the end of a picnic down-
river for tea.   Picnics were the most exciting of all river events:
the thick jam sandwiches in their thin paper coverings and the
tea in the thermos flask were far more thrilling when safely

stowed in a basket in the punt than in the nursery or drawing-room.  The wooden backs were put up facing one another, the cushions arranged on them, paddles laid alongside, and there my mother, perhaps my nurse Julia, and sometimes my Aunt Nina or my Aunt Amelia would settle themselves in, and my sisters and I would jump in after them and push off.  Two of my sisters would sit on the back seat and paddle—until I was old enough to take a hand myself—aided intermittently by one of the grown-ups.  I would let my hand trail in the water, trying to catch at weeds as we passed, sometimes dislodging one from its root, when it would float up to the surface astonishingly long and pale like an invalid emerging from his sick-room.  The big riverside houses slipped by, with their urns of roses and geraniums by the water's edge and their smooth lawns leading down to the landing-stages where a punt or a motor-launch was moored and men in white flannels and straw hats handed their ladies, in wide floppy hats and bright long dresses, into their seats.  We had our favourite spot for picnics, under a line of willows between two lawns only a quarter of a mile down; but sometimes we would go further, to the Cookham bend, where there was another shaded spot that seemed to belong to no one; the swans paddled slowly up and gobbled the crusts we threw in, hissed at the eagerly watching dogs beside us and paddled away again; a river steamer passed with somebody thumping merrily at the piano and somebody pouring slops over the side; I buried myself in my copy of *Tiger Tim's Weekly* as the punt rocked in the wash, and my parents went on talking about their boring grown-up problems.

At last the picnic was over, the bathing was over; we had gone up for our supper and came down again as twilight gathered and the orange flush went out of the sky across the river; Bourne End regatta had been held, and on the last night the illuminations began.  We hung up Chinese lanterns over the raft, and sat on the camp-shedding to watch the punts and skiffs going by, each decorated with its own Chinese lanterns, reflections of red and yellow and green splintered in the dull steel of the river.  A band was playing away to our right, somewhere near Townsend's boat-houses; fish plopped every now and then in the reeds before us, and bats flitted over our heads; my father looked at the gold watch he took out of his waistcoat pocket; and then, remembered as bursting stars of colour against the sky of an innocent world, the fireworks began.

# 6

MY father had a reputation for a certain intolerant brusqueness of manner and sudden moods of stern displeasure that would transform his more characteristic charm and humour; but he was indulgent and easy-going towards his children, and I cannot remember any occasion on which he was seriously angry with me. There was a kind of affectionate detachment about his attitude which made it difficult for him to see our misdemeanours as anything but absurd and entertaining. He could afford detachment, because he took the view that our upbringing was the responsibility of our nurses, governesses and mother; as far as we were concerned, we were there to amuse him. I don't think he showed anger even when it was discovered that I had been secretly ransacking the drawer of his other writing-table in the little back room known as the ' Den '. My stamp-collecting craze had started, and one day, opening one of the drawers out of curiosity, I saw bundles of old letters all with early Victorian penny stamps on them. It was as exciting for me as if I had lit on a cave of diamonds, and for some weeks, whenever I could steal down to the Den unobserved, I went through the bundles with hurrying fingers, tearing off every stamp that had been left in good condition by the postmark. How I hoped to conceal the haul I don't know; but I was overwhelmed with guilt when, inevitably, the theft was revealed, and the joys of stamp-collecting were dimmed for some time. The letters, most of which had passed between my grandfather and grandmother, were precious to my father, but I had, after all, not torn them, only the envelopes, and I daresay the chilliness that resulted was more on account of the furtive side of my character that had been shown up, than of the damage done.

His influence on us was indirect, by encouragement rather than by prohibition, and perhaps all the stronger for that.   He left us to invent our own games, to make our own discoveries, but if it was anything in any way creative, if we were suddenly smitten with an urge to draw, or to paint, or to carpenter, or to write, he never openly laughed at us, but always gently encouraged and fed the urge.   I don't think he ever tried to make us tackle a book when we were reluctant.   He wanted us to have the freedom of his library, would answer our questions as we rummaged among the volumes, and would take out one for us if we asked what we should read next.   Our taste was formed by his taste, simply by the choice of books available. Only on one occasion can I remember that he went further than that.   I think he must have feared that my reading was too much influenced by what my sisters read and by nursery taste for it to be healthy for a boy; one day he returned from London with an old, blue cloth-bound set of Captain Marryat's novels, which he had obviously enjoyed himself when he was my age, and encouraged me to embark on them.   I still have the very worn copy of *Jacob Faithful* out of this set, the pages covered with large greasy stains which fell on them as I ate my bread and dripping at tea-time and followed the appalling moral tale of Jacob's mother who burst into flames through drinking too much gin.   *Mr. Midshipman Easy* and *Peter Simple* were more to my taste; but the swashbuckling adventures of midshipmen in the Napoleonic Wars failed to stir me as David Copperfield's adventures had, or E. Nesbit's stories, which I was in process of discovering, or the yarns of the night-watchman in the orange volumes of W. W. Jacobs' stories that stood on the highest shelf of the bookcase in the hall, and the experiment was not an out-and-out success.

My father, however, fed my imagination by the stories he told me.   He would come in last thing, when I was tucked up in my nursery for the night, and for a few spellbound minutes produce the next instalment of a story he had begun many nights before.   His invention never failed, and I never wanted the stories to end, and had to have them told again as soon as possible.   He used to take me with him when he went out with the dogs in the morning, and as he walked up-river past the

Sailing Club and the meadows, or crossed the river in the punt
and struck out for Winter Hill and the water-logged land
that lay at its foot, known as Cockmarsh, I would demand
another instalment, another story, perhaps from the series
'Richard and the Wishing Cap', and ply him with endless questions about the extraordinary things he told me.   One story in
particular caught my imagination: he pretended that Winter
Hill—a bare, steep chalk ridge that offered very little cover
for anything, let alone fabulous monsters—harboured a
genuine dragon.   As I scrambled up the prehistoric burial-
mound that stuck out of the level field between river and
hill like a bad bump on someone's forehead, and crouched in
the concave hollow on top, the awe-inspiring thought came to
me that the same dragon might actually have seen the unknown
chieftain buried there all those centuries ago.   My father's
stories seemed better, more satisfying than the stories in Andrew
Lang's fairy-books, because they always had something to do
with the world I lived in; but I appear nevertheless to have
developed a slightly sceptical turn of mind fairly early, and I
could never be quite certain that my father wasn't having me
on.   I waited anxiously for the dragon to manifest itself, but
still not even a puff of smoke came out of gorse-thicket or
blackberry bush.   And then one day the cat was let out of the
bag, literally, when I read my father's ballad on the subject,
which appeared in *Punch*: the dragon was nothing but

> A cat, a tortoiseshell mother-cat!
> And a very diminutive cat at that!

It was typical of my father's attitude towards his family that
he used us all quite shamelessly, and to the delight of his large
circle of readers, as material for the verses, and sometimes even
for the prose pieces, which appeared every week in *Punch*.   For
some weeks he encouraged Beatrix to tell him stories on their
walks together, which he would then re-arrange a little and,
imitating her own highly individual spelling, serve up to *Punch*
under the title of 'Stories for Uncles'.   The game was finally
given away by one of the uncles, who told Beatrix of the
plagiarism that was going on, and suggested she should be
sharing in the proceeds; my father, however, turned away her

wrath by pleading a hard-working author's poverty and the
difficulty of paying for all the animals' dinners.  I have reason
to remember one example of this habit of his very vividly
myself.  During the first war he had started a series of sketches
in which we all appeared under aliases but in very familiar
surroundings.  In one of the sketches he described how he took
me up to London one day—I must have been nine years old—
to buy some rare stamps for my collection at Mr. Gibbons's
famous stamp shop.  He embroidered a little, but the story
was substantially as it had happened, and his readers guessed it.
During the course of the next few months, in spite of the fact
that it was war-time, stamps poured in for me from all over the
world, beginning with the Fiji Islands, then from Australia,
Africa, India, Barbados, Dominica and the Falkland Islands.
I was overwhelmed by this stroke of luck far exceeding my most
heated dreams, and became so spoiled by it that I was
thoroughly disappointed when a week passed without more
packets of long-desired exotic specimens rolling in.  Perhaps,
too, the episode sowed in me the seeds of a dangerous belief:
that the printed word can work miracles.

The fact that our childish adventures and imaginings, and
the antics of our dogs and cats, were so frequently written about
made us feel that we lived a privileged life, on an enchanted
island of which my father was Prospero ; a feeling that continued into my school days, for several of the masters at Summer
Fields were fans of ' R. C. L.'  Nothing could exceed my own
boundless admiration for his works.  There were two sketches
in his book *Sportsmen and Others* which I read over and over again
before I reached my teens, convulsed with noiseless merriment
on the nursery floor or in the bathroom where I had locked
myself.  They were called *The St. Bernard Puppy* and *The Black
Kitten* : I doubt if a father has ever given his son more pleasure
than I derived from these two sketches.  He had, however,
made his name as a writer of light verse, chiefly with his rowing
poems, but later also with his animal poems.  Nearly all the
rowing poems belong to an earlier period in his life, before his
marriage, when he was already a legend on the tow-paths of
university rivers, when he founded *The Granta* at Cambridge
and edited it for seven years as a nursery of talent which later

blossomed forth in *Punch* and elsewhere, boxed, fenced, travelled as a special correspondent to distant Balkan wars, went to America to coach the Harvard crew and changed the whole atmosphere of amateur sport in that country,* and made himself that enormous circle of devoted friends by the magic of his personality which long after he was dead I would see reflected in the eyes of strangers who, having discovered that I was my father's son, came up to tell me of the memories they cherished. The rowing poems are still, I fancy, as they were in his lifetime, held to be the best of their kind ever written, zestful, ingenious, inventive, with rhythms rippling through them that suggest at once a light breeze among the willows of a river-bank, and eight young athletes in a racing craft cutting with clean and vigorous strokes through the water:

> To make the rhythm right
> And your feather clean and bright,
> And to slash as if you loved it, though your muscles seem to crack.
> And although your brain is spinning,
> To be sharp with your beginning,
> And to heave your solid body indefatigably back . . .

I came to appreciate these poems later, when I took up rowing at Eton; but by then my father was beyond giving me any practical example or coaching advice, confined as he was increasingly to his chair and limited in his exercise to the very shortest outings with his beloved dogs. He had, however, given me my first lessons in sculling in the skiff—lessons I should have known how to profit by if the same ambition had stirred in me as had fired him in the days of his youth. At least he infected me, as he infected all of us at Fieldhead, with the regularly recurrent leaping fever of excitement about the Boat Race. Every year we grew more and more tense as the day approached, listening as if our lives depended on it to the prognostications of the experts at the breakfast table. I really

* There is an amusing echo of this in *The Personal Letters* of the late President (F. D.) Roosevelt. In 1897, at the age of fifteen, he wrote to his parents from Groton : ' Dear Papa and Mama, last night Mr. Lehmann, the English coach, gave us an informal talk on rowing. He went to Cambridge with Mr. Peabody, and, as you probably know, he is about the greatest authority on rowing in the world.'

believe it was the most important day of the year for my father, a great spring festival and consulting of omens: if Cambridge won, the crops would grow; if Oxford beat them, the future seemed dangerous and dark, only to be redeemed perhaps by the triumph of a Trinity or Leander crew at Henley later on. My father had also loved boxing, and believed that every boy should know how to defend himself scientifically with his fists. I tried dutifully to follow his advice at school, but after a few furious bouts in the gym it was evident that as far as the science of fighting went I was unteachable, and the plan was dropped. He was also very fond of shooting, and often used to go over to Hambleden to shoot with the Smiths and his old friend C. St. John Hornby; but the first rule he had taught us was never to harm an animal, and it was entirely his own fault if the idea of ' bagging ' birds in vast quantities revolted me and I refused to follow in his footsteps. As far as rowing went, it was not only that the dreamier pleasures of the river appealed to me rather than the arduous, and that when I reached Cambridge I found that rowing must be a wholetime devotion to which learning and poetry had inevitably to take second place; but also that my father's reputation as oar and coach was so overshadowing a legend that I felt deep down that I could not possibly compete with it.

The whole rowing fraternity of the Thames in those days was legendary. Nowadays, when so many of the big houses along its banks between Oxford and Windsor have vanished or been adapted to the needs of the Welfare State as institutions, and the river has become the pleasure-ground of week-enders, it is difficult to realize how short a time ago— scarcely half a century—it was inhabited chiefly by the true devotees of the arts of the river, who scorned, as my father taught us to scorn (though we had occasional guilty yearnings), the meretricious advantages of motor and accumulator. At every regatta the same names would appear among the competitors, and the faded Leander caps of fathers and uncles of the great rowing dynasties would follow the fortunes of the younger generation in the judges' launches at Henley and Marlow. The Stewards' Enclosure in the dog-days of July was their place of reunion and celebration; but in my earliest boyhood I can remember how they gathered too at Fieldhead, and round the luncheon table, and reclining afterwards in their deck-chairs beside the raft, would recall the splendours of the past, row over again their famous races, fit together the pieces of history of their friends and companions who had disappeared to the four corners of the earth, and tell again the old stories, always teased a little in the most affectionate way by my father, who loved making fun of them as much as he loved them. Those were the days, too, when the big riverside country houses often created their own rowing clubs. Harry Lawson (later Lord Burnham) had one of the best known at Orkney Cottage near Maidenhead, and under the colours of this club my father rowed many famous races. In 1900 he founded his own, the Fieldhead Boat Club; and many years later, while I was at Eton, my friends and I made up an eight and rowed to Bourne End, where my mother, as President, made us all members—the last members the Club was ever to enroll.

I may have given the impression that my father was the spoilt son of a prosperous family, indulging himself throughout his life in all he liked best, without any other thought or responsibility. He certainly lacked the driving ambition that might have brought him, with his manifold gifts, to more serious fame as an author or as a public figure in the professions; and that easy-going side of his nature was a constant source of annoyance to my mother, with her strong New England sense of the importance of career in a man's life. This impression, however, would be wrong. He was keenly interested in politics from his early youth, became a fervent admirer of Gladstone, and had already stood for Parliament, though unsuccessfully, before he married. With his instinctive sympathy for the victim and the underdog, his belief in fair play and his ever-present awareness of social ills in the mid-Victorian England in which he grew up, it was natural that he should become a Liberal; one of those radical Liberals who in our own time have found their political home in the Labour Party, but are never quite easy about the dogmatic side of Socialism or the inevitable conservatism of the Trade Unions within the new pattern of society. In his day all, or almost all, was still to be won; and I believe that a small voice of conscience was always urging him to do more to push reforms through, to justify his own full and fortunate life.

In all this he found a strong ally in my mother, whom he had met in America during his trip to coach the Harvard crew, at the home of his old Trinity friend, Frank Peabody. She came of the most independent puritan New England stock—on her mother's side descended from John Wentworth, Lieutenant-Governor of New Hampshire between 1717 and 1727, and on her father's from the English family of Burnham—and was of decidedly liberal outlook. She and my father clashed at their first meeting over votes for women, but evidently her forthright progressive views as well as her charm and looks conquered him, and on his next visit he persuaded her to marry him. In those days notabilities received favours that seem almost unbelievable in our egalitarian society: my parents found a special suite had been reserved for them on the Cunard liner in which they returned to England, and a special private coach was attached to the train from Paddington to Bourne End by which they completed their honeymoon journey, all without any intervention on their part.

Very soon after they had settled into their married life at Fieldhead, the Boer War broke out. My father had found the brash imperialism of the end of the century very little to his liking, and in common with most of his political friends, who had long suspected the motives of Cecil Rhodes and the financiers with whom he was associated, thought the Boers were being very shoddily treated, in a way that did no credit at all to England's name. He stood against the war, and many of his most eloquent and impressive speeches at the time were devoted to a destructive criticism of the war party. My mother remembers stormy political meetings in which the audience got completely out of hand. Though the anti-war party had far greater popular support in the Boer War than in either of the World Wars that followed it, it needed some courage to speak publicly in sympathy with the Boers while the fighting was going on, and there were occasions, notably one at Brighton, when he and my mother and others on the platform with them were obliged to make hurried and rather undignified exits to avoid rough handling. During this period Lloyd George offered him the editorship of the *Daily News*, when it changed hands and reverted to its former radical and anti-jingo course from which it had been deflected by the policy of E. T. Cook. He became a director with a financial stake in the new set-up, and accepted the editorship, but only for a short period which he found exhausting physically and nervously. There was continual tension under the surface, and finally, after a series of intrigues behind his back, he threw it up on a point of principle : he was determined that nothing should go into the paper of which he had not approved himself—but the manager thought otherwise. Curiously enough, he had as his assistant editor Harold Spender, brother of J. A. Spender and father of Stephen Spender, with whom I myself was to become so closely associated in the literary world. When one remembers that my father in his work for the *Daily News* was following in the footsteps of his great-uncle W. H. Wills, who had been sub-editor to Dickens on that paper and on *Household Words*, one cannot help being struck by the way in which patterns of family activity and the family friendships that arise from them persist.

These rankling disappointments were finally medicined by the landslide of 1905-6, in which he was at last returned as Liberal member for the Market Harborough Division of Leicestershire. He was popular, he was held in some esteem by Sir Henry Campbell-Bannerman, and everything seemed to point to a distinguished political career; but unfortunately he was already fifty, and his unceasing athletic exertions had been more of a strain on his physique than he realized. He contested the election at the beginning of 1910, and was again returned, but in the crisis of the Parliament Bill and the election that followed so soon after, he decided he could no longer stand the pace and withdrew. I also suspect that the death of King Edward was felt by him as a peculiarly deep calamity : he had the highest regard for that monarch, and considered that the generosity of his temperament, his tact and worldly experience had served the country far better than it knew during a period of exceptionally difficult political change. More practically, he had to consider the expense—no small matter in those days before M.P.s were paid. Only a year after his first election to Parliament he had suffered a serious

financial disaster.   Always generous and rather careless about
money, he had entrusted his affairs to a stockbroker friend who
was unfortunately more of a gambler than he realized.   One
day in 1907 he came back to Fieldhead from London to break
the news to my mother that this man's speculations had failed,
and that they were—at any rate at first sight—all but ruined.
The shock to my mother was overwhelming: she was expecting
another child, and a few hours later I was born.

My father's political life was thus more or less over by the
time I was old enough to be aware of it.   But the whole atmosphere of Fieldhead in my childhood was impregnated with
political feeling.   I saw my father as a crusader for the destruction of intolerable woes:  it seemed to me, unconsciously influenced by the strong radicalism of the early days of *Punch*,
and already beginning my reading of Dickens and troubled even
more by another book I discovered in the library, Charles
Reade's *It's Never Too Late to Mend*, impossible that a right-
minded person should be anything but a reforming Liberal.
Little enough comes back to me now of the two elections in
1910, when I was only three years old, apart from the fever of
canvassing which infected all of us children; but I do remember
the Liberal rosette I wore in my tubby brown overcoat during a
local bye-election a couple of years later, and the pang of misery
and disbelief I experienced when we heard that the rival Conservative candidate had been elected in spite of all our efforts.
I retired, baffled, to the *Children's Encyclopædia*, which so eloquently taught the march of progress and justice throughout the
centuries.

On more than one occasion between 1910 and 1914 my
father was urged by his Liberal friends, officially and unofficially,
to return to the fray, but he always refused, even when it was
suggested that he should stand again for Market Harborough.
His name, though I doubt if he knew it at the time, was on the
list of those Liberals who were to be made peers if the House of
Lords remained immovable about the Parliament Bill in 1911,
and I think it possible he might have accepted this honour, with
the less arduous political duties attaching to it, if it had come to
the point.   One day in July 1912, as he was waiting at Paddington to catch his usual late train home after a *Punch* dinner, he

ran into Winston Churchill, who was off to join the Fleet by the midnight express. Churchill had been brought close to him in the work of the Liberal Association in earlier days, and had, when at the Home Office, appointed him to a departmental committee which looked into the way aliens were treated on their arrival in England. They chatted together on the platform for some time, Churchill enlarging on the pleasure he derived from his association with the Navy. ' Why don't you come back? ' he asked my father. ' You ought to be in the House; come back to us. We're doing very well, *very* well! I think—a strong policy at home and abroad.'

The truth was that my father valued too highly the freedom he had found to devote himself to his growing family, his rowing interests and rowing friends, and his work for *Punch*. Not that the weekly dinners at 10 Bouverie Street were always as merry as outsiders might have imagined. The ' Table ' consisted in those days of Sir Owen Seaman as Editor, Linley Sambourne until his death, Anstey Guthrie, Sir Henry Lucy, E. V. Lucas, A. A. Milne from 1910 onwards, Charles Graves, the three cartoonists, Bernard Partridge, F. H. Townsend and Raven Hill, Laurence Bradbury and Phil Agnew to represent the proprietors, and my father. The real business of the dinner was to settle the political cartoons, and the Liberals were very much in a minority. ' A very stodgy discussion ', ' very sticky last night ' are phrases that continually recur in my father's diary, and on one occasion ' all of us became quite intolerable '. Nevertheless the cartoons were agreed and friendships were maintained—by a hair's breadth. What my father really enjoyed was his writing, the enormous fan-mail it brought him, and the occasions when he took over the editing if Owen Seaman was ill or away or on long holidays, often with Townsend, to whom he was particularly attached, to help him.

I was never really able to discover what my father's religious beliefs had been in the past, but neither he nor my mother ever tried very hard to make us devout Christians. We were, it seems to me now as I look back on it, left to make up our own minds about the metaphysical side of Christianity, but encouraged to recognize Christ as the greatest and wisest of ethical teachers. Strict, old-fashioned church-going, in a

Liberal household, and especially in a family descended from the author of *Vestiges of Creation*, carried with it a slight stigma of an ultra-conservative squirearchy. At the same time, by a curious contradiction, my parents were anxious that we should put in an appearance in church as often as possible on Sunday mornings, though they scarcely ever went themselves; I fancy this may have been more a social gesture of kindness towards the succession of nervous young curates who came to Bourne End, and the vicar we were all so fond of over at Woburn Green, Mr. Unsworth, a fine classical scholar admired by my father as much for his learning as for his human qualities. They did not, however, stand actively in the way of some of their zealously religious friends in the neighbourhood, who showed some concern that we should not stray too far from the flock; but it was my father's attitude of gentle teasing towards them, sharing the joke with us sometimes in secret winks, that I fear won us, and not their missionary endeavours. On one occasion, however, my mother joined forces with them to put on a Christmas Nativity play: my sisters were attired as angels behind and beside the crib, and I had to play the cock in a curious costume with wing attachments for me to flap as the curtain went up. I flapped them; but the ' cock-a-doodle-do ' that was supposed to come out at the same time went wrong in my desperate stage-fright, to the immense delight of the audience and my own shame.

My father was Beatrix's adored hero, while I (there was always some rivalry between us) was unbreakably attached to my mother and rushed to her as my champion in any crisis. I was haunted by the fear that I might lose her in some way, and one of the most terrible moments in my childhood was when she slipped on an icy front-door step as she was about to enter the car one Christmas Eve, and fell in a dead faint. I can still remember the scene: the servants and my sisters rushing towards her, the coachman helplessly twiddling his thumbs and exclaiming ' She's a goner ', and myself lingering paralysed with trembling lips in the background. But my anxiety about her did not need any such dramatic disaster to reach crisis point. She often used to take me with her in the Cadillac when she went for a fitting at her dressmaker's in Maidenhead, ' Myra

Salter '. . . . There was even something strange and sinister to me in the name.   More sinister were the dressmaker's assistants in their tightly corsetted black dresses, who came out to greet her as we arrived.   She disappeared within, and I was left alone in the car with the chauffeur.   I could endure ten or fifteen minutes of her absence, though with difficulty; but after that my fears began to mount, and with every further minute that passed became more and more out of control.   I pictured the most lurid things happening to her: the innocent, hard-working assistants turned into fiends who had trapped her in their den, torturing her, dancing indescribable rites of obscene triumph over her dying body in their black dresses, with Myra Salter herself directing the operation with my mother's long hat-pin in her grip.   Perhaps she had even been turned into a roly-poly pudding, like the unfortunate Tom Kitten in Beatrix Potter's story.   By the time she came out again, if the fitting had been a particularly long one, I was in paroxysms and beyond consolation.

It must, I think, have been these Maidenhead ordeals that made me dislike shopping with grown-ups so violently, and inspired my first poem, written at the age of three or four in a little book my nurse had helped me to thread together out of cartridge paper.   I unearthed it as I was looking through a drawer of childhood remains before starting this book, and found on the first page, in a large uncertain hand, the following terse and simple lines:

> SHOPPING
> SHOPPING
> NEVER
> STOPING

The spelling may be faulty, but I do not think I could ever write a poem of more concentrated expression, of more naked emotion.

# 7

A FOUR-YEAR gap separated me from Beatrix, the youngest of my sisters, and I was very conscious during my childhood of being the baby of the family. My sisters had parties, expeditions and mysterious occupations from which I was excluded, another world which loomed large in my imagination and made me determined to compensate for with a private world of my own. Thus I became rather a solitary, and grew even to welcome the days when my parents took all three sisters to London to see a play or for some other special occasion; it was an adventure I enjoyed to the last crumb to eat with Julia and the staff in the servants' hall, munching a large slice of the caraway seed cake that always appeared on the table there; and I had the garden to myself and could wander up and down the flower border and lavender beds talking to myself, as I looked for my favourite butterflies and bumble-bees, without anyone coming to laugh at me or tear me away.

My pleasure in my own company did not, however, go very deep; I could easily be shaken into a rage of resentment at not being asked to take part in all the exciting things my sisters did, and for the sake of peace I was sometimes allowed to be present, though my childish ways must have been very tiresome to them. I remember there were great sweet-making sessions, presided over by Helen, and I was sometimes allowed to help mix the ingredients, and got myself into a gloriously sticky mess, even though I didn't produce many sweets. More thrilling still, there were the literary sessions, when my sisters retired with pencil and exercise book to write poems and stories, and met afterwards to read them aloud to one another. I couldn't hope to compete, but I minded terribly if I was not allowed in at the final recitation. In my father's diary for 22 May 1910 I find the following entry:

The three girls became afflicted with literature this morning. I had to make composition books for them and they then set to work, Helen to write a story, Rosie a poem and Peggy a fairy-tale.

John distinguished himself by getting lost after lunch. I found
him reclining on two chairs on the Boat-house lawn. He had
wandered down on his own and had taken his cart with him. . . .

I have no recollection of this precise incident, but I think it
quite possible that alone on the Boat-house lawn that afternoon
I was suffering silently from my incapacity to emulate my
sisters, and resolving that I too would one day have a composi-
tion-book and write something in it of which my father could be
proud.    Perhaps the poem I have just described was born that
day.

My sisters also founded a Fieldhead Debating Society, at the
inaugural meeting of which Beatrix distinguished herself by a
passionate and tearful defence of Mary Queen of Scots, arguing
that her execution was especially heinous because it left her
dogs and cats without a mistress.    From those sessions also I
was excluded; but the worst exclusion of all was connected with
one of my father's great friends and fellow Liberals, Wedgwood
Benn (now Viscount Stansgate).    He was adored by my sisters,
and whenever he arrived to stay was dragged off by them at
once to take part in their games and to hear their confidences.
Only a week after they became ' afflicted with literature ', as my
father describes, they hatched a momentous plot with him.    He
invented for them a secret society called The Butterfly League,
for which butterfly badges were devised and even notepaper
printed with a butterfly design on it.    Once a year they went to
visit him at the House of Commons, had tea on the Terrace and
then retired to one of the rooms to conduct their impenetrable
business.    As soon as I got wind of this—everything was
cloaked in the utmost hush-hush and my sisters were remote and
tight-lipped when I tried to find out—it appeared to me unbearable that I wasn't a member myself.    I made such a
fuss, even shouting at night in my dreams about it, that
eventually, it may even have been a year or two years later, it
was decided that I should be allowed to join.    A special
initiation ceremony was invented, which consisted of a kind
of ritual tickling of my leg and removal of my shoe while
Wedgwood Benn and my sisters chanted a doggerel rhyme
together.    If I had not been made so nervous by all the mysterious hints of the ceremony beforehand, I might have taken it

in good part; but I suddenly felt they were all enjoying themselves far too much at my expense and that it was not a true initiation at all.   My soul was pierced by the realization that in spite of the hideous ritual I should never, never know what went on in the Butterfly League, and instead of the gurgles and chuckles they expected, to their horror I turned paler and paler and almost fainted away.   For years after, the sight of a piece of the League notepaper aroused in me anxious thoughts of failure and outlawry.

In spite of this, I sometimes got even with my sisters, as when one April Fool's Day I managed to substitute hollow eggshells for their real eggs on the breakfast table; and I was always ready to be the most fervent admirer of what they did, provided I wasn't kept at arm's length.   They were particularly fond of dressing-up and acting, and plays to which parents, staff and whatever visitors happened to be in the house were summoned succeeded one another with hectic frequency.   To me these plays, when I was allowed to stay up to see them, were the supreme thrills, and no one in the audience took them more seriously, was more utterly purged by pity and terror than I. In fact while the rest were doing their best to suppress mirth, I would be silent, tense and wide-eyed.   Details have grown blurred, and I cannot be sure whether I was present on an outstanding occasion recorded by my father in his diary at the end of August, 1910:

Before dinner there was a theatrical performance in the nursery, to which all the women servants came as spectators.   The programme (written in pencil by Rosie, I think) announced ' Fairy Play;  Dances, Drammatis Event;  The Fairy Queen's Farewell to her Ladies.'   A large screen divided the stage imperfectly from the audience—the whole thing was staged in the nursery—and I had to fold it up and stow it away when the performers declared themselves ready to begin.   The removal of this curtain disclosed Helen, as the Queen, on her throne.   She was robed in a bedspread and had her head bound up with a black and yellow silk band, which was perpetually coming off.   Beside her stood Rosie in a gauzy silvery dress with wings, and at her feet sat Peggy— Prince John was her name as we afterwards discovered—who was got up in a pair of quasi-Turkish knickerbockers, held up by a parti-coloured belt, a white sweater and a knitted green cap.

First the Queen called on Rosie (whose stage name never came out) to dance, which Rosie, after some delay caused by the unreadiness of the musical box, proceeded to do. Prince John was then asked ' to tread a measure ', and did it with great acceptance. A dreadful event then took place. It appeared that, while all this was going on, the Queen's eldest son was engaged in fighting without, for as soon as Prince John ceased from his measure the Queen commanded him to go and see how her eldest son was getting on. He promptly returned and said ' Your Majesty's eldest son has just been killed.' Thereupon the Queen at once fainted, and desperate attempts were made to restore her by means of brandy administered from a clothes-brush by Prince John. This proving ineffectual, Rosie and the Prince blew very hard on every part of the Queen's face, who then raised herself into a sitting position and ordered Rosie to go to the window (Prince John had brought the news of the catastrophe in through the door) and gather further details. Rosie accordingly danced lightly to the window, looked through it into the sky and declared in a perfectly composed and matter-of-fact tone that the Eldest Son was alive. ' It was the other one ', she added, leaving us to infer either that some other son had, in fact, succumbed, or that the Eldest Son's opponent had been killed. Anyhow all was now rejoicing and so remained until the Queen ordered Rosie to tell her what the noise was. Rosie returned with the announcement that it was a gun. ' What is it doing? ' asked the Queen. ' Shooting,' said Rosie. ' Is it shooting at a far distant country,' said the Queen, ' or at this lonely old castle? ' On hearing that the castle was the target, Prince John said loudly ' Then, I'm out,' and walked off in a hurry, leaving the Queen and Rosie together. Thereupon the Queen declared that the drama had now come to an end and commanded me to replace the screen. I don't think I've ever laughed so much.

Sometimes, a year or two later, I was allowed to take part in these plays myself. While Rosamond always cast herself for ultra-feminine parts, Beatrix's dream—perhaps unconsciously influenced by my mother's disappointment when she was told that her third child was yet another girl—was always to play the boy's part, as dashing and adventurous as possible, and she carried me along in her wake, in any subsidiary role she demanded, to feed this devouring impulse. But the time came when I staged shows for myself, in my own nursery. Someone

had given me a box of conjuring tricks, after a visit with my
father to Maskelyne and Devant which had inflamed my
ambition, and I remember an evening when the long-suffering
staff was persuaded to form an audience yet again, this time for
a display of my skill in the conjuror's art. I was suitably
attired in a red dressing-gown and a sugar-loaf magician's hat
which Beatrix had prepared for me; but it proved a terrible
occasion. Over-confident, impatient to prove my ability to put
on a performance as good as any of my sisters', I had hopelessly
misjudged my proficiency and my understanding of the instructions. Trick after trick went wrong, I grew more and more
flustered and incompetent, and when I could no longer disguise
from myself that the under-housemaid was giggling hysterically,
the footman purple in the face with suppressed laughter, and
old Dickie, my grandmother's lady's-maid, enjoying herself
hugely with a commentary that became more and more
cockneyishly caustic, I broke down and abandoned the stage.

Looking back on my relations with my three sisters, I am
amused to see how guilelessly, in my devotion, I opened myself
to their teasing and the traps they laid for me. This persisted
even after I had gone to my preparatory school, and I remember
one morning at breakfast during the holidays when they teased
me so much that I fled the room, scarlet in the face, shouting
' Sirens! sirens! ' Nothing, of course, could have delighted
them more than this romantic cry of anguish. The teasing
came mainly from Rosamond and Beatrix; Helen was always
a little remote, not in the least snubbing or unkind, but just too
far perhaps on the further side of a gulf of years quite to belong
to my country. I think also that Helen preferred the real world
to the world of imagination in which the rest of us spent so much
of our time, and actually wanted to be grown-up as soon as
possible—a thing incredible to me at the age of six or seven.
Rosamond I idolized. She was well aware of this, and took
cruel advantage on one occasion. All three of them were
having a tea-party one day to which Dolly, the head-gardener's
daughter, had been invited. As usual, I was excluded, but
hung about the stairs irresistibly drawn and longing to know
what they were doing. Suddenly the door of the day nursery
opened, and a solemn cortège emerged, Beatrix and Dolly

carrying Rosamond, who had her hands folded over her breast and her eyes closed in the attitude of death. Gloomily they marched past me: I tried hard not to believe that Rosamond had just died, but it all seemed too convincing even for my scepticism, and I bolted downstairs in despair to tell the terrible tale to my parents. I had hardly got to the baize door below when loud peals of demon laughter from Beatrix up above made me realize that I had been had again; but my heart went on thumping loudly for a long time.

Rosamond's early literary efforts filled me with enthusiasm: I was peculiarly susceptible to her high romantic manner, and wallowed in the doomful emotions and mystic intimations with which she filled her copybooks, listening spellbound to her thrilling tones as she read out poem after poem. All through my time at my private school I continued to think these poems the most marvellous I had ever known; and I possess a thin book carefully bound by myself, in which I copied out in Indian ink, in what I thought the most elaborately beautiful of scripts, three of her poems, illustrated in gold and colour with illuminated titles and initials, an achievement on which I lavished hours and hours of devoted labour. The titles of the poems are *Defiance*, *Epitaph* and *Enchantment*, the last-named the most highly wrought and embellished with a black, red-and-gold butterfly and a spider web for the opening verse, which reads as follows:

> Come fearfully among these forest trees;
> Prithee, look not behind; enchantment creeps
> Among the stealthy shadows with the breeze,
> And cloud on purple cloud, in swaying deeps
> The noiseless branches sweep around us—swing
>   To blind our eyes: beware!
> See how the dank, dead-scented brambles cling
> The crawling grass would have us in a snare.
>
> Is there no gleam in all this darkling stir,
> This vast unfriendliness of thorn and fir? . . .

My fanatical belief in her work was rewarded later on when I began to write poetry myself, by her unfailing willingness to read and judge, with the most gently critical encouragement, my own adolescent renunciations and soul-awakenings. But I

never achieved anything as lush as *Enchantment*, though I often
wished I could; indeed, I think that until I was about sixteen it
was my supreme model.

My relations with Beatrix have already appeared in various
incidents: though we both had decidedly independent natures
we were very much together, and I could rarely resist acquiesc-
ing in her leadership in all kinds of daring and mischievous
exploits, inspired partly by her reading of boys' adventure
stories, but also by her extremely fertile imagination. Beatrix
—or Peggy as she was always called, at her own desire, and
after a pony we kept—was also the comedian of the family, with
a gift that developed early for making extremely funny drawings
of everyone we knew and everything that went on in our family
circle, and a knack of burlesquing all the village characters.
Her imitations were ruthless. I loved any kind of comedy
played before me, and I think I must have been the ideal
audience: much of my childhood seems to have been spent in
entranced amusement at the comic performances of others.
My 'Aunt' Amelia, sister of Liza Lehmann the composer, and
daughter of great-uncle Rudolf, had a genius for impersonation
and ludicrous invention, and Beatrix had clearly inherited the
same family strain. I would beg her to dress up as a forceful,
busy-bodying elderly widow who lived nearby, or as the fat girl
of the school in the garden; she appeared once in my bedroom,
when I was supposed to be asleep, as the ghost of this fat girl,
and reduced me to such wails and shrieks of enjoyment that my
nurse rushed to the scene and indignantly banished the per-
former. She could sometimes be persuaded to perform downstairs in the library after tea, for my father enjoyed it almost as
much as I did. Indeed, he encouraged and abetted her in her
dressing-up, and later, during my time at Summer Fields, she
would almost regularly plot with him to hoax me at the end of
term. The idea was to get into my carriage on the train home
from Oxford disguised at one time as an asthmatic old market-
woman or, at another, as a frail and timid decayed gentle-
woman in an almost obliterating veil. And my father, who
had come that morning to fetch me away, when we reached
High Wycombe or Loudwater station, would lean out of the
window on some pretext—to show her where we were. The

extraordinary thing was that though after the first time I was
on the alert, I was taken in again and again—gloriously and
happily taken in—for it was as if the holidays had started with
a burst of the old music of our childhood.

Beatrix liked to score off me with my dreamy ways and innocent gullibility; but I don't think that, apart from sudden fits
of rage and bitter vows to get even, I bore her any malice. In
fact I was a willing slave to the fantasy life she led. On one
occasion she built a ' shop ' in the bushes, carrying about fifty
bricks two by two across the garden for the purpose, and stocking it with all sorts of sweets, ribbons, buttons and odds and
ends: and it even had a bell, hung on the berberis bush, which
one rang as one came in. I became an eager customer, and
my father having presented me with a sixpence, I rushed to the
' shop ' with it and was given in exchange exactly one acid-drop.
As the price of a bag of acid-drops (my favourite sweets) in
those days was about a penny, I was grossly swindled; but so
delighted was I with the ' shop ' that this did not occur to me
at all. On another occasion, during the war, she built a ' field-
kitchen ' in a great pile of earth in the Lovers' Walk. I
followed the construction of this marvel with hypnotized
admiration, and was promised the first soldier's meal that came
out of it. At last one evening a plate appeared of roast potatoes:
they were dry, shrivelled, blackened, smeared with ash and
heaven knows what else, but I gobbled them up with pure
enjoyment, as if they had been produced by the finest chef in
the world. Helen's sweets; Rosamond's poems; Beatrix's
roast potatoes; what in grown-up life has ever seemed so un-
flawed by any fault as these master-creations of my sisters to
childhood's eye of faith?

# 8

MY PARENTS always had a welcome for their friends whenever
they might turn up, and Sunday in summer was apt to be
a crowded day, with chance guests arriving by car, walking
over from nearby houses and even landing from their punts or

launches at the Boat-house, to swell the number of those who were staying for the week-end. Sunday, therefore, was a great day for James the butler, who felt himself to be the central pillar of the establishment, greeting the arrivals at the door with special reminiscences for each. The inflatedly pompous geniality with which he officiated in the dining-room on these occasions, would suddenly be punctured by a violent fit of chuckles—for, like so many butlers of the old school, he took an intimate interest in everything that went on, and would sometimes follow the stories that were being told with such absorbed enjoyment that the service went completely to pieces, the mint sauce being offered as a drink and one whole side of the table being left without vegetables or cheese.

When I look back on that time before the first World War, I see so many faces around the table, or gathered in the library afterwards, or assembled down by the raft in the glittering light of the river—faces that nearly all vanished from my life a great while ago—that I wonder how my father and mother ever had time for their own occupations. But this is only the winnowing action of memory, discarding the days when the family was alone, which must have been many, especially during the week. I remember the week-end parties and crowded Sunday gatherings for the drama they created on the outskirts of my own nursery world, and because as time lengthened away from them they seemed an important part of the special atmosphere of Fieldhead, which, though it was the perfect place for solitary musings and dreamings, was also an ideal setting for my father's generous Edwardian hospitality.

My father's rowing friends, often with their wives and their families, were among the most faithful frequenters of Fieldhead. Rowing prowess, as I have said, seems to run in families: their names echoed through my childhood like the names of the great warrior nobles in Shakespeare's history plays, their legendary exploits were recounted again and again, and great was the rejoicing when fresh laurels crowned an already famous family. My father's most intimate friends among them were the Rowes, the Pitmans, the Beggs, the Nickalls and the Golds; and when I finally decided at Cambridge that I was not the person to make a rowing dynasty of the house of Lehmann, I felt for a long time as if all these heroes, demi-gods and demi-goddesses who had smiled on me among the fabulous lawns and streams of my childhood, were standing at the end of a long vista, accusing me of backsliding with silent and reproachful glances. Most keenly I felt that, perhaps, with the kind, good-looking and gentle-voiced Claude Goldie, whom my father had informally adopted before his marriage as the result of a promise to his dying father, whom he had helped to educate and had coached and moulded into an excellent oar, and who, when my father was too ill to follow my own beginnings at Cambridge, felt that he had a special responsibility towards me.

Of my father's political friends I remember less because his active political life ceased when I was only three or four years old, and he saw less of them after that. The mischievous Wedgwood Benn had an ill repute with me, as I have already described; Jack Seely, Secretary of State for War in the Liberal Government and afterwards, as Lord Mottistone, Lord Lieutenant of Hampshire, had been made my godfather, but I scarcely ever saw him : he was not of that race of godfathers dreamed of by small schoolboys, who descend every term to provide a huge lunch of salmon mayonnaise and strawberries-and-cream and pass a handsome tip as they depart. Nor was my other godfather, Walter James the painter, later Lord Northbourne; but at least he presented me with a fine, gloomily atmospheric water-colour by himself, which hung in my rooms at Trinity beside a reproduction of Brueghel's ' Winter ' and the picture of ducks in flight that Peter Scott had given me.

All these shortcomings were more than made up for by my godmother, Violet Hammersley, who played an important part in the childhood of all of us, and never forgot a birthday or a Christmas. She was the mistress of Abney, the romantic riverside house behind its high walls next door, to which she had come as Arthur Hammersley's second wife soon after my mother's arrival from America. With the raven hair and features of the classic ballerina, a dark musical voice and a strong natural sympathy with the dramatic and passionate, she might, we always thought, have made a famous career on the stage. As it was, all her artistic feeling went into her private life and the entertainment of her friends. Her imitations and impersonations at a moment's notice—sometimes in charades with my sisters or my Aunt Amelia—were transformations, displays of utter possession by the part she had adopted, that left me open-mouthed, and sometimes even a little frightened. She had an immense knowledge of French and English literature, and had, I believe, a considerable influence in forming the taste of all of us. Wonderful above all were the evenings when she read aloud. Reading aloud has always seemed to me a more difficult art than most people imagine, perhaps because in my estimation no one, excellent though my father and mother were, has ever approached the skill of my godmother. Never for a moment could my attention wander as she read chapter after chapter of some famous novel or biography, with just the right variation of tone and the right amount of dramatization and voice-change for the dialogue. If LeFanu's *In a Glass Darkly* and De Quincey's *Murder as a Fine Art* have always haunted me, it has been her doing. A little later a lasting love of Max Beerbohm was implanted in me by her performance— which I obliged her to repeat again and again—of ' No. 2 The Pines ' and ' Going out for a Walk ' from *And Even Now*. Her children, tall Christopher with the look of a romantic Italian nobleman, mischievous David with whom I was later at Eton, and my own special intimate, Monica, the youngest, were our constant playmates in every kind of game of hiding and pursuing and dressing-up; David in particular leading us on in wild games of Red Indians, building wigwams on the lawn from which he and Beatrix would emerge, feathered and painted and uttering blood-curdling whoops. There were also rare, exotic trips in the gondola and the sandolo, which were kept in the Abney Boat-house; for Arthur Hammersley had a Venetian gondolier, Giulio, who came every year for the summer months. As a wedding present, he gave my mother four of those brass sea-dragons that one sees on the sides of gondolas in Venice, to be used as supports for fire-irons; two of them are at this moment serving the same purpose in my London house.

As constant in their visits to Fieldhead as my father's rowing set, were his literary friends and cronies of the *Punch* table, and many writers whose earliest efforts he had supported in the days when he edited *The Granta* and was a director of *The*

*Speaker*. My mother remembers that one of the first big celebrations of her married life was the descent of the whole *Punch*
table to dinner at Fieldhead one night. It was an extremely
festive occasion, and she laughed more throughout dinner than
ever before in her life; but the occasion appears to have ended
awkwardly, for Sir John Tenniel and Phil May, inspecting the
pictures upstairs after dinner, quarrelled violently over a Fred
Walker in her boudoir. Famous quarrels, indeed, form part
of my family's most cherished memories: one of my grandfather's favourite stories was how Robert Browning and John
Forster quarrelled one night at his brother-in-law's house in
Kensington Palace Gardens. The guests, including my grandfather and Landseer, had gone out for a moment with their
host, leaving Forster and Browning in fairly animated argument
over a report by Lady William Russell that the arrangements at Marlborough House, where the Princess of Wales
lived, were in an incredible state of neglect. Forster had
pooh-poohed Lady Russell's story, and Browning, irritated by
his pompous manner rather than impelled by chivalrous instinct,
had rushed to Lady Russell's defence: when they returned, the
astonished guests saw Browning, trembling with fury, about to
hurl a decanter of claret at Forster's head.

Only dimly can I remember the visits of the *Punch* fraternity
in my early years. Sir Owen Seaman, who had made his debut
in *The Granta* and had preserved his affection for my father in
spite of strong political disagreement, I see as an occasional and
rather hurried visitor eager to talk *Punch* shop and hardly entering into our lives. E. V. Lucas and his wife and the Milnes
were much more of our intimate circle. My father's close
friendship with A. A. Milne had started two or three years
before I was born. He no longer ran *The Granta*, but followed
it closely, and had been struck by a serial which appeared in it
under the title of ' Jeremy, I and the Jellyfish ', a piece of
' sparkling and entirely frivolous and irresponsible irrelevancy ',
as he delightedly called it. A. A. Milne was editor at the time,
and when my father wrote to ask who was responsible for the
serial, he confessed that he was the author himself: they met
and became firm friends, and my father keenly encouraged him
to write for *Punch*. But he did not by any means confine his

interest in the younger writers of the day to the ' kindergarten ' of *The Granta* or recruits to the *Punch* table.   He had been one of the dominating influences in *The Speaker* (later merged with *The Nation*) while under the editorship of J. L. Hammond, and had then been closely associated with Augustine Birrell and ' Q '; Barbara Hammond has told me in a letter that she has ' a distinct remembrance of him as the good genius, with strong and excellent pro-Boer and advanced Liberal views, who never made anybody feel that he wanted to interfere about anything said in the paper '.   He followed the work of the new Georgian poets, Wilfred Gibson, Lascelles Abercrombie, Ralph Hodgson, Rupert Brooke and John Drinkwater, with shrewd appreciation, occasionally writing articles on their work in the *Westminster Gazette*.   John Drinkwater was eventually introduced into the Fieldhead circle by his brother George Drinkwater, the painter, who had long been one of my father's most intimate younger friends in the rowing world.   G. K. Chesterton, who lived nearby in Beaconsfield, was an occasional visitor: I can still see his vast form at the luncheon-table, as he held forth and entered into long and amusing disputations with the other guests.   My father had had something to do with his launching into literature; but far more with the early struggles of Alfred Noyes, who, as shy as Chesterton was assertive, would also appear for week-ends and kept up a long correspondence over many years with my father, whom he considered his literary mentor and confessor.

One of the young writers he had helped most effectively through *The Granta* was Barry Pain; of him and his family we saw a great deal, for the good reason that he was married to my ' Aunt ' Amelia.   Aunt Amelia was one of the legendary figures of my childhood, and meant more to me than all my other relations put together.   I can no longer, alas, recapture the peculiar fascination she exercised over me; it was something to do with the voice—it is her voice I first imagine I catch an echo of as I try to live back into those timeless moments when, arrayed in silk blouse and white shorts and silver-buckled shoes, I sat beside her on the camp-shedding at the Boat-house, my eyes fixed on her face, which I would turn towards myself with a determined hand whenever her attention seemed to stray from

my insistent demands; a great deal to do with the fantasy and
absurdity of the stories she used to invent for me; but more
than anything else, of course, due to the fact that a secret sympathy and fondness united us, which transformed everything
she said or did into pure delight.    She loved dressing up, and
there was a long war between her and my father, she employing
every trick to deceive him with her disguises, he determined to
catch her out.    I can just remember one incident, plotted with
my mother, when she appeared at the door as an old woman
selling tracts and got my father to buy one before he discovered
her.    It was only one of numerous similar incidents in the Aunt
Amelia saga, which I often demanded should be repeated to
me with every detail fully described while I rubbed my hands
with joy.    When I was told of her death during the first war,
and of the thoughts of love she sent me, I felt utterly desolate,
and certain that never again in my life would I find anyone
who could mean so much to me, or touch my private world so
magically.

Many other aunts, uncles and cousins arrived to swell the
company at week-ends, but all the younger generation were
nearer to my sisters in age than to me, and I did not get to
know them until many years later.    My father was the last of
his family to marry, and my Aunt Nina, Lady Campbell, had,
for instance, four sons and a daughter who were already grown-
up by the time I was out of my pram and allowed to sit at the
luncheon-table as a special treat on Sundays:  Ronald was
already in Paris at the beginning of his diplomatic career, and
Eddie had gone to India with his regiment, the 60th Rifles, of
which he later became Colonel.    My cousins Nina and Herbert
came closer to my world; I was captivated by Nina's unfailing
sweetness and gaiety, but I always stood slightly in fear of Herbert, who was apt to play malicious practical jokes on me and
Beatrix—and no wonder, as he had to endure the constant
teasing of Helen and Rosamond, egged on by Nina, and must
have felt in need of getting even with us all somehow.    It is
difficult for me now to see the pinching, arm-twisting naval
cadet behind the kind and distinguished Captain of Her
Majesty's Navy who covered himself with glory at the Battle of
Narvik; but during Herbert's visits Beatrix and I felt like two

small allied countries facing a powerful aggressor, and were in constant secret session to be prepared against all attacks. Terrible and memorable for ever was the day when he brought off his greatest coup: I can see, as if it were yesterday, Beatrix swinging alone in mid-stream in the punt, helpless without pole or paddle, and myself, almost blinded with tears, hurling myself at Herbert as he stood laughing and pointing by the raft. Far away up the garden, oblivious of this drama, but its indirect cause, the mischievous Nina was in close colloquy with Helen and Rosamond, telling them things about the grown-up world of which their parents would certainly not have approved.

# 9

IN the years before 1914 my father ran Fieldhead lavishly, with an ample staff which lived in a busy territory of its own behind the green baize door downstairs and the swing-door at the end of the bedroom corridor upstairs. As so often happened in big country houses in the old days, the children were freemen of both front and back territories, and it was inevitable that the leading personages of the staff should loom large in my world. Besides, there were many lumber-rooms, store-cupboards and cellars at the back that had the most exotic attraction for me. For instance, leading out of the kitchen there was a dark little room where the cook kept all her stores: icing sugar, preserved cherries, candied peel, cooking chocolate, and the labelled tins of sultanas, currants and raisins —a cave of inexhaustible delights, all the more alluring because of the shadowy depths into which it stretched. Nearly as good was the larder on the other side of the tiled passage, even more jealously guarded, into which I would sometimes tiptoe to survey the long rows of bottled fruits and jams on the higher shelves, the Virginia hams of which my parents were particularly fond and the remains of cold joints, stewed fruits, jellies and puddings of the day before. It was a risky business, gaining entry into that larder; there had to be an especially active bustle in the kitchen before one could feel certain that one's stealthy turning of the handle would not be heard, but the risk seemed worth taking, not for any quick gobbling of delicious tit-bits, but rather for the æsthetic pleasure of contemplating all those cool and waiting joys of future meals.   Further down the passage, the cellar was marvellous to me, not for the rows of dusty wine-bottles, but because it housed Helen's model railway, powered by a tiny engine which gave vent to a shrill whistle when the water boiled and set off on its always catastrophic journey with hectic speed; and the magic-lantern which under my father's control had brought terror to my earliest years with all too convincingly coloured slides of the history of Bluebeard. But most compelling of all was the telephone-room, so called because it had a huge, immovable early box machine in it beside the cupboards where extra crockery and glass were kept; it was not, however, the telephone on which my imagination feasted, but the safe, which took up the whole of one side of the high, dark room.   Whenever I knew that James was putting silver back there, I would rush down to get a glimpse of the inside of the fabulous treasure-house, before he pushed the heavy door back into place with the muffled ' whoof ' of escaping air.   On the baize-covered shelves I could see all sorts of leather boxes for the knives and forks and spoons; beside them silver and gold salt-cellars, sweet-dishes and cream-jugs, boxes that were never opened and I felt certain contained glittering marvels beyond price, and on the shelves that were far out of reach of my small arms all manner of inscribed trays, challenge cups, goblets and bowls, some of them wedding presents to my parents, but most the trophies that my father had accumulated as oar and coach through all that vista of mythical years before I was born.   Fingering the strong lever that controlled the door from the outside, I would dream that if only I could get in by myself for a few hours, I would discover at the back, behind all the boxes, or up at the top if only I could clamber there, secret chambers that would spring open as I touched a catch concealed under the baize, to reveal treasures that perhaps even James did not know about—heirlooms of my grandparents that might unriddle some of the mystery I felt to cling about my remote ancestry on both sides of the Atlantic.

The pantry in which James lorded it was at the foot of the back stairs. I liked to slip into it as often as I could to peer into the drawer which contained hammers, screwdrivers, clippers and piles of nails and screws of every sort and to watch James polishing the silver under the old Parliament Clock; but my welcome was uncertain, depending on James's temper, which generally in its turn depended on the amount of work he had to do, and I would often creep out again abashed and spend my time instead gazing at the system of bells just outside. In general James was kind, indulgent and sentimental; and he would often give me a penny to run off to the sweet-shop and buy myself a bag of acid-drops. His large, bald, humpty-dumpty head emphasized his pomposity when he was in authoritative mood; it was not, however, the children who suffered from these moods so much as the young footmen and the cook, who had to listen while he droned on instructing them, laying down the law through the kitchen hatch, and reminiscing about the exalted past of Fieldhead before *they* had appeared on the scene. He was my father's oldest servant, except one, and with that one a long, jealous feud was maintained: my grand-mother's lady's-maid, Dickie, who used to come down from London to spend several months with us every year. Though very old, she was the cleverest and neatest of needlewomen, and my mother was always anxious to have her in the house. She also sometimes accompanied the family on its migrations, whether to Brighton or to Paris, as the most experienced, the most widely travelled, the most reliable and most cuttingly amusing of retainers and companions.

Dickie had a room reserved for her, right at the top of the house, with perhaps the most attractive view of all the rooms overlooking the garden. In my memory it is always there that I discover her, though glimpses come back of her brushing my mother's hair under the lamplight in the boudoir, of my going to see her off at the end of her visits at the station, where I would find her settled in the little tin-roofed waiting-room at least half an hour before the train was due, and of her proceed-ing slowly round the garden paths on a summer afternoon, very small, very sedate, and enveloped in her black, bugle-covered dress and black bonnet. Perhaps I remember her best in her own room, because she kept there a little bag of sweets and would offer me one on my visits. While I sucked the toffee or acid-drop beside her, her head slightly nodding, bent over her needlework, she would talk to me, asking me about my own pursuits with a grave and delicate attention, occasionally slipping in a mocking remark about Julia or James as quick as the flickering tongue of an adder, or telling me long stories about my grandparents and the house in Berkeley Square, my father's youth and his exploits in the years before his marriage. How I wish I could remember those stories, for with her sharp cockney eye she had missed nothing in those days, and in her mind, so clear and retentive even in her old age, were stored all the lost chapters of the family past, which after her death I realized too late should have been written down. She would also tell me about her own life, and into her voice there would often come a note of great sadness. She was called ' Dickie ' because her first husband's name had been Dickinson : he had been the father of a boy, the apple of her eye, who had died in childhood long, long before. After Dickinson's death she had married a cabinet-maker from Bohemia called Martin Slezina, and she had actually gone over to Austria-Hungary to share his life. It was only later, after he too died, that she returned to London and entered our family life again. She had outlived all her own people, and was entirely alone : her sister Louisa, who had for a time acted as cook and who, like some other great artists, could not face supreme tests of her skill without the almost incapacitating support of the gin bottle, had also died before my time ; but in addition to her old-world dignity and exquisite manners Dickie had astonishing courage, and lived out her last years in determined independence. She really preferred, I think, her solitary existence in London to Fieldhead, and her visits had to be most carefully negotiated by my mother : only during the Zeppelin raids of the first World War would she suddenly descend upon us by train and reoccupy her room upstairs without any preparation.

The tension between her and James was at its greatest in the servants' hall. She despised him for being woolly-minded and slow in the uptake, for she herself was quick and clever and could never be caught out ; but she was also jealous of him for being so close to my father, and in addition, so to speak, the president or chairman of the staff. He sat at the head of the table and officiated with the joint, while the cook sat at the other end. On those days of happy exile when I had my meals with them, I can remember that her remarks, in the very formal atmosphere of a servants' hall of those days, were always brief and tart, slightly frightening to the housemaids and kitchen-maids, and often puncturing James's ponderous harangues with a neat and scathing efficiency that confused but did not deflect him.

James himself did not live in the house: he had the back part of the little red-brick lodge by the gate at the end of the drive, a mysterious region which seemed rather forbidding: it was, I believe, only after James's death that I penetrated upstairs to his bedroom, and found, to my surprise, a large and well-filled bookcase in which many of the books written by my father's friends—and therefore James's friends also—were prominent. I think this bookcase was his secret compensation for Dickie's thrusts, for she did not, as far as I know, read at all, and I can imagine that when worsted in some wordy contest with her, he might retire to this room and turn over the pages of a book written by one of the guests he had looked after at Fieldhead, and reflect with satisfaction that all this was beyond her world.

The front part of the lodge was inhabited by Mr. Goodman, the head-gardener, and his family. He was a remarkable man, of far too keen an intelligence to have spent his life in such a position. Nowadays a man of his mental energy and under-standing of the world would be bound to have a proper school-ing and rise to a position of wider and more important responsi-bility. Goodman, however, had learnt all he knew of literature, politics and science from books he had bought or borrowed from the house, from newspapers and conversations with my father and his friends; he was tied, too, by a patient devotion to an ailing wife rather older than himself and very much his intellectual inferior. He was a man of independent thought, a natural philosopher. In my childhood a zealous churchman, always keen to assist the local curate in his work, the mass cruelties of the first World War made him feel that something was wrong at the root with conventional religious teaching; gradually

he turned against religion altogether, with a violence in proportion to the fervour of his former conviction, and no one in
clerical garb dared to approach him.   In the 'thirties, when he
was already over seventy but displaying a vigour that many
men of fifty might envy, he had gone so far that it was only one
step more for him, dismayed by the collapse of the Liberal
Party, to become a Socialist.   He read the productions of the
Left Book Club avidly, and followed the fortunes of the Republicans in Spain with fervent attention.   At dusk sometimes
he might be encountered crossing the lawn after locking-up the
Boat-house and the potting-sheds, simmering with a murderous
rage against the established order of things and prophesying
rivers of blood; which did not prevent him remaining an
excellent gardener and on the best of terms with all of us.   In
his old age, after the second World War, when he had crossed the
border of ninety, I think he had seen through the apocalyptic
pretences of Communistic Socialism as well; the story of the
growth and changes in his views and the reasons for them would
have been an unique document.

On the last day before we left Fieldhead for good I went over
to his cottage, and while we sat in his front parlour he called to
mind his own early days and my father's early days at the house.
He had come up from Somerset as a boy, and told me that there
were men in his family who could remember the bad old times
of the press-gangs, and how the rumour would spread through
the villages of their approach and all the able young men
would take to the hills and the woods.   He had been employed
first of all at Abney, next door; the hours were long and he was
always expected to be available, Sundays as well as week-days,
so when he was courting he used to slip off at dusk and walk
many miles up-river to where his girl lived, and come back at
dawn; and one day he came back with the girl herself.   It
was a hard life, he said, but ' we were a stronger lot in those
days '.   He was skilful and knowledgeable as a gardener, with a
little more than the usual head-gardener's strain of independent
obstinacy in his make-up, and a considerable pride in the garden,
which he often reminded me had originally been laid out by one
of the chief men from Kew.   He liked to be consulted about
garden fêtes and functions and put in charge of them, but he

was quick to feel that the neighbourhood was imposing on my parents with incessant requests for every kind of dance, old folks' tea-party, jumble-sale, raffle and sports gathering to be held in the Pavilion or on the lawn. He would be found muttering about ' a herd of elephants ' and ' litter everywhere ' and ' two-legged birds having got into his strawberry beds ', and I used to think sometimes that he would gladly have wrung the necks of some of the most persistent charity-planners—as he wrung the necks of any unfortunate starlings or blackbirds that were caught trespassing under his nets. He seemed rather a daunting figure in my earliest childhood, ever watchful to see that small fingers were not surreptitiously closing round too many ripe figs and nectarines; but he could be wheedled to relent, and would lead me to a special monster strawberry that he had spied lurking under its leaf, or produce an extra-juicy fig he had just plucked from the top of the tree. And on autumn and winter mornings my garden explorations always led me in the end towards his potting-sheds, through the arch-way in the nectarine wall to the yard where the rubbish-heaps were. Perhaps in the sheds the three other gardeners—old Stacey and young Bob, and Godden, who wore his Boer War medal-ribbons on Sundays—were drinking their tea and munch-ing their bread and cheese among the spades and forks and trowels. I would peer through the cobwebbed window of Goodman's own special shed and, finding him there, tap on the window and beg for apples; then he would lead me into the store-room beyond, and I would gaze with wonder at the heaped tiers of apples of every sort, yellow and red and greeny-red and huge ones striped like a dahlia and the little hard, sweet russet ones, and go away triumphant with two or three stuffed into bulging pockets. His special domain, however, always seemed to me the greenhouses; and when I think of him now, the characteristic picture that comes to my mind is of his spare, erect form of medium height, with straw hat slightly tipped over his forehead, busy with his potted bulbs, his toma-toes or his chrysanthemums in one of the two contiguous green-houses. As I grew older, we became firm friends, and on my way back from a walk along the river with the dogs I would look in on him there: he would tilt his straw hat back and his

eyes would twinkle, and we would discuss the latest family news
or the political events of the moment, or the prospects of peace
and war, and he would make his shrewd comments and his
dark prophecies; and with doom ringing in my ears, but stimulated and amused, I would leave him again to his pruning and
potting and watering.   And I am also haunted by an image
of him shadowy in the late summer twilight, with the darkening
mirror of the water behind him, locking up the changing-rooms
and the big roller doors of the Boat-house, suggesting to my
imagination some imperishable country god in humble disguise as in the oldest legends, and the river beside him flowing
like Time into the night.

# I O

MUCH of my boyhood seems to have been spent taking great
danes, spaniels, mastiffs, sealyhams and pekineses for walks.
It became, in fact, an accepted thing that whenever everyone
else was busy, or pretending to be busy, it was my duty,
whatever I was doing, to take the dogs for this exercise.   I
grumbled that I was becoming nothing else but a kennel-boy,
but most of the time I enjoyed it, not merely for the walking
itself, but also for the stimulus I found in it for a dreaming
mind.   I must admit that there is something in Max Beerbohm's criticism of inveterate walkers, that the further they go
the more inane they become; but taken in a leisurely fashion,
alone, and for the first hour at any rate, there is nothing like a
walk for stirring those obscure processes of the mind out of
which poems and stories are born.   When the urge to write
was on me, a long walk by the river or into the woods would
plunge me deep into a fantasy life, where whole trilogies of
novels, epics in twenty-four books and poetic dramas in vast
cycles would hover cloudily before me; dreams only to be
disturbed when a swan was seen angrily bearing down on an
astonished pekinese, or a great dane rushed off to battle with a
bristling enemy dog descried in the distance.

I was never a bird's-nester, though I remember Beatrix
leading me in hushed excitement to some thrush's or black-
bird's nest she had found in a remote part of the garden; but as
I grew older, perhaps between my sixth and ninth year, butterflies, moths and insects of every sort became an absorbing
passion with me. I grew to have an expert knowledge of the
differences between the species and the peculiarities of each
one's life-habits. I learnt to distinguish every kind of caterpillar and knew the plants it was likely to be found on; I kept
several varieties in boxes, the furry ones giving me rashes all
over my hands; I bred silkworms feeding them on the leaves
from the mulberry tree behind the Pavilion, and unwound the
delicate golden thread of their cocoons on Heath Robinson
machines constructed from old cotton bobbins. On walks over
the hills with my sisters, while they were looking for wild
flowers, I would spot from several yards away a rare blue
butterfly or even a chrysalis hanging under a branch; I dreamt
of a farm of giant caterpillars of the Emperor Moth, Death's-
head Hawk Moth and Privet Hawk Moth, but somehow my
parents guilefully managed to prevent me filling my nursery
with these monsters. Nothing intrigued me more than the
mystery of their changes, and sometimes when guests were
present at luncheon or tea I would break into the conversation
and volunteer embarrassing information about the number of
thousand eggs a particular kind of butterfly could lay in a
minute, or describe its mating habits with an innocence that had
entirely failed to relate them to the appearance of babies in
human families. Second only to butterflies and moths, bees,
dragon-flies and beetles fascinated me. At an early age I was
given several volumes of J. H. Fabre's works translated into
English, and I read them over and over again; I got hold of a
copy of Maeterlinck's *Life of the Bee*, and my thoughts obsessed
by his description of the nuptial flight of the queen bee, began
to look for queen bees everywhere, with lamentable results in
multiple stings and dashes to the bottle of Pond's Extract in the
bathroom cupboard; I kept water-beetles in large, weed-filled
bowls in the night nursery, but this had to be stopped because
the housemaids were terrified by the way the beetles, lifting the
handkerchief with which I had covered the bowl for the night,

would suddenly take flight from the water when the blinds were undrawn and zoom noisily round the room—one old char-woman who had come in to help with the spring-cleaning went off into a dead faint one day when this happened. I persuaded my father to give me a microscope, and for hours together would explore the strange ornamentation of moths' eggs and the minute jewelled scales that came off the wings of Red Admirals and Peacock butterflies. I think my parents began to regret that they had encouraged me to take an interest in Nature; but when my schooling at Summer Fields began, this interest gradually faded and died out, and the volumes of *Butterflies and Moths of the British Isles*, with their ever marvellous colour plates, lay neglected at last on the nursery shelves.

While this passion was raging, other inevitable passions of boyhood awoke in me: the bicycling craze, the stamp craze, the Meccano craze, the fretwork craze and the electricity craze. I mastered a bicycle early—in my fifth year—impatient to join my sisters in the sport of accelerating round and round the outer paths of the garden until one came to the final free-wheel past the flower-border, ' Bicyclists' Dashing Hill ' as it was named by us; so intoxicated did I become with this pleasure that at one time scarcely a day passed without my returning to the house and my disgusted nurse or mother with bleeding and scratched knees after yet one more spill. I have already described how the stamp craze landed me in one bad scrape and gave me one unexpected transport of delight. The collecting of stamps is always supposed to be an education in geography and history, and I think it did teach me quite a lot of miscellaneous and moderately useful information; my favourite stamps, for instance, from the point of view of romantic pictorial beauty, were those issued by the Austrian Government for Bosnia-Herzegovina, and I thus had a clear idea at once of the part of the world where the tragedy of Sarajevo occurred. Stamps also opened inviting windows on to the immense variety of foreign landscapes, jungles with elephants and tigers charging out of them, gigantic rushing rivers and mountain waterfalls, totem poles grinning by wigwams, weird-plumed birds perching in tropical surroundings, and savages waving spears below the well-known profiles of King Edward and King George. I

gazed with wanderlust waking in me at the stars over the deep
blue seacoast view, with its sombre mountains and full-rigged
sailing-ship, inscribed Correos de Costa Rica, at the improbable
river steamers on the stamps of the Sudan Postage Tax and the
weird sea-craft of Labuan; I repeated over and over again the
romantic names of Afrique Occidentale Française, Sénégal,
Mauretanie, Côte d'Ivoire, Oubangui-Chari-Tchad, Chamba
State and Nicaragua of the wild desert mountains; but looking
back on it now that the passion has entirely subsided—it was
long dead before I left Eton—what astonishes me is the unpredictably fickle and irrational nature of the lust for possession.
When stamps were the rage, the supremely desirable treasure,
to be coveted above all other possessions, was a dull little three-
cornered stamp without perforation from the Cape of Good
Hope, which entered my daydreams suffused with mysterious
glamour and kept me awake at night; yet only a short while
before, the same glamour had attached to a fat and ugly caterpillar with an absurd spiky tail which if I could only find it
would evolve for me into that beauty of all beauties, the Privet
Hawk Moth; and I was conscious that for some of my friends
a rare bird's egg, totally useless and not necessarily among the
most pleasing æsthetically, exercised the same immeasurable
attraction.   Now that I care nothing at all for the spiky-tailed
caterpillars nor for the little three-cornered pieces of paper, I
am left bewildered by the meaning of it all.   And yet I wonder
whether I have really become very different, for I have to
admit that a rare first edition of some famous author excites my
desire to possess with almost as great a violence; and as any
book-collector knows, the mysterious glamour has nothing to
do with beauty of typography or elegance of format.

My adventures with electrical bells, lamps, magnets and
batteries and coils within coils were fired by the presence of the
machines in the woodshed, where we made our own electricity
in the days before the local system arrived.   I can remember
watching it at work, rather awe-inspired at its humming and
chugging, while Bob or Stacey sat beside it and chopped the
logs in the semi-darkness; and I can remember the lights
suddenly dimming in the house when it went wrong, and James
hurrying to the telephone-room to fetch the green-shaded oil-

lamps that were always kept in reserve. They were also stimulated by the magazine *Hobbies*, which, derided by my sisters, nevertheless seemed to me the guide to endless possibilities of power and miraculous achievement. Reading *Hobbies*, and the more lurid *Scientific American*, bundles of which were sometimes sent over by my New England cousins (who became real engineers and real inventors), I began to experiment with all sorts of chemicals and test-tubes, pieces of Meccano littered the floor, still refusing to make the cranes, bridges and dynamos that the pictures promised me, toy trains came to disastrous collisions in tunnels painted outside to imitate a mossy bank while boiling water spilled all over the linoleum, boxes and brackets laboriously prepared with blunt carpentering tools failed to stick together and stuck to my shorts instead, and at last the fatal fretsaw, first a hand one and then, joy of joys, a big treadle machine worked with furious zeal by my short legs, began its busy, footling activity, transforming beautiful pieces of satin-smooth wood into hideous imitations of crude lace.

And yet all this messing and making and collecting, all these attempts to perform simple magic and to foster the magic of nature, left me unsatisfied. I wanted to do more, I did not know what; there was an itch in my hands, in my mind to shape and change and discover in ways far beyond what I had already attempted; I wanted to master and make use of everything around me for some end that was never plain to me; all the sights and sounds and smells of nature urged me to possess them, to preserve them, to transform them into myself; I kept nature notebooks and laboriously described in them my minute observations about hips and haws and oak-apples and bumble-bees and newts and frog-spawn, but I always abandoned them, feeling that they were an inadequate substitute for some art of communion or transmutation that still eluded me. The Meccano nuts and bolts rolled away under the chest of drawers never to be retrieved, the fretsaw snapped for the last time and was not repaired, the bits of string dangling in strange solutions with crystals collecting round them were thrown out of the window, the beetles were returned to the pond and the female Red Underwings laid their myriad eggs uncounted by my scientific eye. Perhaps books were the answer; all this was a long process, spreading over many years and stretching into the first holidays from Summer Fields; but books, words, gradually seemed more and more to be what it was all tending towards.

# I I

Just before the school was started in the Pavilion, my mother decided that my sisters must have proper French teaching and engaged a Belgian, Maria Jaquemin, to stay with us; it was natural, therefore, that she should eventually become the regular French mistress at the schoool.  ' Mademoiselle ', as she was known amongst us, did not enter my world very much, and I can remember her only as a rather stern and sharp woman, without charm but with considerable intelligence and will-power, her black hair done up in a big coil on top of her head. Her presence in the house made us all French-conscious, for French was continually being talked, French children's books appeared on the nursery shelves, and French songs were often sung.  I shall always be grateful to my parents for creating an assumption in my mind that French was a natural language to talk and read and that there was no virtue in talking it with a crude, Anglo-Saxon accent.  My school days, in fact, were a falling away, and I think I understood French better when I was nine than for many years after I left Eton; I have a curiously distinct recollection of being able to read a book by the Com-tesse de Ségur, which came out of the ' Bibliothèque Rose ', a rather morbid (and distinctly Freudian) story of a little kilted Scottish boy who was always getting into scrapes but really had a heart of gold.  My own education in French, however, properly began when, as the school grew and more and more of our country neighbours began to send their children, Mademoi-selle's younger sister, Bertha, was sent for.  She could not have been more different; many years younger, with red-gold hair, and an easy, laughing temperament without a trace of malice or cruelty in it, she took special charge of me.  She did not live in, like her sister, but arrived every morning from her lodgings in

the village, eagerly awaited by me at the top of the nursery
stairs. I adored her; we used to go for walks together, and
she entertained me with her stories and laughed at my own
absurd imaginings, gently coaxing me all the while to talk a few
words of French, to understand what she was saying in French.
It was therefore a terrible deprivation to me when she and her
sister decided, at the beginning of the 1914 war, to try to get
home to their Belgian village. They vanished altogether from
our lives, and we heard nothing at all until a few years after the
Armistice a letter arrived telling us how the Germans had occupied their village, how they had suffered—but not too tragically
—and how their lives had moved into new patterns since. But
by that time I was at school and the spell had been broken: the
letter came out of a past that was already dim, in which I held
the hand of a girl with a gentle freckled face puckered in
laughter and a head of ripe, golden hair I could never take my
eyes off. It grew dim very quickly: I think I remember almost
as much today of Mademoiselle Bertha as I did when the letter
came, nearly thirty-five years ago.

I must have started going to school in the garden about a
year before the war broke out. There was terror but also
fulfilment in discovering at last what went on in the Pavilion
after watching it from the outside for so long; though shy and
solitary, I made friends in the school fairly quickly, a process
hastened by the fact that I had already met a large number of
my fellow-pupils at parties in the neighbourhood. The family
of a local mill-owner, in particular, was there in full force, the
older children just about the age of my sisters, and the youngest,
Melicena, already my own special companion from many tea-
parties, dances and Christmas parties at their house and at
Fieldhead. Melicena, like Beatrix, had an innate antipathy
to learning from books and blackboards, and Miss Winson's
wrath was constantly descending upon them both, for mis-
spelling four words out of five, for adding up every other sum
wrong, for maintaining that the Irrawaddy flowed down to the
Caspian Sea and that Thomas à Becket was martyred in 1066.
They made these enormities worse by inattention, fits of giggles,
pellet-flicking, caricatures on the blotter and lightning imitations of Miss Winson behind her back; down would come the

ruler on Beatrix's knuckles, and Melicena would be stood 'in front of the curtain'. The latter punishment was considered particularly humiliating, because on the other side of a green cotton curtain that divided the room the elder children were being given superior instruction in a kind of calm Olympus of education, by Miss Edwards. Thus were the Bad exposed to the reproving gaze of the Good; but the punishment did not always work, as Helen and Rosamond would immediately give Beatrix secret signs of sympathy, and Melicena would exchange glances of subversive amusement with her elder sister Thelma. I was, I am afraid, by nature a ' good little boy ', never did any imitations or caricatures and got my sums right; for this reason I was specially favoured by Miss Winson, who would overlook the fact that I was nevertheless revelling in the show put on by the others. On one occasion Beatrix staggered me by the recklessness of her daring. She pretended to be suffering from a cold and concealed a scout-whistle in her handkerchief, so that every time she blew her nose a shrill blast summoned us to Be Prepared and reduced Melicena to even greater agonies of giggles than usual.

# I 2

OUTSIDE the enchanted garden, the world seemed to us on the whole rather ill-planned and unlovely; but there were certain places we visited regularly that had a privileged appeal and were accepted as a sort of extension of the wonders of Fieldhead. Our expeditions to these places had a seasonal rhythm, and when I look back on them now, what surprises me is that even at the age of four or five my expectation of their rhythmic return seemed to be based on an experience stretching far back into the years. We used in spring to make a great foray to a fold in the hills, approached by a winding lane a few miles down the road to Marlow. It was called Winch-bottom, and our excitement mounted as the chosen day drew near when we should pack our picnic boxes and, arming our-selves with baskets and sticks, set out across the fields. Spies had probably been before us to report on the lie of the land and advise on the exactly right moment for attack : for in spring the hedgerows and copses of Winchbottom were covered in prim-roses, more abundantly than anywhere else in the surrounding country, and before dusk we returned in triumph with our baskets filled with sheaves of the soft-petalled, deliciously scented little flowers. Now I do not suppose I can have joined in these yearly expeditions at an earlier age than four, as my short legs would not have been equal to the exertion ; but at least by the age of five or six I can remember I looked on them as if they had gone on for ever in the past and would go on for ever in the future, like the rites of Christmas morning and the joy of waking to find one's bed loaded with boxes and one's stocking hanging stuffed with mysterious packages on the brass posts (surely there can never have been a *first* occasion of that). But the opening of one's consciousness is a secret that I cannot believe will ever be fathomed, unless some genius one day invents a technique of revivifying the buried rolls of memory right down to one's first day on earth—and beyond.

Winchbottom was the supreme expedition of spring, though there was bluebell-gathering too in the woods of Hedsor, but somehow the bluebells never became the centre of such adven-turous and notable experience as the primroses. Summer was, of course, the time for those river picnics and river explorations I have already described, for the noiseless creeping up in a punt in the twilight on the illuminated celebrations that followed the regattas of Marlow and Cookham. There was also a little circular backwater with several arms that wound through what was called the Abbey Estate, once the grounds of an old river-side abbey of which a few relics still remained, but in our child-hood already parcelled out among many secluded little houses and gardens ; to take a canoe up-river to the boat-houses and then plunge under the tow-path bridge into this backwater was a favourite summer outing. The moment one had left the main stream one was in a secret noiseless world : the back-water was only a few feet across, just wide enough for two canoes to pass, and made so many twists and turns that one could never quite remember what was coming next, an overhanging willow tree the leaves of which brushed through one's hair, a smooth green lawn leading to a rose-covered house-front just glimpsed through the shrubs, an old boat-house, a little wooden bridge that made a brief dank tunnel eclipsing the sun that dappled the water through the leaves on either side, a water-front with flower-filled urns, or a miniature lock which one worked oneself, pulling up the sluices by hand and watching the silver-green water cascade through. One dallied in the half-shade, throwing a rope round the branch of a tree and taking out a book, or one saw how fast one could cut through the water and take the bends without making a sound; one gazed into the depths to catch a glimpse of the grey-brown fish flicking through the weeds; one snatched at a blue-green dragon-fly, one put a finger to one's lips as a kingfisher flashed between two branches, or a water-vole suddenly plopped into the ripples along the bank ahead; and then at last one was back again at the opening to the big river, the clatter of skiffs and punts at the rafts, the swans in the reeds and the sailing-boats weaving their intricate wind-dance upstream by the Sailing Club.

At the end of summer an event as important as the primrose-plucking of spring came round: the blackberrying season across the river on Cockmarsh. My father, it seems in the pictures memory has preserved of those years before the 1914 war, was nearly always with us, punting us across and walking surrounded by his dogs and children to the blackberrying ground in the hedge on the far side of the great open field, beyond the burial-mound. He carried the basket-in-chief, while each of us was armed with a chipped enamel mug with which we made our forays into the brambly, fruit-laden depths. Beatrix, intrepid in this as in every other adventure, would plunge into the deepest brambles, emerging with torn jersey and legs covered with thorn-scratches; in the distance, somehow always ahead of us and picking the most by sheer, unspectacular concentration, were Helen and Rosamond; I kept near my father, partly in order to continue chattering away with him, but also very conscious of the disadvantage of being the smallest, and waiting for the moments when he would hook down some high branch, dangling above us with its huge and more unsullied-seeming fruit, and invite me to pick it clean for him. Then, calling in the dogs who were rooting in nearby ditches or plugging a rabbit-hole they had discovered with only hind legs and a furiously wagging tail visible, home we went to the weighing scales in the larder, scarcely able to wait to discover if we had exceeded our score of the day, of the week before.

Cockmarsh was also the scene of the greatest event of the winter: the moment when it froze hard enough for the ice to be safe on the flood-water that lay at the bottom of Winter Hill, lingering reminder of the time, centuries and centuries before, when the river itself had run that way. This was generally in January, and seems to have happened far more frequently in those days than ever since, though I dare say that statistics would prove that this is just one more illusion of memory. All Bourne End seemed to be there on a morning of frosty sun, and people would come from Marlow and Maidenhead and even from London, for the delights of Cockmarsh skating had been famous for years. It was almost a social event, for friends were there in dozens, racing against one another with scarves flying behind, skidding and tumbling to roars of laughter, with here and there a champion skater performing elegant figures of eight with nonchalant skill. As soon as I was old enough to balance on skates I begged to be allowed to join my father and my sisters; till then, I had stood on the bank, watching with tense ambition and disdaining the mere slides made by the village boys. Beatrix dared me on, and the inevitable, endless competition between us began again in the new sport. The earlier joys of the winter, the snowmen modelled on the lawns and the giant snowballs we rolled down the paths together, picking up a wider and wider carpet-strip of snow until they were too big to push any further, seemed trifling beside the winged ease, the abandon, the danger of those ice festivities under Winter Hill. Reluctantly I left them for luncheon or tea, longingly I heard the cries and the shouts still echoing across the river as I sat munching my bread and jam beside my fire; and I dreamed of the return of the days when the river itself should freeze over again, as it had in the legendary years before we were born, when my father had skated down-river all the way from Oxford to Windsor.

Winter, too, was the time of paper-chases all over the valley, led by my father; and the time of the dances in the big houses of the neighbourhood: our own dances, the dances of the Nivens at Marlow, the Mackenzies at Henley (dominated by the awe-inspiring figure of old General Higginson, Margaret Mackenzie's grandfather who had fought in the Crimean War), and the Grenfells at Taplow. These were great occasions for my sisters, but I hated dancing, I resented being dragged out of my private world to be dressed up in frilled blouses and silver-buckled shoes and thrust into a throng of other children so few of whom were my intimates, so many of them bigger and cockier than I was: I was shy, hot, awkward, filled with unreasonable terrors of exposure and mockery; but I came home happier than I went, clutching some trinket that had burst from a cracker or a bigger present—surprise that made amends for all—awarded me from a giant Christmas tree.

Beyond the valley there were holiday lands that seemed to exist in quite a different dimension.

# 13

WHEN I was six years old, we made our first trip abroad together, to Château d'Oex in the mountains above Montreux. I remember very little of the journey, for the good reason that I was fast asleep nearly the whole time. I even slept through the arrival in Paris, where mother broke the journey with Rosamond and Beatrix while the others went on by sleeping car. I slept a deep sleep of the abysm brought about by all the excitement that had preceded the journey; I was shaken, I was stood on my head, I was shouted at, but nothing would wake me up. The only picture that comes out of the depths, is of a huge lake stretching away into the peaks of the sunset, and dwindling below us as the funicular slowly grinds up the mountain side. It cannot refer to any other time, and the lake must have been Lac Leman; but it is strangely dissociated from anything else in my mind, and is nearly all that remains of that summer in the Alpine valleys. And yet it was full of incident and adventure. Together with Archie

Marshall and his family, we made flower-picking expeditions through the pinewoods and the valley meadows, we saw the cheeses being made at Gruyère, and went in for the local sports, to our astonishment winning several events. Helen won the high jump, Rosamond and Nancy Marshall won a three-legged race, Beatrix an egg-and-spoon race, and I, even at the age of six, won a race as well. There exists a photograph of me charging to the winning-post in my white shorts, a look of beatific triumph on my face; but it stirs no shadow of a memory, however much I stare at it.

Far more clearly remembered, because so often visited, with layer after layer of memories superimposed on one another, are our holidays in the Isle of Wight. We went to Totland Bay for the first time as a family in 1910. My father had not been on that side of the island for twenty years or more: he found it more delightful than he remembered, and as the visit was such a success with all of us he decided to make it an annual event. An absurd name, Totland Bay, a new little red-brick village without any charm, that had grown up, rather like Bourne End, round a few old houses; but it had everything to make the perfect holiday for children, and from the very first year it established itself in our mythology as a dream island of enjoyment. Every time we went there, we felt we were discovering it for ourselves: it existed only on privileged maps (our maps), it sprang into life only during the months of July and August, and sank back into the sea again the moment we had all left. And there was nothing of the tidy and spick-and-span plage about it: there was always more to find out, new explorations to be made, new treasure-trove to be revealed on that high corner of land facing the sunset that broke abruptly all round in steep cliffs to the sea.

To begin with, it was approached by a little paddle-steamer, sufficient romance in itself for a small boy. We used to make a cross-country journey from Bourne End to Lymington Pier, to avoid the business of taxi-ing with all our luggage from station to station in London, and changed three times—at Maidenhead, at Basingstoke and at Brockenhurst. It took only about three hours; but to me it was like crossing Africa. I thought about it for weeks before the day arrived, I laid in a store of acid-drops

and caramels, I saved up my copies of the *Children's Magazine*
and *Tiger Tim's Weekly* and as many other comics as my small
funds would run to, and packed them all together with *Jemima
Puddleduck* and *The Wizard of Oz* to be read and re-read during
the long hours while our trains roared us across the vast stretches
of Berkshire and Hampshire; and still it didn't seem enough.
Of course I was so absorbed in everything that was to be seen
from the carriage window, and the journey was over so much
more quickly than it ought to have been, that I never got
through more than a quarter of my travelling library; but I
never learnt, and did exactly the same thing the following year.

And then suddenly we had slipped on to a new plane of
existence, when the little train chugged down from Lymington
pier and the sea-breeze brought us smells at last of salt and seaweed, and we could see the sea-gulls perched on the stakes in
the estuary. Everything from that moment on was of fabulous
interest: would it be *The Solent* or *The Spithead* that was waiting
for us at the landing-steps, with the friendly sailors in their dark-
blue jerseys to help us aboard? I ran at once to the place
amidships where I could peer down into the oily-smelling, hiss-
ing marvels of the engine-room and watch the big pistons beginning to revolve; then up on deck again so as not to miss the
familiar landmarks emerging as we gained the sea: the long
spit of land to the right on which Hurst Castle was built like a
fortress in the desert, and beyond that the jagged advancing
rocks of the Needles with the lighthouse at the end, dark and
sinister against the falling sun. In those days the pier at Totland Bay was still in use, and after the stop at Yarmouth, where
the sailing-boats spread their white wings about us, we went on
in the paddle-boat round the point: abandoning buns and cups
of strong tea in the saloon below, clasping pails and spades and
rain-coats and handbags, we watched the delectable land approach. We could hardly bear not to run down on to the sands
at once, seeing all the other children at play there in the golden
light, building sand-castles and paddling and trying out their
earliest whirling strokes as swimmers; but first our lodgings had
to be occupied, with Mrs. Scovell waiting at the door to greet
us, beds chosen and bounced on, sand-shoes unpacked and laced
up as fast as possible; and then, then at last the wild rush began

for a crowded hour of glorious seaside life before supper, down
the cliff through the ragwort and brambles and on to the beach,
where the red-haired young man in charge of the bathing-
cabins remembered and welcomed us, and our toes first felt
the soft yield of the wet sand under them, the foam frothing up
round them and sliding away again.

There was something to do every hour of the day at Totland
Bay. There was the regular morning bathe, with *petit beurre*
biscuits to nibble as soon as we had dried ourselves; the afternoon walk, either over the fields to lonely Colwell Bay that
somehow looked so old-fashioned and as if a lady in a crinoline
bathing-suit might at any moment emerge from one of the
derelict huts, or up the downs and on to the heather, or along
the road to Freshwater Bay on the other side; and then after
tea a shrimping expedition on the wilder part of the beach
where the downs came plunging in irregular weed-grown
terraces and gullies towards the sea, and the tide left its mystery-
filled pools under the rocks with their wet drooping hair of
rubbery seaweed. Each of us had a shrimping-net, mine the
smallest and most frequently broken, and would concentrate on
separate portions of the beach. Sometimes there would be
a shout from Rosamond, summoning us to observe a particularly beautiful sea-anemone she had discovered or Beatrix
would come running to show me a diminutive crab that had
caught in the meshes of her net; we pushed the nets through the
sand right up on to the ledges concealed by the seaweed, with-
drawing them in tense expectation of the transparent little
creatures left twisting and skipping in them as the sand and water
drained out, with the rare excitement of bigger prawns.
Gradually the sun would sink and the light grow more golden,
the turning tide begin to swallow up the outer pools, and then
the call would come from Julia or Mother to pack up and carry
our loaded pails, with constant glances at our prizes on the way,
up the long haul of the cliffs and back to our lodgings.

Bathing was a shivering, laughing ordeal; shrimping was as
exciting as the pursuit of buried treasure; but perhaps most
marvellous of all were the long picnic afternoons on the heather-
downs. It was a stiff climb; but when at last the heather was
all round us and the great vistas exposed before us on every side,

we felt we were on top of the world.   Away to the north, across
a Solent grown absurdly small compared with our experience
in crossing on the paddle-boat, lay the wooded mainland coast
—the coast of England, as we liked to say—with Hurst Castle
diminished to the size of a nursery toy, stretching away past
Bournemouth distinguishable only at nightfall, when its
promenade lights made a winking diamond chain in the darkness, to a misty outline by Poole.   If we were lucky, we would
see a blurred shape coming out of that haze, and grow slowly
larger until it could be distinguished as a Union Castle liner
home from South Africa, or one of the smaller Cunard liners
that had put in at Cherbourg and could navigate the Solent;
then we would hear the deep echoing throb of the pilot-boat
start up and see it set out for its meeting with the liner, which
would pause in all its majesty almost, it seemed to us up there on
our balcony of heather, within swimming distance.   It was a
tricky channel to navigate, and the biggest liners went round by
Spithead entirely out of our view; there was a shifting sand-
bank in the middle, which in some years disappeared altogether,
but one memorable summer had the wreck of a trawler or
cargo-boat leaning over it in melancholy dereliction.   Then
as we followed the sandy paths across the top, where the bees
seemed to be blown by the sweet-smelling wind rather than
flying over it, marking out a hollow covered with the purple
springy cushions of heather for our picnic later on, gradually
the silvery line of the Needles would come into view and Alum
Bay all sparkling in the shelter of their spears.   Up there, on the
furthest western edge of the heights, Beatrix, peering into the
remains of some old forts built during the Napoleonic wars,
difficult of access, half blocked up, dreamed of tense dawns
waiting beside her cannon for Boney's armada to show up over
the horizon; while Rosamond with a far-away gaze stood
immersed in fantasies of poetry which poured into her mind in
floods as purple as the heather that surrounded her.   I, meanwhile, was on the look-out for rare caterpillars, particularly for
the furry brown caterpillar of the black-and-red burnet moth
that chewed its way through the lacy leaves of the ragwort; but
in later years the scene had much the same effect on me as on
Rosamond.   I longed to make something of it, to marry it to

myself by a poem, or a painting, or a tale of mystery and adventure, to capture everything it seemed to be saying to me, the humming in my senses and imagination, before the experience faded.

The holidays were not complete without at least one pilgrimage across the downs to Alum Bay. In those days the old blackened pier still stood for *The Duchess of Fife* (my favourite paddle-boat) to land trippers from Bournemouth, and sometimes we went in it ourselves. Generally, however, we came over the downs, clutching our jam-jars for the supreme operation of the holidays: the gathering of the coloured sands from the towering, crumbly cliffs with their strange mingling of reds and purples and golden brown. We were busily at work as soon as we arrived, rubbing the fragments of rock we detached until they sifted into the jam-jars in strata of our fantasy. Nothing, I realize, when I look back on it, could be more boring than these jars of sand; but to us at that time they were miracles of achievement, beautiful beyond price, and we carried our booty home with loving care, to stand on the mantelpieces of our bedrooms beside the shells and the green and purple jewels the waves had made out of broken pieces of bottle, that gleamed with the effulgence of emerald and sapphire in our eyes.

Sometimes we bathed at Alum Bay before returning home, with a sense of danger created by the near presence of the Needles and the lighthouse, with the sea-gulls forever screaming round them, and the tiny figure of the coastguard coming out of his cabin on the edge of the cliff. And sometimes, sitting among the decaying lobster-pots and the dried seaweed and the fragments of spars and planks from some forgotten wreck, my father would sing popular songs and Beatrix would dance to them, dances invented on the spur of the moment, while we gathered round and applauded. Then back home again, perhaps taking the road instead of the scrambling path over the heather. This road ran alongside the fields at the foot of the green Tennyson down: another of our favourite expeditions was up to the Cross, where we could see the cliffs of the whole southern coastline stretching away to the east, and creeping cautiously forward on hands and knees, we could peer over the sheer edge and watch the waves boiling and battering far below at the base of the chalky rampart, with a thunderous roar that echoed on and on whether the sea was calm or rough.  And it was along this road that an event occurred in our very first year on the island that has left one of the earliest impressions I can distinguish, though in a confused obscurity, from my childhood.  I must have witnessed it, to have this fading photograph in my mind, but perhaps not on the first day when my parents took my three sisters to make the extraordinary discovery.  Let my father's diary for Saturday 16 July 1910 take over :

> We all walked by road to the Needles.  When we reached the Downs we were told that an aeroplane had just landed.  We pounded up the hill and over the crest and found a Farman biplane lightly perched on the turf and surrounded by an eager crowd.  The driver had left it, but we saw him when he walked to the Coastguard station.  A policeman informed us that ' his flying name ' was Jones.  He used to act under the name of Robert Loraine.  He had started from Bournemouth in order to fly round the Needles and return, but was caught in a rainstorm, lost in a fog and was luckily able to come down safely where we found his machine.  Later the weather cleared and Graham White came sailing along high up, first a beetle, then an eagle, then a dragon.  He circled the Needles and went off on his return.  Sated with all this excitement our party went home . . .

The next day—and I think this must have been the day when Julia brought me along with the rest to witness this curious accident in the early history of flying—my father had to return to the House of Commons, but my mother wrote him a description of the end of the affair in a letter that still survives :

> About 6.30.  Loraine appeared, walked carelessly to his aeroplane, threw off his overcoat, drew on a sweater, buckled a life-preserver over that, climbed as gracefully up to his seat as if he were Romeo ascending to Juliet's window, and waved his hand. The engine was turned on, making as much noise as twenty motor-cars, and suddenly the thing dashed forward on the ground for thirty yards, then began to rise slowly—then faster and faster it flew towards Yarmouth, and then made a circle back again and became a tiny speck in the direction of Bournemouth.  I actually prayed for him as he started, and it seemed a horrible thing for people to cheer as a man hurled himself into space so recklessly. . . .

It was only many years later—for our visits to Totland Bay
continued during the war, and after the war we went again to
stay with the Hammersleys, who had taken a little house at
the end of the turf walk and modelled it into the perfect seaside
home—that Tennyson began to mean something to me, and
the expeditions to the Cross at the top of the downs to have
something sacred about them. I was at Eton then, and
Harold Nicolson's genial essay in revaluation had rekindled, defined and enlarged an admiration I had always had for his
work, for the passionate, simple feeling about love and friendship and death breaking so nakedly through the façade of
bewildered philosophy, for the sensitive response to nature and
the matchless craftsmanship in verse. Before Farringford was
sold to become a hikers' guest-house, I had visited it in reverence
and love; I had stood by the Cross and, facing the sea all alone,
I had shouted out loud to the gulls and the grasses as much as I
could remember of *Ulysses* and *Break, Break, Break*. By that
time Totland Bay had already become a half-buried history
of childhood; I could no longer remember the features of Mrs.
Scovell, that earliest landlady who had once seemed so formidable and so fascinating, nor remember the name of the
tall, fair-haired boy in his teens who had given me his pet
rabbit to fondle on top of a wall (until I met him twenty years
later in Berlin just as Hitler was seizing power); even the
summer soon after the war when we brought father there for
the last time and shared a house with the Somerset Maughams
and played with his daughter Liza, was growing remote. Still,
so strangely, the downs and the rocky shore where I had gone
shrimping as a child stirred in me that feeling of something
undiscovered, something I might understand and penetrate at
last with deep concentration and lonely communion, a secret
behind the heathery hollows, the cold phantom shapes of the
Needles, the mouldering Napoleonic forts and all the wildness
beyond the black runway of the lifeboat house, the ponk-ponk
of the pilot-boat at night and the myriad twinkling lights of the
liner approaching in the darkness.

# 14

WE were at Totland Bay in the August when the war came.
I can just remember my father opening the papers that morning
of the 4th and saying in a rather grim, resigned way: ' So it's
come, after all . . .'

Immediately the wildest rumours ran through the island,
and—to judge from an article which my father wrote the following week in *Punch*—the German fleet was expected to steam up
over the horizon any moment, leaving the British fleet at the
bottom of the North Sea.   The islanders, having a very high
opinion of themselves, were convinced that they would be
blockaded and cut off from the mainland, a special naval
expedition having of course set out from Bremerhaven to sink
*The Spithead*, *The Solent* and *The Duchess of Fife*.   Dire famine
was prophesied, and almost all of the holiday-makers left at
once.   We stayed on, however, my father having kept his sense
of humour and his sense of proportion, though he was a man of
peace and had personal reasons for especially regretting a war
between England and Germany; we battled with the authorities over Maria, the gentle, black-haired German maid who
was with us and whom we eventually got back to her own
country through the United States; and we even came again
the next year and the year after that.   The island changed:
there were detectives to watch people going on the boats,
barbed wire sprouted everywhere, and the military took over
the old Napoleonic forts—which made them even more
exciting to Beatrix and myself.   Both of us, in fact, had a fine
Buchan-ish time during those war summers, as the island was
reputed to be infested with spies, and we conceived that Britannia, incarnate to us in the heroic figure of Bernard Partridge's
cartoons, had given us the special mission of tracking them
down by our own unaided cunning and watchfulness.   We
never, alas, caught one, but we pursued several harmless
gentlemen we found walking over the downs alone, creeping
through the heather and coming up as close as we dared

whenever they stopped or sat down. Everyone in Totland Bay saw the periscope of at least one German submarine popping up in mid-Solent every day, and we waited breathlessly for the stranger to produce a heliograph out of his pocket and start signalling; but we never saw any of our victims make as much as a code-sketch on a piece of paper produced from the lining of his straw-hat.

It was only gradually that the war began to make its changes in our life at Fieldhead. My father was too old to join up, though he over-exerted himself with the volunteers, and thereby hastened his final illness, and I had no elder brothers. Beatrix's scouting ardours as Lone Scout White Owl (she had passed herself off as a boy) were intensified when Helen and Rosamond joined the local troop of Girl Guides, and we all felt that Bob, the under-gardener, had become a hero when he was drafted out to France with the Guards. Sometimes Goodman would claim that when the wind was in the right quarter he could hear the guns booming over the Channel; mornings came when my father looked particularly tense and drawn, having heard of the death of a friend or the son of a friend, and a cold gust blew suddenly closer when the news came that first one, and then another of the Grenfell boys had been killed. Copies of Hilaire Belloc's *Land and Water* were piled up in the library: they meant very little to me, though I gradually became aware that things were not going at all well and that the cheerfulness of *Punch* was beginning to seem rather forced in the face of the mounting casualty lists. Lady Astor organized a big hospital for the Canadians up at Cliveden, and my mother went to work there as a V.A.D., returning with stories that puzzled and frightened me when I overheard them. She also organized a garden-party at Fieldhead for those of the wounded who were well enough to move about, and one afternoon the garden was filled with young men, speaking much more like my American relations than I expected, in hospital blue with bandaged arms, feet or heads, who grinned at me and applauded me when I won in a raffle a piece of a zeppelin that had been shot down over the Thames. It was not till the last year that I began to understand what was really happening; meanwhile, I thought there was something rather adventurous about the shifts we were put to in order to find enough food, the beet we grew to make sugar, the potato cakes and the maize bread made out of the Indian corn my mother had always insisted on having in the kitchen garden. If everyone else made rather a face at the appearance of each substitute novelty, I devoured it eagerly. Like everyone else in the country, we kept hens, and came to long for the day when we could get rid of the intolerable birds; we also made the experiment of keeping two pigs, Marmaduke and Millicent, who were housed in the old dog-kennels. The result could have been prophesied : we became so fond of them that we could not bear the idea of slaughtering them when the moment came. We would gladly have kept them as pets; but with cowardly patriotism we sold them to the local farmer, an act of treachery that disturbed me for many years.

By imperceptible stages only, the war drew everything that had happened before it away to a great distance. Only one event occurred, quite early on, that caused a minor revolution in our lives: the arrival of Belgian refugees to stay with us. Jealous as always of 'outsiders', my sisters and I were dismayed at first, but our impulses to plot malice against the new-comers were checked by frequent reminders from our parents that we must be kind to the unfortunates who had been driven out of their homeland by the wicked Huns. We were good, by a great effort, and in the end settled down to accept the sweet and graceful Madame L. and her two small boys, Serge and Fred, as part of our lives. The boys were a little younger than Beatrix and myself in the count of years, but far older in knowledge of the shamelessness of the world. There were games down in the laurels, accompanied by giggles and conspiratorial whispers in which taboos were daringly broken and mutual inspection made of our small bodies. These games were not, as far as I remember, connected with any conscious knowledge or stirrings of sex, and derived their excitement simply from the sense that what we were doing was forbidden, what we were showing was normally veiled, except from our parents and nurses. They even made Beatrix and me recoil rather prudishly in the end and decide that Belgians were altogether too shocking for the likes of us.

When I was about seven I first fell in love. I have a vivid

recollection of walking down the front stairs at Fieldhead to breakfast one morning, and announcing the fact with fatuous pride to my sisters, who didn't take it nearly as seriously as I had hoped. The object of my precocious affections was a girl of my own age called Margaret whom I met every day at school and dreamed of every night at home. How disappointing to have forgotten so much of one's first passion: all I can remember is that we spent a great deal of time in secret conversation with one another, which made Melicena jealous and ribald at our expense, that as often as possible I asked her to tea with me or went to tea with her at the big house in Marlow, summoned by urgent postcards covered with kisses. We talked nearly all the time about the kind of house we should have when we grew up—I pictured it as a glorified dog-kennel or wigwam—what we should put in it, how many children we should have, and what we should grow in the garden. The truth is that the whole affair was not so much a passion as a very serious and practical contract of marriage, based on affinity of soul and mutual interests, as the best marriages should be. Romantic emotion was far from us; but now I come to a startling feature of my development in my eighth and ninth year. Romantic emotion I did experience: but it was for another girl, and at the same time, and without the slightest twinge of conscience or sense of disloyalty. Alas, it was the story of the houses of Montagu and Capulet all over again, and I dared not approach her: for Marjorie's father was the local Conservative M.P. Over the invisible gulf I watched her every movement in the schoolroom with calf eyes of hopeless adoration: she was slim and pretty, with a high colour in her cheeks, and she stuttered. This impediment seemed to me, in some mysterious way, to heighten her preciousness; I longed to come to her rescue when a word, thick with the prickles of impossible consonants, stuck in her throat; I yearned to stretch out a soothing hand to stroke her hair and cheek; but Mr. Gladstone's portrait in the library with ghostly power forbade.

This was not all: I had a secret tenderness for Imogen Grenfell's freckled nose and boyish head of golden-brown curls, and nothing could prevent me speaking to her, for she was

Beatrix's intimate and my father had long been Lord Desborough's friend; but there was not the same sweet despair in this feeling. Romantic emotion then boiled over in another direction. Perhaps my passion for Marjorie had made me unconsciously feel that the more impossible the longing the more wonderful it could be; for I fell in love with the young mother of one of the boys who had just joined the school. How it started I cannot remember; but she used to come and fetch this boy at lunch-time, and I have a perfectly clear picture of myself lying in wait to watch her pass. The little paved path from the station-gate ran alongside the upper orchard, which was screened by a hedge of hazels. Behind the hazels in early summer the cow-parsley grew tall and thick; and among the light-green stalks I would crouch, invisible to the object of my devotion, just for the happiness of that one moment when she walked by. When she returned with *him*, it was not the same, for they were obviously too pleased with one another's company, and I would slink out of the cow-parsley to avoid this moment of humiliation. I was late for luncheon, but my eyes had feasted. Her glance had not fallen upon me, nor would she have understood if she had glimpsed the son of the house in his curious lair. She might have laughed—terrible thought—and I came morbidly to treasure the pain that her total indifference gave me.

And then came the day when my bags were packed, my mother standing by checking over again the list of clothes that the matron of Summer Fields had sent her, and I left home for the first time in my life. And the whole web of childish friendships, passions and dreams was torn away to become as if it had never existed, as I plunged into the strange and frightening element of boarding-school that was to be mine for the next nine years.

# 15

I HAD had a fortunate childhood. I had not lacked parental love, I had grown up in the midst of a happy family, even though I sometimes wished I had had a brother; I had had all the playmates and playthings I wanted, and I do not think I had been unduly spoiled. I had learnt to exercise my mind in absolute freedom, and my imagination had been richly nourished by books and pictures and beautiful surroundings, by the story-telling gifts of my elders and their love of music and comic invention. If my father sometimes regretted that I so exclusively preferred reading and nature-walks and mooning about by myself in the garden or in a boat on the river to boxing or any other form of athletic endeavour, he was pleased, I know, to see me growing up so imaginative, so fond of animals and so interested in books and the power of words. Before he died, I had shown at school that I could enjoy games like any other boy and be proficient at them too, even drive a powerful oar through the water and feather it cleanly. At the age of ten I had none of the bruises that sensitive children are sometimes unable to get rid of all their lives, and if the gods had missed out gifts at my fortunate birth, I had yet to discover what they were.

It was too good, of course, in view of what the century that promised so fairly was so soon to turn into, was already turning into outside the magic walls of Fieldhead before I left them. And yet, if it was a lucky life for us in money and love and all the opportunities to develop what was growing inside us, it was not a selfish life; my parents' radicalism was not fortuitous or self-interested, but came from deep conviction and deep compassionate awareness of the social injustices of the time and the suffering of others. We were brought up with the sense that if we were fortunate ourselves, we could justify that good fortune only by helping others, in one way or another, to share it, and to diminish the wrongs that still flourished so rankly in other places and other lives. That sense might lead us, at various times in our lives, to espouse false or foolish causes; it might burn with fitful intensity and show itself in obscure ways; but it was always there, as inescapable as a birthmark.

But even when I have said that, I have perhaps left out the most important thing my childhood gave me. I can only describe it as the conception of a complete order of things; a full world. I have sometimes tried to imagine what it would be like to be the only son of divorced parents, living with one parent, perhaps, with the other parent dead, without books or pictures or the immediately available instruments of every kind of pastime or sport, and isolated from the contemporary stream of life; but I cannot, for it is something too completely the opposite of what I experienced myself. My parents' united life, their well-ordered household and contented staff, of whom we were all so fond; the continual visits of aunts and uncles and cousins, some of them from Scotland and America and Germany; one cousin already in the diplomatic service, one making the Army his career, another going into the Navy; governesses from France and Austria to teach us, and a school for all our friends' children in our own gardens; the week-end arrival of heroes of the rowing world, of writers who were famous in the pages of *Punch*, of artists and musicians and political personalities who had fought beside my father in Parliament for the Liberal cause we held so sacred—all this made our family life seem the perfect pattern of earthly arrangements and Fieldhead the very hub of the world, and for a long time I found it difficult to believe that any other real centre of intense life could exist, or that happiness might have to be fought for jealously and ruthlessly; that there could be people who took any sport but rowing seriously, that men of goodwill could be anything but Liberals of my father's persuasion, that the world could honour any writers more highly than my father's friends or that *Punch* was anything but the greatest magazine in the world. This illusion was the cause of some disturbing shocks in the next decade of my life, and held me back from many experiences I might have enjoyed or profited from; but looking back now I believe it to have been a small price to pay for having swum in so clear a pool of contentment. Fieldhead was indeed a microcosm if not the only one in the universe; and when it all broke up, I knew at least what was lacking, and in **many devious**

ways the impulse, not always understood, has risen from childhood depths in my life, to restore, to re-create a focus of harmony and order, a walled garden of meeting and making.

For break up it did. The old life went on in the holidays, but
it was never the same. To begin with, I was not the same:
from the very first encounter, school began to change me,
developing me in some ways and giving me new horizons, but
distorting me in others. And my sisters grew up, Helen and
Rosamond going to Girton and Beatrix at her own urgent
request to a girls' boarding-school, so that the old almost
conspiratorial intimacy as princes and princesses of a private
kingdom could never revive—though it was never entirely
destroyed. The war had changed the basis of our lives, had
undermined the old river fraternity and confused the old
political allegiances; most decisive of all, it had finally broken
my father's health, and the social life of which Fieldhead had
been the centre would not survive against the long years of his
illness, and my mother's preoccupation with nursing him and
looking after our affairs in his place.

It is strange to pause now, to try to recapture it in the middle
years of one's life, to enter a world one had always imagined
was securely preserved in memory and to find it is too late, that
the picture has faded at the edges, that some of the figures are
indistinguishable and later stains have blotted out details of
vital importance. On the hills up above Cores End, where we
sometimes went for a walk, was an overgrown field in which
opened a mysterious deep shaft, the relic of some bygone
mine-working of which no record seemed to exist. We would
creep through the grass to the edge of this shaft, and throw a
stone down: it was several seconds before we heard it strike
hollowly on the bottom, which when we peered over was all
shadowy darkness. So when I peer into the pit of memory, it
is too deep for me to see what lies below with any clear cer-
tainty; I can only throw the pebble of an image, word or
scent down into the depths and wait for the reverberation it may
make. And I cannot be sure that memories which echo up are
all of one season or re-composed from fragments of many
moments that a mood united. So it is with this final picture
that comes to mind and may serve as a tailpiece to the memories

of my childhood: I cannot be certain that it has the truth of an instantaneous photograph, but I do know that it has another kind of truth, the truth of symbols.    It is the end of summer, and the last dahlias, orange and deep crimson and yellow, are flaming in their showy clumps in the borders.    Down in the kitchen garden the little apple-tree with the earliest crop has been stripped of its load of soft apples with their red-veined flesh, the yellow apples are wind-strewn under the oldest tree on the lawn, and the wasps are prodding their way into the bruises.    I am sitting on the dark-green bench under the walnut-tree, which we climbed yesterday to reach the walnuts just bursting from their pungent cases, but now I am good as gold, dressed in my sailor suit, for my Aunt Amelia is telling me one of her funny stories.    We are alone there, among the debris of tea, which everyone has finished: James is coming from the back door to carry away the silver tea-urn, and Goodman passes him with a basket full of nectarines for the dinner-table tonight.    I can hear the click of croquet-balls from over by the Pavilion, where Rosamond and Helen are playing with cousin Eva, Aunt Amelia's daughter.    Under the striped sun-blind of the drawing-room I can just see my mother sitting at her desk and writing letters; and up through the pergola comes my father, wearing his straw hat with the Leander ribbon, accompanied by Lufra the great dane and a flushed triumphant Beatrix—for he has just been giving her a sculling lesson.    Very soon, for the girls, he will propose a bathe before the cool of the evening; but I shall not bathe.    I am still too young.    I shall only watch with Aunt Amelia from the raft.    I should like to watch and listen all my life.

# II
## LUPTON'S TOWER

W HEN I was sixteen years old one of William Morris's early poems, *The Blue Closet*, kept running in my head. I would mutter it to myself on country walks, intone it in my bath and chant it to my friends when the mood came and we were all reciting poetry to one another:

> Lady Alice, Lady Louise,
> Between the wash of the tumbling seas
> We are ready to sing, if so ye please;
> So lay your long hands on the keys;
>   Sing ' *Laudate pueri* '.
>
> *And ever the great bell overhead*
> *Boom'd in the wind a knell for the dead,*
> *Though no one toll'd it, a knell for the dead* . . .

I never found any poem of Morris's maturity, no passage even among the vast epics and word-tapestry weavings that achieved the same quality of pure evocative magic. My secret ear was haunted by the sound of the great bell ' between the wash of the tumbling seas ' tolling by itself in the wind; for bells have always had this power over me, of piercing through to the most sensitive layers of the mind. The sound of the bells of Cookham Church, floating up-river on Sundays across the cowslip meadows, can still bring memories of my childhood that start up out of the darkness, like nesting birds in the church's own ivy-covered tower, with a swoop and flutter of wings. Tears were in my eyes that war-time Sunday when, after so many years of silence, the bells began to ring again far and near, all over London: nothing could have conjured up more poignantly the sense of mortal danger averted and England returning to her ancient island peace and strength.

The clanging of the bells in Lupton's Tower at Eton also has this deep evocative power over me. Since it brings happiness to mind, I now find it a beautiful sound, though it is really rather harsh and ugly if considered without the interference of sentimental associations; in fact I disliked it quite vehemently at first. My earliest room in College at Eton, which by a strange turn of the wheel was next door to my last room, was in what was known as Sixth Form Passage: my ' Election ' was so large in 1921 that we spilled out of Chamber, the long room divided into oak cubicles which has housed the youngest King's Scholars for centuries, into the august precincts of the boys at the top of the school. I was thrilled to be so close to the bloods and stars and heroes, with their stick-up collars and spangled fancy waistcoats and lounging masterful walk, and thrilled to be in a room so large and (to me) so noble; but there was a fly in the ointment, and that fly was precisely the chiming of the hours in Lupton's Tower. The rooms on that side of Chamber and Sixth Form Passage looked out on School Yard and the long, northern flank of Henry VI's unfinished chapel that joins the classical façade of Upper School at one end and at the other stops just short of the older buildings of College Hall and College kitchens and the Provost's Lodge, in the centre of which stands Lupton's Tower—really twin belltowers with the Great Window surmounted by the clock face in between; and in my own room I was nearer to the chimes than anyone else of my Election. They were terrible: every quarter of an hour they broke out remorselessly, unmusically, deafeningly loud. My letters home were full of plaints about the difficulty of getting to sleep. I was a light sleeper, and I worried about getting to sleep: it sometimes seemed to me that only a miracle could submerge my consciousness between the brazen quarters. If I was not asleep at the end of ten minutes, I began to anticipate the clanging that would start five minutes ahead, and as soon as that happened of course I was awake and waiting for it. Sometimes, in the end, I would climb up on to my high window-sill and breathe the night air for a few minutes, and try to penetrate the shadows of the dark-green statue, mottled and marked as if it had been dredged up from the ocean bed, of the pious, luckless King, our founder, in the middle of the Yard; until I felt refreshed for a new bout in my battle with sleeplessness.

This sleeplessness might lead to the conclusion that I was a nervy, overwrought boy at that time. I was certainly introspective and imaginative, but I seem nevertheless to have found enormous enjoyment in the extrovert existence of a young Etonian in his first year. At the end of October 1921—I had been at Eton about six weeks—I wrote to my father:

> Chamber Singing is over!! O Heavens! Now I feel more secure and peaceful. But it wasn't nearly as bad as anticipation, in fact when one's first two verses were over, it was rather fun. But the last two days or so have been rather full of excitement, so I'll start at the beginning. On Friday it was a whole holiday and I played the Wall Game after 12. We had the best game we've ever had, mainly because the sides were so evenly balanced. But another good reason was that the ' Wall caps '—the things we wear to protect our heads and ears from being rubbed to nothing against the wall—were new and so didn't smell bad. I'm sorry to use the expression, but really that is the drawback of the Wall Game sometimes, the caps smell so foully of sweat. But you needn't repeat that, though it is the bare truth. Then in the afternoon I played fives and in the evening I boxed: so I had rather a good day of it. As I am Senior Fag the evenings are rather full . . .

As I have never been able to sing, the ordeal of Chamber Singing, when the new scholars had to get up and sing a song of their own choosing alone in front of the rest of College assembled round the big fire in Chamber, was grim indeed. The dreaded day had been even more eventful for me than the Friday. Some of my Campbell cousins had turned up without warning and given me an enormous lunch at Rowland's; and I had witnessed that extremely rare event, a goal scored in the Wall Game, and to make it more exciting for me it had been scored by my fag-master Bobbie Longden with the aid of George Orwell. ' Wasn't it wonderful? ' I wrote in the same letter, and added, as if to make sure my parents assented to the proper view of the matter, ' It was perfectly splendid. . . . Then as the fateful hour of Chamber Singing drew nearer, I grew more and more nervous, consoling myself with muffins.' That I really rather liked it when it took place, is proof to me now, as I look back on it, that the romantic charm of College was already working on me; a charm derived to a large extent from the sense of living in history, in a nest of ancient buildings, surrounded by the

vestiges of crudely cut names of predecessors long departed
and dead in vanished centuries, the sense of belonging to a
select body of seventy young people who traced their tradition
back through five hundred years to the Wars of the Roses, who
had been at Eton long before any parvenu interloping Oppidans appeared, attracted by the fame of the new school and its
situation so near London and just across the river from Windsor
Castle.   Had not each of us had the special privilege of kneeling
before the Provost to be ' gowned ', while he took our folded
hands in his and adjured us in the ancient Latin formula to be
good, gentle and true?   We were proud of our separateness
from the thousand-odd other boys in their Houses, and gloried
in being thought bookworms, in never having had to pass
through the indignity of Lower School, in trailing about in our
gowns like bedraggled jackdaws, in having our own privileges
and honours, our special places in Chapel, our own inscrutably
ancient game in the Wall Game, and—in spite of the fact that
the top Collegers always made friends with the most intelligent
and socially-minded Oppidans of their own age—in having a
kind of brotherhood of intellectual apartness that united the
boys at the head with the boys at the bottom of College far
more closely than in any of the Houses.   Perhaps it was not
always so; perhaps it is not so any longer; but I arrived at a
fortunate moment.   As Cyril Connolly (who was a year or two
older than I was and had suffered under the earlier *wicked*
régime) has described in *Enemies of Promise,* a revolution had
just taken place, and a group of boys had risen to the positions
of power who thought the rigid tribal disciplines and taboos of
the past were ridiculous, who didn't see why intelligent conversation and friendliness between an older and younger boy
should be limited to the brief exchanges between a fag-master
and his fag, who thought beatings were barbarous and used the
cane only in cases of extreme provocation; who wanted, in
fact, to make College a model of civilized society rather than an
imitation penal settlement.   The Master in College of the
moment accepted this rather than welcomed it, I believe; in
any case he had, under the Eton system, to work through his
Sixth Form and the Captain of the School.   It was the latter
who was the trouble: a tall, blond, good-looking boy without

humour, he was a devotee of the old régime, and it was a fascinating education in politics to see the tug-of-war between the
Dictator and his openly anti-totalitarian Senate.  Though he
managed to devise some pathetic little reigns of terror that collapsed almost as soon as they started, he was thwarted at every
turn, to the delight of the rest of College and particularly of the
*plebs* in Chamber.  Later, when a new Master in College was
installed, an attempt was made with his active encouragement
to revive the old system; but it never fully succeeded, for too
many of us had tasted the sweets of the Golden Age and had
learnt to assume that when it came to the point *we* ruled College.

Curiously enough, I became a martinet myself for a very
brief period under this benevolent régime in which I intensely
believed.  I was the top scholar of my year, ' head of my
Election ', and a year later was made Captain of Chamber, in
which position I was responsible for law and order and invested
with certain minor powers of punishment.  I took these
responsibilities very seriously, far too seriously—but how can a
boy of fourteen or fifteen have the necessary experience and
judgement?—and struggled with fanatical obstinacy to keep
the larkier spirits among my subjects in check.  I was, I think,
just, but severe because I did not see how I could keep control
if I was not.  I was working against my nature and sustained
only by this quite unsubtle conviction of being in the
right.  The result was, of course, that as soon as I laid my
duties down I suffered a reaction and became an extreme anti-
spartan for the rest of my time at Eton.  Saul on the road to
Damascus could not have had a more complete conversion.

It was at this time, when I was battling prematurely with
the eternal problem of order and repression in society, that I
had my first encounter with Cyril Connolly.  He occupied an
isolated room on the other side of the corridor from my own
first room: it was notorious amongst us, dangerous, shocking
and exciting at the same time.  The perfume of Sin that
seemed to rise from it was compounded in my imagination from
the curling smoke of Turkish cigarettes, powerful liqueurs produced from secret hiding-places, risqué discussion of *avant-
garde* books that one could never imagine finding in College
Library, and lurid stories of the forbidden world of cabarets,

night-clubs and dancing girls. Cyril was already fairly high in
the school, and under the tolerant College régime of the time
did more or less as he liked: one of the things he liked was to
invite one or two boys from my Election to come to his study
and join the privileged circle of his friends in emancipation. I
was appalled by this; I felt responsible for the boys—as Captain of Chamber a certain respect was due to me, but my
authority was rather like that of the Paramount Chief of a small
African tribe under British colonial rule, and I could in fact do
nothing—and I was convinced they were being corrupted by an
evilly cynical worldliness, a tone one associated with the faster
and more disreputable Oppidans, only worse because much
more intellectually sophisticated. No doubt this feeling cloaked
a longing to be one of the initiated myself, and Cyril divined it.
In any case he was much amused at my studied disapproval: he
would stand at the door of his room, slim, self-assured, smartly
attired, with a teasing look on his puggish face, and when I
passed would say, in a tone which made the simple greeting
heavy with malice and mockery, ' Well, Johnny Lehmann, how
are *you* this afternoon? ' How could I answer this provocation
from the Devil's emissary? I passed on, head in air, a blush
stealing to my cheeks, with as much dignity as I could muster,
back to the seat of my miserable authority.

In his book Cyril speaks of Godfrey Meynell as one of the
worst of his bullies, though changed later by a severe illness.
His claws had certainly been drawn by the time I appeared on
the scene, and to me he was a figure of pure splendour, epitome
of the Olympian world of Sixth Form and ' Liberty '. He
used to ' mess ' during my first half in the room next to mine,
and would come to borrow my chair every evening for the
occasion. I thought of this as a sublime privilege, the chair
seemed to glow with some sacred invisible fire, and I could not
bear not to be there when he arrived, not to be able to beg him
to accept it when he asked in his off-hand lordly way. One
evening I was a little late in getting away from a rather more
distant classroom, ran all the way and thundered up the stairs
to lean gasping against the wall just as he was helping himself
to the chair. I could not blurt out my joy, but it was written
plain on my face: I think he was slightly embarrassed as well

as flattered by this evidence of insensate devotion from one who, though much younger, was already rather larger than he was.

The drama of the chair added its tints to the romance with which the new world of College was suffused for me during those early days. The light of autumn evenings falls with peculiar beauty on the older buildings of Eton: under the darkening rose- and flame-coloured skies, with the yellow leaves drifting from the elms, the boys returning from practice at the Wall Game, mud spattered on their striped stockings and shirts, huge coloured woollen scarves wrapped round their necks, might have been the young Greek warriors seen through the eyes of a medieval chronicler, as they returned from one more day's heroic assault on the walls of Troy. . . . Then the sound of the shower-baths and padding feet filled the corridors, lights were turned on, meals zealously prepared for fag-masters, school books brought out and abandoned as friends came in to talk and tease and fantasticate. Two or three times every half we gathered before bed-time in the Master in College's rooms for what was known as ' Secular Singing '. There we sang our favourite songs: ' Green grow the rushes o', with its mysterious symbolic presences that had such a hold on my boyish imagination, ' Little Brown Jug ', which in some curious way I managed to associate with my hopeless hero-worship of Godfrey, the song in which Britons, instead of vowing never, never to be slaves, vowed never to be ' marr-i-ed to a merma-i-d at the bottom of the deep blue sea ', and the solemn and haunt-ingly beautiful Agincourt Song, which always sent shivers down my spine as I imagined the victor of Agincourt's mild, unwarlike son looking up towards us from his pedestal in the darkness outside. With him, too, was associated another event that stands out in my memory as part of the troubling poetry of that time. It was the custom that on the eve of Founder's Day, which falls on December 6th, the two top boys of the new Election should carry a sheaf of lilies up to King Henry's tomb in St. George's Chapel and attend the evening service there. It was Freddy Coleridge who went with me, and in our top hats and gowns, tenderly holding the bouquet, we trudged up over the river to Windsor, feeling very proud, very young and rather awestruck, to perform our ceremonial act of piety among the flowering stone arches and the tattered banners, the tarnished colours of which we could only dimly make out above the soft golden candle-stars of the choir. I remember that the Chapel was being repaired that winter, and we had to dodge through the scaffolding to find the tomb, which happened at that moment to be covered by a huge packing-case. The same evening King Henry's statue had the traditional wreath put over it; and twenty-four hours later the senior scholars walked in illuminated procession round the Cloisters before removing it. We were back in the Middle Ages: the evening concluded with a great banquet in Hall, and we were allowed to attend the speeches afterwards, and watch from the Gallery while the Pageant of St. Nicholas was played by the Lower Chapel Choir. . . . Years later, I was to think of this while attending the ' Krampus ' festivals in Austria on the same evening, when St. Nicholas (whom we in England have turned into Father Christmas) appeared, to give presents to the good boys, and the Devil to thrust diminutive birch-rods, painted all over with gold, on the bad boys.

The expedition to St. George's Chapel gave us a strange feeling of escaping from the enclosing barriers of school life into a timeless symbolism, a moment in the sky. Another escape we prized was an invitation to breakfast with the Provost, M. R. James: it was an escape into the spacious dignity of the eighteenth century, and it seemed extraordinary that by walking a few steps across School Yard and into the Cloisters one could be translated out of the struggle so completely and be treated as a friend and a gentleman—instead of an ignorant fag who must buck up and learn the rules—not by a kindly visiting relation, but by the highest dignitary of Eton. The spirit of Dr. Arnold, it seemed, had not touched the Provost: the whole modern development of the competitive, tribal public-school system might never have been as one sat at the table of this genial and amusing super-uncle, who gave the impression of thinking all the dreaded paraphernalia of rules and taboos and marks and examinations rather ridiculous; for surely a young eighteenth-century gentleman would know how to behave himself without all that dragooning and denouncing, and would

*naturally* want to be proficient in the Classics? . . . The faces of
the beautiful young eighteenth-century gentlemen looked out of
their treasured canvases on the walls, and smiled their silent ' of
course '.   And one knew that one could say anything one liked,
provided it was not mean or ill-bred, about anything or anyone
in the school, beaks included, with complete impunity and in
complete confidence: the Provost would chuckle, and offer
one another helping of bacon and eggs.   And then we admired
him, too, for his wonderful ghost stories; he enjoyed a discussion
of these, and I remember telling him at my first breakfast of the
ghost of the nun who had been walled up at the Manor House
(once a priory) at Little Marlow.   Above all he preferred to
talk about detective stories, and had the reputation amongst us
of reading one a day, photographing a whole page on his mind
in the time it takes an ordinary mortal to read two lines.   And
then the clanging of the bell in Lupton's Tower would break in
on the conversation, harshly reminding us that it was time to
return to earth and the forfeits of the present.

All that was in the early enchanted days at Eton: they were
like the upper reaches of a river among delightful and fertile
valleys.   All too soon the mountains gave way to the plains, and
for years one navigated through a flat and dreary landscape,
sometimes feeling the floods rise and carry one violently away
from one's course among the treacherous sandbanks, sometimes
baling desperately to keep from sinking as cracks opened wide
in the timbers, and still the waters came in; far off in the distance shimmered the famous cities of the delta, achievement,
understanding, control; and then the reeds closed in again
and the flood sank, and one was lost.   I think I disliked myself
more than Eton during those years.   I suffered miserably from
the bewildering stresses of adolescence, from an exhaustion that
accumulated out of having worked too hard for my scholarship
and then too hard to keep my place at the top of my Election.
I suffered too from a philosophic darkness that swallowed me
up, in which nothing seemed to have any secure meaning, no
beginning or purpose or end, the darkness being filled with
relentless questioning voices.   But it was not all like that, nor
all the time; there were compensations, and the beginnings of
new solidity, the happiness of friendships, and the excitement

of new discoveries in the world of books and the world of art.

In my abnormally large Election, a number of inner group-ings of special friends gradually defined themselves, though they were never exclusive and were often extended to boys in the Election above or below.   My own particular set consisted most of the time of Eddie Playfair, now one of our most influ-ential Treasury officials and at that time as attached as a spaniel puppy and so bursting with miscellaneous erudition that he could never talk fast enough or irrelevantly enough to lay it all before us; James Brock, quiet, tongue-tied, serious but with a vein of wit that gradually manifested itself as shyness wore off; Anthony Haigh, whose early fanatical obsession with boating fame and the composition of popular song-hits scarcely pre-pared one for his metamorphosis into a distinguished member of Her Majesty's Foreign Service; Patrick Baynes, who had come up from Summer Fields with me, an affectionate and loyal friend who showed qualities of obstinate determination in battling with an impediment of speech that impressed and dis-mayed us at the same time; Dennis Wrangham, who be-came my chief rival and ding-dong competitior all through Eton; Anthony Wagner, whom we teased for his unfailingly unruffled dignity and solemnly lapidary speech, but recognized as the fine mind that has made him one of our most notable experts in the College of Heralds; and Felix Markham, now Dean of Hertford College, whose utter precocious absorption in problems of philosophy and historical speculation was less evident to us than the odd quirks of absent-minded behaviour it gave rise to.   All of us were wetbobs and often competing together in pairs and fours; we played the Wall Game together, some of us getting our College 'Wall' at the same time and playing against the Oppidans on St. Andrew's Day; and we shared many intellectual interests.   We also developed our eccentricities together, making fantastic characters out of one another, evolving a kind of private language of jokes at one another's expense that no one else could understand, and when we were together in our rooms, or eating banana messes at Rowland's, or on the river, or taking walks on Sundays to the Copper Horse in Windsor Great Park, conversing like the 'humours' in an old play with a series of farcical stock responses. Oddly enough, it was only a year or two before that Beatrix had evolved a kind of secret society called 'the Witus' at home, with a silly language private to the four of us which disconcerted my mother and made her sometimes feel (I suspect) that she had given birth to four village idiots. Such freakish growths must often appear in families where the imaginative life has been abundantly nourished, and also often enough among adolescent boys who, as we were in College, are over-exercising their mental powers; but I cannot help feeling that the pressure that produces such an impulse towards nonsensical self-expression was particularly strong in the twenties, in the aftermath of the first war. It was a precious safety-valve, releasing incomprehensible tension below the surface of our lives. I began to write dotty plays for the amusement of the rest of the set, entirely devoted to an even further fantastica-tion of our legends. They were meant to be read, not acted, and read by only half a dozen people at that; if any of our more normal-minded Oppidan friends—who were up to the same beaks at the same time, studying with an equal enthusiasm the Greek dramatists and Roman constitutional history—had looked into them, they would, I am sure, have thanked their stars that they were not inmates of such a childish Colney Hatch. Only one of these plays survives in my possession, an unfinished composition entitled *Toll for the Brave, a Horrible Tragedy*. The first page gives the information that the charac-ters of the drama are: 'William Cutler, Captain of the Boats, etc., etc. (Heroic), Lettuce (Pathetic), Crumb (Villainous); and the subsidiary characters: Mrs. Joyful (a Woman), Mad-with Love (a Corker), Bracken Bury (a Spider) and Bedlam (a poor unfortunate creature who has to cope with Bracken Bury and many others of like calibre in a miserable den full of sound and fury), together with a chorus of Benighted Boaters, Hysterical Historians, and Carsden (a demon probably).' Lettuce, it is clear as the drama proceeds, was meant to repre-sent myself; Madwith Love, Anthony Haigh; Bracken Bury, from his absorption in history to the utter neglect of his person, Felix Markham; and Carsden, the new Master in College H. K. Marsden. The latter played a curiously dual role in our lives. We held him to be a narrow disciplinarian, with too great a fondness for poking his nose into our private affairs and worming our insufficiencies out of us as he balanced on his fender with one long thin leg twisted like a corkscrew round the other; at the same time it was obvious that he was genuinely fond of us, took endless trouble when appealed to, motored us across France in the holidays and entered with enthusiasm and sympathy into our rowing lives. I cannot remember who, if anyone, was indicated in the character of Crumb, Cutler's toadying acolyte and brother of Mrs. Joyful (for whom Madwith Love entertained a desperate passion), nor which beak by Bedlam—to take the nearest rhyming equivalent would be unfair to a sympathetic teacher and salty personality.

The drama opens with an amorous (but scarcely erotic) scene between Cutler and Crumb, reminiscent perhaps of the first scene of Marlowe's *Tragedy of Dido*, in which Cutler, clearly a youth entirely devoid of humour, reveals his great secret plans to be elected Most Popular Man of the Year by making a speech to the Eight after supper so full of witticisms that all will automatically vote for him. As the curtain falls, Crumb is left settled on Cutler's knee, reading from a book entitled *The Art of the Joker*, while Cutler listens with the utmost seriousness. The curtain then rises again on the Madhouse scene. The plot thickens. . . . But there being no Radio Eton, there was obviously no future in these Hogsnortonish dramas.

Meanwhile, however, more profitable literary labours had been embarked upon. I was editing my first literary magazine —unless a mysterious production, unprinted, called *The Pagoda* at Summer Fields can be counted—with Dennis Wrangham as co-editor. *College Days* had been started soon after the war, one number appearing every half or two during the year. There had been ten by the time the departing editors handed over to us, and we produced the eleventh in time for St. Andrew's Day. It was a simple racket. One wrote round to all the well-known authors one could by the furthest stretch of one's imagination claim to be acquainted with, and begged them for a contribution; and they, out of the goodness of their hearts and touched by the schoolboy pathos of it all, generally found something to send. One then wrote to all the firms one could think of which might be interested in an advertising appeal to Eton boys and their relations, and, pointing out how many distinguished authors there would be among the contributors and how many influential visitors would be reading it on St. Andrew's Day, or the Fourth of June, suggested they should buy space. To our never-failing astonishment a large number did, and even bought it again on the next occasion. The result was that if one displayed enough energy and a moderate amount of canny business sense, one made money, more money than we had ever dreamt of falling into our laps at that time, making possible the purchase of many long-desired books and pictures, new cushions for our ancient wicker arm-chairs, new ties for the holidays at Devereux or New & Lingwood and a round or two of banana messes for our friends. It all went quickly enough, but it was a heady excitement while it lasted. As far as I remember, the contributors did *not* share in these profits. At the same time, to be fair to myself, I must add that it would still have been exciting if we had made only sixpence—or even lost sixpence. Nearly all intelligent boys, I imagine, enjoy the chance of making a magazine of their own, but to me there was the special stimulus of at last achieving something that I had longed to do since childhood: the beaver had built its dam, the tom-tit had found its letterbox to build a nest in. But I have to admit we did not do well enough by *College Days*. Our first number was a gallant attempt to produce a kind of Eton *Punch*, with contributions from my father's old friends Barry Pain, Archie Marshall and Alfred Noyes. I think it went down well enough; but I am dismayed to find that by the fourteenth number, produced in my last year, the proportion of outside contributions had increased. The names were splendid feathers in our cap—John Buchan, Rose Macaulay, Eva Gore-Booth, and even the Headmaster himself, C. A. Alington—and significantly enough we had stopped trying to be *Punch*. But why had we not done more ourselves? Our work looks very tame beside *The Eton Candle*, that outsize *avant-garde* chapbook, bound in boards of the purest Brighton-rock pink, with a postage-stamp area of elegant type to an acre of page, with which Brian

Howard, Alan Clutton-Brock and Harold Acton had made the mortar-boards of the staider beaks dance on their heads only a short time before; and tame, too, beside what Peter Fleming was simultaneously making of the official weekly *Eton Chronicle* in a different vein. The truth was that since the departure of Cyril Connolly, Peter Loxley, Alan Clutton-Brook, Noel Blakiston, George Orwell and their friends, the literary stew had gone off the boil in College, the moment of discovery was past.

The chance to buy long-desired books meant for me at that time the works of Bernard Shaw and Lytton Strachey, which I read till late into the night under the bed-clothes with a torch, my mind in a whirl of over-stimulation with all the revolution-ary ideas propounded in Shaw's prefaces, and receiving a shock of almost sensual pleasure from Lytton Strachey's style. I lusted grossly after Hakluyt's *Voyages and Discoveries*, having had my imagination inflamed by an early nineteenth-century compila-tion of ancient voyages—with a delicious musty fragrance of old paper—which I had found tucked away in the library at home; but I was never able to run to Hakluyt, nor to any of the really interesting old maps of which I bought catalogues at the same time, in spite of the super-profits of *College Days*.

Long-desired pictures meant at that time colour reproduc-tions of the works of the Early Flemish painters. I cannot remember exactly how this craze started, but it must have had its germ in a little book we were once given as holiday reading, Arthur Clutton-Brock's Home University Library study of William Morris. I still think it a remarkable work, for its skilful compression and presentation, for its eloquence and clarity of style, and for its imaginative insight; but at that time Clutton-Brock's exposition of William Morris's criticism of modern industrial society and the death of pleasure in good craftmanship, opened entirely new vistas to me. The effects were profound and long lasting, with many ramifications, lead-ing to the love of printing and the making of books that was as much as anything else the origin of my publishing career. I began to be interested in all things medieval, illuminated manu-scripts, Gothic cathedrals, the vanished abbeys of the Thames Valley, wood-carving, Chaucer and crusades; and for many years I was prevented from appreciating the beauties of Renaissance and Baroque art by this exclusive fanaticism. The Early Flemish painters, of course, belong to the disintegration of the medieval tradition and are already several centuries away from Morris's golden age of medieval civilization; nevertheless enough of the medieval spirit survives in them, and the spark jumped the gap at once when I bought one day as a prize (the admirable Eton system was to give the prize-winner a book-plate signed by the Headmaster and a chit with which he could choose his own book up to a certain value) a book called *The Early Northern Painters*, an introduction to the Flemish, Dutch and German painters of the fifteenth and sixteenth centuries as they could be studied in the National Gallery. I had discovered a world utterly unknown to me before, as unknown as Australia to Captain Cook when he first sighted its shores: the world of Jan Van Eyck, Robert Campin, Dirk Bouts, Roger van der Weyden, Hans Memlinc, Gerard David, the Master of St. Hubert, the Master of St. Giles, Joachim Patinir—names that gleamed in my imagination with all the brilliance of those exotic birds and flowers and beasts the early explorers of the antipodes found on their unknown shores. I searched in the School Library for more information, and as luck would have it one of the first books I came upon was J. M. Huizinga's remarkable study of *The Waning of the Middle Ages*. That a historian should consider a whole epoch as a psychological *case*, with confusions of belief and neurotic symptoms that obviously have their parallels in our own day, was a revolutionary idea to me. The stimulus Huizinga's book gave me mixed in a seething effervescence with the excitement that grew as I explored further into Van Eyck-land, and developed into what became for a time a total infatuation, keeping me awake at night long after my forbidden torch had been extinguished and the padding footfalls of H.K.M.'s last nocturnal inspection of the corridors had died away. I devoured Weale's monograph and read and re-read my favourite chapters in Sir Martin Conway's fat green volume which was also in the School Library, even embarking upon Friedlander's austere, monumental series, which (as far as it went) had the best illustrations of all. Hardly any of my friends knew what I was doing, buried in the Library for so

many hours on every half-holiday—no guilty vice could have
been indulged with more secrecy of passion—but it was because
I expected little sympathy or understanding from them, their
tastes at that time inclining more to Giotto, Botticelli and
Rembrandt, if they inclined to the great masters at all.  I
spent long mornings during the holidays in the National Gallery, and bought all the reproductions I could afford at the
Medici Galleries and Pulman's shop in the Marylebone Road,
collected them in folders and had some of them framed to hang
in my room at Fieldhead as well as at Eton.

What seems to me extraordinary when I look back at this
craze, is that while it lasted I found more to satisfy me in the
more obscure and indifferently gifted of these Early Flemish
painters than in almost any of the great masters of other schools.
To come upon a small and dubiously attributed work by Petrus
Christus, or a follower of Geertgen Tot Sint Jans or the Master
of the Death of the Virgin in a foreign gallery was a fulfilment
for me incomparably greater than the first sight of a famous
Giotto or Rubens.  Standing now in front of some of the most
crudely painted of these panels, I am at a loss to understand
how this taste had developed so violently in my teens—though
my love of the greatest pictures of the school has persisted ever
since.  I can only try to distinguish the various elements in it.
Above all, I believe, I was seduced by the delight Van Eyck
and his followers show in landscape and the outdoor view before
they had come into their own as independent branches of
painting, by foregrounds of lovingly painted flowers and grasses
—not a blurred outline or tone among them—and by the exquisite views of medieval towns and river-valleys glimpsed
through open windows or between the pillars of porches and
arcades in a smokeless air, moments of long-vanished time
arrested with such fidelity to nature that I was almost surprised
to find the figures in the same places when I looked again, and
yet transformed and purified by an artist's vision.  I could
never have enough of the tiny medieval town one sees through
the casement behind Robert Campin's ' Virgin and Child ', the
workmen mending the roof, the woman standing in a shop
doorway, the gaily clad horseman and the road winding over
the hill beyond the church spire, past the white farm-house and

into the blue-green distance; nor of the landscape of ' The
Legend of St. Giles ', the misty castles with their pale-red roofs
in the folds of the green-hazed mountain distance, and the
clump of purple-blue irises and the yellow mullein in the foreground. The wonderful Van Eyck ' Madonna and Child ' (the
Rolin Madonna) in the Louvre seemed to me one of the greatest
pictures in the world, not for the important figures that dominate the foreground but for the river view on to which the hall
opens beyond, a view so dazzling in its jewelled light and atmosphere, composed with a million precise touches of drawing and
colour, that it is like a hymn to the beauty of the world. Today,
looking into it again, I see it, with its delight in the world made
by man as well as the natural world, as an achievement that
would be all but impossible in our alienated modern age, not
an irrelevant exercise with which the artist could not resist
transforming a solemn subject which bored him, but in fact the
*meaning* of the picture, an image of the joy of creation in the
birth of its Saviour.

The dotty plays were not my only dabblings in authorship
at this time. I wanted to express—I did not know what. I
wanted to write—I did not know whether in verse, or prose,
in stories or novels; but words fascinated me, and what they
could evoke when cunningly chosen and ordered in the rhythms
of a sentence, a paragraph. Learning Latin and Greek, care-
ful construing of Lucretius and Vergil and Catullus (my
favourite Roman authors) and Homer and Euripides (my
favourite Greek authors), and being obliged to write verses
myself in these languages, had taught me to narrow the focus
of my response and care more and more for the colour and
sound and texture (I did not call it that until I read Edith
Sitwell a few years later) of each individual word. I had also
been greatly influenced by Robert Graves's little book *On
English Poetry*, which first introduced me to the ideas of overtones
and ' under-patterns ' in poetry, the manipulation of the letter
' S ' and the psychotherapeutic theory of imaginative literature.
It explained to me, in a novel and stimulating way, why I
liked certain passages of poetry and was bored by others; and
at the same time inhibited me—from writing reams of bad
verse. In fiction I had grown increasingly interested in the

descriptive passages: a landscape, a storm, a walk through the woods described with sensitive feeling came alive to me as nothing else on the page.    I began to write stories and sketches, but the real object of them was always to paint some natural scene or effect, and my problem more often than not was to fit some plausible story round these passages, to give them a point which was not the real point at all.    They were influenced by Walter de la Mare's stories in *The Riddle*, a book which I especially prized at the time for its fastidious prose and the poetic evocation in its descriptions.    To his poetry I had been introduced even earlier, while I was still at Summer Fields, by Rosamond, who was always gently trying to draw me away from the *Oxford Book of English Verse* to contemporary poetry.    *The Listener* was the first volume of his poems I read, and I can still remember the pleasure I had in the discovery that poetry could make so vivid an appeal to the eye and the ear by such simple means—by a vocabulary where no word seemed to be without its sensuous content and its imaginative overtones.

Besides Rosamond, I had had another unofficial teacher of contemporary literature before I came to Eton, and it was not until I went to Cambridge that I met anyone again to direct my reading and awaken my sensibility with such discriminating sympathy.    Leonard Strong became an assistant master at Summer Fields soon after my arrival there.    He did not teach English literature, though a poet himself, but I think he soon spotted my greed for reading and my imaginative inflammability.    I had also become a kind of story-teller to the school, and in our dormitories at night, assuming my role of ' Great White Chief ' or ' Sosoko ' (I cannot any longer think why I chose that name), I spun endless tales of terror and romance to the listening beds.    This must have tickled his fancy; I on my side was intrigued to find that he wrote poetry, and, as usual, I was at the feet of anyone who could tell me funny stories and make comic drawings and caricatures for me.    When I discovered these gifts in him, I accepted him at once into the sacred company of entertainers which included my father, my Aunt Amelia and my sister Beatrix.    I talked to him for hours during our free time on Sundays, and would sit beside him in the playing-fields in summer while waiting to go in to bat, listening to his persistent coaxing that I should get beyond *The Hound of the Baskervilles, Prester John* and *She* and learn something of writers who were trying to create a new literature and express a modern sensibility. It was all done very gradually, over several years; but by the time I left Summer Fields he had introduced me to Yeats, Housman, Flecker, Synge, Robert Graves, Rupert Brooke, W. H. Davies, had made me understand something of the mood of the young poets who had been in the war, and of the reasons why one writer was good and another bad. When I protested that he didn't think much of the *Punch* gods of my childhood, he told me that there were people who didn't think much of the gods he had introduced me to either, that there were even more advanced modern writers he hadn't mentioned; a reply which stunned me into silence. For many years after I left he was a shrewd and encouraging critic of my own earliest efforts, and I came to regret that I never found his equivalent at Eton.

Of course I wrote poetry as well as plays and stories at Eton; but though the longing was desperate, the achievement was nil. I could not find myself, even in the precocious imitativeness with which some of my contemporaries managed to fill the pages of Oppidan rivals to *College Days*. Actual verse-making seemed to me appallingly hard, and I got stuck emotionally in the inevitable sentimental nostalgia for romantic friendships, the futility of which I took far too seriously. In addition, I read too much Shelley, not only because the mood of his last poems chimed in with my mood but also because I had become particularly interested in the poets who had been at Eton and in whose work I found a feeling for the familiar and so well-loved landscape of river and lush river valleys. I used to read over parts of *The Revolt of Islam, The Question, Spirit of Night,* and *O World O Life O Time* to myself night after night: what more fatal models could there be for a young man trying to write in 1925? Nevertheless, I cannot regret the hours I spent getting to know one of the greatest poets in our language, nor that the fact that Swinburne was also an Etonian drew me to *Poems and Ballads* and *Atalanta in Calydon.* I selected Atalanta's speech beginning ' Men, and the chosen of all this people ' for my own contribution to

speeches on the Fourth of June in the year I left; I have re-read
the poem again and again in succeeding years, and the better I
know it the more beautiful it seems to me, a more astonishing
work of genius the more I understand the harmony of its parts,
and the problems Swinburne overcame in writing it.

My last year at Eton was also important for two new worlds
of æsthetic enjoyment into which I entered.   I had become a
member of the Shakespeare Society, which was run by Henry
Luxmoore.   He had long retired from his House and from
teaching, but he still kept his home behind the Chapel and also
his exquisite garden on a little island in the river just opposite,
where I spent many afternoons of peaceful contemplation,
reading a book, dropping it to talk to a friend who had also
come to enjoy the garden's seclusion, taking up the book again,
and brooding on what I was going to do when I left Eton.   It
was Luxmoore, I think, who was responsible for the strong
pre-Raphaelite note that had crept into Chapel and was so
formidably challenged by the genuine medieval wall-paintings
that were uncovered while I was there; a bent, impressive
old man with a sepulchral voice and flowing white hair, he had
little humour, but great kindness, a passionate devotion to the
traditions of Eton and a sincere love of art and literature; I
remember him telling me how much he objected to being described as ' ring-bedizened ' in Shane Leslie's *The Oppidan*, but
if his rings were actually few, it is curious how strongly he suggested that impression.   The Shakespeare Society was re-
cruited from the top layer of Collegers and Oppidans, and met
once a week in his house.   He chose the plays we were to read,
and allotted the parts; the day before we met an envelope
would arrive for each member, which contained a small slip of
paper on which was written in a spiky, gothic hand the character to be impersonated.   He seldom took a leading part himself, generally confining himself to reading the stage instructions
in his slow and ponderous voice, with results that were sometimes too much for us.   He did not at all like merriment in the
wrong places, as in some of Shakespeare's more salacious
innuendos, but as he was growing rather deaf and kept his
eyes glued to the text, he was not always aware of it; when,
however, we were reading *Cymbeline* and he pronounced,

with the solemnity of a judge passing sentence of death, *Exit pursued by a bear*, the explosion of giggles that followed was too violent for him to ignore and we were in bad odour for the rest of the session. But we all enjoyed the play-reading evenings, and I certainly benefited from them. It helped me to lift Shakespeare out of that fatal classroom atmosphere—there is something intolerable to the junior British schoolboy about the Forest of Arden and Ophelia floating in the brook—in which for many he remains gassed for ever. I already knew many of the Sonnets by heart, and now began to learn some speeches from the plays as well. I trace back to those evenings the fondness for Elizabethan drama which developed rapidly while I was at Cambridge and has remained with me ever since.

The other world I discovered was that of classical art and its revival in the Italian Renaissance. The flash-point was a trip in a private yacht in the Mediterranean at Easter; but obviously the train had been fired long before, in the gradual growth of my feeling for Greek literature and the civilization of Athens. I remember being rather surprised during my first half at Eton to find that nearly all the emphasis was on Greek and so little on Latin; I was lucky, for in the thirty years since then Greek has gradually been fading out of the schoolboy's curriculum and will soon no doubt be extinct altogether; it is true that I came to feel by the end of my time at Eton that one could have too much of it if it excluded modern history and one's own literature, but I have nevertheless remained unrepentantly of the opinion that without a knowledge of the Classics no one can call himself properly civilized or acquire that finer sense of distinction between the creative and meretricious in his own literature. Weeks, months, years of boredom with Livy, Cicero and Xenophon had not prevented me responding to the Greek and Latin poets and dramatists; and suddenly, in the light and colour of the Mediterranean and the great Italian museums, it all burst into meaning and joy.

My sister Rosamond had married Leslie Runciman, and I became very attached to him. I was invited to join the family on the *Sunbeam*, which was then in the possession of Leslie's grandfather, the old sea-dog Lord Runciman, in a trip down the Italian coast from Genoa to Naples. In the end I went on

board at Portofino : the next evening, in the still, velvety darkness, unseen by us, a little boatful of musicians and singers
slipped out from the harbour to our moorings, and suddenly
began to play.   The surprise, the warm Italian voices rising
from the obscure water, the gaiety and southern nostalgia of
' Santa Lucia ' and ' O Sole Mio ' cast a spell on me that lasted
to the end of the trip.   We put in at Elba, explored the flower-
grown ruins of Napoleon's miniature summer palace and made
an expedition into the mountains to see the old farmstead where
he lodged for the night when engaged in secret signal communication with his partisans in Corsica.   When we finally reached
Naples, I spent a long day looking over Pompeii and another in
the museums.   The statues, the bas-reliefs, the mosaics were a
revelation to me of poetry and harmony, of the world as it can
be dreamed separated only by the hair's breadth of unclouded
inspiration from the world as it is.   I fell in love in particular
with the marble bas-relief of Paris and mighty-winged Cupid
before Aphrodite and Helen, and with two mosaic bas-reliefs,
one of the young Mercury with a ram and the other of a draped
figure of a young girl called Hope.   Unfortunately, very soon
after we reached Rome I fell a victim to ' Roman tummy ', and
was stuck in bed while Lord Runciman was received in audience
by Mussolini, an experience from which he emerged to praise
Fascism, the disciplined ardour of youth and the punctuality of
the trains in the once so happily insouciant land of music, art
and wine.   Nevertheless, I managed to see the Sixtine Chapel,
and returned home with Michelangelo's sybils, prophets and
heroic male figures whirling in my head amongst the statues
and the bas-reliefs.

My state of mind during my last summer half was curiously
divided and troubled.   The cities of the delta had at last been
reached, but they had an unsubstantial and disappointing look
—at least in certain lights.   The charm of Eton persisted,
though showing to me others of its many facets than those I
had been so aware of during my first year.   The sense of living
in history, of becoming a part of very ancient traditions had
to some extent faded.   It was rather of Eton as a beautiful
setting to grow up in that I thought continually at that time ; of
Eton as a place where boyhood friendships were made that one

dreamed of lasting far into one's life beyond its walls; and above all, now that many of the friends of my first year had already gone out into the world and at the same time I had reached the point where I had come to know the most interesting among the Oppidans of my own age, as a place where one was trained to make history, which naturally led into the council chambers where the world was governed and fate was decided. Some people may think of this as a hang-over from the eighteenth century, when Etonians—as the names carved on the walls of Upper School and all those smiling, assured young faces that look out of the canvases in the Provost's gallery prove—ruled England, made its Empire and saw themselves as the inheritors of Rome. It is nevertheless an interesting fact that all through the last hundred and fifty years during which the opportunities of rule have been spread far beyond the jealously guarded circle of the eighteenth-century aristocracy, Etonians have remained prominent, not only in the seats of power as cabinet ministers, governors-general, ambassadors, field-marshals and captains of industry, but also in the arts. It is not easy to give a simple explanation of the discovery that was made during the Festival of Britain that, of the ' Hundred Best Books ' chosen to represent English literature of this century, more than one in ten were by Etonians: a proportion not approached by any other school. Each of the great schools has its own special virtues, and it is not my intention to belittle them; but I find it striking that one of the very oldest, and the most famous of these in the eyes of the outside world, should still show such unflagging vitality while complaints are raised even louder that they are out-of-date, effete, unsuited to twentieth-century democracy, and so on *ad nauseam*. There may still be privileged ways into public life, though they have certainly decreased with remarkable speed during the last thirty years; but it is a very long time since birth or wealth provided a passport to Parnassus. During the brief five years of my own career at Eton, among my contemporaries were a surprisingly large company who were to make distinguished names for themselves in the world of books, including Cyril Connolly, Anthony Powell, Eric Blair (George Orwell), Henry Yorke (Henry Green), Harold Acton, Rupert Hart-Davis, the Fleming brothers Peter and Ian, Alan Pryce-Jones and Freddie Ayer.

My own dissatisfaction was to some extent due to the feeling that I was less well equipped to make a fitting contribution to this tradition in my last year than I had been during my first. I was proud, and could not bear the idea of being second-rate in anything I took up, but the introspective side of my character had for the time being the ascendancy over the aggressive, and I was haunted by the conviction of being a failure. I was in Sixth Form, my reports were good, but I had kept my place at the top of my Election only by the skin of my teeth and an all-round ability rather than exceptional gifts in any one subject. I had got my ' Upper Boats '—I was in the *Prince of Wales*—but the Eight was definitely not within my reach. All during my years at Eton the desire to be a poet had grown, but I knew that I had produced nothing that was of any value or even promise; it was all inchoate, and I could not find my proper means of expression. This was as true of my ' real ' career as of my literary ambitions; I knew I had to have a career while I learnt to be a writer, but the idea of becoming a diplomatist like my uncle Ernest and my cousin Ronald, a project favoured by my parents at the time, left me cold— though certainly not as icily cold as the idea of going into business.

This conviction of failure was at the same time, of course, largely subjective, an aftermath of adolescence, which is rather like an infectious disease attacking some victims extremely severely and letting others off with hardly a rise in temperature. I believed at the time—and on looking back I still believe I was right—that I had outgrown Eton, and I was full of restless impulses to go to sea for a year—to spend six months as a dock-hand—to be trained as a compositor in a printing-house. I wanted to work with my hands, to rough it and to get to know another kind of life. These impulses may have been laughable, but they were symptoms of a real malady. I do not think my experience was unique. A public school is designed for young boys, but by the time one is seventeen or eighteen the restrictions and limitations of experience (even in such a broad-minded school as Eton) that are suitable for a boy of fourteen or

fifteen have become absurdly inhibiting. I feel more than
ever convinced now that after the age of sixteen a boy should
begin to live the kind of life that he will lead at Oxford or
Cambridge, and it seems to me as warping to his nature to be
still in monkish segregation and under narrow discipline as to
be allowed to exercise that discipline over boys a few years
younger than himself. Sex is not the only problem, but it is
one of the most obtrusive. The sex-problem in the public
schools has been written about again and again, statistically,
prudishly, sensationally and sentimentally, and has become
rather boring; but it is still there. Two stories may illustrate
the absurdly distorted perspective into which sex is thrown for a
public-school boy. The first did not occur at Eton, but was
told me by a friend at another school later on. He was caught
making some rather salacious drawings of naked women. This
was of course the most ghastly type of offence. He was solemnly
denounced before the whole school, and then flogged. That
was the result of a normal sexual impulse seeking a mild,
frustrated outlet. If instead his sex had found an abnormal
outlet towards his own schoolfellows, he would have been
expelled. If in despair he had turned in on himself, he would
have suffered appalling guilt and anxiety, with the warnings
of his elders and masters that madness and imbecility would
rapidly overtake him echoing in his ears. And this at an age
when, we are told, male sexual energy is approaching its
height. . . . The other story shows the tension generated by
the inevitable tendency towards inversion in a society which
excludes females and at the same time throws young men of
eighteen together with boys of fourteen, worships athletics, and
holds up the civilization of Greece and Rome for boundless
admiration. The Headmaster, Cyril Alington, a man who
delighted in intellectual surprises and paradox, took as the text
of his sermon one day in Chapel Oscar Wilde's story of the
Happy Prince. When the name of the prisoner of Reading
Gaol boomed forth in those hallowed surroundings one could
immediately sense the change in the atmosphere. Scarcely any
boy dared to look at the opposite pews except in a glazed, rigid
way; jaws were clenched, and blushes mounted involuntarily
to innumerable cheeks. It was a moment of horror and panic:

no one knew what was coming next, and everyone was thinking
exactly the same thing.   Luxmoore cleared his throat like a
thunder-clap, and the ancient Dames in their traditional pews
bowed their heads—as if about to be executed.   Only Sir
Galahad continued to look soulfully out of Watts's picture up
near the altar, with a gentle feminine innocence.

The friendships of the early years had now been extended.
The 'Jolly Boaters' still kept together, but our circle had been
enlarged by many other friendships the river had brought us.
I rowed in School Pulling my last year with the brilliant and
caustic Jasper More.   The year before I had rowed with an
Oppidan, Peter Wilding, who had been found for me by the
assiduous Marsden : no chance could have been greater than
that which brought us together, but he turned out to be a
neighbour of ours in Buckinghamshire, with a mother already
familiar to me by look in one of the great Sargent portraits of
the Wertheimer family, and we struck up a friendship that has
lasted ever since.   The top of my Election had now coalesced
with the Election above, and I began to see a great deal of
Anthony Martineau, excellent classical scholar, tall, dreamy,
blue-eyed, with a nose placed crooked in his face that somehow
added to its charm, who shared my tastes in poetry and was a
fellow-member of Luxmoore's Shakespeare Society.   The old
rows between the Spartans and the anti-Spartans in the government of College had broken out again : I was on the extreme
anti-Spartan wing with Anthony and most of the Jolly Boaters,
and was continually getting involved in clashes with the Captain of the School, Quintin Hogg (now Viscount Hailsham), who
had all the moral force behind him of the Master in College's
approval.   ' It would be idle to pretend that I think his ideas
about the government of College are the same as mine,'
observed the latter tolerantly enough in his final report to my
parents, ' but he is a strong Liberal in both politics and practice',
a judgement which must have pleased them more perhaps than
he meant.   Quintin was an extraordinarily pugnacious boy,
who grew truculent, noisy and excited in argument the moment
he found himself opposed, hurling personal insults and sar-
castic innuendos across the room, a wild gleam of aggressive

joy lighting his eye and his chin jutting bull-doggishly forward
as he became more and more incoherent with his own violence.
It was already easy to picture him as a brilliant barrister and
parliamentary skirmisher, but there was some explosive force
in him that was never completely under control and in conflict
with a naturally warm and easily wounded heart.  The odd
thing is that in spite of the scenes that were always taking place
during supper, while Quintin was threatening a new wave of
summary trials and executions among his juniors for offences
real or imagined, we were in fact very fond of one another, and
were often together in the most amicable and affectionate way.
One spring he had been deeply upset by a personal bereave-
ment, which affected him to such an extent that he had to give
up his school work; and I remember I used to go out with
him to Fellows' Eyot and sit under the elms by the river talking
to him and consoling him as best I could.

One of the most pleasant aspects of Eton for me was that I
was never completely cut off from home.  Fieldhead was only
ten miles away and linked by the river.  My mother, and my
sisters when they were staying there—for both Helen and
Rosamond were now married and Beatrix had started her life
as an actress—would often motor over on a Sunday or a half-
holiday afternoon and take me out with them; and I managed
to get permission to pay many brief visits home in between
' absences ', and was sometimes even motored over by Marsden
himself.  This proximity also had its disadvantages: my relatives were apt to appear without due warning, and, growing
to feel familiar with Eton, would ignorantly flout some of the
most sacred taboos.  There was a terrible afternoon when my
mother brought Helen's eldest child, my dear niece Maureen,
then a small baby, over with her nurse.  She came in to find me,
and left nurse and child outside with the car parked by the low
wall that runs between the yard outside Upper School and the
road.  No one was allowed to sit on this wall except the members of Pop: an electric wire of privilege, of the highest voltage
but visible only to the Etonian eye, ran along it.  As I emerged
through the gateway of Upper School with my mother, a
shock of the utmost consternation and dismay went through me.
I would rather have sunk into the ground than see what I

did see, and desperate plans of immediate escape and renunciation of my family for ever ran through my head: for Maureen's
nurse had taken her out of the car and was encouraging her,
with cooing baby noises, to toddle along the top of the holy wall.
Nearly all schoolboys are, I believe, hyper-sensitive about the
appearance and behaviour of their relatives, but perhaps I
was peculiarly so: I remember how I boasted at Summer
Fields about the beauty of my sisters and the smartness of the
world they already moved in, and the disgrace I felt when
Helen came to visit me soon after her marriage with her husband, Mountie, who was wearing—an old deer-stalker hat.
But the disgrace about Pop Wall was far worse and far more
profoundly disturbing.

Few Etonians enjoyed my special kind of luck in having their
homes so near; but all of us as we grew older, with London so
accessible and Windsor just across the river, had the agreeable
feeling of easy contact with the outside world.   And yet we
were curiously insulated at the same time.   The General Strike
caused hardly a ripple in the calm pool of Eton, and very few of
us had any idea of the size or importance of the issues involved:
we rather wished we had been allowed to volunteer as engine-
drivers or printers, and that was nearly all.   Some of the beaks
enrolled as Special Constables, which struck us as very amusing;
our food continued as bad as, but no worse than, usual; and we
had to make some small economies in light and heat.   I
accepted Arthur Cook at the valuation of *Punch* as a black-
guardly villain, but my liberal instincts revolted when all the
fuss was made of Baldwin afterwards.   Of the 'twenties as the
'twenties we were scarcely conscious, and I look with wonder
at the satires and caricatures of the period which are done
nowadays, as at something I cannot have lived through.
Monsieur Coué made an almost State visit to Eton and attended
Chapel, and everyone went about muttering ' *ça passe, ça passe,
ça passe* ' for some days after, without any noticeable effect on
their conduct or nerves.   I thought Noel Coward's *Hay Fever*
the most glorious play I had ever seen, quite outclassing *Chu
Chin Chow*, and fell in love with Marie Tempest. . . . There
was a wild evening at the Café de Paris at Bray with Beatrix
and Tallulah Bankhead, but I found I was temperamentally

unsuited to keep up the pace when the husky-voiced beauty from the Deep South began to be surrounded by smashed glasses. One of my more spirited aunts suddenly took to a one-man, or rather one-woman jazz-band, which she carted about with her everywhere and played with hideous verve—but not at Eton.

The rage for Shakespeare in modern dress had a curious freak progeny at Eton, where, at the end of the Christmas half in 1925, we put on a production of *Androcles and the Lion* in modern dress, in School Hall, with the Matron in College, Miss Oughter-son, as producer. I played the Captain in topee and khaki shorts, Rupert Hart-Davis a frighteningly convincing Ferrovius, Peter Fleming doubled Spintho and the Lion, and Quintin Hogg Megaera and the Editor of the Gladiators. *The Eton Chronicle* observed:

> Lehmann, 'the handsome captain' and one romantic character, restricted to the silvery rather than the caustic side of his tongue, was a distinct success, though he did not put enough variety into his first speech to Lavinia and contrast his private and official feelings. Of the male Christians, Hart-Davis and Fleming claim chief praise. The former with a face of brilliant red gave a real impression of the fierce fighter with his lust for battle vainly struggling to subdue flesh and spirit to a meek and unresisting death; and we all wished him the best of luck on his final pro-motion to the praetorian guard. Perhaps his serious acting did more than anything else to make the play interesting as well as amusing. Fleming, as Spintho, with a face of parchment, pro-ceeded terribly on his course of progressive mental derangement, and the audience were relieved to hear from Ava—the despairing lion-keeper, responsible for his beast's appetite—that Spintho's final exit was into the lion's jaws; for not only was Fleming's acting real enough to make us chary of seeing him mad on the stage, but his success as the Lion, whether roaring in chase or lying meekly on his back having his tummy scratched, deserved to be rewarded by a meal.

I went back for my last Summer Half at Eton reluctantly, having tried to persuade parents and tutors to let me leave. I knew I couldn't get into the Eight, I had won my Exhibition at Trinity, and I felt that the old round of exams in Latin and Greek was a waste of time for me. They won me over by flattering hints of my being a ' good influence ' in College and of the need of my juniors to be coached by me in the fledgling stage of their rowing careers; also by arranging that I should join the History Specialists for half my time, which was at least a novel experience.   As a matter of fact I enjoyed it, though I felt that I was marking time in everything except the strengthening of many friendships.   I was oppressed by the strange, despairing feeling of having been through huge cycles of experience without getting anywhere at all; but the cycles were in my own thinking and the experience was of the void.   In that void neither conventional religion nor social attitudes nor moral values seemed to make any sense at all.   If I was still an unhesitating Liberal in practice it was because I hated to see or hear of other human beings in either physical or mental pain.   That still rang solid in the darkness, as did the experience of friendship and the experience of beauty.   All the aims in life so passionately pursued by so many millions of people seemed to me extraordinary illusions; all except one, the writing of poetry or painting of pictures, because in art there was something that stayed real, resistant to the remorseless inner questioning, when everything else that men made or did was dissolving.   It was to art, therefore, that I was drawn more and more, and the conviction was growing in me that Cambridge and the future would be tolerable only if the pursuit of imaginative art took the chief place in my life, if necessary ousting everything else except the need to earn my bread and butter.

Sitting up on my window-sill, in the room next to the room in which I had started my life in College, on summer mornings well before the work of the day had to begin, I used to watch the sun beginning to gild the weathercocks on the Chapel opposite, and think sentimentally of my earliest days, the November mists gathering as we heaved and gouged and struggled in our padding in the mud by the Wall, the roaring fire in Long Chamber and the words of the Agincourt Song:

> Deo gratias Anglia
> Redde pro victoria
> Owre kynge went forth to Normandy,
> With grace and myght of chyvalry . . .

Now, as I looked down on the statue of the Founder, I felt
more sympathy with him than his martial father, and thought
of the words Shakespeare puts into his mouth when abandoned
on the battlefield:

> So minutes, houres, dayes, monthes, and yeares,
> Past over to the end they were created,
> Would bring white haires unto a quiet grave.
> Ah, what a life were this? How sweet? How lovely . . ?

I felt that the famous speech expressed some rhythm of contentment and harmony that I had missed too, and imagined
myself into King Henry's melancholy as he watched the shep-
herds under their hawthorn bush.   And yet that summer itself
was experienced as a kind of poetry, and was happy for me
because it escaped from the time-pressure and competitive
struggles of the last few years almost into an absolute air of its
own.   Luxmoore's garden epitomized the feeling: one had
reached an island garden out of the hurly-burly where one could
pause for a precious moment, and through one's melancholy
savour something in the circle of one's friends that the past had
been secretly distilling inside one, drop by drop.   And the
garden too was against the background of the river, surrounded
by the river, as the whole of that summer was suffused with
light off the water.   It trembled in reeds and willows and swallowed our limbs and the arrows of the light racing-boats in
which we rode into its own substance, as we paused on a cloud-
less afternoon to gather breath in mid-stream on our way from
Monkey Island or Queen's Eyot, or to rise and fall on the roaring
sluices of a rose-festooned lock:

> I'll sing you three, o,
> Green grow the rushes, o,
> What are your three, o?
> Three, three for the rivals,
> Two and two for the lilywhite boys
> Clothed all in green, o.
> One is one and all alone
> And ever more shall be so. . . .

Never had Henley seemed more magical, a poem of rambler

roses and ripe strawberries and dark leaves of elms reflected in the ripples of a punt-crowded reach : in the state of one listening to romantic music I watched the eights and the pairs and the scullers flash by to the cheers from Phyllis Court and the Steward's Enclosure which did not quite drown the hurdy-gurdy tunes of the fairground behind, while the gold of afternoon turned into the copper of evening and the old rowing heroes in their Leander caps climbed out of the launches and conferred together, comparing the battles of the day with the battles of long ago. Never had the Fourth of June seemed more like an echoing ballad, as we dressed self-consciously in our white ducks and our striped vests and little jackets of old-time sailors and tipped our flower-festooned straw hats with their gold-lettered ribbons on the backs of our heads, and *Monarch* and *Victory* and *Prince of Wales*, followed by *Britannia*, *Dreadnought*, *Thetis*, *Hibernia*, *St. George*, *Alexandra* and *Defiance*, like the roll-call of a fleet Nelson might have commanded, passed under Windsor Bridge in procession and rowed out of sight down river to the feast spread out in the meadows :

> Skirting past the rushes,
> Ruffling over the reeds
> Where the lock-stream gushes,
> Where the cygnet feeds,
> Let us see how the wine-glass flushes
> At supper on Boveney meads . . .

In the gathering twilight Windsor Castle loomed behind us, dominated by the silhouette of the Round Tower, and we thought of the old, mad king, George III, who had loved Etonians so much and in honour of whose birthday it all took place as it had taken place when he could watch it from his terrace. And then when darkness fell we climbed into our boats again for the great ordeal and triumph, returning for the densely packed rows of friends and relations on Fellows' Eyot suddenly to be revealed to us, a strange sea of motionless illuminated faces in the ruddy glare of the fireworks as we floated by standing erect in our boats ; and the catherine wheels beginning to turn and the rockets and star-shells soaring up above the elms to make their soft twin explosions in sky and river, reminded one young oarsman, holding his breath for anxious balance as he rose to his feet with his seven companions and cox, of regattas long ago when he had watched with his father on the river-bank at Fieldhead for the dance of the coloured stars to begin.

# III
## THE DILEMMA ITSELF

# I

MANY were the vows that the Lehmann children had made to themselves at Fieldhead to find fame and honour by their deeds in the world of art, music and literature; and now at last, in my first year at Cambridge, a vow was to be accomplished, a dream fulfilled. Rosamond had for some years past abandoned poetry for prose. She wrote several sketches and *nouvelles*, and, with a determination worthy of Althæa, mother of Meleager, cast them on the flames as juvenilia. And then, with Girton behind her, and a new sense of what it was all about and how it was all to be done, she began to write a novel into which she was pouring all the treasures that had accumulated in the bulging trunks of memory and imagination. When report reached us that some of her new literary friends, to whom she had showed her work in progress, thought very well of it indeed, we were gripped with a dread excitement. I identified myself with her to such an extent in her career as an author, that I was as tense, alternating between wild hopes and anxious fears, as if I were writing the book myself; and when Chatto & Windus finally accepted her manuscript, I was as happy as on the day when I won my top scholarship at Eton—indeed far happier, because then I had had a nervous collapse. Rosamond's success was somehow a triumph for all of us, *Dusty Answer* was our book, and not merely because so much of it was an imaginative transposition of the world we had grown up in together.

Encouraged by the acceptance, Rosamond began a new book before *Dusty Answer* was actually published in the spring of 1927. She wrote me a characteristic letter from Cap Ferrat in January, giving the news:

> My cold was awful on the train, my head hammered, my eyes watered, my patience was terrific; but I drank hot whisky and lemon by the gallon, and took aspirin, and when next morning came, with sun and all the excitement of new things, I recovered

almost completely. . . . This country makes one feel rather mad.
In this painted world of blue sea, blue sky, orange groves, roses
and toy houses, values are all changed, and one feels lost: and,
which is more dangerous, *safe* as well.   Absolutely safe from the
real world, and blissfully detached from it.   Everything must
in a moment begin to happen just as one wants it, and nothing
ever go wrong again; and everybody will sit round in a circle in
the sun and feel light-hearted for ever. . . .

O these little enchanted villages dreaming and secret inside
their walls, very old and luminous, perched high up on mountain
tops, Eze, La Turbie, St. Paul.   You didn't get as far south, did
you?   They are all old forts built against the Moors.   And
Vence.   You must have seen paintings of it. . . . As for me, I
have begun writing a new book, in a great burst of rather feverish
excitement.   I wish I could stop.   I shall try to, now that I see it
all clearly.   Beneath my window the sea sighs, crashes, murmurs.
I look out in the morning and see nothing but a multitudinously
twinkling sheet of blue water. . . .

The new novel was *A Note in Music*.   Meanwhile proofs
arrived of *Dusty Answer*, but I was only able to snatch a few
glimpses of them, and had to wait for advance copies to read the
whole book.   As the day of publication approached, I could
scarcely control my impatience to know what everyone else
would think of it.   Waiting for reviews was an agony: and some
of the earliest were lukewarm or even hostile.   In the middle
of May, Rosamond wrote to me:

It is sweet of you to keep me posted with news.   Mr. Raymond
writes that the first sales have been promising (550 in the first
week) but of course all depends now on the reviews. . . . It is
curious that some people have been shocked.

A few days later a review of the utmost enthusiasm, written
by my father's old friend, Alfred Noyes, appeared in the *Sunday
Times*.   News of the result came to me from Rosamond very
soon after:

A letter from Chatto this morning says the Noyes review has
swept them off their feet.   All the first edition (1,500) is gone, the
second (2,000) is ready and they've even ordered paper for a
third.   The Times B. Club took 300 in 3 days and can't cope
with the demand.   For the *first* time this morning I had a faint
passing thrill.

If Rosamond found it difficult to be thrilled, I was bursting with pride myself, and I think the whole of that summer I walked on air, the world transformed for me by Rosamond's success, our success, our justification. I read the book again and again, and then read it in the miraculous French translation by Jean Talva, and once more in the American edition. I was beginning avidly to assimilate contemporary novels at that time, looking for something that would make articulate and put into perspective the experience and feelings of our own generation, our sense of being cut off from the past by the war and endowed with unique sensibility and revolutionized values we did not expect our parents' generation to understand; and everything else seemed cold, artificial or sententious after I had read *Dusty Answer*. Evidently, to judge from the reviews and the sales and the letters Rosamond was getting, a large slice of the English and American public—and perhaps even more the French public—agreed with me and found that Rosamond had spoken for them as no one else had. Cynics who do not know the book world intimately, may be inclined to say that this extraordinary international success of a first novel by an unknown writer only proves that readers will believe anything they are told to believe by a critic they are prepared to follow. The truth, however, is that no amount of praise, even of the most hysterical kind, will move the public to read a book they find they do not like: it is the combination of the right praise at the right time with the *right book* that causes the avalanche at the lending libraries.

All during my Cambridge period Rosamond remained the most patient and understanding critic of my own writing, especially of my poetry, in which I was at last beginning to find out what was worth saying in what I wanted to say, and how to say it. She would spot at once when I was using someone else's poetic style (generally Walter de la Mare's) and when my adjectives and metaphors were second-hand or 'thought' rather than felt or seen. 'You suffer,' she wrote to me on one occasion, ' as I always did, from a fatal facility. It is so *easy* for us to write. Don't you find that? I personally am only just beginning to find it terribly difficult, and feel a little more hopeful.' And again, a little later, when I was in one of my recurrent glooms of indecision about my future career:

> I *don't* want you to go into the Diplomatic. I can't bear you to go on being inwardly torn. . . . I am confident that you can make a success of a literary career. It may be a struggle, and it may mean never being rich—but you don't mind that. . . . If I can help in any way you know I always will. The great thing is to have confidence in oneself—and I think you have. The *London Mercury* success is a great encouragement. What you'd do well would be to edit a paper. . . .

The little ' *London Mercury* success ' she referred to was that I had had a poem illustrated by myself accepted by that magazine. I had begun to do wood-engravings; and my first efforts so surprised all my friends, who had never thought of me as having even a glimmering of a draughtsman's instinct, that they urged me to go on. It was a curious sudden outcrop of a vein that failed to prove very rich, but it had a remarkably satisfying and soothing effect on me at a time when my prevalent mood was rather tense and morbid. I acquired a set of lino-cut materials, found that I enjoyed playing about with them, and quickly went on to wood-engravings, encouraged by Wogan Philipps, who helped me to buy the right instruments and an assorted pile of the little highly polished box-wood blocks on which the engravings are done. Nobody was more astonished than myself to discover that I could make designs and patterns that pleased within the diminutive dimensions of the blocks. I studied everything that I could find about the history of wood-engraving, unearthed in the library of Fieldhead old copies of Bewick's *British Birds* and *Quadrupeds* that had been given to my father when he was a boy, and developed a passion for the eccentric old Northumbrian illustrator's work that all the years of deepening knowledge and appreciation of art and artists have done nothing to destroy. Bewick's vignettes of the life he observed round his Newcastle home, in which he managed in a space no larger than a couple of square inches to convey so subtly the feel of the countryside in all its moods of winter snow, spring rain and wind, and leafy summer sunshine, the melancholy of a troupe of ragged musicians strumming outside the walls of an elegant garden, or the joy of children playing at soldiers in the mud, set me an impossible standard of technical skill; but I also studied the works of modern artists in the medium, which was enjoying a sudden popular revival at this time, and began to see how to adapt their favourite techniques of rich sensuous blacks and fine white cross-hatching to my own ideas. I strained my eyes at it in the end, and had, after several years, to give it up; but not before I had designed book-plates for many of my friends, made a number of patterns for end-papers and cover-papers that I never exploited, and produced a set of broadsheets of my own early poems (of which the *London Mercury* poem was one) with an engraved block at the top and the bottom of the page. I even had a vision of myself, in a moment of manic optimism, as a new William Blake, developing my poetry and engraving side by side in an artistic marriage where each enhanced the interest of the other. Of course I really had no notion at all; as I had had no artistic training, the whole thing was a flash in the pan; but I still sometimes wish that I could pick up my old engraving tools and design tail-pieces for my own and other people's stories—as I commissioned many genuine artists to do when I was editing *Penguin New Writing* and *Orpheus*.

In this new development of mine, Rosamond, as usual, was full of sensible encouragement and appreciation. In the spring of 1928 she was again on the Riviera, and wrote to me from Le Lavandou:

I've meant to write to you for ages. I loved your last letter, and the description of spring in the garden—especially the tadpoles, broken egg-shells and the wych-elms in new leaf made me see it all so clearly—and I felt suddenly homesick. I expect your time abroad seems quite unreal now. How incredibly easily, after the first wrench, one adapts one's personality, and how quickly the once-near becomes remote. And how queer it is that some places and people should expand one's ' ego ' and act and react on it and give it a soil to root in and its *own* food to eat (whatever mysterious substance that is), while other places and people do *nothing* to it, give it nothing, shrink it up. Where in the world do you feel most ' yourself '? Sainte-Maxime would give me a chill in the imagination if I lived there fifty years—while this little place a few miles from there along the coast is pure romance and delight to me. . . . I liked the woodcuts *very* much.

Some months later, when she had at last finished her second novel, *A Note in Music*, there was even a project that I should do an engraving for the title-page or cover:

> I've been correcting my 3rd typed copy to send you.   Helen is reading it now and is going to send it on to you at once.   I do hope you'll like it.   P. 151, the paragraph beginning "These were once . . ." to the end of that little story—is the key to the whole thing and is vaguely the subject I want for the cover. . . . But of course L'auteur propose, Chatto dispose.   They are lyrical about it.

But I decided I could not produce anything worthy of the occasion, and Wogan Philipps designed an appropriately romantic little emblem for the title-page instead.   Already at that time my feeling that I could be an artist as well as a writer was starting to fade, and the letters exchanged between Rosamond and myself were more and more occupied with my poetry and her novels.   She sometimes told me, after reading the book reviews and the articles I was beginning to get published, that she wondered whether perhaps I ought not to concentrate on prose more exclusively; but the knot of my will had formed round the desire to make poetry.   If only I could one day write one lyric that would take its place in English literature—that seemed to me worth more as an achievement than any fame prose could bring me; and in any case I felt that Rosamond had established novels as her territory in a way that I could never possibly rival.   It was not only my own admiration for her books that taught me that; but her fans and fan-mail, in which letters of perceptive, heart-warming praise from shrewd critics were mixed up with bedlamite outpourings of hysteria, reckless intimate confidences from unknown pilgrims of eternity of both sexes, proposals of marriage from the Colonies, unsolicited illegible manuscripts from aspiring authors who saw her as soul-mate and star disclosed by Heaven to guide them, demands for immediate cash support and love-sonnets from remote Alpine monasteries.   She used to keep the plums for me, and we passed hours of innocent enjoyment in reading (and acting) them over to one another.   No prose I could write would ever, I knew, evoke such a response, and it

was not only from the fan-mail that I learnt this. Strangers
had once come up to me to declare that they had known my
father, to lavish on me for a moment a devotion that had started
perhaps long before I was born; now began another experience
of adulation by proxy, but this time the worshippers were more
often very little older than myself. 'Are you any relation of
the author of *Dusty Answer*?'—'You are the *brother*?'—the
fanatical light would kindle in the eye, I would feel as if a
bucket of something warm, sweet and frothing were about to
be emptied over my head, I was transfixed like St. Sebastian
by flying arrows of passion meant for another—'*Ach, wie
wunderbar!*'—'*Comme vous êtes heureux, je rêve chaque nuit à votre
sœur!*'—'Say, Mr. Lehmann, you sure are the luckiest man in
the whole world; when I think that I've shaken hands with
Rosamond Lehmann's brother!' And then the identifications
would start, and I would be reminded of the little boy in this or
that novel who had been sitting up in bed doing his knitting,
who had been trundled across the lawn in his pram, who had
been danced up and down in the waves by his mother at the
seaside while his teeth chattered, and I would do my best to
join in the general merriment and ecstasy. It was hard; but
I reminded myself that it was far, far harder for Rosamond;
and even when I acquired a little modest and specialized fame
for myself, I believe the pang of pleasure remained in the midst
of embarrassment and wounded conceit. But by then I had
grown a kind of sixth sense, and could detect in the front rows
of a lecture-hall even while I was speaking the harpy who would
pounce at the end, and would plan evasive action. I pictured
Rosamond's dismay if she had been present herself; and resolved that to be a lightning-conductor of all this emotion was
the least I could do.

# 2

CAMBRIDGE was for me a great release and new beginning. I floundered badly during my first term, broke away, and came back, and must have been a spectacle for my friends of overwrought nerves and spiritual confusion. By the winter, however, I had seen that it was impossible for my University life to be a continuation of my Eton life. I finally abandoned Classics and turned, not to English, which I determined should be my private rather than my official subject, but to history and modern languages. And I made the discovery that if I was to be a successful rowing man, closely watched by many an older pair of eyes on the tow-path for signs of my father's flair, I could not devote my leisure to anything else at all. Not without sentimental regret, but with a profound feeling of a burden at last slipped off the shoulders, I gave it up, though at home I still continued to find enjoyment sculling along the familiar reaches in the deliciously light and speedy racing-craft Claude Goldie had presented me with. Alone in a 'whiff' I could dream about poetry; walking and bicycling with friends I could talk about it; but it shows the extraordinary hold that the idea of violent competitive exercise has on a boy who has been through an English public school, that I felt I was being rather daring and laying myself open to almost moral criticism in abandoning in one reckless *seisachtheia* rowing, fives, football, tennis, boxing, the hundred yards, the high jump and even the egg-and-spoon race for ever.

With the attempt to be a model public-school boy now finally behind me, I plunged myself with impatient zest into all the intellectual and æsthetic experiences that Cambridge offered. One of the chief of these was the Festival Theatre, which had recently been opened under the eccentric and stimulating direction of Terence Gray. Week after week, and often two or three times a week, I would trudge up the hill with a friend to revel in the modernistic decoration of the three bars, programmes on transparent paper that could be read in the

dark, multiple sets, illuminated cycloramas, austerely plain
back-cloths with melodramatic spot-lighting playing on them,
scene-shifters doing their work in full view of the audience, and
the continuous bombardment of ideas and contrasts in dramatic
style from all countries and periods provided by Terence Gray's
bill of fare.   Norman Marshall was then beginning his important work in the theatre, as assistant producer to Herbert Pren-
tice.   Ninette de Valois, with the founding of a British school
of ballet still in the impossible future, was choreographic director
and producing from time to time a programme of ' Dance
Cameos ' of her own invention, with Ursula Moreton and Hed-
ley Briggs as her chief dancers. Sophocles, Congreve,
Tchekhov, Wilde, Ibsen, Shaw, Yeats, Synge, Maeterlinck,
Strindberg, Kaiser, Dunsany, Elmer Rice, Capek, C. K.
Munro, Flecker and Victorian melodrama were all in the
repertoire;   and as the theatre's success and self-confidence
grew, many young actors were introduced who were later to
become world-famous, notably Flora Robson and Robert
Donat.

One of the plays that stirred me most was C. K. Munro's
*The Rumour*, that bitter, disillusioned play of two Ruritanian
states that are precipitated into war with one another by the
machinations of sinister political and commercial interests
behind the scenes.   The atmosphere of intellectual Cambridge
at that time was strongly pacifist, there were many younger
dons who had been through the war or had had some of their
dearest friends killed in it, and admiration of Cambridge's
darling poet, Rupert Brooke, was at a low ebb: the memory of
horror and the sense of futility and waste were uppermost.   I
had read C. E. Montague's *Disenchantment*, and I was ploughing
through Goldie Lowes Dickinson's study of international diplomatic intrigues in the years immediately preceding the war,
*The International Anarchy*.   *The Rumour* completed the revolution
in my thought against the conventional judgements about war-
guilt that I had shared until then;   not as yet towards Socialism,
which was by no means the implication of Lowes Dickinson or
Munro, but to the ideals of the League of Nations.   I suddenly
saw, or seemed to see, that war might come about, not because
one nation deliberately planned it, but because of the anarchy

that was inherent in the idea of sovereignty and the unchecked competition of great industrial interests, national in scope and repercussion but controlled by private individuals or groups. Not the Kaiser and the German General Staff plotting to master the world, but the industrial kings instigating armament races and fomenting old hatreds and jealousies became for me the villains of the world political scene. From that time I realized that what had happened in 1914 might happen again at any moment, and became permanently haunted with war-dread. I discovered Wilfred Owen, a revelation to me as much for expressing the mood of disillusionment and human pity transcending frontiers that was antidote to Rupert Brooke, as for his experiments in the technical devices of poetry. I devoured R. H. Mottram's *The Spanish Farm*, Zweig's *Sergeant Grischa*, Edmund Blunden's *Undertones of War*, Edward Thompson's *These Men My Friends*; it seemed to me that Joe Ackerley's *The Prisoners of War* led to unanswerable conclusions against modern war; I was deeply moved, even without seeing it on the stage. I tried to get anyone I knew who had been through the war to tell me about his experiences. My chief source was Pitson, a reserved, rugged-faced mechanic and chauffeur who had taken over our old stables and coach-houses at Fieldhead to transform them into a garage and petrol-filling station. He used to come to fetch me at the end of term in my mother's Morris. Stimulated by my continual questions, he would describe the Western Front as he had seen it as an army lorry-driver: a steady flow of reminiscences, all the grimmer for being uttered in his habitual undertone and without any dramatic heightening or trace of personal emotion, gradually built up in my mind the picture of that blasted landscape of massacre. I tried not to believe it; I tried even harder to believe that it could not present itself again; but in my heart I knew that I was fooling myself.

I have always hated a passive attitude in the face of imminent danger, and I determined to associate myself with the only immediate kind of positive action that seemed feasible: the exposure of armaments intrigues and the building of a supra-national society through the League of Nations. Such a reaction, however, was out of tune with the mood of that

powerful side of intellectual Cambridge which formed a kind
of Bloomsbury-by-the-Cam.  I do not think that Goldie himself had much hope; but many of his younger friends and colleagues adopted a far more defeatist attitude, treating enthusiasm for the League of Nations as slightly absurd, like putting on
shorts and scouting with the boys in middle age.  When I look
back on it, it seems to me that the Cambridge I knew was
haunted inescapably by the old war; it was always there in the
background conditioning the prevalent sensibility, with its
preference for tragedy and bitter wit, its rejection of cosy pretences and its refusal to accept any criterion of behaviour except
one: does your action cause suffering to another?

Profoundly disillusioned and pessimistic about ideas and
human folly was the atmosphere in The Pavilion, West Road,
where one of Rosamond's friends, the novelist E. B. C. Jones,
known to us all as ' Topsy ', and her husband Peter (F. L.)
Lucas, poet and devotee of poetry at that time preparing his
great edition of Webster's plays, were living.  Tea at the
Pavilion was one of the events I most looked forward to in my
early years at Cambridge.  ' Topsy ' would lead the conversation, fixing her guests with a bright, determined, searching
gaze and firing leading questions at them in a deep voice,
probing their intimate personal secrets and their views on
literature and their friends' affairs, demanding frankness (and
giving an unalloyed example of it herself) and assuming that all
cards would be put on the table, even those most tightly clutched
to one's bosom.  I was embarrassed but nevertheless delighted:
here one could talk openly, and listen to talk of passion and
wit about modern poetry and modern novels, and (once one had
plucked up courage) freely unburden one's heart of all that had
choked it, while ' Topsy ' uttered a throaty chuckle or a sympathetic comment that showed how exactly she understood
what one was going through—even though her Freudian interpretations and pagan suggestions for remedy dismayed on
occasion a sensibility still too tender for this bracing air.  It
was ' Topsy ' who introduced me to Yeats's later poems which
were coming out at that time: a gift for which I shall always
be deeply grateful.  Peter put in only the most fleeting, ghost-
like appearances: noiselessly he materialized from his study,

took a cup of tea, maintaining an alert silence or partaking briefly in the conversation, like a bird swooping down to shake its wings for a few seconds in a bird-bath, and then as suddenly and swiftly was gone.   His book of collected essays, *Authors Dead and Living*, was a key to many treasure chambers hitherto unknown to me in modern poetry, and I longed to draw him out: but as vainly as Hamlet tried to stay his father's ghost.

Peter's brother, however, who had rooms in Gibbs's buildings became a close friend.   Far less articulate than Peter, or indeed than anyone I had ever met before, Donald smiled silently while he twiddled a lock of falling hair in his finger, and then punctured my enthusiasms or despairs with a gentle shaft of disillusioned wit.   ' Vanity, all is vanity ', was written invisibly over his door; disconcerting for me at first, but good when he persuaded me to read far more deeply into his favourite author, Thomas Hardy, than I had before.   He was one of the many friends I made at King's: it was my spiritual home in the new phase of my life, but I retreated gladly when the gay, stimulating, malicious parties were over to the ample, dignified bosom of my own College.   Trinity was too large for the complex web of gossip and scandal that was spun so closely over the denizens of King's, and seemed spiritually as far distant from that animated world as a stately country house in the eighteenth century from the coffee-houses of the capital.   Of George Rylands, one of the youngest dons of King's, I saw a great deal. He had long been a friend of Rosamond's and took an incredible amount of trouble to direct my reading in English literature and to give shrewd advice about the poetry I was writing.   I owe more than I can say to his coaxing, teasing sympathy; when he praised I knew it was because he sincerely admired, when he found fault he did it so gently but with so sure a precision of analysis that it was impossible for me not to be convinced.   His *Words and Poetry* was just the book I needed to read at the time: it was an antidote, with its emphasis on the importance to a line of the weight, colour and overtones of every single word, to Peter's more sentimental view of poetry, and brought me down to the earth of craftsmanship and truth— truth of eye and heart—from some of my windier cloud-wanderings among abstractions and emotional clichés.   We used to go for walks together, discussing every poet under the sun, E. M. Forster's and Virginia Woolf's novels and Lytton Strachey's biographies and the works of all the other authors I envied him for knowing in London; and I found that he shared my interest in printing and wanted, as I did, to own a press of his own.

Eddie Playfair was one of the Eton friends who had come up with me at the same time, and gone to King's. The Jolly Boaters still saw a great deal of one another: I shared rooms with Anthony Martineau and then with James Brock. With Anthony, and sometimes with Stephen Hawtrey, I bicycled all over the flat East Anglian countryside, with its huge skies and lush pastures, visiting its countless riches of old churches and toiling as far as Ely, the cathedral towers of which would gradually push themselves up over the horizon as we pedalled away, reminiscing about Eton and planning our future. James Brock acquired a car, and we motored further afield, to the little towns of Suffolk with their great churches that recalled a Huguenot prosperity long since vanished, and across the turnip-sown Bedfordshire wastes to Oxford. Eddie sometimes accompanied us; and through Eddie, in my second or third year, I came to know the young poet with whom I struck up the most intimate intellectual friendship of my Cambridge years. Julian Bell was the elder son of Clive and Vanessa Bell, a nephew of Virginia Woolf, and one of the most gifted of that fortunate second generation of the Bloomsbury giants who inherited the well-laid-out gardens of ideas their elders had created, and basked in the sunshine of their artistic achievements. Julian was a great, untidy, sprawling figure of a young man, awkward in manner and dressed always in dishevelled clothes with buttons rarely meeting button-holes at the neck and wrists. He imposed, nevertheless, by charm of expression in the smiling, intelligent face under the curly tangled hair, by natural force of temperament and by an obstinate persistence of intellectual curiosity—to which was added a conviction that the arguments he defended had the authority of graven tablets of the law: the tablets of Bloomsbury. He had had a Quaker schooling, followed by a period in France, but Bloomsbury had been his real education. An instinctual power, as strongly growing as a wild thicket of hawthorn and briar rose, was at war in him and never completely tamed by the rationalist ideas that his father, Clive Bell, Roger Fry and their friends represented. To act from reasonable motives that were clear to oneself and to avoid confused irrational emotions; to treat chastity and the sense of sin in sexual matters as relics of the barbarous dark, as uncivilized as religious superstition or any of the fashionable mumbo-jumbo mysticisms; to be a pacifist because war was futile and absurd as well as painful and destructive of beauty—all these principles were already inscribed on his banner, which he waved demonstratively in one's face during his first year at King's. And yet he had a passion for nature at its wildest, and the poetry he was writing at that time was remarkable because it was an attempt to let the countryside, the moods of wind and weather and life outside the cultivated human pale, speak for themselves without any interference of the poet's own moralizing thoughts. ' We receive but what we give '—perhaps; but if so it was the non-rational intuitive side of his temperament that Julian was finding in nature. As time went on, the struggle in his mind was almost completely resolved in favour of the eighteenth century, in my opinion much to the detriment of his poetry; but I am convinced that if he had lived there would have been a new turn in the struggle and a new creative phrase. No one who knew him at all intimately could doubt that he was born to lead in some intellectual sphere: I remember that a French poet who stayed at Cambridge for some time was so struck by him that he exclaimed, ' Julian Bell is not a young man like other young men, he is a force of nature.'

A letter he wrote to me in the spring of 1929 shows in an amusing way the conflict in his mind between his poetic sensibility and his fear of being found guilty of romantic emotions. He was staying at the Bells' villa, La Bergère, at Cassis:

> I am leading a thoroughly primitive and simple life here, which means one has too much of those commodities of civilization of which one has no need, and one has to walk ten miles to get a nail or a box of matches—which is not strictly true, but at any rate near enough.

> I asked Michael to let you have *Winter Movement* when he had

finished with it: I hope you have it safely. I find it very hard to do any work here. I get conscience stricken about staying in-doors, and then in the evenings I become sleepy. However I'm getting my hand in again by translating one or two of Ronsard's sonnets. He is a poet for whom I have suddenly developed an absolute passion. I hope you like him, for I foresee I shall be boring everyone about him next term. I feel half tempted to write you a short essay about him but refrain. Meanwhile the country here is delightful. Spring has just begun, the almonds are in blossom—so pretty that one suspects them of being dressed for the occasion, and of making up on the sly—wild purple anemones and grape hyacinths, with endless birds singing and a most Shelleyan Aziola—which I stalked last evening and, to my great joy, identified as Scop's owl—hooting in a melancholy manner to the sunset, whilst Aristophanes' frogs—but I'm really getting too literary—sing choruses all down the valley. And the most incredibly romantic views, with hills, pines, sea, sunsets and distant mountains. Yet the whole affair done in the best grave, sober, French classical style, laid out by Cézanne, with the ghost of Racine at his elbow. So I get the best of both worlds, to say nothing of first-rate French cooking and red wine. Or rather of all three, for I don't believe that even in Greece itself would one be more likely to come on Pan and the Dryads—or my classical prototype, Silenus. Indeed, I discovered Parnassus only the other day, the most enchanting deserted oliveyards, high up in the hills, with open grassy lawns under the trees and a tiny stream falling from terrace to terrace.

Lord, what an appalling rhapsody. I shall have to take to writing shilling shockers in mock-Stevenson next. Appalling!

If he had not allowed himself to grow fat (though he was certainly not a Silenus), Julian would have been strikingly good-looking. An impish smile lurked about his lips when he was engaged in the arguments he loved to pursue; if someone else put forward a point of view that seemed to him difficult to refute the smile would momentarily fade, and one was conscious only of the intent clear gaze of the reflective eyes. He was a hesitant but obstinate debater, never voluble or overbearing; he was too anxious to discover the truth and too conscious of the importance of good manners in argument to want to gain a victory by the tricks of rhetoric. And yet strong emotions were held in uneasy control under the smile, and his nature was more complex than these discussions at first revealed. At one moment he seemed full of indolent charm, a sensualist who cared only for the good things of life; at the next one saw an entirely different side emerge, ascetic, hard-working, ruthless and battlesome. We kept up an enormous correspondence for years, mostly concerned with problems of poetic technique and the philosophy of poetry. Writing in an untidy, sloping, almost illegible hand, he would one day attack my own poems for woolly romanticism; another day he would declare that I would still be read in three hundred years' time, a compliment I ill deserved, but typical of his sudden spurts of generous appreciation of somebody working on lines he could not entirely approve. As his career at Cambridge progressed, and he felt his ideals challenged by the followers of Eliot and Pound or the surrealists among his contemporaries, or one of the anti-Bloomsbury pundits, his letters became full of malicious cracks and angry verse-satire in the best eighteenth-century manner with no holds barred. At the same time the challenge, the furious wrangles in which he involved himself, accentuated his rationalist stand and drove him even further away from the kind of imaginative writing with which in reality he had a strong instinctive sympathy. He finally reached the point where he would have liked to blot out the whole of the romantic movement and the century and a half of poetry that followed it. 'Altogether', he wrote to me in the autumn of 1930, 'I'm beginning an education whose end is to be the full enjoyment of classical poetry—not because of its romantic beauty, but for a beauty of its own. When I shall really be able to read it as if I had been born before 1798, I don't know—but I feel that it may not after all be too long.' Pope was finally established as his god of poetry, and his rage descended, with ludicrous and wilful exaggeration, on Shakespeare. 'Talking of the grand simplicities,' he wrote during one long vacation, at the end of a terrific diatribe about commonsense, precision and the eighteenth-century virtues, 'I am obeying Peter's instructions and reading all Shakespeare's plays. I am astonished to find how right I am about them. What can be said at this time of day for a person so utterly lacking in all notions of construction, half whose lines mean nothing at all, and who has only the vaguest notions of metre. An intelligent earwig with a gift for blank verse could do as well.' At this I blew up (perhaps I was meant to). I was staying with a French family at Fontainebleau at the time, as part of my vaguely sketched education for becoming a diplomatist, and nearly choked over my breakfast *croissant* when his provocation reached me. I wrote in answer one of the longest letters I have ever dispatched to anyone. I told him how fatal I thought it to try to resurrect the eighteenth-century mentality in our own time, how monotonous and inadequate the end-stopped couplet must become for a modern poet if indulged in to the exclusion of everything else; and then in refuting his criticisms of Shakespeare called to my aid two of his favourite modern critics, Lytton Strachey and Charles Mauron, and flung at him as many quotations from his own seventeenth and eighteenth century authors—Dryden, Dr. Johnson, and even Pope—as I could remember, all praising Shakespeare for the qualities Julian denied him. The result was typical and comic. Another long letter arrived, written in even more illegible pencil all up and down several sheets of crumpled notepaper, with an even longer tirade about the advantages of a course of the pre-romantic poets for a modern who wanted to learn his craft, but ending, almost as an afterthought, ' But the greater part of your argument remains unanswerable'.

The book by Lytton Strachey from which I took my ammunition was the luminous little masterpiece of interpretative criticism he wrote for the Home University Library, *Landmarks in French Literature*. I had already met him by then, through Dadie Rylands and my sister Rosamond, and I think it was he himself who suggested that I might find the book of use, as I was embarking on a deeper study of French literature. It taught me, as no other book could have, how to find excellence in the French tradition even if one were a devoted believer in the English tradition, and why Racine was a great poet and dramatist even though his greatness was so totally different from Shakespeare's. My enthusiasm for the book was the origin of an amusing occurrence that very summer. I was deep in it on the boat-train on my way back to England; and I noticed that a distinguished-looking lady dressed in black, who was sitting next to me, was unusually interested in me and the book.

Finally she leaned over and asked me what I thought of it. She looked French, and yet she spoke perfect English without any trace of accent: I was intrigued, and immediately launched into a rhapsody about the book, adding, with all the naïve vanity and pride of youth, ' You see, I *know* Lytton Strachey personally.' This seemed to delight the unknown lady, who proceeded gently and skilfully to draw me out on the subject of the author. . . . It was only when we reached Calais that she revealed, to my total confusion, that she was in fact his sister, Dorothy, married to the French painter Simon Bussy, the *traductrice accreditée* of Gide, and many years later famous as the author of *Olivia*.

Paradoxically enough, in the same letter in which Julian had written so unpardonably about Shakespeare, he told me he had thoroughly enjoyed *Wuthering Heights*. It was rare for him to like or even read a novel at all. He admired his Aunt Virginia's work with strong Bloomsbury loyalty, and yet he was made uneasy by it. It was a surprise to me, therefore, a year later, to find that he had been reading Rosamond's just published novel, *A Note in Music*, and evidently *Dusty Answer* as well. He wrote to me from Charleston:

> The fifth symphony is going on, much against Clive's will, but really just now Beethoven is the only musician I can endure, for I'm suffering from—not melancholy but black blood, the black blood of the Stephens, I suppose, that Virginia talks of, and only hardness, strength, tragedy are endurable. In fact I've had an overdose of romance and beauty. Cures: Beethoven and ten-mile walks in big boots, and the slaughter of innocent birds. . . . I've just finished your sister's book—which happened, heaven knows why, to fit into my mood, so just now I am confident it is a work of indubitable genius. My opinion on novels, tho', isn't worth very much. But it must really be pretty good to have affected me at all. You know, you're rather alike in imagination . . . you've both got a same quality, midsummer in gardens—trees—water and parties I should label it—which is fascinating.

When I read over today the letters that Julian and I exchanged in such numbers at that time, I find them full of the most detailed arguments and theories about couplets, quatrains, blank verse, free verse, cæsuras, rhythm and counter-rhythm, realism and romanticism, dialogue in verse and description in verse, clarity, obscurity, ambiguity and all the other subjects that two eager apprentice craftsmen in poetry can find to discuss with one another. The light has faded from them, the ashes are dead. And yet it was the most exciting colloquy in the world: the whole future of poetry, we felt, depended on these arguments; we were remoulding English literature nearer to our own hearts, and even our great differences of approach seemed to promise a spark of fusion out of which the new way of writing, the completely modern poem would be made. In the release of Cambridge life I gradually found new energies in myself, and began for the first time to write poetry that gave pleasure to others whose opinion I respected, that disturbed, however slightly, the common pool of the creative imagination. I have experienced only three or four such periods in my life; and this, the first, was inevitably the most exhilarating. I began to drain off the romantic excess of my dreamings and to be far more successfully what every poet or novelist must learn to be: the critical objective spectator as well as the actor, discovering thus how to give words and images a newly charged life and significance. I read all Eddie Marsh's volumes of Georgian Poetry through, and Squire's fat volumes of Selections from the Georgian poets again and again in order, not merely to find the real and nourishing food I wanted, but to purge myself, by surfeit, of all contemporary clichés of attitude and metaphor and phrase-making. Of course I cannot pretend that I did completely purge myself, but many years later, when I found so many young poets ardently returning to all the stale poeticizings of the 'twenties and believing that the dew of dawn was upon their writings, I wished I could have persuaded them to take the same course. Inevitably my poems were colder and more impersonally dry for a time than the norm of temperature I knew I had one day to reach; but joyfully exploring modern French literature I longed to blend the complexity and vision of Rimbaud with the passion of Baudelaire and the pictorial power of Heredia. I urged Julian in my letters to read La Fontaine rather than Boileau, and Valéry on the subject of La Fontaine, and Peter Quennell's all-too-slender volume of poems to see how a gifted poet could be modern as well as

traditional, a symbolist and a classicist at the same time.   I
dreamed of writing poems beyond those I was at work on then,
which would have the intensity and packed imaginative rich-
ness of Yeats, Wilfred Owen, Valéry's *Charmes* and Gerard
Manley Hopkins's shorter poems (which I had just discovered).

Julian and I used to carry on endless discussions whenever
we were together as well as by letter: walking along the Backs,
in his room at King's or in mine overlooking the Great Court of
Trinity.   I lured him during the vacation to Fieldhead, and I
visited him in return at Charleston.   Life at Fieldhead in those
days was not very formal, but nevertheless a sense of the formality of big country houses in Edwardian times still lingered
about the softly carpeted corridors and the dining-room with its
silver candlesticks on polished tables and its ring of onlooking
family portraits; even though the occasions were rare when we
dressed for dinner, and old James with his serio-comic grand
manner and jingling keys was no longer there to carve the joint
on the sideboard.   The contrast of Charleston's bohemian
atmosphere was an agreeable stimulus to me.   I have always
enjoyed being able to be the citizen of several worlds at the
same time, and found a special pleasure a few years later in
being accepted intimately in the working-class life of Vienna
and the literary life of London.   It amused me at this time to
move between Charleston and Fieldhead and the even more
traditional atmosphere of my sister Helen's comfortable home
in Northamptonshire, from where I wrote to Julian: ' I'm here
in the middle of the hunting country,' when I would sometimes
find myself, inexplicably, discussing the merits of the various
Hunts in the Southern Midlands with one of the grooms.   There
were no grooms touching their caps on the porch at Charleston,
nor pink coats hanging up in the cupboards, and the discussion
was about *The Nature of Beauty*, *Vision and Design* and *The Ego and
the Id* rather than the way in which the Grafton or the Bicester
was run by the latest M.F.H. or the impact of rich American
horsey enthusiasts on the ancient pattern of country life.   The
half-finished canvases by Duncan Grant, or Julian's mother
Vanessa, or his brother Quentin piled carelessly in the studios,
and the doors and fireplaces of the old farm-house transformed
by decorations of fruit and flowers and opulent nudes by the same

hands, the low square tables made of tiles fired in Roger Fry's
Omega workshops, and the harmony created all through the
house by the free, brightly coloured post-impressionist style that
one encountered in everything from the huge breakfast cup one
drank one's coffee from to the bedroom curtains that were
drawn in the morning, not by a silent-footed valet or housemaid
but by one's own hand to let in the Sussex sunshine, excited
the suppressed painter that lurked in my breast. They
seemed to suggest how easily life could be restored to a paradise
of the senses if one simply ignored the conventions that still
gripped one in the most absurd ways, clinging from a past that
had been superseded in the minds of people of clear intelligence and unspoilt imagination.

Julian was often alone in the house while his parents were
in London or down at La Bergère. ' My own life is utterly
monastic,' he warned me before my first visit, ' except for letters.
I work three hours a day, walk four, and get meals, make fires
and bath in two.' But this was just what I looked forward to,
an ideal way of life and perfect surroundings if one wanted to
write and think about writing. We went for long walks over
the downs with their distant views of a hazy sea, accompanied by—for Julian, like all sensible bachelors, possessed, or
rather was privileged to enjoy the company of a spaniel bitch—
Clinker, who at that time was carrying on a protracted and
embarrassing love affair with a fine gentleman from the neighbouring farm at Tilton where Maynard Keynes and Lydia
Lopokova lived. ' Clinker is with child by the Keynes's cur,
what a life! ' grumbled Julian in a letter to me after I left.
Clinker would return from her distant trysts in a state of the
wildest elation, running round the kitchen and barking at the
top of her voice, while Julian cooked me delicious ham ome-
lettes. After dinner we both laid our pens down, and took up
again the endless argument of Pope versus Shakespeare, Herrick
versus Keats and Shelley, and plotted a magazine of our own
which Julian saw as a counterblast to the crimes committed in
the name of Eliot and Dr. Leavis by his contemporaries. . . . I
had a dream one night that Edmund Blunden (who had
recently accepted a poem of mine for *The New Statesman*) was
going to speak about this magazine through a megaphone, and

that I had been given, as a great favour, the post of Editor-for-Scotland. . . . But we were both already deeply involved with other, real magazines in Cambridge.

# 3

THE ' Michael ' of Julian's letter from La Bergère was Michael Redgrave, and the paper for which he was holding Julian's long poem ' Winter Movement ' was *The Venture*, a magazine edited by himself, Robin Fedden and Anthony Blunt.   It was during the long vacation of 1928 that I received a letter from Anthony, who was already establishing a reputation for himself in Cambridge as a formidable and disputatious art critic, informing me that a new magazine was being planned and inviting me to contribute, not poems but woodcuts.

The first number of *The Venture* appeared in November, and from that moment till I went down it occupied a central place in my interests.   Many of Julian's best poems appeared in it, some poems of mine (most of which I had the good sense to tear up later), and nearly all the passable woodcuts I designed in my freak career as engraver.   Michael contributed poems, as did Robin Fedden, John Davenport and Basil Wright, and Anthony, I remember, an impressive article which was my first introduction to Johann Fischer's baroque masterpieces in Bavaria.   *The Venture* was extremely pleasantly produced, and the illustrations, by Raymond McGrath, Douglas Davidson and Guy Barton as well as myself, made it very easy on the eye.   It was, I think one might say, a magazine of the ' centre ' in what was already being called a Cambridge poetic renaisssance.   The extreme left started its rival magazine at exactly the same time, and for the next two years a furious battle raged (in our minds at any rate) between the protagonists of the two magazines.   *Experiment* disdained wood or lino-cuts, but had reproductions of paintings by abstract and surrealist artists.   There were surrealist and imagist poems, many pieces in which the influence of Eliot was glaringly evident, and nearly all of them offended against Julian's canons of clarity, concrete imagery and commonsense. In spite of the rivalry, a number of contributors managed to live comfortably in both camps, and were contemptuously dubbed by Julian ' the Mercenaries ': they included Basil Wright and Humphrey Jennings. There were also early poems by J. Bronowski, Kathleen Raine and Hugh Sykes; but by far the most interesting of all the contributions were those by William Empson, including the extraordinary early poem *Camping Out*, which begins, ' And now she cleans her teeth into the lake '. Nothing more original was produced in our time, and yet these rare blooms had poison in the stalk for those who plucked them. I was fascinated by their formal skill, the poetic discipline which controlled the off-hand conversational manner, giving it a subtle texture and music; not, however, having received, as Empson had, a training in mathematics or science, I was all too often baffled by the extended specialist metaphors which he carried through with sure cunning; and I looked with a suspicious and unbelieving eye on those of my friends who claimed that they understood them. No such frustrations arose about the extracts which Empson also allowed to appear in *Experiment* from the book on which he was at work, *Seven Types of Ambiguity*, which I still consider one of the cardinal books of my initiation into the deeper mysteries of poetry, as important for me then as Robert Graves's *On English Poetry* had been at an earlier stage.

In spite of Empson, *The Venture* remained my spiritual home; and through *The Venture* I became a close friend of Michael Redgrave, the most versatile in his talents of the group of gifted young men at Magdalene at that time. Tall, slim, with curly chestnut hair and a romantic profile, he was an engaging embodiment of the ideal conception of what a young poet should look like and how he should behave; but the stage was in his blood—and would out. When he became editor of the semi-official *Cambridge Review* during the following year, I joined him as his assistant, and we had a great deal of fun turning the staid *Review* almost into an adjunct of *The Venture*, livening the inevitable reports of University doings and the University Sermon with poems and reviews by all our circle (including, for we felt we could count it neutral ground, Empson and some of the other stars of *Experiment*), theatrical criticism by Dadie Rylands and Michael himself, articles on modern French writers by the learned and enchanting Jean Stewart, daughter of Dr. Stewart who was guiding my official steps in French literature, and polemics in which Julian took a lusty part.

The perishable nature of play production being what it is, and the impossibility of comparing one production with another, as one can compare one picture or even one film with another, making all judgements highly uncertain, I can only record my subjective conviction that the *King Lear* which Dadie Rylands produced for the Marlowe Society in the early spring of 1929 was one of the most moving and beautiful of our time and without much doubt the one truest to the spirit of the poetry.    Michael's playing of Edgar revealed a quality that put most clever undergraduates' acting in the shade : it was easy—at least it seemed so to me—to prophesy a brilliant stage career for him after that experience.    But the production was also remarkable for the acting of Lear by Peter Hannen, the son of Nicholas Hannen and Athene Seyler.    It has always lingered in my mind, and I think in the minds of most of those who came to see it that week, and made us feel that Peter's death so soon after was a tragic loss for the English theatre.    I can still hear him uttering the famous line ' Pray you, undo this button,' and feel the constriction of heart that assailed me.

Michael pursued his triple career as poet, player and editor with astonishing verve.    In the winter he was in another production of Dadie's, Milton's *Comus*, for which his beautiful speaking voice was well suited.    He wrote to me just after Christmas, to tell me of its success at the end of term, and added :

We did it again on the 19th at the Keynes', with Duncan Grant scenery, and *all* Bloomsbury in the auditorium—including Shaw, Sickert and Strachey.    Lydia spoke an epilogue and danced, and she and Maynard did a pas-de-deux which brought things to an end uproariously.    Afterwards sausages and beer in the supper-room, where Robert and I wanted to examine the Sickerts, Seurats, Derains, Frys and Grants which hung on the walls, but thought it would be impertinent, with all those famous people paying full attention only to their sausages.    Miss Matheson of the B.B.C. was there, and I have since received an invitation to

' try the Microphone ' with a view to broadcasting poetry. I should like you to tell me what I ought to broadcast, if I am allowed to do so.

Some of his poems appeared in the volume of *Cambridge Poetry* which was published by the Hogarth Press the next year, and in which the so furious-seeming contestants of *Venture* and *Experiment* were made most unprotesting bed-fellows. And yet, for all the pleasure they gave those readers who were attuned to them, I find it difficult to doubt that he made the right decision in devoting his mature energies to the theatre, where the peculiar originality and force of his temperament found a far more unimpeded outlet. Michael was educating himself all this time in taste and understanding, and I am sure this apprentice-ship played a vital part in making him what he has since become: one of the supreme interpreters of the poetic on the English stage of our time.

# 4

I HAD chosen History and Modern Languages when I gave up Classics, chiefly because I still had my eye on a diplomatic career, but also because—with Rosamond and Dadie and ' Topsy ' to advise me—I felt I could take care of English literature by myself while learning something about French and German literature. My appetite reached out in all directions, and dictated a meal more gigantic than any supervisor would have dared to set me. Sitting up in the window-seat of my rooms overlooking Great Court early in the morning and late into the evening, with the sound of the fountain as gentle musical accompaniment, I went *at* English literature as one of Walt Disney's woodpeckers tackles a tree-trunk, with the chips flying out in a ceaseless hail. Volume after volume of the Mermaid series of Elizabethan and Jacobean dramatists was swallowed to the last morsel, one century after another of English poetry was cleared off my plate as a hungry dog licks its bowl clean of the crumbs. I found a special delight in the prose of the seventeenth century, from *Urn Burial* and *Centuries of Meditation* to Dryden's essays; and when I came to the novel, exploring huge territories my boyhood reading in the Library at Fieldhead had left untrodden, I looked more and more for what was distinguished by a poet's fastidious sense of style and care for the individual word. I carried home from Bowes & Bowes every volume or anthology of modern poetry I could afford to purchase, with red-letter days of treasure trove—such as the day on which I discovered Roy Campbell's *The Flaming Terrapin*. I made my first serious explorations into the world of the contemporary novel: only Conrad had been added to my reading pleasures at Eton, and D. H. Lawrence, Aldous Huxley, E. M. Forster and Virginia Woolf were entirely unknown, and excited me by their ingenuities of approach and artistry to a whole new series of ambitious dreams of revolutionary novel-writing. In addition, I had my long reading list of French and German books, and was trying to swallow Tolstoi and Tchekhov at the same time. I also began to read some books of Shakespearean criticism, stirred by Wilson Knight's *The Wheel of Fire*. The more I read the more interested I became. I began to feel I wanted to master the huge scholarly and interpretative literature in an orderly fashion; but I realized at the same time that to do this I needed a discipline and an objective I could not find in any higgledy-piggledy private reading. I therefore welcomed Dadie Rylands's suggestion that I should spend one long vacation working for the Charles Oldham Shakespeare scholarship. Generally this scholarship attracted very few entrants, as the prize was not great and the time involved in preparation might swallow up a whole summer; but for that very reason the few were keen, hard-working, would-be experts, and it was not at all an easy plum to shake from the tree. This was not really the point in my mind: my instinct was that I must *know* Shakespeare through and through, and if at the end I could say I did, that would be reward enough for having ' stayed in after school ' during three holiday months of summer.

I stayed in. And I have seldom enjoyed anything so much, or felt so deeply satisfied with the results of an effort made, even though I only achieved the position of runner-up to the winner. The whole Shakespeare panorama unfolded before me, like a new landscape or the further side of a mountain pass —new, because, though many details were already familiar enough to me, I had never seen it as a whole before—and my mind was changed by the experience. In no other way could I have understood that Shakespeare was the key to the whole of English literature, the master mind that determined its course and depth and vitality so fundamentally that we can hardly conceive what our imaginative life—perhaps even our moral values—would be like without him. The pedants and witch-doctors moped and mowed round him in ever-thickening hordes, but if one raised one's eyes and ignored their mumblings and dervish howls, he towered still above them, a figure striking a rock: and the whole of our civilization since his day fertilized by the streams that came gushing out. What excited me as much as anything else was the discovery that even those minds which seemed most unlike his, Dryden's or Dr. Johnson's, were not only compelled into admiration in the study of his work, but were also brought to know themselves more deeply—as if his genius were radio-active, penetrating immediately beneath the surface layers of varying historical circumstances and fashion. No one had prepared me for this experience before Cambridge, nor would I, with my sceptical turn of mind, have been ready to believe what the necessity of reading every play (and every apocryphal play as well) two or three times in the order of writing—and following step by step how that order had been established—so miraculously presented to me: the incredible flowering of his genius and the immeasurable amplitude that flowering reached. Even if there had not been this revelation, which was almost like the revelation of a new dimension to existence, the summer would not have been lost. On the contrary, it was transformed into one of the most memorable summers of my life, because the whole of my surroundings seemed to exist within Shakespeare's vision. I spent a great deal of it at Kidlington, near Oxford, where Rosamond, now married to Wogan Philipps, had taken the old grey-stone manor-house, and from there we used often to motor over to Stratford. Even in those days, before the great revival of Shakespearean production and acting we have enjoyed in the last dozen years, one could see productions that never lacked something to delight or illuminate a student at the height of his passion for his subject.    I was like a lover who finds even blotchy and badly developed photographs of his beloved precious and fascinating.    I was ready to forgive more in the way of bad, dim-witted acting and crude, unimaginative sets than ever before or since.    And the delight I found in the ripening orchards and golden cornfields of the countryside between the Chilterns and the Cotswolds, the sheep-farms on the slopes and the water-meadows below, the old villages huddled round their Crusader churches and the little towns basking in the afternoon sunshine of July, with their inn-signs swinging a welcome as ancient as the Wars of the Roses, the towering umbrage of oak and elm in the parklands and the lanes so deeply furred with wild flowers leading up to the beechwoods on the horizon, were enhanced and consecrated by Justice Shallow and Hotspur and Falstaff and the music that haunted a wood near Athens.    It was a time in my life when the identification of poet and landscape was one of the greatest sources of imaginative pleasure to me.    My eye blotted out the pylons and ribbon development that encroached apace on the ' Russet Lawns and Fallows Gray ' of Buckinghamshire, and I saw them with the vision of the young Milton :

> Meadows trim with Daisies pide,
> Shallow Brooks, and Rivers wide.
> Towers, and Battlements it sees
> Boosom'd high in tufted Trees. . . .

The river and the wooded slopes round Marlow were filled with the presence of Shelley composing *The Revolt of Islam*, and his magic boats sailed under the willows, reducing to ghostly vanishing point the spooning spivs with their raucous portable gramophones oozing sentimental jazz.    On the downs of the Isle of Wight the rhythms of *Maud* and *Crossing the Bar* were what sounded in my ears, and not the back-firing, the honking and brake-screeching of the char-a-bancs that carried their loads of trippers on the daily advertised tours down lanes that were made for shepherd and farmer's cart.    I lived in a timeless England of ideal presences, where all the centuries joined hands to praise ; and learnt to understand the meaning of that *absence* which poets have lamented in countries like New Zealand, so dazzlingly beautiful but so entirely (as yet) without spiritual significance.

In my third year at Trinity, my father died, after ten years of illness bravely borne, but tragic for his family and friends to watch, who could remember the man so devoted to active pursuits, so surrounded by health and energy and the hope of youth. Strangely enough, as I stood by his bedside—I had failed to arrive from Cambridge in time to see him in his last moments—though the face before me seemed infinitely remote, centuries and the space of stars distant, some element that his illness had obscured and confused for so long reigned there again, giving an unforgettable impression of triumphant resolution and the calm that comes from having won through all obstacles and sufferings; something I had never expected to see on a dead man's face, which pierced me to the heart with a sense of communication. We were alone; I had never felt so close to him, nor so strongly the archetypal power of the bond between father and son, at the very instant when it had been broken—for me—for ever. I consoled myself by making a selection of his verse over the next few months: the little book was published by Blackwood and prefaced by Alfred Noyes. It contained the famous ode he wrote on the birth of a son to Dr. Butler of Trinity: that son happened to have become, by an odd turn of fate, my own tutor, Jim Butler, and had written to me only a short while before: ' Will you convey my respects to your father, and tell him it is the sorrow of my life to have failed to live up to his poem about me.' It would have needed some doing:

> Though no doubt he'll be a stoic or a modern Pocahontas
> (This allusion is τι βάρβαρον) when cutting his ὀδόντας,
> Yet *if* he when his teething time approaches should to cry elect,
> He will cry, I am persuaded, in the purest Attic dialect. . . .

My wanderings about Europe had now started in my vacations. I stayed in a family at Munich to learn German, which I still found a difficult and ugly language (and only discovered the beauty of a year or two later when I could read Rilke's poems in the original), and fell in love with Nymphenberg but *not* with the family or the Bavarian character even in that pre-Nazi period. Incautiously one morning at breakfast I made an approving remark about the League of Nations, which provoked a terrifying explosion about the wickedness of the Versailles *Diktat* from the cropped-headed ogre of a paterfamilias, backed up by his dour student son of lean and sallow countenance already slashed by duelling. A peace was patched up by the mother, and we were all courtesy again at lunch time, though the conversation did not flow. I had learned something, that did not quite square with the idealistic beliefs I had acquired at Cambridge, about the causes of modern war. On another occasion I was taken round Nuremberg by a young student, who spent the whole day trying to persuade me that the French had no lavatories and never washed. This seemed rather a caricature of the great *bidet*-loving nation over the frontier which he himself had never crossed, and I tried shyly to say so. A fatal move. When he saw me off on the train in the evening there was a look of despairing contempt underlying his polite smile. I also stayed with a French family at their home in Fontainebleau and in their lodgings on the sea-coast at La Baule, to steep myself again in a French atmosphere while studying French poetry. Michel, the son of my own age, was a pleasant companion, but the family was grimly *petite bourgeoise*, and I felt constrained all the time. One day the news arrived of the death of a child relation, a distant cousin of the mother. I saw her open the letter and discuss the news with the rest of the family without any sign of great distress, before leaving the table. A few hours later Michel came into my room and told me she would like to see me. I was astonished to find her in her room with her hair carefully disarrayed, her rouge very obviously wiped off her lips on to a handkerchief with which she was dabbing her remarkably dry eyes. I had been called in to witness a conventional scene of mourning and to offer conventional condolences. I knew by then what genuine grief was like in the presence of death, and the episode left a disagreeable taste in my mouth. But I had learned something again; and whenever I come up against the extraordinary, undying English legend of the frivolous, loose-living ' frogs ', cocking a snook at those rules of conventional decency that keep John Bull so superior, I think of that scene in Madame's room.

I had scarcely finished this round of Europe when Violet Hammersley reported that she had heard of a vacancy in the Prints and Drawings Department of the British Museum: would I be interested to try for it? We had often discussed together what I was going to do, and she knew that my thoughts were turning increasingly towards something more closely connected with the arts than diplomacy. The views of her friends in the Foreign Office *milieu* were discouraging: a diplomatist had become nothing but a letter-box since the war, they asserted, but at the same time much harder work was expected of him than in the days when he had a genuinely influential role in international affairs. Unlike the Quai d'Orsay, the Foreign Office did not seem to favour literary creation, at least until the conventional book of memoirs appeared, like an egg in an elderly hen's nesting-box, out of ambassadorial retirement. I was fascinated by the world of diplomacy, but I had a passion for art, and surely in a career at the British Museum I should find sympathetic surroundings and time to write my poetry. So the argument ran; and I found it persuasive. The job seemed interesting and well-paid, and the people who interviewed me charming, even if the whole atmosphere had for me, faintly, the dusty smell of a mausoleum. Off I went, therefore, on their advice, on another round of Europe, this time chiefly to study the great foreign collections of prints and drawings, in the Louvre, the Kaiser Friedrich Museum in Berlin and the Albertina in Vienna. By natural inclination I specialized in the drawings of the Early Flemish school, but I found new delights in the work of Tiepolo, Guardi and other Venetian artists of the eighteenth century, an affection that began to grow and rival my early love of Van Eyck and his followers. In the Albertina I encountered for the first time the attractive but thoroughly formidable Fräulein Spitzmüller. She ruled the room in which we studied the drawings from the dazzling collection under her care as firmly as any schoolmaster dealing with an unruly class of small boys: an invisible cane seemed sometimes to rattle in

her desk.   I was sensible of her Viennese charm, but rather
frig :ened of her, reduced to awful guilt when it was discovered
that I was trying to introduce a magnifying glass into the room
and a pencil not previously approved.   Fifteen years later,
with two Austrian revolutions and a world war between, she
was re-installed at her bomb-battered desk by the British, and
brought over to England on a visit; and I was amused to find
that a faint sensation of alarm mingled with my pleasure at
seeing her again.

I lived rather a solitary life during these visits; by choice as
much as by the way things fell out.   I read a great deal of
poetry; I liked to think of myself in the guise of the imaginary
figure Dickens invented for *Household Words*, ' The Shadow ',
moving invisibly through the great cities, learning the pulse
of their life, the aura of their history and literature and art that
encircled them, trying to find the European mood and to see
them in the perspective of the tragedy they had just been
through, the tragedies that yet threatened them.   How could
one individual help to avert those tragedies?   This problem
was always present in my mind, baffled by the growing feeling
that politics were impure and diplomacy powerless.   At least
one could raise a voice, and give ' *un sens plus pur aux mots de la
tribu . . .*'   I spent long afternoons in the parks of Schönbrunn,
Nymphenberg, Chambord, letting myself be invaded by the
nostalgia they exhaled, feeling for the beginning of poems into
which these inchoate intimations might crystallize:

> Beyond the furthest Naiads' row
> Flame red the sun began to glow,
> Flame red in mirrors round the bare
> Pilastered halls, on marble stair;
>
> No voice they heard, where lips were stone,
> No sound of stepping, but their own;
> Diana, in green solitude,
> Changed not her chiselled attitude. . . .

And so poems did slowly emerge from all the false starts and
scratchings out, a few in which emotion and observation
seemed at last to be matched by words and technique; but
only a fraction of the vast series that struggled within me for

expression. These poems were affirmations wrung with end-less struggle out of the void that still oppressed me, little islets with a single palm-tree on each pushing out of a fathomless ocean. Still I could write in my note-book: 'A day of utter self-torment—leading nowhere, NOWHERE!' And then suddenly, with pencil and paper before me, the dance of the words would start, and the solidity of the impalpable envelop and assuage me:

> Now memory, a butterfly, whose wings
> Folded within the mind are fallen leaf,
> Opens her peacock eyes, melodious tints
> Dark purple, rust and blue; here love submerged,
> A silver florin, wavers through the pool
> Bright among filaments of olive weed. . . .

Home again, I began to spend more time in London, brows-ing among the bookshops in the Charing Cross Road and buying more books than I could ever read. In the intervals of work in the Museum, I would sometimes visit Lawrence Binyon and his family next door: his pretty, vivacious daughter Margaret, who inherited so much of her father's gifts of imagination, was just about to marry an old schoolfellow and close friend of mine, Humphrey Higgens, who had gone straight into the City from Eton and used to write me long letters about the books he read to keep up his spirits. Beatrix had been launched some years before on her theatrical career, to our great excitement; she played for several seasons at the Gate Theatre under Peter Godfrey's direction, where I remember she made a deep and characteristic impression as Blazes in Robert Nichols' *Twenty Below*; and at the little Royal Court Theatre in Sloane Square played in *All God's Chillun Got Wings*, her first appearance in a play by Eugene O'Neill—who was to be the playwright of her greatest triumphs. I was a frequent visitor, renewing thus the pleasures I had first tasted at the Festival Theatre, in Cam-bridge, of the experimental modern theatre. In fact, I had come to the point where I could scarcely bear to see any play in an ordinary West End theatre with conventional production—unless Noel Coward was the author or Marie Tempest the actress. My godmother had now taken Sargent's house in Tite Street, and in the great studio which she had converted

into the most sumptuous and elegant of living-rooms she gave
parties at which, shy but keyed up, I was introduced to some of
the notable literary figures of London, including Arnold Ben-
nett, Somerset Maugham, Desmond MacCarthy—whose
daughter Rachel, soon to be married to Lord David Cecil, had
been a fellow-guest at Charleston—Osbert Sitwell and Raymond Mortimer.   There also I met Lord Esher, who, with his
ceaseless behind-the-scenes devotion to English literary and
artistic life, was at that time supporting *Life and Letters* under
Desmond MacCarthy's editorship.   *Life and Letters* often had a
wayward and unfinished air about it, but with only the rarest
editorial comments or contributions from Desmond MacCarthy
himself, nevertheless succeeded in being impregnated with his
personality, his standards of taste and style, and his enormous
range of literary enjoyment.   I spent hours brooding on the
problem of how the magic worked: my uncertainty at that
time about my own literary gifts had not killed the strange dream
that persisted, like a vision of cabbage leaves in a common-or-
garden white butterfly's brain as it emerges from the chrysalis,
of an editor's chair, a telephone at the elbow, a pile of manuscripts and a blue pencil.   The first cabbage leaf was nearer
than I knew.

# 5

DURING my travels in late summer of 1930, after I had come
down from Trinity, I was deeply preoccupied in my inner
self with the preparation of a book of poems.   At last it
seemed in sight: the gradual adding of poem to poem had
been a painfully slow process, but now, as I anxiously sifted
through and re-wrote lines and stanzas, I could begin to
imagine that the total had passed the absolute minimum for a
young poet's first, very slender volume.   It hovered before me
in fantasy with all the effulgence of an impossible apple from
the Garden of the Hesperides.   Gusts of hope and despair
swept through me with alternate violence, rising to gale force

when Julian's book, *Winter Movement*, was published by Chatto & Windus. On my return to Fieldhead from Paris at the beginning of November I wrote to him:

> Here I am, immensely glad to be back, in time to see the last act of an English Autumn. *And* in time to see the publication of *Winter Movement*: I have seen a copy, and I think it looks admirable—Chatto have not failed you. I re-read the first twenty-six pages—to which I am deeply devoted—on the spot. You must let me know what reviews there are—keep them for me. I have not seen anything myself yet, but the Lords of Reviewdom take their time about poetry—if they condescend to notice it at all. I must say I think in some ways Keats was rather lucky to have so many important pages of abuse devoted to him. . . .

Julian himself, flushed with triumph though he was that autumn at getting his book out, did not cease to coax and encourage me to try my luck as well. He considered that my poems to a large extent vindicated his own principles in his crusade for the ' eighteenth-century virtues ' against the technical licence and intellectual obscurities of the school of Eliot that continued to excite his bellicose derision, just as they had when he turned the pages of the undergraduate magazines at Cambridge. I was an ally, perhaps a disciple; but the ally, alas, was slipping, for in the same letter I made the dangerous admission that after re-reading his poems I was beginning to believe that the imitation of Pope was a wrong turning for him. ' The couplet pieces ', I wrote, ' seem small beside the splendour of the earlier pieces.' In fact, this treasonable thought had never been far from my mind, and when I re-read Julian's poems after his death I felt convinced that, amusing and stimulating though the whole campaign had been, he was never meant to write couplets or even satiric verse at all. There was something untidy and untameable about his deeper nature that was wounded by this forceful grafting on of alien stock for the formal garden; his instinctual power seemed never to be as strong again as it had been in the early poems, which were unlike any nature poetry written before or since in their precise and loving observation and absolute lack of any prettification or poetic sentimentality. They created, I thought, a new kind of poetic ' stuff ', the precipitate of an unusual and difficult, but exciting way of experiencing the objective world.

Julian's belief in me buoyed me up, as did my sister Rosamond's, in that last lap before the almost unbelievable goal; and great was my joy when, the finally winnowed pieces having been carefully typed out and sent to be scrutinized by my most exacting and sensitive judge, Dadie Rylands, the verdict was favourable. What was more, Dadie promised to show them to Leonard and Virginia Woolf.

Then began the rapid sequence of events that was, as it turned out, to determine the course of my life for many years to come. Dadie had worked in earlier days under Leonard in the Hogarth Press, and shared the interest in printing that had woken in me when I first began to read about William Morris. He had helped the Woolfs print some of their booklets of poetry on their own hand-press, and for a long time we had schemed to have a printing press together. We had even gone to see a manufacturer about machinery and type. He guessed that I was really more interested in printing and publishing than in prints and drawings and diplomacy, and when the Woolfs told him that they were again looking for a manager who could run the Press under their supervision and eventually become a partner, he immediately suggested that the young poet whose work he was bringing them (and about whom they already knew quite a lot from their nephew Julian) might fill the bill.

The result was that one morning I received a letter from Leonard, which informed me not only that he and Virginia liked my poems very much and wanted to publish them, but also that they had heard that I might be interested in working in the Hogarth Press, and would I come and discuss it with them? I wrote off triumphantly to Julian:

> I have heard from the Woolfs, and they say they will be glad to publish my poems. Bless them. I'm cheered, I don't mind saying. It won't be till the autumn—I'd rather it were the spring—but it scarcely matters, will be an admirable experience in patience for myself, and I'm grateful to have them published at all. I gather they are now being inspected by Lady G. Whether, if she disapproves of them, they'll publish them on

their own, I know not. But I suppose having said they'll publish them, they will. Bear with my selfish pleasure.

' Lady G.'—Dorothy Wellesley (now the Duchess of Wellington), to whose patronage the series of Hogarth Living Poets owed its existence—announced her approval in spite of my fears. Gone at once were the rather sobering visions of a lifetime dedicated to etching and aquatint in the dusty recesses of the British Museum, banished forever the idea of following my uncles and cousins into the service of His Britannic Majesty, as I rushed off to see the Woolfs in 52 Tavistock Square at the beginning of January. Immediately I sent a report to Julian:

> I would have written to you before about your poems, if the end of last week had not been so hectic—interviews—consultations—calculations. I expect you know substantially what the offer of the Woolves was going to be: I was surprised when they made it to me—on Friday, at tea, when I met them both for the first time, and thought them most charming, Virginia very beautiful—and not a little excited. I've now decided I'm going to make every effort to accept the offer. . . . I really can't imagine any work that would interest me more, and to be a partner with them, with a voice in what's to be published (and how) and what isn't—it seems an almost unbelievable stroke of luck.

The consultations and calculations continued intensively for the next few days. There were problems to be solved about raising the money, but I found my mother sympathetic in general and pleased to see me launched on something that I obviously cared about so much. Looking back on it now, it seems to me that everything was settled with astonishing speed, for only six days later I could announce to Julian:

> This week has been a fevered one—I emerge with an agreement in my pocket, by which I become Manager of the Hogarth Press in October—if not fired after eight months of apprenticeship. And I have the option of becoming a partner in a year or two. And I start in on Wednesday as ever is! Your advice was just what I wanted—very welcome. As a matter of fact Leonard had lost confidence in his first proposition even before my Trustee turned a dubious eye on it, so I think both parties feel better under the present agreement that we argued out in a series of interviews. I pray that I shall be a success: hard work, but congenial . . . and

Leonard is giving me good holidays, long enough to get some writing done, I hope. But there's so much I want to say, that I can't say it all in a letter, and must wait till I see you. I was charmed by both Leonard and Virginia, and hope they liked me.

# 6

THE year before, I had been staying in London with my sister Beatrix in St. George's Square. Now I moved into the house in Heathcote Street, just off the Gray's Inn Road, that was occupied by Douglas Davidson, the painter, and his brother Angus, skilled translator from the Italian and author of an excellent book on Edward Lear. There the room which had previously been occupied by Dadie was made over to me. The advantage of Heathcote Street was that it was only a few minutes' walk from Tavistock Square. Every morning I set out to reach the Woolfs' house at 9.15 a.m., passing through a disused graveyard filled with ancient tombstones of the seventeenth and eighteenth centuries, its half-effaced inscriptions and funeral ornaments dappled with moss and lichen. The Burial Ground of St. George-the-Martyr had become a quiet garden, and some old people used to sit there all day when the sun was shining: I would see the same faces on my return after work as I had observed on my setting out.

At No. 52 the Press occupied the basement, formerly the kitchen and servants' quarters; a friendly firm of solicitors were installed on the ground and first floors, while on the top two floors Leonard and Virginia had their own living quarters. The basement was cold and draughty and ramshackle. My own office, as apprentice manager, was a small back room that had once been a pantry and cupboard room—the cupboards were piled high with the dusty files of the activities of the Press ever since it had started in 1917. It was badly in need of re-decorating, it had a jammed window that looked out on a narrow outside passage and a gloomy wall, and a decrepit gas-fire in front of which Leonard would attempt, without any striking success, to warm his hands when he came in to see me with the day's correspondence soon after my arrival. My mother was appalled when she first visited me there; but to me nevertheless it was sacred ground. I was at last part of a publishing firm, and the one that seemed to me the most glamorous of all; I was associated every day with the—to me—legendary Leonard and Virginia Woolf; in the former scullery up the passage an actual printing-machine was installed, with its trays of type beside it, and there on many an afternoon Leonard could be found rolling off the firm's stationery, writing paper, invoices, royalty forms and review slips; while every now and then Virginia herself could be glimpsed setting the type for one of the small books of poetry that the Press still produced at home—at that time it was, I think, Vita Sackville-West's *Sissinghurst*—in spite of the fact that it had grown into a large business dealing with many of the biggest printers and binders. All round me, in all the rooms and down the dark corridors, were the piled packages of finished books as delivered from the binders. It gave me a special pleasure to explore among them, noting on the labels the names of books that were already precious to me, such as Virginia's *Monday or Tuesday* (not many of these) and *To the Lighthouse* in their original editions, and occasionally coming across a single, opened package of some early publication that had long been famous, Ivan Bunin's *The Gentleman from San Francisco*, or E. M. Forster's *Pharos and Pharillon*, or *The Notebooks of Anton Chekhov*, though not, alas, Katherine Mansfield's *The Prelude* or T. S. Eliot's *The Waste Land*, long out of print but tantalizingly advertised at the back of some of the other books. And I persuaded Leonard to allow me to make a collection of the early hand-set volumes of poetry, all different shapes and sizes in their prettily decorated paper covers, John Crowe Ransom's *Grace After Meat*, Herbert Read's *Mutations of the Phoenix*, Robert Graves's *Mockbeggar Hall*, curiosities such as Clive Bell's *Poems* and Nancy Cunard's *Parallax*, and many others, of which I can think of one instance, Fredegond Shove's *Daybreak*, unjustly forgotten today. By far the largest piles were in the studio room at the back where (as I have described elsewhere) Virginia had her work-desk; and I would slip in, with carefully controlled eagerness and as silently as possible, to hunt out some books that were suddenly needed on the packing-table in the front room, feeling that I was entering the holiest part of the house, the inmost ark of its presiding deity. I was even allowed, later, to work at the desk when they were both away.

No one could have been a kinder or more sympathetic teacher than Leonard. There was no nonsense of formal ' business relations ' in the Press, and he would explain to me how to prepare estimates and contracts (on his own highly individual patterns), how to design a book-page and an advertisement and how to organize the flow of books to the shops, with steady patience and an assumption of intimate interest in everything we published. He described the authors, the printers' and paper-makers' travellers and all the other people with whom I was to have to deal, including the persistent and unsnubbable bores, at length and with characteristically caustic comment. The absurd conventions of the trade, the prejudices of certain important booksellers and reviewers, the inexplicably chancy ups and downs of success and failure in the fortunes of books, would rouse him at all times to exasperated and withering wit; and it was due to his teaching that I learnt early on to face with a certain detached philosophy the irrational behaviour that almost everyone who has to do with books is so frequently capable of. In fact I learnt the essentials of publishing in the most agreeable way possible: from a man who had created his own business, had never allowed it to grow so big that it fell into departments sealed off from one another, and who saw it all as much from the point of view of an author and amateur printer as of someone who had to make his living by it. If Leonard had a fault, it was in allowing detail to loom too large at times. A small item that could not be accounted for in the books, a misunderstanding about a point of production would, without apparent reason, irritate him suddenly to the extreme, he would worry it like a dog worrying a rat, until indeed he seemed to be the rat and the detail the dog; and betray, I felt after one or two such experiences, the long nervous tension he had lived under in caring so devotedly for the genius of his wife.

My relations with Virginia began with an ardent youthful hero-worship; but gradually, as I got to know her better, this turned into a feeling of real affection as well as respect. At first she was irradiated in my eyes with the halo of having written *Jacob's Room*, *To the Lighthouse* and *Mrs. Dalloway*. No other books seemed to me to express with anything like the same penetration and beauty the sensibility of our age; it was not merely the conception that underlay those works, of time and sorrow and human longing, but also the way she expressed it, the paramount importance in her writing of technical change and experiment; almost everything else seemed, after I had read them, utterly wide of the target and inadequately aware of what was needed. I was influenced, of course, as a poet, by the skill with which she managed to transform the material of poetry into the prose-form of the novel; but that in itself seemed to me one of the major artistic problems of our time, arising out of the terror and tension, the phantasmagoria of modern life. I devoured the three novels again and again, and always with fresh delight, valuing them far higher than *The Common Reader*, *A Room of One's Own*, *Orlando* and even *Flush*, which, much as I enjoyed them and popular as they were, seemed to me of far less significance. In those early days I revered Virginia as the sacred centre, the most gifted and adored (and sometimes feared) of the Bloomsbury circle. But, as time went on, the feeling she inspired in me was more one of happy release than of reverence. I found her the most enchanting of friends, full of sympathy and understanding for my own personal problems and the problems I was up against in my job, with an intense curiosity about my own life and the lives of my friends in my generation (many of whom were, of course, known and even related to her). She liked to hear all about what we wanted to do in poetry, in painting, in novel-writing. She would stimulate me to talk, she had an unique gift for encouraging one to be indiscreet, and would listen with absorption and occasionally intersperse pointed and witty comments. Some of the happiest times I can remember in those years were the luncheons and teas I would be invited up to in the Woolfs' part of the house, where the walls were painted with frescoes by Duncan Grant and Virginia's sister Vanessa Bell, discussing the plans of the Press, the books submitted to us, and all the histories and personalities involved. She was always bubbling with ideas, longing to launch new schemes and produce books that no one had thought of before, that would startle the conventional business minds of the book world.   She found an all-too-ready response in me, and had sometimes quietly to be checked on the rein by Leonard.

There were days, however, when she seemed withdrawn behind a veil, and it was hard to draw out her interest in the activities of the Press or ignite the gaiety which at other times was so characteristic of her.   Sometimes this veil concealed her preoccupation with the problems of whatever she was writing at the moment;   at other times it was darker and more opaque, bringing an uneasy atmosphere of strain and misery to the house.   It is not for me to explain or explore the moods of fathomless melancholy that overcame Virginia Woolf at various periods during her life, and nearly always began with a series of acute headaches;   I can only record the anxiety and distress they caused me for her own sake and for Leonard, who had fought them with her for so long, and my wonder that she managed to achieve so much with that perpetual threat hanging over her, always dropping nearer when she was in the throes of her finest creative achievement.

One of the worst of these fits of melancholy attacked her in the last stages of her work on *The Waves*, and Leonard decided that she must abandon it altogether for a time.   The crisis passed, and she was able to get the book, to me the most daring if not the most successful of all her experiments, ready for press in the late summer.   I could hardly contain my impatience to read it;   it was for me the great event of the year, even though my own first book of poems was coming out in September.   At last, at the beginning of the month, the advance copies arrived, just after I had spent a week-end with her and Leonard at Rodmell, and in writing to thank her I mentioned that I was in the middle of reading it.   She immediately sent me a note insisting that I should write down for her exactly what I thought about it.   I was deeply stirred by the book, and wrote her a long letter in which I tried, no doubt naïvely, to describe the impression it had made on me.   In the same letter I suggested that it was high time for her to define her views about modern poetry, which we had discussed so often together.   I received the following letter in reply, dated 17 September:

Dear John, I'm most grateful to you for your letter. It made me happy all yesterday. I had become firmly convinced that *The Waves* was a failure, in the sense that it wouldn't convey anything to anybody. And now you've been so perceptive, and gone so much further and deeper in understanding my drift than I thought possible that I'm immensely relieved. Not that I expect many such readers. And I'm rather dismayed to hear we've printed 7,000: for I'm sure 3,000 will feed all appetites; and then the other 4 will sit round me like decaying corpses for ever in the studio (I cleared up the table—for you, not the corpses). I agree that it's very difficult—bristling with horrors, though I've never worked so hard as I did here, to smooth them out. But it was, I think, a difficult attempt—I wanted to eliminate all detail; all fact; & analysis; & myself; & yet not be frigid and rhetorical; & not monotonous (which I am) & to keep the swiftness of prose & yet strike one or two sparks, & not write poetical, but purebred prose, & keep the elements of character; & yet that there should be many characters & only one; & also an infinity, a background behind—well, I admit I was biting off too much.

But enough, as the poets say. If I live another 50 years I think I shall put this method to some use, but as in 50 years I shall be under the pond, with the goldfish swimming over me, I daresay these vast ambitions are a little foolish, & will ruin the press. That reminds me—I think your idea of a Letter most brilliant—'To a Young Poet'—because I'm seething with immature & ill considered & wild & annoying ideas about prose & poetry. So lend me your name—(& let me sketch a character of you by way of frontispiece)—& then I'll pour forth all I can think of about you young, & we old, & novels—how damned they are—& poetry, how dead. But I must take a look into the subject, & you must reply, 'To an Old Novelist'—I must read Auden, whom I've not read, & Spender (his novel I swear I will tackle tonight). The whole subject is crying out for letters—flocks, volleys of them, from every side. Why not get Spender & Auden & Day Lewis to join? But you must go to Miss Belsher, and I must go to my luncheon.

This is only a scribble to say how grateful I am for your letter.

Yrs
Virginia Woolf.

Virginia need not have been so anxious about the sales of *The Waves*, for it was an immediate success; I find myself complaining in the middle of October to Julian that an accident to

my hand was ' all very unfortunate with your Aunt's book
booming and high pressure of work in the office, the public
apparently having decided that to be IT one must have *The
Waves* on the drawing-room table.'   Naturally, in the excitement of the preparation for the book's publication and the first
public reactions to it, the idea of a ' Letter to a Young Poet '
did not get very much further; but Virginia was turning it
over in her mind all the time, and was changing her views about
the ' deadness ' of poetry, for when I sent her a copy of my own
*A Garden Revisited*, she wrote:

> I am a wretch not have thanked you for your book, which will
> not only stand on my shelf as you suggest but lie beneath the
> scrutiny of my aged eyes.   I want to read it with some attention,
> & also Auden, & Day Lewis—I don't suppose there's anything
> for me to say about modern poetry, but I daresay I shall plunge,
> at your bidding.   We must talk about it.   I don't know what
> your difficulties are.   Why should poetry be dead? etc. etc.   But
> I won't run on, because then I shall spurt out my wild theories, &
> I've had not a moment to read for days, days—everybody in the
> whole world has been here—the Easdales in cartloads etc. etc.
> And now I should be packing.   And then we go back.   And
> then there'll be all the books fluttering about us; alas: it's going
> to be a bad season, I'm afraid.
>
> But I want to go into the question of poetry all the same. . . .

# 7

THE publication of my first book of poems had a further
unexpected consequence, which, like one bowl hitting another
bowl that in its turn knocks all the other bowls into different
places, was to set a series of events into motion not without
historic interest for the curious student of literary movements and associations in England between the wars.   One
of the letters I received was from someone I had never heard of
before, called Michael Roberts.   He wrote that he admired
the poems, had been watching my work for some time, and
asked if I would care to come in to see him in his flat one evening
to discuss them.   An irresistibly flattering call for a young

author: a few days later, after dinner, I knocked at his door, and found myself in the presence of a tall young man in glasses who reminded me at once of a giraffe that had taken to the serious life of learning, a university don of a giraffe. The presence was solemn as well as freakish, but the rare, contracted smile that played across the sharp and concentrated gaze was sympathetic. We plunged into talk about modern poetry at once, and I discovered that he had read all my contemporaries, and what was more had an idea that they belonged together more closely, in spite of the wide apparent differences, than I, in the middle of the *mêlée* which Julian made so dramatic, had detected. The more he talked, the more flattered I felt at the thought of belonging to a revolutionary movement in the arts, and the more my fresh publishing ardour was inflamed by the possibility, which began to grow in my mind, of presenting all of us in some way as a *front*, so that the public, notoriously sluggish in its appreciation of individual poets, should be obliged to sit up and take notice. I went home with many ideas humming in my mind. During the spring and summer we had endeavoured to get a Cambridge Miscellany together, but the project had collapsed at the last moment: out of Michael Roberts's theories I saw an admirable substitute, with far more possibilities, emerging. During the next few days I talked it over with Leonard and Virginia, proposed an anthology of poetry by all the young writers whose names had been mentioned that evening, got their sympathy and provisional support, and then wrote to Michael Roberts and suggested he should edit it for us and write an introduction.

The project that was eventually to take shape as *New Signatures* was on. It was not meant to be a presentation of entirely new poets, but rather the tracing of a pattern, between a number of young and recently published poets, which had escaped notice before, which was in fact becoming clearer, under the gathering winds of the epoch, all the time. The three ' Oxford ' poets who roused Julian's bristling suspicion— Cecil Day Lewis, Wystan Auden and Stephen Spender—were to be in it; Julian and William Empson (who was in Japan at the time) and Richard Eberhart and myself from Cambridge; and two writers I had got to know since I came to London,

A. S. J. Tessimond and William Plomer.   When I was being
frank with myself, I had to admit that the links that joined us
seemed rather frail; but Michael Roberts stoutly maintained
that in spite of what I might say in my moments of misgiving,
they were real.   Three Cambridge poets, leading lights of
*Experiment*, he excluded because he thought them too close to
T. S. Eliot and to the French surrealists Eluard and Tzara.   In
his view, however estimable their aims might be, we were on a
different tack that he was convinced would in the long run
prove more important.   We all represented a reaction against
the poetry that had been fashionable hitherto, we were united
by a desire to assimilate the imagery of modern life, and even
when we wrote, as Julian did, of country life, we meant something very different from what he described as the sentimental
country clichés of our predecessors.   The precision of thought
and expression characteristic of the eighteenth century re-
appeared in our work, he said; and we were trying to make a
new intellectual and imaginative synthesis that would be positive, not negative and pessimistic in its attitude to the problem
of living in the twentieth century.   Only the slightest hint, in
all this, of the radical politics which so very soon after were to
appear as the label attached to most of us.

Julian, battlesome to the last, did not at first like the idea at
all of appearing under the same label as the ' Oxford ' poets.
In reply to my invitation to contribute, he wrote me a long,
growling letter about what we had stood for hitherto and the
danger of condoning the heresies of Spender and Auden.
As the poets of *New Signatures* have so often been assumed to
have started off as a ' school ', or to have imagined themselves
a ' school ', it is perhaps worth quoting my retort to Julian,
written on Christmas Eve 1931 :

> Thank you for your damned intransigent and intractable letter.   I
> enclose a copy of the blurb for the book which will show you how
> deeply you will commit yourself if you offer any poems to it.   The
> net is meant to be wide, and naturally the poets are not meant to
> form a *School*—an idea totally ludicrous.   Are we to expunge
> your name from that provisional list?   I hope not—but your
> letter in tone might have been that of a French General arriving
> in the Ruhr, 1923.

Cecil Day Lewis was already one of the poets published in the Hogarth Living Poets, so to recruit him was easy.  His volume, *From Feathers to Iron*, had appeared at the same time as my own volume, and the interest it roused in inner literary circles was enormously magnified by an approving remark from T. E. Lawrence, which managed to get into the papers.  It is perhaps unfair to a remarkable book to say that it was one of the first to show the strong current of Auden's influence; but *From Feathers to Iron* marked a decisive change in Cecil Day Lewis's poetry from what he had written before, and the new imagery of mysterious skirmishes in a landscape of industrial decay, railheads, frontiers and escapes across them came unmistakably from the bursting warehouse which Auden had thrown open.  Auden's first book, *Poems*, had come out only the year before, but because it focused the growing restlessness and dissatisfaction of his generation coming to manhood in a world erupting with economic crisis after crisis and heading for another war, and focused it with dramatic imagery in poetry that already had its own distinctive rhythmic life and tone of voice, because in fact with the arrow aim of genius it exactly touched the nerve that no one had touched before, it had an overwhelming effect.  All of us were to show the marks of it in the next few years, and Cecil for a short time far more deeply than in *Feathers to Iron*.  What is remarkable to me about that book as I look through it now, is the way Cecil assimilated the first potation of Auden's strong punch: the poems are not quite as good, I think, as those he was to write in the early years of the war, but the theme is worked out with great skill and subtlety through twenty-nine poems, the voice is consistently masculine and optimistic without that undertone of romantic despair that could still be heard in Auden's book in spite of its ' message ' of break-away and renewal.  And all is presented in a clear, sharply defining light, rather as in Donne's early poems, without any mists of musing and dreaming fantasy, any poeticizing, to blur the edges and confuse the colours—something that my own poetic impulse of the time responded to immediately.  Much of the paraphernalia of dynamos and trains and tractors may seem a little out-dated now, but nevertheless how refreshingly alive compared with all the old poetic tinsel, all the Christmas-tree baubles that so many young poets began to drag out again during the war (and were applauded for hanging on their dead branches).

I had met Stephen Spender for the first time during the Christmas holidays of 1930, when my sister Rosamond had brought him over from Ipsden. We went for a long walk together by the river in the direction of Marlow: I found him the most rapidly self-revealing person I had ever met, in fact he seemed to be devoured by a passion for presenting his *cœur mis à nu*. Very tall and slim, with a huge head of curls, he loped along beside me in the mild winter landscape, pouring out his views on the world, on how to find fulfilment and how to write, and graphically described the life he had adopted in Germany, where he spent most of his time. My father and his (as I have already related) had been colleagues in the old heyday of Liberalism, in both politics and journalism, and everything he said struck uncomfortably home: we came from the same matrix, we both had a blood connection with Hamburg, and his so very different solution to our common problems was bound to have a violently disturbing effect on me. In his view Germany, because of defeat and ruin, had escaped from the mortal sickness of Western civilization, and there youth had started to live again, free of the shackles of the past, a life without inhibition, inspired by hope, natural humanity and brotherhood in the springs of being. In England we were chained still by guilt, ossifying bourgeois conventions, and philistinism. If only I came out to Germany I would see the beginnings of the new world for myself. . . . He talked a great deal about Auden, who shared (and indeed had inspired) so many of his views, and also about a certain young novelist called Christopher Isherwood, who, he told me, had settled in Berlin in stark poverty and was an even greater rebel against the England we lived in than he was, and had been closely associated from the beginning with himself and Auden.

Since that first meeting we had exchanged letters from time to time, and had met abroad, and I had read and admired his early poems in spite of the large difference which I felt existed between what he was trying to do in poetry and what I wanted myself. He was enthusiastic about the idea of the anthology,

and he wrote to me in January of 1932, from Berlin, to tell me
that he and Christopher Isherwood had sent Auden a joint
letter urging him to contribute as well.   In the same letter he
said that he hoped I would stay at the Hogarth Press, as one
or two intelligent young publishers were badly needed; but he
realized that his and Christopher's eagerness for me to stay put
was purely selfish, and if I felt the work was seriously interfering
with my writing, I ought to go.   How familiar this note was
to become in my life: like a slowly tolling bell, I was to hear it
for the next twenty-one years, and indeed still hear it.   Rung
by one or other of my friends, or by some friendly reviewer or
critic, always it reminded me of the unresolved dilemma of my
life: was I to be the impresario of other people's creative work,
or a creative writer myself?   .Each time I had some success in
the one direction, I was to feel the need of effort in the other;
and perhaps one day I shall discover that the dilemma itself
was all the time the real pattern, the figure uniquely my own
I had to write on the sand before the tide washed it away for
ever.

So it was that *New Signatures* took shape, with surprising ease
and an exciting cumulative impetus.   But even as its outlines
emerged, the stream was changing course, and with extraordinary rapidity.   Ever since Cambridge I had been turning
gradually away from the Liberalism of my upbringing, towards
Socialism.   My arrival at the Hogarth Press hastened the process.   Leonard Woolf was a convinced and proselytizing
Socialist and anti-Imperialist, active in the inner councils of
the Labour Party, and many of the non-literary publications
of the Press, especially the pamphlets, were propaganda for the
Socialist point of view and exposures of the wrongs due to British
Imperialist exploitation of other races.   My conversion was
partly the result of my deep-seated horror at human injustice
and cruelty, a feeling that none of us brought up in the atmosphere of Fieldhead could ever escape, quickened into new life
by these luridly documented cases for the prosecution, revealing
how our Empire-builders and their followers had behaved in
India and in Africa; and partly the effect of the more abstract
economic theories of the intellectuals of the *New Statesman*, with
whom Leonard and most of the leading lights of Bloomsbury

were so intimately associated, theories which seemed to prove
conclusively that social injustice and economic crisis and the
wars of colony-grabbing Great Powers could be abolished only
by the triumph of Socialism.    By the time of the General Election in 1931 I was already sufficiently converted to share to the
full the consternation and gloom that settled on all our circle at
the collapse of the Labour Government.    I remember a party
on Election night, where faces grew longer and longer and
prophecies of doom more and more despairing as the results
came in, and the impenetrable, evil-tasting, olive-green fog
that had blotted London out during the whole day seemed to
me a symbol of the ominous obscurity of our future.    But even
as I reached this point of intellectual conviction, I began to
move away from it, further to the left.    The discredit of Labour
made even staunch supporters of the Party in Bloomsbury mutter
that perhaps far more radical measures of Marxism were necessary to defeat reaction and stop the drift towards a new war.

It was under the first wave of this disillusionment that work
on *New Signatures* began; and Stephen Spender's contributions
were portents of what was to come.    In Germany of the
Weimar Republic, in the last spasms before it gave birth to the
Third Reich, the class-war that we felt was now approaching
so much faster in our own country was far more nakedly
apparent; the Communist Party was a great force, engaged in
actual, ceaseless battle with its opponents; and from living with
the ordinary working people of Berlin and Hamburg, Stephen's
so fine and sensitive poetic intuition had penetrated to the purest
elements of the hope and idealism that underlay the Communist
faith in action at that time.    I was deeply impressed and moved
by the poems he sent us, the now famous exhortation beginning
'Oh young men, oh young comrades', the Lawrence-like 'I
think continually', and the celebration of a Communist
funeral ' Death is another milestone on their way '.    They had
a visionary ardour and sincerity that could not fail to quicken
the turbulence of thoughts and emotions that had already been
stirred up in my mind—and in the minds of many others moving
along the same lines in my generation; though, as Stephen
insisted, they were the issue of *poetic* sympathy, and in no way
proof that the poet himself had assented to the whole Communist

faith or wished to become an active political worker. In fact, he made it quite clear (in letters) that he thought it essential for an artist not to commit himself in that way. Now, twenty years later, when Stephen and I have long come to see how unscrupulous and ruthless the power-urge was beneath the idealism, and how cynically the realities of Stalinist Communism contradicted the hope, these poems still seem to me to retain their poetic validity; in fact I find them even more poignant because of the disappointed dream that haunts them today.

Over some of these poems, I remember, a controversy blew up with *The Listener*, to which paper Stephen had already promised them. The little crisis was resolved by the tact and sympathy of the assistant editor of that time, Janet Adam Smith, who was keenly interested in the work of all of us, and a most useful patron for young poets at a period in their career when every guinea counted. An anthology of the poetry she had selected, which was published after she had ceased to be associated with *The Listener*, shows how sensitive and intelligent her taste was. One of the pleasanter accidental by-results of the *New Signatures* venture and the encounters that arose from it, was her marriage some years later to Michael Roberts.

It was part of the romantic mythology in which Stephen delighted to cloak his contemporaries, to present himself as a learner at the feet of Auden, the great prophet, but to suggest that behind both of them stood an even greater Socratic prophet, cool in the centre of the stormy drama of remote Berlin: Christopher Isherwood. When he had first mentioned him to me during our winter walk by the river, he had told me that after his disappointment about the way his first novel *All the Conspirators* was received, he had abandoned England, written another novel, failed to get it published, and thrown it into a bottom drawer in despair and disgust. He talked about this unknown novel with enthusiasm: it was called *The Memorial*, and was, Stephen said, an extremely important work for our generation. My curiosity was aroused, and when I joined the Hogarth Press I persuaded Stephen—who in fact needed very little persuading—to write to Christopher and ask him to let me see it. In due course the manuscript arrived; I can still remember the eagerness with which I took it home with me to read. I was completely won over by it, and immediately decided to hand it on to Leonard and Virginia with a very urgent plea that we should accept it for publication.

During the course of the next few years Christopher became such an intimate personal friend and also such a close associate in my publishing and editing activities, that I find it very difficult to recover the impression he made on me when he first came to see me in my back room at the Hogarth Press. Much shorter than myself, he nevertheless had a power of dominating which small people of outstanding intellectual or imaginative equipment often possess. One of my favourite private fancies has always been that the most ruthless war that underlies our civilized existence, more ancient than the opposition of Teuton and Slav or Moslem and Christian, more ruthless even than the sex war, a war never to be concluded or halted by any but the most temporary and contemptuous of truces, is the war between the tall and the short. Does not example after example of conqueror and dictator in modern history—Napoleon, Dollfuss, Stalin among the foremost—demonstrate how unassuageable and remorseless is the lust for power when it wakes in a breast only four feet from the ground? Has it not been proved again and again that the small man on the war-path regards nearly all tall people as amiable loons with their heads in the mist, incapable, in the state of mushy good nature and confidence which their inches give them, of discerning in time the small foot put out so cunningly to trip them? There were moments when a look crossed Christopher's face which seemed to suggest the stirrings of this ancient and implacable urge. . . . And then, immediately after, a smile of extraordinary breadth and charm would flash across it and the deep-set eyes below the high forehead would twinkle with tenderness and fun, with that sense of the total absurdity of everything in the world which has always broken in irresistibly even on his most serious and passionate discourses, and led him away without warning on recklessly unbridled comic fantastifications: an element intoxicating to breathe with him, and entirely belying the formidable authority of his imperial nose. It is almost always true that unless one puts down at the time some record of first impressions in such friendships, one confuses them with later impressions of a personality that may imperceptibly be changing all the time; as I write I cannot exclude from my mind the picture, only a few weeks old, of Christopher delivering a short talk into a B.B.C. microphone on the opposite side of a table from me, the same look of impish fun alternating with the tense concentration of the prophet with a message; and I have convinced myself that I noted this compelling contradiction and complexity in our earliest meetings.

It was impossible not to be drawn to him: I was attracted by the warmth of his nature, and by the quality which appealed to me so much in *The Memorial*, an exact feeling for the deeper moods of our generation with its delayed war-shock and conviction of the futility of the old pattern of social life and convention; his capacity—the pressure he was under in his imagination—to invent the most extravagant dream-situations of comedy for everyone he knew, evoked a response at once in that part of me that had produced the dotty fantasy plays at Eton; and at the same time I had fallen under the spell of his Berlin legend. And yet for some months after our first meeting, in fact until I actually joined him in Berlin after the break with the Hogarth Press, our relations remained rather formal: perhaps it was the sense of alarm that seemed to hang in the air when his smile was switched off, a suspicion he seemed to radiate that one might after all be in league with the ' enemy ', a phrase which covered everything he had, with a pure hatred, cut himself off from in English life, or even a mutual shyness that took quite a different form for each of us. In any case, the bonds between us were not yet very close: one mutual friend, and my enthusiasm for his work. A fruitful enthusiasm: Leonard and Virginia had decided, after some hesitation, to publish *The Memorial*, and early in 1932 it came out in an unconventional brown-paper jacket designed by John Banting, one of the most original of many beautiful designs he did for the Press to the delight of my friends and myself and the dismay of the booksellers. The book made a deep impression on our circle, and one or two of the critics were quick enough to spot a future winner; but it did not sell more than a few hundred copies. Christopher took its financial failure with a philosophy uncommon among young authors. When I sent him a report on the sales in the summer, he wrote back: ' Please don't suppose that I'm disappointed by the sales of *The Memorial*. They are actually £1 more than I'd reckoned.' Some years later, of course, when he'd made his name on both sides of the Atlantic as the creator of Mr. Norris and Sally Bowles, the edition sold out and even became a rarity.

Meanwhile, *New Signatures* had come out and had an un-expected success. The reviewers were impressed, the public bought it and there was a general feeling in the air that Some-thing had happened in poetry. We even had to print a second impression within a few weeks. Several of the poets were already known individually; but the little book was like a searchlight suddenly switched on to reveal that, without anyone noticing it, a group of skirmishers had been creeping up in a concerted movement of attack. Some of us were, perhaps, as surprised as the public to find that we formed part of a secret foray; Michael Roberts himself felt that one or two of his contributors had let him down by failing to provide poems that quite came up to his dramatic billing of them, and that his preface was inadequate and imperfectly worked out. As so often happens, however, an impression had been made on the public that no amount of reservations or protestations on the part of individual contributors could efface, and from that moment we were all lumped together as the ' *New Signatures* poets '. In retrospect, what surprises me is that, while much was made of the sense of social shifting and upheaval in the poems, so little notice was taken of the sense of menacing war, implicit or explicit in so many of the contributions.

The success gave me confidence as a poet, more confidence than the rather soggy reception *A Garden Revisited* had the year before. More important at that time, I think it gave Leonard and Virginia confidence in me, and made them feel that whatever private criticisms they might have of the aims and achievements of the new writers, their works were worth publish-ing. They were also shrewd enough, I believe, to divine a success to come behind the partial flop of *The Memorial;* and they saw that our joint enterprise, the Hogarth Letters, was turning out lively and popular. At the same time they had observed with approval, if also with a certain amusement, the avidity with which I had learned all the details of the publishing business, the possessive passion I displayed for all Hogarth authors, and the enthusiasm with which I launched myself into every new development, undaunted by the cobwebs of my basement and the continuing need to save pennies. They decided they would be able to do something that had seemed too difficult for years : to take a long holiday abroad while I looked after the Press for them.

They set out for Greece in the spring, with Roger and Margery Fry. It was by no means unwillingly that I was left in charge, even though the trusty Miss Belsher, head of the front office, was absent much of the time. The omens for the future might have seemed as good as could be when Virginia wrote to me from Athens :

I have written to you several times (in imagination) a full account of our travels, with a masterly description of Byzantine and Greek art (Roger is all for Byzantine) but I'm afraid you never got it. The truth is it's almost impossible to put pen to paper. Here am I balanced on the edge of a hotel bed, with Marjorie and Roger popping in and out to suggest excursions, and Leonard ranging the sponge-bags with a view to packing.

I'm afraid you've had the devil of a time, with Belsher away, and the doors standing open to bores of every feather. I've often thought of you with sympathy when one wheel of the car has been trembling over a precipice 2,000 feet deep, and vultures wheeling round our heads as if settling which to begin on. This refers to the road into the Peloponnesus. Then we went to Delphi, to Nauplia, to Mycenae—it's all in the letter I never wrote. I can assure you Greece is more beautiful than 20 dozen Cambridges all in May Week. It blazes with heat too, and there are no bugs, no inconveniences—the peasants are far nicer than the company we keep in London—it's true we can't understand a word they say. In short I'm setting on foot a plan to remove the Hogarth Press to Crete. Roger is the greatest fun—as mild as milk, but if you've ever seen milk that is also quicksilver you'll know what I mean. He disposes of whole museums with one brush of his tail. He plays chess when the dust is sweeping the pawns from the board. He writes articles with one hand, and carries on violent arguments with the other. It has been far the best holiday we've had for years, and I feel deeply grateful to you, for sitting in your doghole so stalwartly meanwhile. Excuse scribble. Love from us both.

Virginia.

# 8

THE two years of my apprenticeship at the Hogarth Press
were so entirely absorbed into the zealous learning of my
trade, into reading up the past publications of the proud little
firm and ploughing through the manuscripts that came to us,
into planning and preparing and discussing with the Woolfs
and my poet friends, that when I search my mind for images
of the period, I see all the time the house in Tavistock Square
and the short walk across Southampton Row and through the
old graveyard that connected it with the studio flat, a little
further down Heathcote Street from the Davidsons, into which
I had moved.   The first year was a very busy and happy time,
in fact, and like so many times of contentment has left very few
detailed traces behind it in memory.

   And yet during those active months I was meeting a great
number of people in the artistic and literary London of those
days, and getting to know better many others I had originally
met in my Cambridge days, in Cambridge itself or with Rosamond or at my godmother Violet Hammersley's house.   There
were evening parties at the Woolfs', where I was introduced to
Roger Fry, eagerly spinning his theories about painting and
poetry and discarding them again with the greatest good
humour when Leonard exclaimed that they were ' grotesque '
and began to pick holes in them; Aldous Huxley, a tall, rather
willowy figure who struck me as a little austere and remote as
he leaned against the painted mantelpiece in his horn-rim
spectacles and discoursed learnedly about everything under the
sun—though, as a devotee of *Crome Yellow* and *Antic Hay*, I
listened in fascinated awe; Lytton Strachey's beautiful niece,
Julia, whose so original and rarely flavoured novelle, *Cheerful
Weather for the Wedding*, was soon to be published by the Press,
and her husband, the gifted and tragic sculptor-poet Stephen
Tomlin, known to us all as ' Tommy ', who died so early and
left so few examples of his work to stand as lonely promise of all
he might have achieved if the cloud of melancholy had lifted at

last; and the formidable and legendary Lady Ottoline Morrell, whose strangely garbed figure, deep voice, predatory smile and aristocratically ruthless 'attack' in her manner towards young poets she was meeting for the first time, conquered but terrified me. After my first encounter with her, I wrote to Julian:

> Do you know Ford's lines, something like ' not like the ruins of his youth, but like the ruins of those ruins '?—She made me think of that. Virginia as usual made outrageous remarks and as usual I wanted to fall down and worship. Tommy was there and said all Romantics were pursued by a sense of guilt. I thought rather sweeping. We had a long argument.

This was not very gallant, but implied, nevertheless, wonder and awe; and whenever she summoned me to her famous salon in Gower Street I hastened thither, drawn by her powerful personality and the expectation of meeting some of the great men of letters who had frequented it so long, above all W. B. Yeats.

There were also parties which Ottoline definitely did not attend and into which Leonard and Virginia were rarely drawn, late-night parties at the studios in Fitzroy Street or elsewhere in the neighbourhood, where the younger members of Bloomsbury predominated, danced, dressed up for charades and skits on their elders—of which Angelica, Julian's sister, was more often than not the leading spirit—and argued, glass in hand, into the dawn. No one, I firmly believe, has ever succeeded in retaining a coherent recollection of such a party, or has been able in after-years to distinguish one party from another that followed it a few weeks later, unless some ineffaceably awful disaster or crisis occurred at one of them; even falling in love does not make a party memorable, for one only remembers a blur of faceless figures behind the chosen, the unique face; and because they were happy parties, and I happily rode on the crest of the wave, I remember them only as if they were a series of tapestries, in which many of the same figures are repeated again and again against a background that varies only in detail, tapestries woven out of the bright colours of our life at the time, before Hitler and another war changed everything, and all of us moving to a rhythm that seems now

broken for good and part of the history that no one ever dis-
covers again, a tune unique and beyond all exact evocation,
even of the most brilliant pen.    They were the parties, above
all, of the artists who had been grouped by Keynes's
shrewd and ingenious shepherding into the London Artists'
Association, who every Christmas put on a show at the Cooling
Galleries where one could buy as presents what I look in vain
for now—trays and match-boxes and all sorts of small objects
made delightful and precious in the transformation of the
fanciful designs and colours they had been given.    I still possess
a tray painted by Douglas Davidson, which I would not part
with, even though it is now covered with stains and the paint
has flaked from rough usage, and a desk match-box by Robert
Medley that looks as fresh as the day I bought it.    One could
also buy objects that bore the unmistakable stamp of Duncan
Grant and Vanessa Bell, John Armstrong and John Banting,
and strange, poetic collages by gentle, witty, red-haired
Quentin Bell, of whom I saw much in those days, both in London
and down at Charleston, where he was forever engaged in a
mysterious board game, known as the ' War Game ', with his
brother Julian.    All this painting of trays and designing of cups
and vases and firing of decorative tiles was the aftermath of the
Omega Workshop enthusiasm, that has not been replaced by
anything as good or delightful since.
    In the middle of this brotherhood of two generations of
poets, critics and painters, linked together by an easy community of artistic beliefs and ethical values, by an athletic
intellectual curiosity and a passionate faith in the sensuous
world, a tragic gap was soon to be torn.    I had continued to
see Lytton Strachey since my arrival in London, and egged him
on to tell me many fond and malicious stories of Leonard, one
of his oldest Cambridge friends : in those early days at the Press
everything that could add to my knowledge of my two employers
and future partners was vitally important to me.    We used to
meet in his rooms at 51 Gordon Square, or at his club, the
Athenæum, which I already knew from meetings there with my
cousin Charlie Chambers, who over tea would put out the most
cautious Scottish feelers about my joining the ancient and
honoured family publishing firm.    A few years later I became a

member of the Athenæum myself, owing to my father's foresight in putting my name down at a very early age. I felt myself to be the most insignificant member, the very baby of the club, with nothing to protect my insignificance except a thin volume of poems, as I walked up the huge staircase under the golden statue of Apollo, or edged my way into the dining-room through the assembled ecclesiastical dignitaries, or tiptoed to a vacant leather-covered chair some way from the fire in the drawing-room, in order not to disturb the somnolence of eminent civil servants, officers of learned societies and retired Empire-builders of literary leanings from whose hands had fallen a copy of *The Round Table, The Nineteenth Century and After* or *La Vie Parisienne*. At this time, however, in the wake of my distinguished host, whose beard seemed capable of challenging the pretensions of any of those forbidding, semi-prostrate forms, no shrinking assailed me. I was in a glow of pleasure and amusement as Lytton, in his high, thin but authoritative voice ordered an excellent wine and we settled down to a long discussion about the past of Bloomsbury and Lytton's Cambridge days, about poetry (which Lytton wrote copiously, though modestly and in secret), or modern French literature, in which he sadly found all the vices of German literature and very few of the great traditional French virtues. I also visited him at Ham Spray, and explored endlessly in his library while he worked, and afterwards would go for walks with him, during which we renewed our discussion—or rather I renewed my eager questioning and he his judicious and witty answers to the ever-unsatisfied disciple.

During the late autumn of 1931, however, he fell seriously ill, and nobody quite knew what was the matter. At Christmas he rallied, and Rosamond, who with her husband Wogan Philipps was a constant visitor to Ham Spray, wrote to me describing the Christmas celebrations at Ipsden:

> That evening was the first for a week when the feeling of being in a bad dream lifted a bit—as we had just heard that a miracle had happened and Lytton had pulled round after being given up by everybody. I feel now he will live, though the danger is still acute. The bottom would fall out of the world for us if Ham Spray was no more.

But the danger was more acute than anyone guessed, and he began to sink again.   Towards the end of January he died: the post-mortem revealed that he had been suffering from cancer of the stomach, that all the diagnoses had been wrong and that nothing could have helped him.   It was a shock and great sorrow to me, but more for what might have been than for what had already matured between us in the way of friendship. Others among my intimate circle felt the true sharpness of a blow that oppressed the whole of Bloomsbury.

One of the most interesting sides of my work at the Hogarth Press was meeting the authors who were already published by the Woolfs, or who had very recently been taken on.   Just about the time I arrived a remarkable manuscript of a novel by an entirely new writer had been accepted: *Saturday Night at the Greyhound* by John Hampson.   The author of this book, which scored a hit at once and has since been reprinted in many forms, had had an extraordinary life and had finally settled in as a male nurse to the incapacitated son of an intelligent and well-to-do merchant in the provinces.   His real name was John Hampson Simpson: he wrote to us always in a curious brown ink I have never known anyone else use, and informed us that he did all his novel-writing in the early morning, in bed, before the day's responsibilities began for him.   It has always seemed to me that this was an excellent solution to the everlasting problem of how an author without private resources should earn his basic living, with only two drawbacks: one, the necessity of waking with the lark, and two, the inability to move about, travel abroad, renew the store of impressions and experiences that a writer must never allow to become exhausted if he cannot—and who but the most exceptional genius can?—rely entirely upon the memories of childhood and early youth. Later on, I became very good friends with John Simpson, and out of his encyclopædic reading in modern literature he wrote some excellent articles about ' the underworld ' for *Penguin New Writing*.

One of the first books that Leonard urged me to acquaint myself with, was a short novel called *Turbott Wolfe* by William Plomer, which they had published five or six years before.   I was impressed when I read it: I felt that the emotional design was more chaotic, the execution a great deal rougher and more haphazard than appealed to my rather orderly taste; but how I envied the passion that swept through it, the ferocity of its rejection of prejudices and conventions that stand in the way of human justice and the natural flowering of human feeling. I eagerly turned to a collection of short stories that had followed it a couple of years later, *I Speak of Africa*, and found in it one story that compelled an even greater admiration: 'Ula Masondo'. In this story of a young Zulu boy who goes to work in the gold-mines, is nearly killed in an underground fall of rock, is quickly corrupted by his associates and returns home only to reject his family and native upbringing, the material seemed to me more completely under control, but the fire, the vision no less intense. Especially I admired the bold impressionism of the story's telling, the spare, vivid description of African nature, and the imaginative power with which the author penetrated into the primitive mind of Ula himself, his prose passing over by natural transition into poetic rhapsody and poetry in the scene where Ula loses consciousness while imprisoned in the mine. The preface he had written to *I Speak of Africa*, describing his collaboration with Roy Campbell in the magazine *Vorslaag* and the hostility some of the stories encountered when published there, was attractive enough to a person of my age and ideals in its uncompromising Elizabethan contempt for 'business men, party politicians, paint fanciers, half-dyed blue-stockings, and half-witted catchpenny inksprayers', but I was immediately drawn to him by something deeper, an element which I have always found in his work, and which many years later was to appeal to me in the work of an otherwise very different writer, the young American Paul Bowles: a capacity, a need in his temperament to go outside the traditions and assumptions of his own race and class and enter imaginatively into the minds of people living by an entirely other, less sophisticated pattern of impulse and belief. That seemed to me his triumph in 'Ula Masondo'; and when I knew his work better I found the same power in his stories of Japan and Greece, the same dramatic presentation of the subtle undercurrents and submerged reefs in the relationships of differing civilizations as they work out in individual friendships and associations.

The opportunity to meet him came very soon, as the Press was at that time preparing to publish his novel of Japan, *Sado*, and his book of poems *The Fivefold Screen*. What struck me at once about the rather burly figure with the deep voice who came into my office one morning, was the shrewdly observant look behind the spectacles, the sensitive mouth and the humour that would leap into the whole expression of his face at the slightest lead from whoever was talking with him. As I got to know him, I found his delight in anything eccentric or fantastic, the continuous bubble of crazy commentary that he would keep up in responsive company, completely irresistible. I noticed, too, that when I was with him things would happen, people would appear, that were exactly the right food for this kind of foolery: as he approached the ticker-tape news in the Athenæum, the machine would make a misprint that reduced the whole sentence to absurdity; as one went out into the street with him a woman would pass wearing a hat that looked as if it had been lifted entire from an amorous nook in the parrot-house in the Zoo. Like so many other people of lively personality, he seemed to create his own surroundings. Or is it simply that one doesn't notice them in that particular light until such a person points them out?

When I was preparing the publicity for *Sado*, I asked him to send me some details of his life. In his reply he wrote:

> Please say that I am English, *not* South African. My age is 28. My career, though chequered so far, has not been without its oases—or is that a mixed metaphor? I was at school at Rugby, I haven't attended a university, and don't intend to do so. I have been a trader in Zululand and an apprentice farmer in the (rugged) mountains on the Basutoland border. I have been unemployed in Japan, a tourist in Russia, and an alleged Λόρδος in Greece. I once saved a nun from drowning, I seldom eat tripe, etc., etc. What *am* I to say? . . . If you mention that I have written verse, please say I never pretended to be a poet—even to myself.

All (or nearly all) this he was to describe in living detail during the war in his autobiography *Double Lives*; but I think he was wrong about not being a poet. Poetry has informed the best of his novels and stories, and if in the medium of verse his control of formal design has not always been so sure, some of his poems achieve that absolute rightness of concentrated effect that only a true poet can bring off. By far the most remarkable sections of *The Fivefold Screen* were those groups of poems inspired by Africa and Greece. They owed their success, I believe, to William Plomer's direct response to what is primitive, vivid and elemental, so that his gifts have always seemed to me by comparison muffled and uncertain of themselves in the mists and half-tones, the temperateness of England—all his gifts, that is, except his gift for satire and comic portraiture.

Even in his humorous ballads, with their violent resolutions in which the grotesque and the terrible so oddly mingle, one feels the same response at work. And yet it would be unfair to stress this side too much; William Plomer is a writer of deep compassion, and no one of his generation has shown a more emphatic respect for the civilized virtues of scepticism, tolerance and patient understanding. As with other writers who owe a great debt to E. M. Forster, he takes seriously the poet's and novelist's role of philosopher and interpreter of life, and it came to be of increasing importance to him after the early books. I could wish that I had paid more attention at that time to the view of life, of the integrated man's attitude in the modern world, which he puts forward in *Sado* :

The present chaos of transition in East and West offers four chances to the individual. One can be a reactionary, and seek security in the past. One can surrender oneself to the opposite extreme, and live in a hypothetical future of communism and standardization, with a view to making the best of things. One can stop thinking, drift with the crowd, and play the fool with more or less energy, thus turning oneself into an irresponsible. Or lastly, one can strive to think, to keep one's balance, to treat past and future with equal respect, committing oneself to neither but trying to seize the best from each, questioning much, admitting only what rings true, working and living with an enthusiasm at once steady and lively, ready to face the worst, ignoring politics, despairing perhaps of human beings ever behaving rationally, but at least trying to base every thought and action on a sound understanding of what is constant in and necessary to human

nature—a proper balance between heart and head, the need for
religion and idleness as well as for work and science, and the
recognition that it must always take all sorts to make a world.

William Plomer soon became one of my closest friends, a
cool and humorous judge of some of my excesses of enthusiasm,
but always that so much desired and so rarely won phenomenon,
a critic who approached all my works and projects with an
intuitive sympathy *from the inside*.

The moods, the pleasures and preoccupations of the early
'thirties are so far away now that they seem beyond recapture;
but as I turn again the pages of the little booklets of the Hogarth
Letters, it appears to me that they preserve, like a row of jam
jars on a larder shelf, the essence and the flavour of the time.
Raymond Mortimer's *Letter on the French Pictures* brings back
that great exhibition at Burlington House which dazzled the
whole of London with a light that took years to fade, which we
talked about at every luncheon and dinner and evening party,
arguing whether we preferred Poussin and Claude and Watteau
or Ingres and Delacroix and Daumier or Courbet and Manet
and Seurat, or Degas or Toulouse-Lautrec or Monet or
Cézanne, and which was the great festival and triumph of the
devotees of the French tradition in the arts who reigned in
Bloomsbury.   The watchwords of rhythm and design, of personal vision and the frank enjoyment of the ' terrestrial
nourishments ', the creed of a religion which offered an
intoxicating release from the stuffiness and pretentiousness of a
Royal Academy orthodoxy—so effectively reinvigorated since
then by some of the artists and designers who learnt in the
Bloomsbury school that it is difficult to remember just how dull
it was—all is brilliantly expounded in this little essay: ' Art ',
concluded Raymond, ' is like a tiger.   And if your eyes were
once opened to these pictures, you would find in them not an
escape from reality, but an escape into reality, and then you
would be in deadly danger.'   This creed, however, did not
confine itself to attacking the effete artistic tradition in England
at the time.   There was rather a scolding and superior note in
the voice where almost all things English were concerned, and
an assumption that everything was better ordered across the

Channel: an excellent tonic when taken with a grain of salt, but apt to be disastrous when swallowed unmixed. Frankie Birrell provided a fairly concentrated dose in his witty *Letter from a Black Sheep*. ' Your morals, your taste in colour, most of your novels, your historical information, even your scientific chitchat are all so damned antiquated,' cries the Black Sheep to his cousin John, and laments the great ages when English taste was the taste of all Europe and English products had the world as their market. Exaggerated it may have been, this case for the prosecution; but if anyone dismisses it now as a frivolous mood of affectation, the falsity of which was shown up by the events of 1940, he should reflect that the almost mortal peril of those days might never have confronted us if there had been more Black Sheep in the land to wage a truceless war against complacency and to warn against that hardening of the national arteries that comes out in self-righteousness, philistinism and inept foreign policy. Frankie anyway loved England, for all his digs; and if the buzzing of this bee in his bonnet was music to most of us in those days, I myself was curiously aware that an opposition group was emerging among the younger writers, waging war with equal zest against the Black Sheep's enemies, but looking for. succour across the Rhine rather than to France: poets whose works Virginia was already quoting, with doubtful approval, in her *Letter to a Young Poet*.

That letter, more personal in its message for me than any of the others, brings back all the fervour of the great poetic debate the young poets of my generation were taking part in at that time; and Leonard Strong's *Letter to W. B. Yeats*, as persuasively reasoned and perceptive a tribute as was ever paid the great Irish poet out of loving admiration, awakens again the excitement I felt at the discovery of the Byzantium poems and the other masterpieces of *The Tower* from the first moment I read them at Cambridge, and also the pleasure it gave me to be able, a publisher at last, to make this gesture to a man who had taught me what to look for in modern poetry so long before, when I was only a small schoolboy with an incoherent need to find in literature something that spoke, not out of the calfbound past but out of the world around him. And Rosamond's *Letter to a Sister*: there are passages, written in that fresh and lyrical prose of sensuous evocation that has always been one of her most striking gifts, that immediately recall the happiness of country-house week-ends, that combined arcadian, timeless pleasures of garden and river, whether at Fieldhead or Ipsden or the houses of other Thames devotees, with strenuous reading and discussion on every conceivable problem of art and literature and politics. . . .

> Discussions on the lawn, arguments at the breakfast-table, debates at midnight, dissensions in the bath. What enthusiasm for painting, what views on writing, what sidelong, discreet but yearning glances at enigmatic music; what inability to stick to the point—and what dreadfully ribald jokes, what absurd laughter! I thought of the blissful fortnight of hot weather—of picnics, and deck-chairs in the shade, of packing into the car to go down to bathe before dinner, to plunge from the trodden grass bank into the warm lit evening water, of the infinitesimal flecks of gold-dusty midge-swarms; the glimmer, the clinging touch, like a soft threat on the limbs, of the ribbon-weeds; the swallows and willow-herb, and the reflections.

And there, beside the *Letter to a Sister* in my shelf, is Viscount Cecil's *Letter to an M.P. on Disarmament* to bring another note in, to remind me that even then we were aware that those timeless summers were in peril, that beyond the deck-chairs and the flower-filled urns that overhung the dreaming water, the armaments were piling up, and in Geneva the nations with all pomp and circumstance were failing to agree, and the dragon's teeth sprouting apace.

# 9

IN those first few months of 1932, when the fruits of my entry into the Press were beginning to show, when our worldly fortunes looked bright enough with a Book Society Choice in the shape of William Plomer's new novel *The Case is Altered*, and a second volume of *The Common Reader* to follow the success of *The Waves*, when I was beginning to feel an entirely new self-confidence in practical affairs as well as a new hope

for myself as a poet, all should have been well. I had great
ambitions already to draw all the new writers to the Press,
I wanted Stephen's prose if I could not have his poetry, I was
jealous that the magnet of T. S. Eliot and *The Criterion* had
drawn Auden to Faber & Faber, I worked as hard as I could to
persuade the Woolfs and Dorothy Wellesley to take on Louis
MacNiece's poetry, and I heard with the tremor of excitement
that an entomologist feels at the news of an unknown butterfly
sighted in the depths of a forest, that behind Auden and Spender
and Isherwood stood the even more legendary figure of an
unknown writer, Edward Upward. I determined to catch him
in the Hogarth net. And yet even while Virginia was writing
so happily from Athens and I was sitting in my ' doghole '
revolving these schemes, things were beginning to go wrong.
Under the surface my restlessness was increasing, and as the
time loomed nearer for the decision about my partnership with
the Woolfs to be taken, difficulties and doubts began to arise on
both sides. Leonard and Virginia might approve in general of
the new authors I was bringing to the Press, and encourage the
new schemes I was so eager to propose; but their sober check on
all this youthful foisoning of ideas would, it was clear, be much
less effective when I was an equal partner—in an enterprise
which was their own child and had never been shared so far
with anybody.

Very soon after Leonard and Virginia returned from Greece,
I left for my own holiday abroad : it was a trip that did nothing
to lessen my growing doubts about the harmony of future
relations at 52 Tavistock Square, and did much to increase my
restlessness. My plan was to go through France into Austria,
and then up from Salzburg through Germany to Hamburg
and Berlin, and end with a visit to Stephen Spender (and
Christopher Isherwood if he was there) on Ruegen Island on
the Baltic coast. I stayed only a few days in Paris, and then
went on by the Arlberg Express to St. Anton in Tirol. Even
though I was alone, the sense of release and exhilaration I felt
at getting into Austrian Alpine surroundings was extraordinary,
all the more so as I had no interest in ski-ing or mountaineering
(and have never been bitten by either sport). Even today I am
not quite sure why Austria became a passion for me, was in fact

already a passion before this, though I had visited Vienna only once, two years before, on my tour of the Prints & Drawings departments of the great European museums. Was it an obscure recollection of the summer we all spent at Château d'Oex just before the war, the sunset over Lac Leman a small boy caught forever in his sleepy eye as the funicular ground slowly up the mountain-side? Had all this been stirred again by the story of the ruined Empire, that was bound to draw the children of those who had fought on the other side? Perhaps it was Rilke's poetry, which I had come to know since I had joined the Hogarth Press, a poetry so evocative in itself and so intensely redolent of the old Austria, that had quickened all these seeds lying deep in my mind; that had created the illusion that the country itself was more beautiful than any other, the inhabitants more sympathetic, more deeply civilized and yet closer to the natural rhythms of life than anywhere else in Europe. Whatever it was, illusion or reality or childhood haunting, it grew into an infatuation strong enough to turn the whole direction of my life, that survived the knowledge that came to me later of poverty and squalor in a discarded metropolis, of social dissension and a fecklessness that made the Austrians the easy prey of their powerful and pushing northern neighbours—a people to whom I was more closely allied in blood.

My first morning in St. Anton the mist blew away and I saw blazing snow-peaks against the blue sky, and slopes of fresh green below the dark pine-woods. I spent the day climbing up through the high meadows, following the roaring, narrow torrent full of spring's melted snow, while the arch of sapphire above me seemed to grow deeper, more incandescent in the purity of its tone: only on the topmost peaks little clouds were still clinging like attendant spirits, like Ariel to Prospero. Next morning, in Innsbruck, I looked out of my window to see a sheer wall of mountain rising straight up behind the houses; the white-powdered rock-face shot clear above the freshly opened buds on the chestnut trees in the town's park spaces, where I sat at midday with a Baudelaire unread in my hand and watched the beautiful Tirolean young men and girls saunter past with their strong mountaineers' placing of foot on ground, laughing and chattering together. I was keyed up by the pure air, and

I felt for a moment as if I had always been in Innsbruck, as if the bells I heard begin to ring called back innumerable such days in years gone by: my happiness was so great, I felt an urgent need to gather and store the emotion, as if I could make a reservoir of it strong enough to drive a mill-wheel, a turbine. Then the train took me twisting down through Alpine meadows so thickly woven with spring flowers they seemed to me like Bokhara carpets or the glittering fragmentations of light in the medieval rose-windows of the great cathedrals, dazzling harmonies of deep violet and silver-yellow and pure cloud-white and every shade of coral and rose; and landed me in Salzburg, a crystal city of sun and open spaces and towering architecture so white in the sun it might have been made of snow.

Everyone seemed burnt and transformed by sunlight in Salzburg, with a fiery warmth in sharpest contrast to the pale faces I had left behind me emerging pastily from a London winter. The handsome features of the Salzburgers seemed open with the openness of sunlight, their fair hair had the glint of the sun, the ruddy darkness of their cheeks, their necks, their sturdy legs and arms were like a honey extracted from the huge flower of the sun, as they whirled recklessly through the streets and over the bridges ringing their bicycle bells, or leant against the pillars of a white baroque colonnade laughing together in the sun, or lay on the edge of the baths (but not bathing) luxuriating in the rays that poured down ceaselessly out of a sky without a cloud. In the evenings I wandered into the Mirabel gardens, where a concert was being held and all the statues were illuminated and the fountains changed from green to red to purple and back to flashing silver; and watched the people strolling in and out of the focus of light, standing quietly listening round the band with absorbed faces, or talking under the trees in groups of three or four, or leaning over the balustrades and chaffing one another. I was a spellbound watcher of a conjured scene, and my imagination began to weave patterns of poems out of them, to invent stories of their lives that would capture as if by accident something of the magic element in which they seemed to exist.

I began to think again of the poetry I wanted to write. For a long time I had intended it to become more personal, following

more fluid rhythms of thought, my thought, responding to
and in harmony with the nervous, complex, unmonumental
awareness of my own European generation, the tunes that
travelling, that watching and brooding on the lives of strange
people in new countries started up in my mind; a mingling
of outer and inner, of the beleaguered past and the dissolving
present, of the conscious mind with the irruptions of the unknown rain-maker in the deeper intuitive mind, that the couplets and quatrains I had been writing at Cambridge disciplined
too rigidly—though the discipline had been necessary.  I felt
that my wanderings—and they had essentially to be undertaken
alone for this purpose—released springs that I had instinctively
known to be welling up inside me for some time; I wanted, as
it were, to travel light in my search for whatever the truth was
that I craved, and poetry to be as simple and informal as marching songs, and yet, like the sublime lyrics that suddenly break
out of the prose in Rimbaud's *A Season in Hell*, or Yeats's *Words
for Music Perhaps*, to concentrate experience and vision in a few
lines.   That, in an age when prose was staking claims all over
the lazy ancient lands of poetry, was surely poetry's proper
destiny and technique for survival.  I was haunted by the
words that Rilke puts into the mouth of Malte Laurids Brigge in
the famous *Notebook*:

> In order to write a single verse, one must see many cities, and men
> and things; one must get to know animals and the flight of birds,
> and the gestures that the small flowers make when they open
> out to the morning.  One must be able to return in thought to
> roads in unknown regions, to unexpected encounters, and to
> partings that had long been foreseen; to days of childhood that
> are still indistinct . . . and to mornings by the sea, to the sea
> itself, to oceans, to nights of travel that rushed along loftily and
> flew with all the stars. . . .

Only then, it seemed to me, as the train followed the swirling,
opaque ochre-yellow waters of the Danube on the way to Passau,
when one had trained one's imagination to turn one's life, one's
experience into legend in that way, could one write a truly
modern poetry.

And yet it was not enough merely to be a watcher of other
people's lives from the outside.  One must, I thought, be able

somehow to enter into them, to lose oneself in them until one could hear inside one's own heart the rhythms and music to which they moved, until their hope and dismay touched one on the quick of one's own nerve. And then the poetry that was still out of reach would lean out towards you and take you and create itself through you. Of all places, the Austrian provinces I had just been through inspired me with the greatest longing to accomplish this act of self-loss and self-renewal. ' Towards the heart of the fire '—that was a phrase that kept repeating itself in my mind, and the fire was the suffering, tension and bitterness the ordinary working men and women of the world were enduring, the creative despair and the revolutionary ferment that seemed to increase like a hammer beating louder and louder in the economic crisis of the 'thirties. A poet, if he was to accept all the implications of being a poet in our age, could not run away from that, but must set out towards it. When I reached Hamburg (where I made a pilgrimage to discover the paintings of my great-grandfather in the museum), the sight of the masts of all the ships in the harbour that had been lying up for so long unused, and the clusters of unemployed sailors and port-workers who slouched round the quays in their dark blue caps dully watching those masts and funnels, stirred these thoughts violently again. And I remembered that in Vienna an experiment was being made by the Socialist Municipal Government to prove, what had become so doubtful to us in London, that the working masses could find welfare and civilized conditions of life without a Communist revolution. Another reason to know Austria intimately—another magnet pulling me into the heart of Europe.

For some time I had been telling Stephen and Christopher in my letters that I was beginning to wonder whether my life as a publisher in London was compatible with the life of a poet, as I now felt it should, in the world and at the time in which we lived, be ordered. Our debates about the nature of modern poetry, the way the poet should prepare himself to create it, began again as soon as I reached Stephen on Ruegen Island While I had been travelling, Leonard and I had exchanged letters about the future, half exasperated with one another, half unwilling to break up what had started so promisingly. Stephen was sympathetic to my desire to be more completely a poet, but also clearly believed that there was much to be said—from the point of view of all of us—for having me planted in the centre of publishing and editing in London.   Sensibly, he preferred not to influence me too strongly, and in spite of the turn my thoughts had been taking and in spite of the living example Stephen himself was, in so many ways, of my idea of 'travelling light' as a poet, I might, even then have plumped for the back pantry; but, alas, there was more to it than just my restlessness.

We went for long walks through the gently sloping, wooded landscape of the island, where fields of barley alternated with pastures of black-and-white Friesian cattle and water-meadows full of yellow irises and yellow mustard.   We climbed the high cliffs on the northern edge of the land and came down to sand dunes and a cobalt sea stretching out towards invisible Scandinavia.   Stephen, who always went about with an open collar to his shirt and was often without a shirt at all, was now burnt a deep brick-red, which, contrasting with his large, deep-set, bluish eyes, gave him a demoniac look, particularly when his face was split by a huge pantomime grin at some absurd recollection or some remark of Gerald Hamilton, who was also holidaying on the island.   We talked all through the walks, about poetry, about politics and what was happening in Germany, about his friends in Berlin and the way they lived, about Bloomsbury and our mutual circle in London, about a magazine I wanted to launch to carry on what *New Signatures* had started. Stephen did not exactly monopolize the conversation, but he had the lion's share.   When he was excited, perhaps about some opinion he thought outrageous on politics or poetry, his words would pour out, grating on the ear like pumice-stone; and then suddenly he would check himself and fall into a gentler, more receptive, almost diffident mood, and his expression would soften as his voice became more harmonious.   In the evenings we would go on talking in the local café where the German sailors danced with their girls, or in his room, where, in a sudden outburst of confidence and intimacy, he would rummage wildly in the chaos of his work-table and the wardrobe, and out of the jumble of pens, papers, ties, torn shirts, unpolished shoes and undarned socks would fish up poems, photographs and letters, all to be heaped upon me for my admiration or critical inspection.

Christopher was not on Ruegen, nor in Berlin when I passed through, and I returned to London without seeing him. The situation between myself and the Woolfs seemed to have got worse since I left, and it continued to deteriorate during the remainder of the summer, some weeks of which I spent in convalescence, after a persistent fever, at Fieldhead. It seemed impossible to find a compromise that would satisfy Leonard and myself, and thinking it all over again during my rest, I saw only too clearly that if I stayed, my relationship with him and Virginia would almost certainly be poisoned for good; and I did not want that. I was far too happy in my relationship with them as a literary beginner sitting at their feet; and this relationship did indeed continue to the end as if nothing else were growing up between us. The *Letter to a Young Poet* had come out, and Virginia and I had many discussions about it. I maintained that there was no harm in the ' dressing up ' she had attacked in the Letter, it was a good stimulant, and had been practised by many excellent English and French poets in the past. . . . She replied that gin and bitters was as good as a stimulant, and that the trouble about it was that it became a habit and froze one into ridiculous poses as one grew older. I claimed that there was no harm in a poet publishing early, because it wiped the slate clean and gave him a new start: her argument was that, on the contrary, it engraved the slate in a fatally enduring way. Our chief point of difference was over ' Mrs. Gape ', the symbolic char-woman figure she took to represent the intractable realistic material we were trying to use in our poetry. I felt that this was the weakest part of a brilliant piece of work: Mrs. Gape was a fantasy of Virginia's, who corresponded to nothing we were trying to assimilate, and her idea of ' beauty ' was oddly conventional. In her reply (in a letter to me at the end of July), she admitted she had chosen quotations that were weak for her argument, but returned—and I think effectively—to the attack by saying that her complaint was that the poet, in tackling this new material,

> doesn't dig himself in deep enough; wakes up in the middle; his imagination goes off the boil; he doesn't reach the unconscious, automatic state—hence the spasmodic, jerky, self-conscious

effect of his realistic language.   But I may be transferring to him
some of the ill effects of my own struggles the other way round—
with poetry in prose.   Tom Eliot I think succeeds; but then he is
much more violent; and I think by being violent, limits himself
so that he only attacks a minute province of the imagination;
whereas you younger and happier spirits should, partly owing to
him, have a greater range and be able to devise a less steep and
precipitous technique.   But this is mere guesswork, of course. . . .

In spite of these absorbing exchanges, I knew that an
impossible situation was approaching.   So it was that, impelled
partly by disappointment and bitterness, partly by a need to
prove to myself whether I was a poet or not, partly by currents
that ran too deeply under the surface of the time for me to be
entirely aware of them, currents that were affecting in greater
or lesser degree all our friends and all our world, I finally
decided to make the break.   I knew it meant abandoning all
my hubristic schemes to make the Press the centre of literary
publishing for my generation, and, more particularly, abandoning the chance of having a share in the book to follow *New
Signatures* which I was already discussing with Michael Roberts
(and which was published the following year as *New Country*,
with some of my poems in it).   I minded bitterly.   I thought I
was leaving the Hogarth Press for good.   It would have
appeared fantastic to me if someone had suggested that six
years later I should be back, better friends than ever with
Leonard and Virginia, and in a stronger position as a publisher,
with the enterprise of *New Writing* successfully under way.

During my convalescence I had lain awake one morning,
hearing the reveille sound from the camp up-river by Little
Marlow, and thought how far and how rapidly the events of the
last two years had taken me from Eton: the memories of it
seemed no longer charged with the same potency, though I
knew that one day I should possess them all again.   And then,
just before I left for Vienna, I had a curious dream about Eton.
I was in one of the schoolrooms, and had just been wrongfully
accused of some fault and was hotly defending myself.   It was
only when I was able to make a joke of it that everything came
right, the class broke up and we went upstairs to Chamber and
clambered round one of the high windows.   Down below in

School Yard there was a good deal of noise, many people running to and fro, and it seemed as if the commotion had something to do with the O.T.C. Suddenly a friend beside me flung himself out of the window, and I cried out in horror: but the air was like water, and the boy's death-leap turned into a graceful dive which did not even touch the cobbled yard below. I remember most vividly that as he plunged he appeared to be dressed in matador-like mauve satin tights; and that the dream teased me for days with a feeling that it had some under-meaning I could not elucidate.

# IV

## TOWARDS THE FIRE

DURING my first autumn in Vienna in 1932 I was feeling my way towards a new life, trying to learn to be the poet that Rilke had ideally imagined in *The Notebook of Malte Laurids Brigge*. That book, Yeats's last poems, Arthur Waley's translations from the Chinese, a collection of Rimbaud's works in prose and poetry and Wilfred Owen's poems were, I think, my most constant companions: books I wanted to absorb into my bloodstream and be the food of the poetry I planned to write. I lived in a *pension* in the Josefstadt where the chief lodgers were a group of Indian students. We used to meet at lunch, and, to my surprise—for I had never had anything to do with Indians before—they could not have been more amiable or more indifferent to the fact that I belonged to the race that ruled their country. As they all came from different parts of India, English was the language they used amongst themselves: as I chewed my *naturschnitzel*, I was amazed at the crackle of gaiety that went on between them, the gentle mutual teasing, the witticisms and flights of fancy. Gradually my reserve was thawed, and my preconceived picture of the Indians as sullen and mystery-enwrapped or darkly servile faded into thin air while an occasional shaft of unmalicious wit landed also in my breast: the first practical lesson I had had in the absurdity of the assumptions of an imperial tradition. In spite of these midday relaxations into English, however, I was determined to avoid the society and conversation of my fellow countrymen, in order to learn to speak and read German as fast as possible, and in particular that seductive variation of it known as *Wienerisch*. I used to settle in a café for an hour, morning and evening, with my lexicon beside me, and struggle to understand the jargon of the Austrian newspapers, adding about twelve hideous words to my vocabulary every day. In between, I went out to learn the ordinary speech of the Viennese, and whenever I visited the park of Schönbrunn or the Belvedere, or took a trip up to the Kahlenberg or to the *Heurigen* of Grinzing,

endeavoured to get into conversation with Viennese people
who looked as if they would *not* be able to speak even the most
pidgin English.   So little by little, as the golden, dusty days
of that perfect September slipped away and the piles of grapes
on the fruit-stalls in the streets grew scarcer, I made my
first steps into intimacy with the city that had fascinated my
imagination for so long.   At last I managed to penetrate to the
outer circles of habitation, discovered the Karl Marx Hof, and
made friends with a family that occupied one of the flats.   The
young son, Karl, was an electrician and a fervent member of the
*Schutzbund*, the armed defensive organization that the Social-
Democrat Government of Vienna, knowing itself surrounded by
enemies who had already shown their teeth, had created after
coming to power.   He showed me all over the beautiful tenement, the only one I had ever seen that did not remind me in
any sense of a barracks, and proudly described the achievements
of his Party in social welfare and education.   He was absolutely
confident in their power to resist any attacks of the Austrian
fascists; confident, too, in their natural leadership of the
civilized forces of progressive Socialism—which seemed more
like radical Liberalism to me—throughout Europe.   Like all
Viennese with even only a smattering of culture, he was at the
same time entirely un-chauvinistic and naturally curious about
other peoples: he questioned me without cease about the
customs and eccentricities of the English, who still, in his
mind, lived in a land of top-hats, beefsteak, Derby Day and
fog.

It was Karl who, flashing his gold tooth at me, first brought
home to me the reality, the increasing desolation of unemployment in the little Republic.   It was difficult to believe, in that
beautiful country, with the sun laying its benediction day after
day on baroque domes and dahlia-filled parks, that anything
could be wrong: even the bands of young singers and musicians
with their accordions, who wandered all day through the streets
picking up a few *groschen* here and there, seemed to be more
part of a sad, timeless pageant at first than raw human evidence
of the same urgent tragedy that had overtaken the unemployed
in England, who seemed so much more denatured, plunged
so much deeper in squalor:

The singers wandering before the door
Come empty-handed from shut factories:
Suffering is in their faces, but no greed,
Their voices are not strong, but like the wind
Straying in gusts about the littered road.
Yesterday came three boys from an Alpine village,
Fair, with brown skins, and one had a violin;
They moved like twigs that fall in a sluggish river,
They held out caps for coins and passed by,
And the violin grew faint, as the voices now;
Tomorrow these too will be gone, but more will come. . . .

Those autumn months convinced me, nevertheless, that in
the life I envisaged in Austria I could not only find the food I
needed for my poetry but also that close-up view and understanding of the human and social problems of the time that had
become so important for me.   Towards the heart of the fire . . .
There, in Vienna, I should find the way.   In the New Year, I
decided, after returning to England for Christmas, I would look
for a more permanent abode in Vienna.   But another, unexpected card was to be dealt me before that, rearranging the
whole outlook I had so carefully planned for myself.

Christopher Isherwood was still in Berlin, and again invited
me to visit him there.   I decided that it would be a good plan
if I stayed for a few weeks on my way back to Vienna.   I
arrived at the end of January, and within a very short time
found myself in the midst of the last agony of the Weimar
Republic.   In my lodgings off the Nollendorfplatz, stung by
Christopher's claim to be able to write a thousand words a day
and give English lessons to earn his bread and butter as well
as live an agreeable social life, I laid out my exercise book and
my pens every morning.   It was not much use: what was
going on in Berlin was too novel for me, too tense and too
ominous.   The crucial elections were approaching, and bloody
conflicts between the Nazis, the Communists and the Social-
Democrats were taking place almost every day in some part of
the ice-bound city that was laid out like a patient about to
undergo an operation without any anæsthetic at all.   Now that
I was close at hand to the battle I had read about and heard
so much about from Christopher and Stephen, I noticed some-

thing that I had not foreseen, an element, puzzling and disturbing, that had been left out of the reporters' reckonings of Right versus Left, reactionary capitalism versus the working-class movement, and so on.   All over Berlin, especially in the middle-class shopping and residential districts, huge pictures of Hitler were displayed at night in windows illuminated by devout candles.   As I wandered along the streets with Christopher, muffled up to the eyes against the flaying wind, the crude likenesses of the Man of Germany's Destiny, row upon row above us, were like altars dedicated to some primitive demon-cult, and seemed to menace far more terror than had been conceivable in the rational, easy-going atmosphere of London.

A few nights later I was in a bar near the Zoo, when a friend who had been to a cinema came in, and said ' The Reichstag's on fire! '   I followed him outside, and could see the glow of flames eastwards against the black sky. . . . It is not my intention to tell again here the story that is known so well, of the Nazi *putsch* that followed the trumped-up crime and Hitler's inevitable triumph and appointment as Chancellor after the hollow voting had taken place; only to describe some results it had for me.   For the events of the next few days, until I left Berlin for Prague and Vienna about a week after the elections, laid a searing mark across my mind.   Christopher, who so skilfully managed to have friends or acquaintances in all the warring camps, had of course a number of friends among the Communists and their sympathizers: they were in immediate danger of arrest, exile in concentration camps and death. Their plight in hiding, their sudden disappearances never to be explained, the tales they told of the brutality that the victorious Nazis were indulging in towards their opponents in the secrecy of barracks and prisons, the ruses that had to be invented to remove them to some kind of temporary safety, the Jew-baiting, sabre-rattling, hysterical tone of the Press—all this illuminated for me the hour that had struck in Europe with blinding clarity, and keyed me up to one of those rare moments of vision when I could almost have broken into prophecy.   Indeed, when a broadcast by Vernon Bartlett on the new Germany was reprinted in *The Listener*, I wrote a letter in which I denied

all his hopeful and comforting conclusions and said roundly
that Hitler's success meant war sooner or later and we should
very quickly find all the treaties torn up in our faces. From
that moment it seemed to me desperately urgent to do all in
one's power to help build some kind of dam against this torrent
that was sweeping down towards war, and in spite of governments if governments were half-hearted about it. From that
moment, too, I was obsessed by the political terror that had
broken out: it was almost as if I had been a victim myself, so
keenly, on the raw of my nerves, did I feel the abomination of it
and the need to prevent it breaking out in other countries. And
I experienced for the first time the strange paradox of life maintaining its smooth and smiling surface—so smooth that it
could apparently hoodwink a publicist from England as intelligent and humane as Vernon Bartlett—while out of sight
thousands were being tortured and broken, and edifices of political liberty that had taken generations to build up were being
sent crashing to the ground. These experiences haunted me
incessantly; I was experimenting with prose poems at the time,
and in several of them I tried to master and make artistic shape
of what was going on in my mind :

> In the days before Easter, the haze vanishes early before the sun,
> and innumerable tips of branches are set glowing with a soft
> green flame. But when we look out of our windows, we see the
> trees as if they were dripping blood.
> Down there, below the lilac bushes, rank ivy creeps and sucks
> among the bulbs of the crocuses. Over the first folded heads of
> daffodils a shadow seems to hang, that will not turn with the
> turning light.
> A body lies on the cobbles of an industrial city's suburb, covered
> with a stained green coat, and casts its shadow over these fields.
> The mind, quickened by horror, darkens here and now with
> shadows of the images of other time and place.
> There is a horror to be fought, to be wrenched away as the ivy
> is wrenched away from the crocus-bulbs by the gardener. . . .

I spent several months of 1933 in Vienna, where I eventually
found a small flat in a modern block off the Arenberg Park. I
lived there in rather absurd austerity, with little more than a
bed, a few chairs and a table built for me by an out-of-work

carpenter of the district. The austerity was not the result of principle, or really of poverty, but of the restlessness and uncertainty that the *putsch* in Germany had so enormously increased in me: in Prague and in Paris I met again some of those who had been fortunate enough to escape from the new Third Reich, and their tension and gloomy forebodings deflected me even further into the political anti-fascist movement that was now beginning to gain an international impetus. The dream of making myself into Rilke's poet seemed shattered: the dangers of the future had taken such a huge bound nearer, I found myself, with my own friends and Christopher's friends, so deeply involved, plunged so far into the swirl of refugee, underground and above-ground, anti-war and anti-fascist activities that I could only fitfully recapture the mood of the previous autumn—rare little islands that would suddenly be overwhelmed by a gigantic wave of alarming news. Christopher, exiled from the Germany he had made his home, suffered acutely from now on from traumatic anxiety about the explosive state of Europe. He pitched his tent in various European cities—Lisbon, Copenhagen, Brussels, Amsterdam—never staying very long, listening to the darkest prognostications of the refugee friends from Berlin who nosed him out, prostrated every seven days by the grisly international low-down that Claude Cockburn served up in his skilful little news-letter *The Week*. The burden of his letters was always the same. ' What do you think of Europe? ' he wrote from Copenhagen. ' I am utterly unable to judge, having lapsed even deeper into a state of utter inert horror. I read all the newspapers and listen in to the wireless in all languages, even those I don't understand; hoping somehow I shall get a clue from the peculiar intonation with which the Lettish announcer pronounces the word Alexander. . . .' And again from Greece: ' Is there going to be a war? This question may well be answered before you read it. Anyhow, I can't judge anything from the scrappy paragraphs at the back of the Athens *Messenger*, whose leading articles are generally about Lord Byron, " Sir Codrington " or a French poet's impressions of the Ægean. . . .' Or from Tenerife: ' I read the most alarming reports. When and where will the war start? K— has ceased to write to me, and his silence is more terrifying than his worst prophecies. Wasn't there an Oracle which foretold disaster and then suddenly shut up altogether—and the Assyrians arrived and killed everybody? But perhaps I am getting mixed. . . .' It was a mood that only the Spanish war was to make intelligible to most of our contemporaries in England, and even then only in the most gradual stages. And yet during these years Christopher was writing his first plays in collaboration with Auden, and working at the material in his Berlin diaries which was soon to make his name known far outside the small circle that had admired *The Memorial*.

The ominous year passed with ever-growing anxiety in Austria. The Austrian clerical-fascists and their Heimwehr, with the picturesque but adolescent throw-back Prince Starhemberg at their head, seemed to derive as much comfort from the change in Germany as the Pan-German Austrian Nazis. No wonder the morale of the Social-Democrats trickled away: they continued to make brave gestures and statements in public, but being above all men of peace, they allowed their outer fortifications to be taken piecemeal and without a struggle as autumn deepened into winter. I had espoused their cause emotionally, and tried hard not to look the future in the face. Again and again there came up before my inner eye memories of Berlin: a patrol of S.A. men breaking into a bar one night, and young Jews being taken away while one Nazi stood at the door covering us with a revolver—lorries full of political suspects driving top-speed towards the Alexanderplatz—the monstrous effigies of Hitler candlelit at night. . . . No, this could not happen in Vienna, it would require too violent a reorientation of one's thinking, too horrible a menace to all one had already grown to be so fond of and to admire in Austria. . . . At the beginning of February, 1934, stopping off in Paris on my way back from Vienna to London, gloomily convinced that the Social-Democrats in Austria would in the end surrender without a fight, I found myself jammed one evening in a huge, excited crowd by the Madeleine, the bells of the ambulance ringing incessantly as they tried to nose their way through: at the bottom of the Rue Royale in the distance I could hear the roar of the rioting demonstrators in the Place de la Concorde, while near me in the shadows the blue-cloaked police reserves shifted and muttered uneasily. I did not then realize that this upheaval in Paris would have almost immediate results in Vienna; but the last inhibition that restrained the Austrian fascists from the *coup de grâce* they had so long prepared to give the Socialists, was anxiety about the reaction of the French Radicals. This inhibition was now suddenly lifted, while Parisian politics were in turmoil. Only a few days later I was agitatedly telephoning through from London to find out if my Viennese friends were safe, while the guns were bombarding Floridsdorf and the Karl Marx Hof, and Schutzbundler Karl's dream was smashed for ever into the rubble.

In my book *Down River*, published a few weeks after the outbreak of war in 1939, I attempted to describe in some detail the political imbroglio that led up to the events of that February and the results they had in Austria during the years of strange, suspended animation between then and Hitler's invasion. I do not propose to go into them again here, especially as I now disagree with many of the conclusions to which I felt inevitably driven at that time, and see the extraordinary, confused, romantic underground battle, in which tragedy and terrorism were mixed in such characteristic Austrian fashion with *schlamperei* and farce, in a slightly different light. I want, rather, to give some idea of the impact of this experience on my way of life and my thinking at the time; an impact which in one way or another, sooner or later, so many of my generation were to feel.

For the time being the experience seemed to create an irrecoverable and widening distance between myself and those of my friends in England who had not been through it, who had not learnt the mysteries I had learnt. I felt as if I was looking through the observation car at the end of a train that was gathering speed, making familiar landmarks diminish and bringing mountains to light beyond them on the horizon, mountains I had not known before existed. I tried to explain the why and whence of my new extremism in my letters, especially to Julian, who had remained sturdily by his belief in the Labour Party and the gradual revolution, and anyway had a deep suspicion of almost everything that emanated from beyond the Rhine. I wrote sometimes pleadingly, sometimes priggishly and intolerably: underneath it all lurked an unhappiness that events should be separating me from the friend who had been closest to me in the life of poetry—the most real life of all hitherto. I think Julian sensed this, for he wrote to me in December, 1934:

> . . . All your old Cambridge friends are asking after you and hoping to see you. When we met we didn't find much chance to talk about poetry, which was a pity, because I feel that it's probably our best subject of agreement now. It's very hard for me to share your feelings about politics because we live in such different worlds. . . . But I've always felt that there's a certain intimacy between us as poets that should be able to last through any other difficulties of communication. Incidentally, do remember this difference in our lives when you feel that I'm unsympathetic. None of my friends are in danger or hardship, and it's hard for me to imagine what I should feel if they were.

A strange perplexity overcomes me as I reach this point in my story; for the seven years of the war and its aftermath so completely buried my life in Vienna, that it is as if I needed superhuman strength to lift up the stone slab that presses on it. How can it be that so many years of one's life, so full of varied and intense experiences and discovery, in human relations as in intellectual exploration, should be as completely cut off from oneself as an arm or a leg left on the battlefield? The total loss of even small details is curiously bewildering: my telephone number in Vienna, or the registration number of my car, which seemed somehow to symbolize the solidity of my day-to-day life. Why should I have cared so passionately to scour so many papers every day for information that would piece together into some kind of coherent picture of the international situation, to know so much about it and to have forgotten and to care so little about those dramatic details today? How is it possible that people in the centre of one's happiness in those years should have vanished without a trace, and one's life go on, still so busily and so urgently? The great biographies and the great novels give the impression that every character and every experience in the first act of one's life will play a part in the last act, bringing all to harvest and meaning; but in this again we discover how dangerous it is to mistake art for life.

It is, then, with a kind of agonized detachment that I find myself exploring the six years during which Vienna was the centre of my life; wondering whether there really are fortunate people who have never experienced such obliterations on the path they have trodden. It dismays me not to be able to remember in clear sequence how my thinking changed, not to be able to disentangle all the threads that contributed to the emotional texture of that time, which gave certain kinds of action an imperative necessity and made others unthinkable; for these things are more complex than most people in their recollections are willing to admit—far more complex than the critics of a generation that comes after, who judge by the result in the present and not the possibility in the past, are ever likely to see.

In the reasoning that between 1933 and 1934 led me, not alone among my contemporaries, to believe that the solution to the troubles and dangers with which we were faced lay in Marxism, and even in Moscow, I can still, nevertheless, distinguish the strongest of the intertwining strands. First, we had seen three successive and cumulative failures of ostensibly radical régimes, but reforming rather than revolutionary, to survive against the counter-offensive organized by the privileged and the possessors in the economic crisis: the collapse of the Labour Government in England in the face of (what we at any rate believed was) the trick-scare of the ' your savings are in danger! ' election—I have already described the consternation this reverse caused amongst the Labour partisans in Bloomsbury; the elimination of all liberal and social-reforming parties in Hitler's triumph in Germany; and now the inch-by-inch encirclement of Vienna's Democratic Government by the reactionary forces which had gathered in the provinces, with their private armies and their cynical use, in the final thrust, of heavy artillery smuggled in from abroad to crush the last struggles of a régime that had been too civilized—and too hopeful of civilized behaviour in its opponents—to take the offensive while it was still possible. These three defeats seemed to point to one conclusion: that if it was in serious danger, capitalism would stop at nothing to turn back the wheels of democratic progress and social justice and establish its puppets in power.

Another essential strand in our reasoning, an inference to which the combination of all these events all too easily led, was the belief that the attacks were part of an international conspiracy in which all capitalist countries acted in secret concert; and that out of fear of the propaganda value of the sheer existence of the ' one Socialist country ', even more than from a perception that rearmament and only rearmament offered an easy solution to the economic crisis, all capitalist countries were preparing to launch a war against the Soviet Union. This inference was reinforced, for a generation that had been brought up on the idea that it was primarily the wicked intrigues of arms manufacturers, oil companies and banks that had been responsible for the First World War, by the continual uncovering of international armament deals and what appeared to be the connivance of the Western Powers behind the scenes in the flouting of the rearmament clauses of the Peace treaties by the Central Powers; and then, at a later stage, by the Abyssinian and Spanish wars. Society was sick, it was sick unto death: it had called in the thugs as doctors: the thugs were preparing to sweep away all the traditional liberties of Western civilization and use force to destroy the one country that was not in the grip of economic crisis. That was one part of the argument in which we saw the trend of the times summed up and exposed; and the other was: society is sick because it is organized on capitalist lines; every crisis will be succeeded eventually by an even worse one, because that is the nature of capitalism; the only country that is not subject to these crises is the Soviet Union, because it has gone the Marxist whole-hog, and totally eliminated capitalism. Those two parts of our argument came to form our intellectual climate, as we searched for a means to make an end of the horror of recurrent unemployment and a way of escape from the narrow tunnel that we knew was leading to war. It was the climate of Auden's *The Dance of Death*, that witty, brilliantly simplified and partisan 'picture of the decline of a class, of how its members dream of a new life, but secretly desire the old, for there is death inside them ', which ends with the entry of Karl Marx (with two young Communists) announcing: ' The instruments of production have been too much for him. He is liquidated.'

What completed the change in our thinking, was the apparent supineness of our own Government in the face of the fascist menace, even its collusion with the fascists in the hope of deflecting this dynamic away from itself and against the Soviet Union. We were deeply suspicious of the motives of Whitehall; and everything that happened, up to and above all including the Munich agreement, confirmed our suspicions. Not all of us pretended to superior wisdom about the international chessboard, but with Eden's eventual resignation and Winston Churchill campaigning against the policy of Whitehall, we felt that honest men ' in the know ' supported our case.

Of course there was another side to the story, and factors we missed; but it wasn't particularly easy to see them in the conditions of the 'thirties. The *bona fides* of so many of those who presented the other side seemed suspect. The factors we missed were missed by thousands who did not hold our views. It did not occur to us that the dynamic released by Hitler's revolution might be more anti-rational than anti-Russian, or that Wotan and Marx were capable, at a given moment, of finding the democrats and imperialists of the West more contemptible than one another. We never imagined, having seen the reforming régimes collapse, that a solution to the endemic crisis of monopoly capitalism other than Marx's revolution might be found. We missed the absurdity of the apocalyptic nature of the Communist doctrine—an absurdity that had long become clear to such canny and cynical dictators as Stalin. None of us, not even George Orwell, had as yet grasped the fact that in the proletarian paradise all citizens might be equal in theory—but some ' were more equal than others '. And we astonishingly deluded ourselves into believing that Moscow had not only established all those liberties and opportunities that were the breath of our being, but had established them beyond the possibility of destruction.

The delusion that ' Moscow, of all places, was the sole source of light ' came partly from wish-dreaming; partly from the absence of adequate facts on which to base our views (the facts were to come thick and fast in the next decade for those who had eyes open enough to see them); and partly from the extremely skilful and widely ramified propaganda emanating from

Moscow. In Russia itself, one might have thought, one
would see the facts for what they were; but once across the
border at Negoreloye the propaganda was non-stop and exclusive, and so intense that it was difficult to remain in a frame of
mind where one could coolly question; besides, there was
much to be applauded and much that was absorbingly interesting, and on these features one's visitor-eyes were carefully
directed.  There were certainly no freebooting Prince Starhem-
bergs, no Jew-baiting Streichers, and no private empires were
being built out of the profits of trade and industry.  What one
saw was a Welfare State being built up with heady Slavonic
enthusiasm, backward compared with the Welfare State we
have since created in Britain but starting from much further
back.  What one did not see then were the moral and intellectual conditions of the material progress: the total absence of
political freedom, the fatal lack of open critical check in
bureaucratic one-party government, the concealed poisoning
of truth and corruption of values, the paralysing power of the
secret police which produced one kind of life for those who were
not suspect to the régime, and another of the most cruel and
unjust order for those who were.  In 1934, when I made my
first trip to Russia, there was an impetus and zest to Socialist
planning in such marked contrast to the economic stagnation
and political despair of the Austria from which I had come,
that it was impossible not to feel there was ' something in it '.
This active optimism excused for me spectacles of poverty in the
outskirts of the big cities as squalid as any in Vienna; the
development of a privileged class one couldn't fail to notice in
the course of long journeys in trains with their sharply distinguished levels of comfort; and the electric-light switches
that didn't work, the plugs that didn't pull, and the taps that
came away in one's hands in the new hotels into which one was
ushered with such a flourish of pride.  In the future lay the
Trials, the new terror (old terror admitted as soon as a new one
started), the betrayal of the Spanish War and the Nazi–Soviet
Pact, not to be guessed at that time.  I had seen the Schutz-
bündler, who had fled to Russia after the February risings,
marching in the formidable May Day parades and dedicating
themselves to fight fascism until they could return to a liberated

Austria.    It was a heart-warming sight if one had been personally involved in the Austrian tragedy;    and though half-
formulated questions were already stirring uneasily at the back
of my mind, I came home feeling that there was more than
' something in it '.    I decided that in some way or other I must
myself be identified with the same cause.

The impact on me of that first visit is clear enough from the
prose poems I experimented with on my return.    In one of
them, called *The People of Moscow*, I wrote:

> *We are winning*, they seem to say, as they swarm in cool white
> clothes against the early warmth of May, through the noisy shops
> and past the roughly moulded statues, the painted models and
> decorations that mark the stations-to-be of their underground
> railway, as they crowd before the windows where the plans of a
> hundred new buildings are displayed.    *We are winning at last* is the
> mood of the dancing processions that pass, with their many-
> coloured streamers and effigies, under the huge-written slogans of
> a still unfinished revolution.    Their new life, in its long-awaited
> splendour and prosperity, like a chestnut tree after the winter,
> begins to break into leaf and flower around them.
>
> The cars that carry guests and delegates from every country,
> halt at the street-crossing as a detachment of soldiers march by,
> roaring out their songs.    And over the bridge another company
> advances, singing in German, still carrying through exile the blue
> shirts of their world remembered battles.    At night, while some
> fill the theatres, some the cinemas and concert-halls of the workers'
> clubs, they join the dense masses in the illuminated square to
> watch, with strange feelings, the films that show their distant,
> shell-torn homes. . . .

Recurrent as malaria, a serious bout of rentier-guilt, the
characteristic malady of my class and generation, laid me low.
I began to feel that even my poetry was a frivolity unless in
some way it was *useful* to the anti-fascist and anti-war cause.
Already, after the Hitler *putsch* in Berlin, I had come into
contact with a new international movement, Communist-
controlled, though trying (with only varying success) to pretend
that it was not, that held its baptismal congress in Amsterdam
and called on all who were opposed to war and fascism, from
whatever class they came, to unite under its banner.    I had
been introduced to its Paris offices, where I tried to persuade

the dishevelled, overburdened political workers as they struggled with bursting files, broken-down typewriters and a dozen different languages, *gauloises* forever drooping from their mouths and nerves forever on edge, of the sincerity and ardour of my wish to help. I doubt if they quite knew how to take this strange six-foot animal from unpredictable England, who loomed up through the tobacco-smoke into the focus of their horn-rimmed spectacles; a poet talking enthusiastically in unidiomatic French of revolutionary English poets they had never heard of (and would not have understood if they had), an Old Etonian with public-school manners and a copy of *L'Humanité* in his pocket, as persistent as he was shy. I was suspected of being an agent of the famed *Intelligence Service Britannique*, an adventurer in search of cash, or just an eccentric nuisance; but one Polish girl believed in me, and I was eventually taken in to the inner sanctum to shake hands with Henri Barbusse, who had been persuaded to be the movement's figure-head, and received his blessing to act as their secret correspondent in Vienna. For I had determined that the best way I could serve was by making myself a channel of information from all the underground parties and sects in Austria (even of the Nazis if their news proved valuable) to their friends in the outside world. The idea of this work acted like an aspirin on the rentier-guilt: I felt I could pursue my literary activities and enjoy my life in Austria far more happily if I had this matter-of-fact association with the new movement, working in a way for which I intended specially to equip myself and in which I already had certain obvious advantages. Besides, the triangular struggle in Austria, between the so-called Clerical-fascists, the underground Social-Democrats and Communists, and the underground Nazis had begun to fascinate me in itself; and I had been seized by the wild ambition to explore all through the countries of the old Hapsburg Empire and make myself an expert on Danubian affairs.

With all this in mind, and feeling, after the collapse of the Nazi insurrection in Austria in the summer of 1934, that the struggle would be of longer duration than had seemed likely even three months before, I made up my mind to look for a more permanent home in Vienna. So it was that, when one of my friends introduced me to a young Viennese architect, an apostle of the neo-Viennese *Wohnkultur* but intelligent enough to listen to a client who did not want cacti sprouting all over the place from cosy little plywood cupboards that turned into dinette-tables or extra beds for midgets at night, I decided to enlist his help to find an old studio or attic that could be converted into a flat to live in, and entertain in, and work in: a proper headquarters, and not just a waiting-room at a station in transit.

The place I eventually found was at the top of a big building in the Invalidenstrasse, that belonged to a rich Czech mining concern. It had originally been used for offices, and I was told that the room which took my fancy had served, oddly enough, as the directors' dining-room. The great feature was a wide semi-circle of tall windows, from which one could see all over Vienna as far as the heights of Kahlenberg. Herr Grünbaum spotted its potentialities in a flash, and carried the day by his eloquently persuasive description of what it would look like when he had waved his (not extravagantly expensive) wand over it.

A few months later it was ready, and I moved in, to remain there for the rest of my years in Vienna. At the window end of the room a raised platform had been built to make it possible to sit in a chair and enjoy the view. On this platform a large desk jutted out from one wall, and above this desk I arranged a wall-paper of maps: large-scale maps of Vienna, Austria and the surrounding countries, smaller ones of England, France and the Caucasus. Down below the platform there was a bedroom on one side, closed by a curtain, and a big L-shaped settee on the other with table and chairs and a massive Austrian stove: the whole had been ingeniously arranged by Herr Grünbaum to give the impression of three rooms in one. There was more than a touch of *Wohnkultur* about it, but the transformation was not fussy or affected and marvellously improved the amenities. The door at the end led on to the hallway with a new built-in cupboard; through that to the kitchen and the showerbath, and out to the back, where there was a terrace which we surrounded with a trellis and boxes of plants to make a screen from the other roof-tops in summer and autumn.

I was lucky enough to find a paragon of a housekeeper in a
plump, cheerful-faced woman of Czech blood by the name of
Frau Chval, who plunged into her work like a high-powered
tank going straight across country through copses, hedges and
spinneys.   There was never a speck of dirt in the flat, nor a hole
in a sock, nor a button missing from a shirt, and I never had to
remind her about these things.   She arrived on the dot in the
morning, and produced delicious breakfasts, *Jausen* and luncheons, which I would dread to face now, with their fattening
Viennese delicacies, all manner of *torten, nockerln, nudel-suppen,
zwetschken-knödel, palatschinken* and so on.   Mysteriously, I
thrived on them then, and my weight remained steady.   Her
son Toni became a sort of secretary-chauffeur to me, and when
there was anything to be done—a job of painting, plumbing,
carpentering, shoe-making, repairs to the car or provision of
wines—he immediately produced a friend from the district
to quote what I was assured was a bargain price.   Unemployment was by then diminishing from the worst, but very few
of these young men had regular work, and I was glad enough to
give them the jobs and thus, as they were friends of Frau
Chval's family, extend my knowledge of the working people of
Vienna.

Toni also had a near relation of his own age, whose plight was
an epitome of the worst that had happened to a generation
that seemed to have been simply struck out from the roll of
human fortune.   He had *never* had proper work: after training as
apprentice to a shoemaker, he was flung on to the streets as soon
as his time was up to earn a *schilling* or two here and there by
any odd job he could scrounge, no matter how squalid or
sweated.   Sometimes he did not have more than a few hours
work in a month, and would sit in the cheapest and most
villainous cafés smoking an occasional cigarette made out of
ends picked up from the gutter, and paying for a malt-coffee
and a roll—sometimes his whole food for a day—with a few
*groschen* he had wheedled out of Toni or his parents, who were
extremely poor themselves and lived in a tumbledown shack in
the Lobau.   He had grown moody, bitter, unemployable and
felt permanently ill.   He had made several attempts at suicide
and had long gashes on one of his wrists; he would often

involve himself in brawls with the police solely in order to get into prison and have a few days' prison food. There were thousands like Heini in Vienna. As the iron winter of Central Europe closed down, the desperate, rotting horror of their existence, without adequate food or heating or clothes, seemed to me to reach its climax; as I watched the first snow falling on the roofs and domes of the city from the windows of my new eyrie, only prison thoughts came to me, a clenching of the fists to live through this evil time, for all those I knew and loved in Vienna to survive to better days; and yet, paradoxically, the arrival of the snow was a moment of relief and opportunity, for the Municipality had sudden need of an army of auxiliary street-sweepers, into which Heini and his unemployed friends were all likely to be enrolled for a few days.

It was not only in the cities that unemployment had made its ravages. One winter I went up to Puchenstuben in the foot-hills of the Alps; and I remember walking down from the inn one day to the village, through the utter stillness of the sparkling untrodden white, the branches of the tall pine-trees loaded down with lumps of snow that looked like whipped cream in the afternoon light, and having a long discussion with the young man who ran the general store. Most of the inhabitants of the surrounding country, he told me, earned their living in the timber industry, and conditions had gone from bad to desperate, and some of the peasants had had no work at all for months; in the farms it was just as bad, costs of transport were high and to compete with foreign produce in the Viennese market was almost impossible. Hundreds of lean, hollow-eyed young peasants came down from the mountains to join the ranks of the ' ausgesteuerten ' in the Viennese doss-houses.

When the work of converting my new home was completed, Toni produced a young student from art school, a friend of his girl-friend (whom he eventually married), an amusing boy of irrepressibly comic vein called Richard, who decorated the back wall of the house giving on to the terrace with fantastic pictures of jungle life—some of which were certainly not for the shockable eye. When he had finished them, I remember, we all celebrated with several bottles of Gumpoldskirchner on the terrace on a sunny afternoon; we were like a pack of cards for

Happy Families, with Frau Chval beaming, arms akimbo, in the background. . . . How few years later war had sundered us and carried us away to opposing destinies: some, like Richard, who disappeared into the hell of Stalingrad, forever.

Far away, out in the Atlantic, his movements made more and more eccentric by loyalty to *émigré* German friends and their passport difficulties, Christopher Isherwood was also trying to make a home and a plan of work for himself.

Here, amidst the flowers, our Rousseau life goes on [he wrote from the Canaries]. This place is a sort of monastery. It is run by a German of the Göring–Roman Emperor type and an Englishman who dyes his hair. The Englishman loathes women so much that he has put up a barbed wire entanglement across an opening in the garden wall, to keep them out. . . . My novel is exactly three quarters done. I hope to finish it on the day war was declared in 1914. It is a sort of glorified shocker; not unlike the productions of my cousin Graham Greene. . . . I am very happy here, and then, because I am happy, I feel sad. As long as we stay on this island, or somewhere equally remote, life is so charming and pleasant and calm; but nowadays a retreat seems artificial and wrong. As long as I work on a book my conscience is partially relieved, because I feel I'm doing a job to the best of my ability and helping in my tiny way. But I wish I were you. . . . I admire passionately the people who are standing up now and telling the truth; especially I find myself warming to Cockburn—I get *The Week* regularly. Misinformed or not, he does slash out at these crooks and murderers, and he's so inexhaustibly cocky and funny; like a street-boy throwing stones at pompous windows. . . . It is Sunday, and the moron Englishman and his guests are playing the gramophone in the bar, effectively sabotaging my attempts to work. '. . . What does it matter?' says the Englishman, when I expostulate: '. . . In fifty years we'll all be dead. . . .'

Now that I had a real home in Vienna, I felt much more settled and in harmony with myself; and though I still used to spend several months in every year in England, I was always glad to get back to my big desk with the wonderful panorama of the city I had become so infatuated with. In the rainy winds of late winter the line of hills, washed of their habitual mist, stood out behind the Stephansdom and the Karlskirche in sharp, blue outline all round the horizon; as spring advanced I could see the trees in the Stadtpark filling out with the fresh green of new leaves; and as evening came, I would raise my head from my work to see the falling sun had covered the maps on the wall with a dull, red glow.    Here I worked on my book about the Caucasus, *Prometheus and the Bolsheviks*, on my novel with a Viennese setting, *Evil was Abroad*, and on the articles about Vienna under the Dollfuss–Schuschnigg régime and about Danubian problems which were to form the basis of my book, published in the autumn war broke out, *Down River*. Here, too, I collected and sorted all the news that came to me from the underground parties, that reached me by word of mouth from people who arrived in my flat for a few hours and then vanished again, and by the innumerable little forbidden news-papers and pamphlets disguised as catalogues, religious appeals and medical advice that were thrust into my letter-box by invisible hands.    The living truth of Vienna haunted me, like the reality of one's beloved: I was always trying to enlarge my knowledge, to define it, to encompass it in all the changing facets it presented me with, forever perplexed and fascinated by it.    I wrote poems about it, and tore up more than I kept; poems in verse, and poems in prose, of which this one, now that I read it again nine years later, seems to me to hold more of the truth of that time than any other:

Seen from under the trees of the mountain slope, lying densely in the deep cleft of the hills, the myriad buildings of Vienna might be those of a dead city, with no single breathing inhabitant.    At five o'clock in the afternoon, there is neither visible nor audible sign of the many hundred thousand human beings, whose activity can never for a moment cease.

Deliberately, the mind assembles pictures to counter this decep-tion: innumerable feet, at five o'clock hurrying from work along the pavements, some with narrow high heels, some with heels broad and low, mixing with feet that move with slower, more uncertain impulse, and heels long worn away and broken; detach-ments of auxiliary police, in their drab uniforms, tramping with music over the street-crossing, while the crowded trams wait; the chatter and rattle in and around shops at closing-time; taxis hooting and an ambulance ringing its bell; the noise of printing machines and radio concerts heard suddenly from open windows; weeping, laughter, voices raised in anger.

A mile away, under the trees, all this has vanished. Even the murder of a Chancellor, the execution of a Socialist, can have happened unheard and unseen.

It is strange to imagine, under that still appearance, the despair of the bankrupt shopkeeper, or the student who knows he will find no post, the mixture of curiosity and revolt of the unemployed leather-worker, as he passes the entrance to a fashionable restaurant. And startling to remember the suffering in overcrowded prisons, the words of darkness repeated in court after court. A mile away, while the breeze ruffles the branches ever so slightly, the look of tension or wretchedness on the faces of many hundred thousand men and women, might be only the memory of an ugly dream.

And now the lights begin to come out, scattered or in groups and strings, evidence indeed of life but as inexpressive as the stars. Just so they glitter now, while the heavily armed police restlessly prowl the streets and the revolutionaries are whispering under their feet, as they would were the city echoing at last to shouts of *Freedom*, and the tramp of exiles' feet returning.

Sometimes, while I was away in England, friends would take the flat over: Stephen Spender, who had become deeply interested in Viennese underground politics since he had written his poem *Vienna*, was installed one summer, and his travel-shattered wardrobe was transformed and made new—' as if by a miracle ', he exclaimed—by Frau Chval's furiously busy hands in a couple of weeks. Various members of my family arrived to stay, and we would go off to the Salzkammergut lakes, scattered round which most of London could be found at one time or another during the season of the Salzburg Festival. I remember driving in to Salzburg very early one morning from the Attersee, to meet Rosamond, who was arriving by the express from England. It was long before breakfast, not a soul was stirring in the opalescent light, and curtains were still drawn in the inns and villas where foreigners were staying. Only, as I approached the big hotel on the Mondsee, I noticed a solitary female figure at one of the tables on the deserted terrace. As I flashed past, I recognized with amazement that this early bird was none other than Sybil Colefax, indefatigably scrawling her summonses to luncheons and teas and dinners, postcard after illegible postcard, to catch the first post.

I was so deeply absorbed in Austria in the life of the hounded and the unemployed, all those living on the furthest outskirts of fortune, that when, on these summer expeditions, I moved again amongst the personalities of English social life, familiar acquaintances from the world of London salons and country houses, I sometimes had the curious sensation of visiting a country I had known only in a vivid dream.   There, in the Austrian lakes, bringing with them their money, their jokes and the gossip of their class—the class to which I belonged by birth and education—the difference from their surroundings not obliterated but made only more striking by the adoption of a *dirndl* or a pair of *lederhosen*, they moved in a kind of protective cellophane, insulated from the deep, troubled, transforming currents of Austrian life, that roared with only the faintest of echoes beneath the confidence of their holidaying feet.   I knew I must find the connection; but I felt often like an actor who cannot remember which is play and which is reality of the two existences he leads.

One of the channels through which I tried to make the connection was *New Writing;* but that story belongs to another chapter.

# V

## THE CONSTANT ELEMENT

# I

IN 1935 my restless, confused plans for a magazine, which had haunted me ever since the success of *New Signatures*, began to crystallize. I think it was bound to happen: no one can be so obsessed by a craving without taking steps to satisfy it. Indeed, I had been obsessed for so long, and had fed myself on so many fantasies about it, and devised it in imagination in so many different ways, that I can no longer remember exactly when the precise seed that was to grow into *New Writing* was sown.

I had talked it over, in one way or another, with my sister Rosamond, with Stephen Spender, with William Plomer and many of my friends abroad; and above all with Christopher Isherwood. Since the days of *New Signatures* a great many changes had taken place in my life. My *Wanderjahren* had begun and, as I have described, I had come to know a side of life in the big European cities that was entirely new to me. I had seen popular uprisings and counter-revolutionary repressions, and I had even made a pilgrimage to Moscow with the reasonable intention of trying to understand the other side of the picture. I had made the acquaintance of many strange figures in the revolutionary ferment that called itself anti-fascism, idealists like Henri Barbusse—whose terrible, uncompromising novel of the war, *Le Feu*, seemed to me the only one I had read that really dared to tell the truth, and in that way comparable with Wilfred Owen's poems—and mysterious agents of the Comintern like Bramson, who was probably known by a dozen different names to other people and who had a habit of sitting down at the next table to one in Paris just when one had heard for a fact that he had been arrested in Berlin.

Like so many of my contemporaries, I was haunted by the feeling that time was running out before a new world war. ' How to get out of this trap? ' I noted in a journal at the time. ' How to find sanity and a clear thought again? How to defend oneself, to be active, not to crouch paralysed as the hawk descends? But there must be hundreds, thousands like myself in every town in Europe, wrestling with this nightmare.' And I was inexplicably bewitched by the idea that writers and artists had a large role to play in the struggle to prevent it. The literary side of Barbusse's anti-war movement fascinated me; *Monde* and *Vendredi*, where the politics were interspersed with stories and reportage by a group of clever young writers, including André Chamson, Paul Nizan, Jean Giono and Louis Guilloux, seemed to reach a far higher literary level than *Left Review* in England, which had certainly not attracted many of the younger writers of parts. Why should there not be a magazine in England round which people who held the same ideas about fascism and war could assemble without having to prove their doctrinaire Marxist purity? Why not a magazine to which the writers of *New Signatures* and *New Country* could contribute, side by side with writers like Chamson and Guilloux, and other ' anti-fascist ' writers from other countries? In *Left Review* the politics came, fatally, first; I wanted a magazine in which literature came first, with the politics only as an undertone. I believed it would serve the triple purpose of providing a platform for the *New Country* writers that *The Criterion*, the *London Mercury* and *Life and Letters* could not be expected to provide; of introducing foreign writers, who had excited my interest during my travels, to an English audience; and of serving as a rallying point for the so rapidly growing anti-fascist and anti-war sympathies in my intellectual generation.

It was natural that it should be with Christopher that the first schemes should be sorted out, the first steps taken. He was living in Amsterdam at the time, and invited me to visit him on my way back to England from Vienna. We had talked it over vaguely before, we had written about it in our letters, but during that visit I suddenly felt that it was no longer a pleasant daydream, but something about to become real. He promised me his own collaboration, which seemed to me essential, and agreed to help me in getting the active support of Wystan Auden and Edward Upward. One point which had nothing to do with the aims I have already mentioned was also, I think, settled on this visit: the magazine should, if possible, provide an outlet for short stories longer than most magazines were prepared to take, and also for all forms of imaginative writing in prose that were rather too unconventional in style or approach to find a home easily elsewhere. We both admired the *novelle-*length short novel that was so popular in Europe, and Christopher had in mind to write several himself; and at the back of our minds was also the possibility of publishing some of the ' Mortmere ' fantasies that Christopher was later to describe in *Lions and Shadows*. And where in England could one publish prose-poems of the sort that so many of my poet friends admired in the work of Rilke and Rimbaud and other, living, French writers? I dreamed confusedly of our magazine growing famous for publishing modern English equivalents of *Les Illuminations* and *The Notebook of Malte Laurids Brigge*. . . . I dreamed, too, of being the author of some of them myself.

For a long time we could not settle on a good name. We called it originally our ' Chapbook '; and then for a while it became ' The Bridge ', as a symbol of the work we wanted it to do in bringing together writers of our own class and writers from the working-class, writers of our own country and writers from abroad. At this distance I cannot remember what finally decided us to choose ' New Writing ', a name that had been mooted early on and then abandoned for a time; perhaps the publishers. I had had fairly close relations with The Bodley Head over *The Year's Poetry*, which I edited for 1934 and 1935 with Denys Kilham Roberts of the Authors' Society; and it was he who suggested that Allen Lane and Lindsay Drummond of that firm might be interested in my plans. To begin with, I put up the suggestion of a quarterly of about 160 pages at a fairly cheap price, 3s. 6d. or less, but Lane and Drummond found when they worked out their estimates that this was impracticable, if there was to be a provision for editorial expenses as well as payment to contributors at even the smallest reasonable fee. The letter containing this dismal news was sent to me in Vienna early in September, 1935. I had been so certain that The Bodley Head were sold on the idea that I had told Christopher that we were all set to go. I was therefore appalled at the letter, and realized that unless fairly vigorous action was taken at once all our plans would collapse.

So I packed up and returned to London as fast as I could;
and by the end of the month we had come to an agreement, and
the project emerged as a book in stiff covers which was to
appear twice a year with a guarantee of three numbers.    I was
given £60 a number, to cover editorial expenses (roughly
estimated at £15) and all contributors' and translators' fees.
Needless to say that sum was always exceeded by me, though I
believe that it was as much as The Bodley Head could risk on
such a venture in those days; and if it had not been for the
indulgent sympathy and provision of my mother—whom I
was able to pay back in full many years later—*New Writing*
would have been on the rocks in a very short time indeed.

The moment the agreement was in the bag, I wrote round
with the news to the authors who had provisionally promised
to contribute, and in triumph to Christopher:

> Your own contribution can be anything between 3,000 and
> 12,000 words long.    However deeply Wystan A. may have
> involved himself with the Empire-builders and their film-hacks,
> he must not be allowed to leave for our far-flung territories
> without producing something.    He will probably write it while
> you stand over him one evening.    My homage to him when he
> comes.    I think the moment has arrived for me to write to
> Edward Upward myself, now you have prepared the way.    Can
> you give me his address?    And will you find out from Stephen
> whether his contribution is finished, or nearly finished?    Put
> the pen in his hand if not.    I'm reckoning to be able to pay each
> contributor (of prose more than 3,000 words in length) at least £4
> on account of royalties.

At first I had wanted him and some others of our friends to
form a sort of Advisory Committee to be announced beside my
name.    He was against this, and had written:

> Certainly I will be most honoured to act on the advisory com-
> mittee, if you don't think my absence from England disqualifies
> me?    But let me urge you, once more, to take as little notice
> of us all as possible and be very autocratic.    I'm *sure* it's better.
> Need you, in fact, have a formal committee at all?    Why not just
> consult people informally, whenever you want an outside
> opinion?

The idea of a committee was dropped.    Christopher's advice
was, in the circumstances, with so many of us scattered so far

from each other across Europe, sound; but I am inclined to think that, apart from the ideal aspects of the matter, he had, with his usual quick perception, divined that I was likely to prove an autocrat anyway.

Gradually the manuscripts accumulated from all the sources that were available to me. I sifted a huge pile of French and German magazines and books of short stories to find works suitable for translation and authors to write to for the future. If you have rather strong ideas about the character you want your magazine to have, the first number is bound to be the most difficult. So many of the authors whose natural home it will be are still invisible to you, and will appear only when they have read or heard about your first number: the magazine then quickly acquires its own impetus, bowling along with little more needed than a firm hand on the steering-wheel, an alert eye to avoid the pot-holes and interpret the confusing sign-posts, and a hard heart to refuse to slow down for the shady individuals thumbing a lift. Even so, before make-up time arrived I found many more contributions in my hands than I could get into the limits to which The Bodley Head were sensibly determined to keep me. My suit-cases were full of them as I travelled between Vienna, Paris and London, and my mind contentedly revolved scheme after scheme of selection and arrangement for the first volume. I think those were some of the most happy-anxious months I have ever spent.

In spite of having abandoned the idea of an ' advisory board ', it seemed to me extremely important to get the magazine's ' Manifesto ' accepted beforehand by all the people who had formed the ' shadow committee ' in my mind: apart from Christopher, Stephen, Rosamond, William Plomer and Ralph Fox—who had promised to help over modern Russian literature (about which he knew a great deal more than any of us) and to introduce me to some of the French contributors to *Monde* and *Vendredi*. When it came to putting our aims into words, I found the problem a good deal trickier than I had envisaged. Almost everyone had objections and suggestions about the draft I made, and rightly; in the end, deciding that some definition, some pointer to the direction in which I intended to go, was better than none, not satisfied, but hoping that controversy over the manifesto would be more likely to stimulate interest than choke off potential readers or future contributors, I put this on a page by itself at the head of the first number:

NEW WRITING will appear twice yearly, and will be devoted to imaginative writing, mainly of young authors. It does not intend to concern itself with literary theory, or the criticism of contemporaries.

NEW WRITING aims at providing an outlet for those prose writers, among others, whose work is too unorthodox in length or style to be suitable for the established monthly and quarterly magazines. While prose will form the main bulk of the contributions, poetry will also be included.

NEW WRITING is first and foremost interested in literature, and though it does not intend to open its pages to writers of reactionary or fascist sentiments, it is independent of any political party.

NEW WRITING also hopes to represent the work of writers from colonial and foreign countries.

The third paragraph, I see now, was all too imperfectly expressed, and only indirectly contained my intention, which was to appeal to all those writers to whom, in the catastrophic impasse of the 'thirties, Keats's famous lines applied:

> Those to whom the miseries of the world
> Are misery, and will not let them rest.

It brought me some sharp raps over the knuckles when the reviews began to come in; but the ' Manifesto ' as a whole succeeded in arousing the controversy I had looked for.

## 2

FAR more abundantly than any of us had hoped, *New Writing* was a success. In its ingenious, multi-coloured poster-jacket devised by Edward Young, it began to sell, it was talked about, it was reviewed at length, more often than not with an enthusiasm that surprised us. There were slaps and buffets too: Cyril

Connolly in the *Daily Telegraph* gave me an admirable little lecture on the place of propaganda in art, dubbing my offending third paragraph ' disingenuous ', while Geoffrey Grigson snarled in the *Morning Post* that it was ' sad jargon '. Nevertheless, most of the critics agreed that *New Writing* had avoided the crudities of propaganda and justified its claim to be interested in imaginative writing before politics. I longed to offer the minority who did not agree a copy of the Russian *Internationalnaya Literatura*, or one or other of the continental magazines of the same sort, to show them what happened when the order of priorities was reversed.

In recent years a fashion has grown up for authors to be asked to reply to their critics in long articles. Though this practice offers dangerous pitfalls for the author with a grievance, it has its advantages: if he has some reputation or the book has created a stir, the very diversity of reviewers' opinions brought together and contrasted in this way is fascinating in itself. Looking through the early press-cutting books we kept for *New Writing*, I have felt as if I had suddenly found myself back in a room where a babble of discussion was going on; discussion that was still interesting for the light it threw on the times and for the effect it had on the fortunes of an enterprise that was to last, in one transformation after another, through the next fifteen years. Of course *The Nowaks*, as it justly deserved, received bouquets from everyone; but there were many strands woven together in the book, and it gratified us to see one critic seizing on the opportunity it provided for long short stories as the most interesting thing about it, another on the inclusion of so large a proportion of foreign writers, one on the realism he found to be the keynote of many of the contributions, another on the imaginative intensity that struck him in other contributions. It was heart-warming to be told by the *New Statesman* that if we could ' keep up this standard *New Writing* will deserve the sales of all our other literary periodicals together ', and by V. S. Pritchett, professionally spotting that the way things were said was as important in our intention as what was said, that ' there is in nearly all these pieces a refreshing speed and vigour of narrative which are what the English novel had lost '. But what encouraged us most was the recognition, in so many of these reviews, that we had succeeded in our object of making our readers realize that there was a new awareness among imaginative writers which transcended frontiers, an awakened conscience and interest that impelled them to look for their material in new fields, and produce, as Ifor Evans said in the *Manchester Guardian*, ' a literature arising from the violent conflicts of human life in our time ', even when it was only by implication, as in the reactions of the tutor in Edward Upward's piece to the stuffy household in which he was employed. The *Methodist Times* sadly observed that ' there is scarcely a gleam of simple beauty '; a remark that I must admit I found almost as satisfactory as the long estimate of the book's intention which *The Times Literary Supplement* printed, and which still seems to me to interpret with extraordinary insight the fundamental impulse behind it:

> That, the conception of an effective brotherhood born between victims of oppression, is the constant element, or the nearest to a constant element, which gives this miscellany its claims to unity. The oppression takes various forms—sometimes it is war, sometimes it is fascism, sometimes the social system, sometimes human nature or even the hard earth itself; but always it is this sense of broader comradeships breaking through the hard skull of confining, destroying individualisms, which is the basic creative thing, ' a new life bursting through the old. . . .' Whatever the limitation in this case or that, the impulse is there, giving direction, movement and force to these stories, manifesting itself as ease and power of narrative. For in the best of the items emotional identification—the essence of brotherhood—is no mere aspiration; the writer himself has experienced it, entering into the lives of his characters.

We were lucky on the whole in our reviews, especially at the beginning, and those which showed an imaginative sympathy with what we were aiming at gave me confidence even when they were critical. I have an obstinate nature, and I doubt if I was often deflected by its public critics to one side or other of the path I thought *New Writing* should take; I made my own discoveries of faults in my own time, and I was more likely to be swayed by the private advice of those whose judgement I respected and solicited; but I remained inordinately sensitive to the tone of the reviews nevertheless. A thoroughly hostile review, and I began at once to wonder whether it would not be better to give the whole thing up after all; a praising review followed, and my needle swung back to Set Fair in an instant.

Sometimes when a batch of reviews had arrived by the morning post in Vienna, I would take them with the rest of my mail to the café round the corner, and study them with manic-depressive anxiety over a *mokka*. 'We should ask ourselves, for the sake of lucidity and order, whether this documented fiction is fiction at all, or a red herring trying to pass itself off as a grilled sole.' *Down.* . . . '*New Writing* sets itself apart; it does not describe the bright and easy world of the successful magazine tale. These, rather, are stories in which the authors' teeth have been set on edge.' *Up.* . . . 'The temporary amorality of the junior fictionists makes their work strangely juiceless.' *Down (though a trifle bewildered).* . . . 'The outspoken or imaginative author has, today, about as much chance of getting into the average editorial fortress as a convict has of getting out of Parkhurst; and my only criticism of *New Writing* is that its appearances are absurdly infrequent.' *Up again, strongly.* . . . 'New in what sense? The total effect is one of sprawling.' *Down, down.* . . . I was anxious, too, for the individual authors, as much as for the volume as a whole. When a critic in *The Criterion* said: 'Mr. Auden's fable was probably thrown off over a meal or in his bath, but bears traces of his genial sadism', I felt low again. I began to wonder whether authors blamed editors for the reviews they got, casting back in my own experience (I have since learnt how strong the impulse to blame publishers is, if a book is badly received). I held on to a letter that had just come in from one author: 'I think you are my patron saint. Since you published my story, people publish as much as I write. . . .' The faint halo of a patron saint banished the doubts about Auden, the gloom caused by that nasty word 'sprawling'. I felt strong enough to go back to that pile of manuscripts upstairs in my flat, and polish off a dozen of them before luncheon.

# 3

THE contribution in which the *T.L.S.* had found that the
spirit seemed to crystallize ' most forcibly of all ' was a long
Chinese story by Tchang T'ien-Yih, *Hatred*, which I had put
last in the volume.   I had discovered it in a French magazine,
and had been deeply impressed by the simplicity and power
with which it described the sufferings of peasants and soldiers
somewhere in the huge spaces of China, at some timeless
moment in what seemed an eternal civil war: almost unbearable, so absolutely naked of all inessentials, and yet so
beautifully done, so full of human feeling and at the same time
so completely without sentimentality that it seemed to me a near
perfect example of writing that drove its implicit lesson home
far more effectively than any straightforward propaganda could,
by being a work of art.   I decided to translate it myself; and
discovered a new pleasure in the quiet, semi-creative work that
this provided me with.   The work was rewarded by the
impression the story made; but it would have been worth it if
only for the fact that I did it myself to my own satisfaction.
For with the first number of *New Writing* my long, still truceless
war with translators had begun: as time went by and more
numbers came out, I found myself increasingly irritated by the
frivolity of those who contracted to do translation work for me,
or even solicited it with a parade of plausible credentials.
There were exceptions, of course—and John Rodker, who did
supremely well the English versions of André Chamson's
stories, and my sister Rosamond, who contrived to make a
little translating masterpiece out of Jean Cassou's *Letter to
Cousin Mary*, were among those I most gratefully remember—
but again and again, after hours of laborious checking with the
original and days of correspondence about small but vital points
not only of exact meaning but also of English idiom, I was
reduced to wishing I had saved time and exacerbation by
tackling the job myself.   The exchange of letters would run
something like this:

*J. L. to Translator:* I wonder whether you would have another look at pages 3, 4, 6, 7 and 8 of your translation of so-and-so's story? I have marked a number of small points that are worrying me: you will see in the margin that I sometimes query for accuracy (I don't pretend of course that my knowledge of French/German/Italian is anything like as thorough as yours), and sometimes also for the sound of the phrase *in English.* For instance, doesn't ' fils ' mean *son,* and not *threads* on p. 6? Again, on p. 3, doesn't ' it was inescapable for him to gain the wherewithal of his daily butter ' sound just perhaps a little clumsy in English?

*Translator to J. L.:* Thank you for your letter. I'm sorry you should be so pernickety about my translation. I can assure you I *sweated blood* over it. Monsieur So-and-so is one of my oldest admirers and friends, and has always expressed complete confidence in me—I can show you the letters. Nevertheless, I have carefully thought over your objection to my rendering of ' fils ', and after consulting a number of authorities, have decided that perhaps in this case you *may* be right. At the same time I should like to point out the admirable hint of veiled obscurity the rendering ' threads ' gives the passage. As for your second observation, I really cannot believe it was serious. How can you not have seen that my typist left out ' bread and ' before ' butter '? I'm afraid I have had to reject the other suggestions you made in the margin.

*J. L. to Translator:* It was good of you to make that change about ' fils '. I hope you won't mind me having made one or two other small alterations here and there. My publishers were, by the way, most insistent about this. You will of course see these in proof and be able to challenge them. Again, my warmest thanks.

*Translator to J. L.:* I received the galley proofs of my translation last night, and was so indignant I could scarcely sleep. I tell you this frankly, as it is a serious matter in view of my long friendship with Monsieur So-and-so. You mentioned ' one or two small alterations ', but I find that quite extraordinary liberties have been taken with my text. I prefer to think that the worst is really the work of your publishers, who are obviously ignorant philistines. Anyone will tell you that I am an extremely broadminded and tolerant person; but if this is how an editor's function is to be interpreted by you, I cannot collaborate in the future. It is not worth the annoyance and sleeplessness. P.S. I have restored ' threads ' for ' son '. So-and-so is a much *subtler* writer than you have guessed.

It is true that most of my trouble with translators occurred in later years; and if my strictures may appear ungrateful to the many enthusiasts who worked for *New Writing* with all too small return, I am sure that those who did good work will know very well already, from my letters, that I appreciated it. Nevertheless, in nearly twenty-five years of editing and publishing I have been appalled at the lightness of heart with which Tom, Dick and Harriet will present themselves as capable translators, and even more appalled at the success some of them have had in getting their grotesque travesties of distinguished foreign authors printed. Translation is an art, not a cosy pastime for those who want some excuse to live abroad: this was borne in on me with peculiar force during the early years of *New Writing*, as the plan depended so much on introducing writers from abroad, and suggesting a movement, or mood, that was common to many countries and many languages. With No. 1 I was working to some extent in the dark—for like would soon attract like when people could see in front of them what kind of a magazine I was trying to create—but I had good helpers in Christopher, Stephen and Ralph Fox, and there were three German stories, by Alfred Kantorowicz, Egon Erwin Kisch and Anna Seghers, one anonymous Italian story, two Russian stories, by Nicolai Tikhonov and Nikolai Ognev, and one Russian poem, and André Chamson's *My Enemy* from France as well as the Chinese story to take their place in that first number beside Ralph Bates's *The Launch*, Christopher's *The Nowaks*, Stephen's translations and poems, Edward Upward's *The Border-Line*, William Plomer's *Notes on a Visit to Ireland* and several other English stories. As yet nothing from America or any other English-speaking country overseas— that was to come later—but enough from abroad to set the international stamp on it quite firmly. I may even have toyed for a time, in the early planning stages, with the megalomaniac idea of creating a new international literature. I was brought down to realities out of such insubstantial clouds by Ralph Fox, who, when recommending various writers and editors for me to get hold of in Paris, said: ' Are you clear what you want to do? Is it something new for European literature you're after, or something new over here? ' It was a few seconds before I answered: ' No, of course it's English literature I want to do something about.' It was a salutary shake he gave me: it helped to keep my compass pointing more steadily in the years to come.

# 4

LOOKING back through the early volumes, it seems to me that the reputation I gained for introducing entirely new names was not altogether justified.   I did publish some first poems and stories by unknown writers (though many more later, during the war); but my success, such as it was, lay rather in creating a kind of magnetized area round the magazine which attracted the best from young writers who had already begun to be known, and manuscripts that had failed to find a home but were destined, when published in *New Writing*, to bring their authors fame.   I still think *The Nowaks* (which was too long for any other magazine and was written specially for me out of the fragments of the great unfinished Berlin novel, *The Lost*, left over when *Mr. Norris Changes Trains* had been made into a separate novel) is the best thing Christopher Isherwood ever wrote.   I felt that I had brought off a small coup in landing André Chamson's *My Enemy* for the first number:  everyone praised it, E. M. Forster remarking that ' when the French do remember their boyhood it can be quite extraordinary ', and Christopher that it ' makes one feel that a real artist can write about absolutely anything and still produce all the correct reflections about fascism, nationalism, etc. in the reader's mind, a trite observation but it always comes as a fresh surprise '.   The fun, however, really began when No. 1 had been widely read and discussed.   Encouraged by the opportunity *New Writing* gave him, Christopher had started to work as hard as he could on turning the remainder of the wreckage of *The Lost* into stories.   ' There is another section of *The Lost* ready,' he wrote before he had seen more than the contents list of No. 1, ' about an English girl who sings in a Berlin cabaret, but I hardly think it would suit the serious tone of *New Writing*.   It is rather like Anthony Hope: The Dolly Dialogues. It is an attempt to satirize the romance-of-prostitution racket.' It was not, however, till the end of October that *Sally Bowles* reached me, and though I was enthusiastic and did not agree in the least that it was too frivolous for *New Writing*, there was a difficulty about its length. Some futile proposals for cutting it were discussed and (luckily) abandoned, and in the end I published instead the first part of the *Berlin Diary*, which Christopher described as ' only mildly dirty ': *Goodbye to Berlin* was slowly taking shape.

As soon as No. 1 was out, however, Christopher began to blossom with ideas. ' Now I must really try and earn that extra guinea as member of advisory com. ! ' he wrote from Portugal. ' What about publishing, at long last, Upward's " Railway Accident "? Wystan tells me he quotes it often at lectures—sometimes very extensively—and that the bowdlerisation needed would be very slight: but after all it is one of the most magnificent pieces of narrative prose produced since the war.' And again a few weeks later: ' The Accident is pretty long. A good 15,000 I should say. But I do hope you'll print it, if it can be revised: not merely for his sake and art's sake, but because I have a quite vulgar hunch that he is about to be " discovered " with a resounding to-do.' *The Railway Accident* was the last and the most elaborate of the ' Mortmere ' fantasies, as Christopher explains in *Lions and Shadows*, and certainly the most brilliant; evidence of an imaginative gift in ' Chalmers ' the fate of which one will never cease to mourn, slowly killed in the Iron Maiden of Marxist dogma. Upward, however, in spite of my persuasions, came down against publishing it; and it was only many years later that it was printed in full in America by James Laughlin. I tried again and again to get Upward to contribute more, reminding him of the interest that *The Border-Line* in No. 1 had aroused; but nothing would deflect him from the job of completing the novel,* of which that contribution formed the first part, the slow Laocoon-like tussle with the symbolic presentation of the philosophical problem underlying it.

Meanwhile, other contributions were being brought in by

* *Journey to the Border.*

the wave *New Writing's* publication had created. It was an exciting morning when George Orwell sent me a short piece, which has since become as famous as anything he wrote, called *Shooting an Elephant.* Urged on by Christopher, and full of admiration for *Burmese Days,* I had written asking him to contribute (I do not know whether he remembered the ardent fan of his football prowess fifteen years before), and he wrote to me in answer:

I waited before answering your letter, as a friend in London was endeavouring to get me a copy of *New Writing,* but evidently she hasn't succeeded yet. What I was going to say was, I am writing a book at present and the only other thing I have in mind is a sketch, (it would be about 2,000–3,000 words), describing the shooting of an elephant. It all came back to me very vividly the other day and I would like to write it, but it may be that it is quite out of your line. I mean it might be too lowbrow for your paper and I doubt whether there is anything anti-Fascist in the shooting of an elephant! Of course you can't say in advance that you would like it, but perhaps you could say tentatively whether it is at all likely to be in your line or not. If not, then I won't write it; if you think it might interest you I will do it and send it along for you to consider. I am sorry to be so vague but without seeing a copy of *New Writing* I can't tell what sort of stuff it uses.

Encouraged by this letter, I sent him a copy of the first number of *New Writing* at once. It found favour with him, and a fortnight later the typescript of *Shooting an Elephant* was in my hands. Equally rewarding was the morning when V. S. Pritchett, who had written such a generous and perceptive review of No. 1, offered to send me a story which he told me had no hope of being accepted by other editors:

I've got a story I want to send you for *New Writing* but I'm not sure whether you want to see unsolicited MSS. It's about 7,000 words long and this and either its manner or its subject or both, give it little chance as far as I can see with the monthly reviews. May I send it to you? We met, if you remember, at the *New Statesman* the other week. I was covered in books and bottles. If you are this way come in and have a drink one evening. Give me a ring. I've just been reviewing your book in the *Fortnightly Review* and I liked it immensely. Thank God, no editorial notes!

The story arrived, and I immediately wrote Pritchett an enthusiastic letter of acceptance. I apologized that I could only offer him a fee of three guineas, a miserable payment by to-day's standards but all I could provide out of what my publishers gave me. There was also a problem about the title, as another contributor had already staked a claim in his original title. He wrote back:

> I'm very glad you liked ' The Commercial Traveller ' and that you are going to put it into *New Writing*. The fee is all right—that is to say, it's damn little for weeks of hard work, but the people who pay me 15 and 20 guineas for stories would certainly not publish this one; and then I don't like their magazines as well as I like *New Writing*! So go ahead. And call it ' Sense of Humour ', if the other chap sticks to his title. This is perhaps more acutely descriptive. When does the next number appear?

After that, Pritchett became a close friend and collaborator, and we published several of his most remarkable short stories, including his masterpiece *The Sailor*, which was not only greatly admired when it appeared in *New Writing*, but seemed as fresh as ever, and almost completely stole the applause in many reviews when it was reprinted in *English Stories from New Writing* after the war. But it was not only such ' realism ' I was after, though to break with the ' mandarin ' style, to support bold experiments in the ' vernacular ', was one of our chief aims. When I went to see Cecil Day Lewis at his country home, to persuade him to write for us, he told me that his friend Rex Warner had written a novel, *The Wild Goose Chase*, in a fantastical or allegorical manner, and was finding great difficulty in getting anyone interested in it. We persuaded Rex—whom I did not meet personally for some years—to pick out one or two more or less self-explanatory episodes for *New Writing*, and I remember feeling, when they came in, that an entirely new event, comparable with Edward Upward's *Journey to the Border*, was taking place in the imaginative writing of our time. Upward was trying, by the use of shifting images of reality, to present an upheaval of thought occurring within the mind; Rex Warner, by the use of even more highly-charged dramatic symbols, to work out an allegory of contemporary politics in action outside the mind; taken together they seemed to add a new dimension to the novel. *The Football-Match* was printed in No. 2 with Pritchett's *Sense of Humour* and Orwell's *Shooting an Elephant*, and soon after, under the impetus of this acceptance, the whole novel was bought and published by Boriswood. When it came out, this novel, which, like *The Memorial*, had had so much difficulty in pushing to the light, was treated by the press, and *The Times* in particular, as a work of the most disturbing significance. I can still remember the extreme surprise—and equal satisfaction—I felt, as I sat in a Viennese café one morning and read the long review, almost a whole column, which *The Times* devoted to it.

Another young writer, of just the kind of talent and promise we were on the look out for, whom the appearance of the first volume of *New Writing* led to me in those early days, was Tom Hopkinson, then Assistant Editor on *Weekly Illustrated* and married to Antonia White, the author of that harrowing, brilliant novel *Frost in May*. When I read the manuscript of *I Have Been Drowned* I was struck by the terse, dramatic simplicity of the way it was written and the extraordinary imaginative intensity with which the experience of drowning was described. Tom, however, had never been on the point of drowning: this he confessed to me, to my astonishment, very soon after I had got in touch with him. Three years before, he told me, he had been seized, as he was walking along by the river, with the desire to possess a boat. When he bought one, he did not even know how to moor her up, or put the sails on the spars, or start the engine; but he gradually taught himself and began to sail in the Thames between Chelsea and the sea. The key to the story was that he was a bad swimmer, and was constantly obsessed, whenever there was bad weather on these expeditions, with the idea of death by drowning. Once he had fallen into the water, and had had a struggle to get back into the boat: from that moment he felt not so much a wish as an urgent need to write about being drowned. When I heard this story, I felt even more certain of Tom's promise as an imaginative writer.

# 5

THE success of *New Writing* was crucial for me.  I felt that I
had at last justified my decision in breaking with the Hogarth
Press, at last fulfilled a life-long ambition, and had also done
something which was specifically mine in the common effort
we felt we were all engaged in towards a solution of the crisis
and tragedy of the 'thirties.  Since leaving London I had not
only continued to review for *The Listener*, *The Adelphi* (then
under Richard Rees's sympathetic editorship) and other
literary periodicals, but I had also begun to write a great many
articles for various papers on Austrian and Central European
affairs: I had wanted the outside world to know what it felt
like to be in the desperate situation of the Viennese after the
collapse of the February Rising, and turned myself into a
journalist to make my own contribution to this missionary work.
This was the ' open ' side of the work which had its ' underground ' side in the information I collected from the political
agents hunted by the police.  I happened to feel very strongly
about it, and believed I knew more intimately what was going
on below the surface than most other writers;  but while
journalism was the job of many others more efficiently trained
for it and experienced at it than I was, *New Writing* came out
of my own special capacities and interests.  It also seemed to
me that it could do more than any poem—any poem that I
could write—in the short time still left to us.  The fatal error
made by so many thinkers from Plato to Wells, Edward
Sackville-West once observed when discussing *New Writing* in a
sympathetic review, is to imagine there is anything better to
be than a poet.  Deep down, in my heart, I knew this to be
true;  yet I felt that poetry was a channel through which only
part of my energies could flow, for the channel was not broad
enough;  and I sometimes reminded myself of Thomas Lovell
Beddoes' remark: ' Apollo defend us from brewing all our
lives at a quintessential pot of the smallest ale Parnassian.'
When the preparations for *New Writing* were being made I

remember feeling a curious sense of repose and relief at the broad channel being at last discovered. And the success filled me with an extraordinary sense of explosive power; but a power that used me rather than a power I had developed myself. Always at the back of my mind was what was perhaps the most important discovery of all those I had made in my years of turning myself into ' the Shadow ' among the submerged masses of Central Europe. Talking with Karl and his friends of the Social-Democrat movement, and with the unpolitical younger generation I came to know through Toni and his family, again and again I was struck by their eagerness to understand, to take part, to rifle the honeycombs of civilization's knowledge and power, to learn to enjoy in art and literature what we of the fortunate educated classes enjoyed as our birthright. There were times when it seemed to me like an irresistible force of water slowly piling up against a dam, and filled me with feelings of alarm and wonder at the same time : alarm because of the power it gave to false prophets and self-seekers to deflect it for their own evil purposes, wonder for the sheer beauty of the instinct and desire behind it, the potentialities of creative renovation that stirred in its darkness.

For the next few years, *New Writing* controlled my movements; when I journeyed across Europe I was in search of new contributors or new collaborators, whether in Paris, or Prague, or Amsterdam, or Moscow, or Tiflis, whether working in London or Vienna, the two poles of my wanderings. My earlier ambitions still remained, but rather, now, as an undertone to all this editorial activity. The political idea, however, continued to be strong; and I was to make many mistakes, when I failed at first to see that an author whose political attitude was exactly what I sympathized with was not, from the point of view of creative power, a good author. And yet, I believe, I was constantly saved from the worst excesses of ' political literature ', which flourished so rankly in many periodicals of the time, by a deeper instinct—or perhaps a deeper wish—to be pleased rather than to be edified. My response to imaginative literature has always been more instinctive than intellectual; and confronted with some new poem or story that bothered me ideologically, I could never resist it in the end if it excited me, if it seemed to me to break new ground imaginatively; though I would sometimes invent farcical pieces of casuistry to justify my ideological qualms.   When I first read the stories of Jean-Paul Sartre (whom Ralph Fox had mentioned to me), the impact on my imagination was terrific and I felt it was absolutely necessary to enrol him as a contributor; we eventually published *La Chambre* in John Rodker's translation; but I remember one morning in Paris, saying rather anxiously to Paul Nizan, his great friend: 'I suppose one could call Sartre a humanist?'—and Nizan, with a grin spreading over his face, flashing back: 'If you do, you'd better not tell him!'   I remained suspect, therefore, and capable of flagrant heresy, to the exponents of the pure doctrine of socialist (or proletarian) realism; inarticulately aware as I was all the time—though this practical experience was helping me gradually towards a formulation—of the difference between a literature that is an interpretation of its time, and one that transforms it.

# 6

SOON after I left the Hogarth Press in 1932, I had given up my studio flat in Heathcote Street, and transferred my books and furniture to Fieldhead, where I eventually converted one of the old nurseries at the back of the house into a *New Writing* work-room.   I had, therefore, no place of my own in London, and being too awed in my early years as a member of the Athenæum to introduce my bohemian literary friends into its solemn archiepiscopal atmosphere, I used to meet them in Bloomsbury cafés, Soho restaurants and also in the little *avant-garde* Parton Street bookshop run by the ever-welcoming but tongue-tied David Archer.   There I bought the first, slim green collections of poems by Dylan Thomas and George Barker long before I met either of them, and was taken by Ralph Fox next door to visit the publishing offices of Lawrence and Wishart, where the poet Edgell Rickword (whose *Invocations to Angels*, since sadly neglected, I had long known and admired) was always to be found sunk in profound and almost wordless gloom. One day I was browsing among the books, when I was suddenly confronted by a small fresh-faced youth, in whose expression innocence and truculence were curiously mixed, professing eagerness to write for me: he turned out to be Esmond Romilly, then in the first flush of his defiance of the Public Schools, with a copy of *Out of Bounds* in his pocket.

Archer's bookshop was also the rendezvous where I at last came together with Rex Warner, who looked—to my first, surprised but admiring glance—more like one of the powerful three-quarters in his own *Football-Match* than the author of it, as I had imagined him; and with David Gascoyne, in whose company, after a shy, rather limp hand had been offered me with an almost inaudible mutter, I retired for tea over the road. David was at that time only twenty or so, but was already the author of a novel and a number of poems that had been published in various London papers. He was particularly interested in the French surrealists and wanted to prepare some translations for us from that phase of surrealism where it suddenly embraced revolutionary doctrines. We had planned a surrealist section, but it all came to nothing, partly because (I must frankly admit) the French poems did not seem to me all that good, partly because we failed to get Edward Upward to contribute *The Railway Accident* and there seemed to be no other English author sufficiently identified with the movement. Unlike English painting (though even there only to a small degree), English poetry never took kindly to surrealism, in spite of the strong 'nonsense' tradition in the nineteenth century; David's own poems of that period have remained an almost completely isolated 'sport'. His first contribution to *New Writing* was his short poem *Snow in Europe*: a beautiful and imaginative piece of work, but which only faintly foreshadowed the philosophical and mystical preoccupations that were to give his poetry its extremely rare and individual flavour. David himself, tall, broad-shouldered but excessively slim and slightly bowed, with his beautifully regular oval face and large, greenish-grey eyes in which sparks of light flickered as the tumble of his conversation gathered speed, following his thoughts like the spray of a fountain tossed by contrary gusts of wind, gave me the impression at one moment of an ultra-æsthetic poet as imagined by the cartoonists of the 'nineties, at another of a hunted hare. The introspective suffering of a highly strung sensibility was in his expression when in repose (and how rarely it was in repose), but would suddenly give place to a look of darting, malicious humour—an element that emerged in his poetry only at a later date. His hands attracted one's attention at once, with their long, elegantly articulated fingers. He has described them himself in his poem *The Writer's Hand*:

> . . . See my hand
> The only army to enforce your claims
> Upon life's hostile land: five pale, effete
> Æsthetic-looking fingers, whose chief feat
> Is to trace lines like these across the page:
> What small relief can they bring to your siege!

I did not see David again until two or three years later, in Peter Watson's apartment in Paris. He seemed then overcome by his nervous tension, unable to get anything out at all because so acutely anxious to define his subtle metaphysical meanings with precision; but perhaps he was in fact nervous as well, as someone in a neighbouring apartment had given a fire-alarm and the firemen, mistaking the address, suddenly burst into Peter's sitting-room in their enormous brass helmets, waving axes and making the floor shake with their ponderous, booted steps. We all rushed about looking for the fire, except David, who remained quivering and silent on the sofa in the midst of this vortex of purposeless activity.

It may seem strange that poetry played such a very small part in the earliest volumes of *New Writing*. I had, after all, started as a poet, poetry meant more to me than any other form of literature, and my first action as a publisher to present the writers of my generation had been the anthology of poetry, *New Signatures*. And yet in the first volume of *New Writing*, apart from Alec Brown's translation of Pasternak's long poem *1905*, only Stephen Spender was represented by poems, and three out of the four were translations from Hölderlin. In the second volume there were no poems at all, though Wystan Auden was represented by his ' cabaret sketch ' *Alfred*.

This was partly because, when I launched *New Writing*, I believed prose to be much more important for my purpose than poetry. It was in prose that the idea of ' an effective brotherhood born between victims of oppression ' and the ' sense of broader comradeships ' was most clearly to be traced, especially in its international parallels; modern English poetry, at that moment, seemed to me to be following a more complex ideal, in which the champion influences of Eliot, Hopkins and Rilke fought against the transparency I looked for (and found) in prose, and the ideas of Freud and Lawrence—and perhaps Groddeck and Homer Lane as well—were as important as the new ' revolutionary ' awareness that had been the theme-song of *New Signatures*. Privately, in my capacity of poet, I found this complexity and ' density ' of supreme interest, but I did not think them compatible—at any rate on the rather narrow front I proposed to break through on—with the intention of the prose. Later, as *New Writing* acquired its own momentum and became more broadly representative of all my generation's ideas, and at the same time their poetry itself performed an evolution towards the spirit of the prose, poetry was to come into its own. But the domination of prose at the beginning was also due to the fact that the poetry of my contemporaries already had its own magazine, Geoffrey Grigson's brilliant, eccentric, inestimably valuable *New Verse*, the first number of which had come out in January, 1933, offering twenty pages of poems and criticisms about poetry for ' 6*d*. every two months '. The strong, mustardy flavour that *New Verse* very soon acquired, and maintained throughout its existence, was as much due to the violence of its Editor's prejudices, and the nervous polemical fury with which he expressed them, as to his absolute devotion to the interests of (what he admired in) modern poetry. Its aim was entirely non-political; but it is an amusing comment on the mood of the times that so large a proportion of the poems sent in for the first number were so unequivocally revolutionary in tone (including Wystan Auden's *Poem* and Cecil Day Lewis's extracts from *The Magnetic Mountain*) that Grigson was obliged in his second number to insist that ' if there must be attitudes, a reasoned attitude of toryism is welcomed no less than a communist attitude '.

Nevertheless, by the time I was preparing the third volume for press, more poetry had come my way and more poets who felt strongly that they belonged to the world of *New Writing*. No. 3 presented seven poets, including three Spaniards and a Pole; and from that time on poetry played an essential part. Some of the best poems by Stephen Spender, Cecil Day Lewis, Louis MacNeice (including his beautiful *June Thunder* and *Meeting Point*) appeared in the eight volumes that had been published by the time the war broke out; but by far the largest number of poems by any single author were from Wystan Auden. I had started with what many people (myself included) still think one of his most beautiful and original poems, *Lay your sleeping head, my love*, in No. 3; and in No. 4 came *Under the fronds of life* and the extraordinary ballads *Miss Gee* and *Victor*—perhaps a little too much of the ' genial sadism ' in the former, but the latter would have made any poet's name immediately and sensationally if he had written nothing else: in Wystan's case it showed only another extension of the scope and inexhaustible fertility of his genius. All these poems came to me copied out on long foolscap sheets in Wystan's minute, squashed handwriting, more like the recordings of a highly sensitive seismograph while a road-drill was breaking up the street outside than an attempt at human communication. We rose to a bumper harvest of eight in the seventh volume, and from America he sent me three, including the famous *In Memoriam Ernst Toller* and *Refugee Blues*, for the eighth and last volume of the new series, published only when the war had already broken out.

Reading through these poems of Wystan's again, I am even more impressed than I was then by their variety, their intellectual power and formal skill. By the time he started contributing to *New Writing* he had outgrown the arcane doom-laden telegraphese of his first book and *Paid on Both Sides*; had passed very rapidly through the phase of the bullying, Marxist bogeyman exhortations and emerged unscathed into the clear sunlight—so clear that it is only necessary to recite two or three of them to silence anyone who complains that modern poetry is too obscure and esoteric to bother about,—the midsummer's day of his genius. In that full-flowering moment, feeling, thought and technical mastery were, it seems to me, in perfect balance; before his passion for rhetorical personification of abstractions like 'glory', 'desire', 'hunger', 'the will', began to devour his invention, and the transplantation to America dried up the sensuous sap and made his utterances for a time seem more like the delphic riddling of a disembodied mind. Each of these astonishing poems was a new discovery about the world we lived in, and seemed to illuminate whole stretches of experience that had lain in a kind of twilight confusion before; disturbing, as all good poetry must be, to accepted ideas and habitual sentiments, by the unexpectedness of its psychological insight—not merely into the behaviour of individuals but also of classes and nations—and the images it brought together to act as symbols for that insight. There was a kind of dismay mixed with my delight as the foolscap sheets came in: I envied as well as admired the smoothness with which the cylinders of his poetic engines worked, compared with the pinking, backfiring and sudden total non-functioning of my own—even though I knew I was after something rather different. Other poets of this century may have shown more fastidious care in the polishing of the texture of their poems, line by line, and the proportioning of the architecture of the whole, than Wystan with his Byron-like exuberance and fluency; some may have penetrated deeper into their specialized areas of experience; but none, I believe, has shown such an extraordinary capacity to speak through poetry, with a poet's vision, about the whole of life. The vision of his generation was, in fact, largely formed by him; and if one has been more often than not disappointed in the poets who have come after him it is, I think, because they have lacked this particular power that every generation needs to find in its imaginative creators, and have seemed, by comparison, for those who had lived in the age of Auden's great poetic outflowing, to be little more than neat annotators on the margin of life—and art. Auden has his weaknesses, as his critics are never tired of pointing out: his occasional slap-dash, his adolescent lapses of taste, his obsessive ideas, a fondness for the sententiousness of the pulpit that is apt to overcome him; but when I turn, in the pages of the old volumes of *New Writing*, from the lyric sublimity of *Lay your sleeping head, my love*, with the wit that counterpoints the ecstasy, to *Victor*, that transforms old ballad forms so skilfully to modern uses and contrives to extract tragic passion out of grotesque case-history, and then to the emblematic reflections of *Under the fronds of life*; from the folk-song rhythms of *Refugee Blues* that so poignantly accent the despair of the theme, to the sonnets on *The Novelist*, *Rimbaud* and *A. E. Housman* that illuminate with such unforced economy and apt symbolism, in fourteen lines, the whole complexity of difficult lives; it seems to me that each mode would be a respectable achievement for a modern poet by itself, might even be thought to be by different poets in an age that expects no miracles, if all were not united by the peculiar unmistakable cast of Wystan's imagination.

Reflecting on all these triumphant poems of Auden's, on Louis MacNiece's effortlessly airborne songs, with their colloquial freedom and gaiety—a tone of voice that he alone has discovered and no one can imitate—that carry the subtle metaphysical probings of his mind with such easy assurance, and on George Barker's highly wrought coruscating elegies; hearing the strange, half-muffled music of David Gascoyne's philosophical meditations, and delighting in the wit of William Plomer's *French Lisette*; I am struck not only by the range of achievement but also by the absence of that ' naïve radicalism ' of which the poets of the 'thirties have so often been accused by those who argue from undiscriminating general impressions or, less disinterestedly, wish to conjure away awkwardly formidable presences before they present their own shadow-shows. If you want to condemn people wholesale, it is an excellent principle to lump them together under some slogan, some half-truth that obliterates individual differences. It would be easy to compile a dunce's anthology of foolish and shallow and affected effusions by the poets of these years (one could compile a similar one from the off-moments of most of the outstanding poets of former ages), and they would sound especially ridiculous in the entirely altered conditions of today; but every artist has the right to be judged by his best, as the scientific explorer is judged by the experiments that come off, and not by the hundreds which go astray before or after; and the best that Auden and MacNeice and their contemporaries contributed to *New Writing* and *New Verse* in the brief, agitated, exciting and tragic period between Hitler's rise to power and the outbreak of the Second World War, stands for judgement as art independently of all topical considerations. ' Occasional verse ', said Dr. Johnson, ' must be content with occasional praise '; but I firmly believe that when their occasional verses have long been lost in the turbulently running waters of our time, the poets of the 'thirties will still be remembered by poems that for imaginative vitality, intellectual backbone and innovating technical resourcefulness—for the creative power of the word—have certainly not been excelled, and only rarely equalled, by their successors.

# 7

THE British contributors who met in the pages of *New Writing* could be roughly divided into two teams: those who, like Christopher, Stephen, Wystan, George Orwell and James Stern, had a background of middle-class education (though not necessarily public school followed by university), and already moved to some extent in metropolitan intellectual circles; and those, like George Garrett, B. L. Coombes, Leslie Halward and Willy Goldman, who started without any of these advantages, and when they wrote of mines, seamen, factory workers or East End tailors, were writing from the inside, out of their own experiences. These I was particularly interested to encourage; it was, in my view, one of the main reasons for the existence of *New Writing* to break down the barrier between these and the other team, to provide a place of cross-fertilization of their talents. The way was hard, and the harvest was not abundant; but that we were able to publish such stories as Leslie Halward's *Arch Anderson*, Willy Goldman's *A Youthful Idyll* and George Garrett's *The First Hunger March* before the war came to obliterate so much of the distinction between the two teams, gives me the conviction that it was worth while.

One of the chief difficulties was, of course, money. Very few of these writers had anyone who could support them, even with the most meagre weekly subsidy, in fact the older ones among them generally had families which looked to them; they at all events could not afford to devote more time to learning their craft as writers than a few hours after work in the evenings, with children squealing and romping around in the clatter of dishes being washed and all the other noises and smells that cannot be escaped in crowded tenement flats with thin dividing walls. Sometimes the writer was on the dole: this provided more time all right, but made the purchase of even such minor instruments of the trade as notebooks and pens an almost impossible extravagance. I tried to devise all kinds of stratagems to get round the difficulties when I believed that the writer really had 'got something'; but I had not the means at my disposal to do more than occasionally produce a tiny allowance, as advance on a remotely envisaged fee, for a limited number of weeks. One wrote to me, with savage despair, that if he didn't get a job, or a promise of acceptance from a publisher in two or three weeks' time, he knew it would be impossible to go on; that on twenty-five shillings a week he could only produce a twenty-five-shilling job, and he knew it wasn't good enough; and that anyway he could not go on doing all the 'taking' without any 'giving' in return. Another told me that not only did he have five small boys of his own, but that next door there was a family of eight children, and above him a family of nine; and that through the ceiling and the walls he could hear not only the normal noises of boisterous tenement children, but also roller-skates, marbles, coal-breaking, firewood-chopping, the roar of the lavatories being flushed, and worst of all the piano being played out of tune. If he tried to write during the few blessed hours—being out of work— when most of the children were at school, there was a constant stream of callers, canvassers, pedlars, hawkers, rag-and-bone men, coalmen, buyers of old gold, and equally unemployed neighbours coming to pass the time of day; if he told them he was trying to write, he would merely become an object of special curiosity, and they would come all the more. If he tried to do his writing in the early hours, when everyone had gone to bed, he was too exhausted the next morning to cope with the household chores and necessary visits to the U.A.B.

Bitter was the disappointment when the writer one was trying to keep going had to throw in his hand before any work was sufficiently complete to make a proposition for a publisher. Sometimes, totally defeated and discouraged, he vanished altogether from my ken. If George Garrett, Liverpool seaman and heroic battler against impossible odds, should by any chance read these words, I should like him to know how much I have always regretted that he found it impossible to go on with what he had so vigorously begun; and I should like him to tell me what happened to him.

The ' About the Contributors ' pages of each volume were a catalogue, often, of trades extraordinary for writers: leaving school at fourteen or fifteen, they had been carpenters, die-sinkers, tool-makers, railway-men, dock-hands, plasterers, metal-turners, racing tipsters and sewer cleaners. Glamorous indeed these origins beside the humdrum acknowledgement of vain years as a private-school teacher or hack reviewer or clerk in an advertising agency, that came from the other side. There were the keen political workers, too; one young author, a dockyard apprentice, described to me his struggle to find an evening or two a week for writing against the claims of political study-circles and organizing the Labour League of Youth, door-to-door collections for ' Arms for Spain ', making speeches at the Co-operative Guild and running a stall at the Labour Party Christmas Fair. It was *not* a good programme for an intending author; but he had endless courage and energy to obscure for many years the impossibility of running three careers at the same time.

There were, of course, those who made it, in spite of all obstacles. Most remarkable of these, to my mind, most significant of the moment in English history in which he lived, was B. L. Coombes. This small, hard-bitten miner, with his small, square head, his pale, rough-hewn, serious face, was the son of a Herefordshire farmer; he had set off for Wales at the age of seventeen to work in the mines, and in his thirties had decided to take up his pen and describe, for the world to know, the life in the lost country of the coal-face, where

Many hearts with coal are charred
And few remember.

He had a wide experience to draw on : he had worked in almost every type of mine, had narrowly escaped death or mutilation many times himself, had seen others escaping—and some fail to escape. He had been in charge of the installation and working of the new coal-cutting machinery, and when I first came into contact with him was responsible for dealing with accidents underground. In Resolven he was a member of the workmen's committee, the cricket and dramatic committees, played a violin and was assistant conductor of the local orchestra. A man of quite unusual gifts, but above all the gift of imagination, which perhaps worked so freshly and vividly in him because he had come as a young countryman to the mines, his senses attuned to the clean air and green fields and slow, natural rhythms of the Herefordshire farmlands, he was plunged into the darkness of the tunnels deep below the earth where men worked in continual danger for a wage that had no relation to the endurance and skill demanded of them. After many years crowded into a squalid miner's lodging with his wife and children, forced to type in the bedroom in any odd half-hour he could snatch, he had at last got a room of his own for writing, in a lodge which belonged to an old castle. Later, when he had made his name and sold many stories and articles, and had had his autobiography *These Poor Hands* made a Left Book Club Choice by Victor Gollancz, he bought a small farm and there returned, happily, to the life from which he had started.

What struck me at once about *The Flame*, the first sketch he sent me late in 1936, was the simplicity and unforced, quiet movement of the writing with its occasional small touches that revealed the natural way of talking of the West of England. This rare quality—for men who have had no formal education beyond elementary school too often use the jargon of newspapers and the lurid style of cheap novelettes when they try to write—was allied, as story after story showed, with a capacity to make you feel exactly what it was like to be alone in a mine and see ' a thin flame—dancing and blue as the flame that one sees on a coal fire '—suddenly flicker out of the darkness and approach the end of a fuse one had just laid; or to have to gather with your mates round an obstruction in a gallery where twenty tons of coal had fallen, knowing that when you had moved it you would find the broken body of a friend underneath it:

> Griff seemed to be no more than half his usual size. Someone takes his watch from the waistcoat hanging on the side. They hold the shining back against what they believe is his mouth. Thirty yards away another stone crashes down on top of the others, and the broken pieces fly past us whilst dust clouds the air. The seconds tick out loudly through that underground chamber whilst forty men watch another holding a watch; when he turns around someone lifts a lamp near so that they can see. The shining back is not dimmed. . . .

Coombes felt very deeply about the wrongs of the miners during the years of unemployment, their neglect by the country as a whole, and the need to modernize the mines, not only to speed up production but also to reduce accidents and to make conditions more tolerable—in what is, perhaps, after all, an intolerable occupation. He was active in the political struggle to improve the miners' lot: but what was admirable in his writing was the absence of propaganda and deliberate over-painting of suffering and injustice. I was one of many who had their imagination awoken and their heart stirred by the vivid human appeal of these stories, their sensitive, un-hysterical truth with a just perceptible undercurrent of stolid bitterness; and as a story or a poem is like a pebble dropped in a pond, its effect spreading out from those—perhaps a small circle but influential in forming opinion—who are interested to read it, to hundreds of thousands who may never read it, so I believe that B. L. Coombes' writing about the lives of the miners may have had much to do with the great stirring of national conscience which eventually made the nationalization of the mines a priority no party could withstand.

One of the chief pleasures of editing *New Writing* was the discovery, not simply of individual writers, but of pockets, or fertile valleys of them hitherto unsuspected. It was good to find that the mines could throw up two such original talents as B. L. Coombes and Sid Chaplin. Hopefully, I looked for the same phenomenon appearing in other areas of industrial and working-class Britain; greedy that there should be other writers besides Willy Goldman from the East End of London and George Garrett from the ports and the sea (I published several stories by that erratic genius James Hanley, but then he had already made his name). When G. F. Green's first stories came in, both Christopher and I were eagerly interested, because we felt that here was a writer (of our own class) who could look into the minds of working-class adolescents and reproduce the flavour of the speech of his native Derbyshire in the prose of his short stories. We were disappointed that so little had as yet developed in Scotland from the impulse that Hugh Mac-Diarmid and Lewis Grassic Gibbon had given to a local literary revival—many years were to pass before it was obligatory for a literary critic to assume familiarity with Lallans. It was surely absurd that I expected so much so suddenly, but nothing could quench my faith: I was like a water-diviner walking over country where springs and wells had always been few and far between, absolutely convinced that his rod would twitch again and again. In the mines, on the sea there was something to quicken the imagination, it was natural to look for young writers in those directions; least of all did I expect that my rod would twitch over industrial Brummagem and the ants' nest home of the Austin Seven. Yet there, centred on the University where Louis MacNeice had been teaching, a group of local writers had appeared, all the more interesting and significant to me because they were outside the magic (and tyrannical) triangle of London–Oxford–Cambridge. John Hampson—who helped to lead me to this discovery—I already knew from Hogarth days; Walter Allen, whose first novel Michael Joseph were to publish a few months after I got in touch with him, had already had one or two of his stories published in *New Stories;* Leslie Halward, who had also appeared in *New Stories*, was to send me one of the best ' proletarian ' stories I ever published, *Arch Anderson*; and there were other promising talents, many of them contributors to the

*Mermaid*, the University magazine, in which later on, at the beginning of the war, I came for the first time on the work of Henry Reed, who had written a skilful and penetrating review of Auden's work.

No one, I believe, has ever satisfactorily explained how these sudden flowerings occur. It is, of course, no more mysterious that a group of people with exceptional imaginative gifts should suddenly emerge in Birmingham or Aberystwyth than in the older universities. Uncommon teachers, extraordinary books, processes of influence and opportunity too complex to unravel to the end of the skein produce a moment when Auden, Spender, Day Lewis, MacNeice, Warner, Bell, Isherwood and Empson all appear together at Oxford and Cambridge; but there, because of their centrality, and because one has the habitual expectation of an almost annual crop of talent, it seems less remarkable—at any rate until many years later. Once the process starts, however, wherever it starts, it appears to generate its own momentum, and more and more people come forward who might never have thought it worth while to develop those particular gifts in themselves—or perhaps even realized they possessed them. We had welcomed Mulk Raj Anand and Ahmed Ali as young Indian writers who held the same ideals as ourselves; we had found one or two writers of unusual gifts in the West Indies; but the British Empire is vast, and was a great deal vaster when I began to edit *New Writing*, covering in fact a quarter of the world's land surface. Why was it then that out of all the hundreds of towns and universities in the English-speaking lands scattered over the seven seas, only one should at the time act as a focus of creative activity in literature of more than local significance, that it should be in Christchurch, New Zealand, that a group of young writers had appeared, who were eager to assimilate the pioneer developments in style and technique that were being made in England and America since the beginning of the century, to explore the world of the dispossessed and under-privileged for their material and to give their country a new conscience and spiritual perspective? It was William Plomer who had first drawn my attention to a little pamphlet called *Conversation with my Uncle*, which had been sent to him by an admirer in New Zealand by the name of Frank Sargeson; and I was struck at once by the wit and the style of the short pieces, the skilful use of the vernacular idiom, and the tension between rebellion and acceptance underneath which lay an extraordinary warmth of feeling for the New Zealand scene: miles away in its attitude to the world from Katherine Mansfield, and yet unmistakably out of the same orchard. As a New Zealand critic, E. H. McCormick, was to write a few years later in his *Letters and Art in New Zealand*:

> Despite their kinship with American analogues, there is in Frank Sargeson's Kens, Toms and Neds and in their outlook something that is deeply rooted in this country. Its origins may be imperfectly seen in the letters of labouring immigrants of the 'forties and in goldfields literature, though it has rarely reached the printed page.

William Plomer himself observed that, though Sargeson owed something to Hemingway, especially in his use of repetitions and constant variations on a single thought or phrase to give a rhythmic strength to his prose, ' the lilt and rhythm are his own and not Hemingway's, nor anybody else's '.

I got in touch with Sargeson at once, and he soon became a frequent contributor to *New Writing*, as well as a delightful correspondent, his letters full of illuminating and entertaining news about his own country and lively comments about literature in England, which were especially stimulating because they came from so far outside the fashionable judgements of the metropolis. Through him I learnt a great deal about the circle of young writers of like mind who found a generous and enthusiastic patron in Denis Glover of the Caxton Press; and I eventually published poems and stories by several of them— Charles Brasch, Roderick Finlayson, Allen Curnow and A. R. D. Fairburn.

A number of other New Zealand writers, closely allied with this group, appeared during the war, perhaps the most interesting being Dan Davin, to prove again that the area of such an explosion continues to be radioactive long after its original force has spent itself. It gratified me immensely to print the New Zealanders; for not only did I want to make *New Writing* world-wide in its scope, but I was also obsessed by the conviction, based more on faith than on reason, that the climate which had produced our English, French and German writers had spread all over the world, and therefore should be ripening talents of the same flavour wherever literature was alive at all. There are, of course, several fallacies in this view which I see more clearly now than I did then; but the New Zealanders were at any rate a proof for me that I was not altogether mistaken in my faith, nor entirely foolish in my desire to be without metropolitan exclusiveness and snobbery in my responsibility as an Editor. I was less successful in my search for American contributors (though Americans were often included), partly, I think, because at that time I did not know the American scene well enough to look in the right places, partly also because so many of the American writers who were in the same line of business as my other contributors—the Hemingways, Steinbecks and Caldwells—were already famous and earning big money for whatever short stories they produced. It was a particular disappointment, because Alfred and Blanche Knopf had been interested enough to take sheets of some of the early volumes, and they had been well received. I longed to be able to mobilize the Americans round the standard of *New Writing*; and I can well remember the stab of pleasure it gave me when a spy reported that Hemingway had been observed in the Place de l'Odéon deeply engrossed in the first volume.

# 8

THE five years before the outbreak of Hitler's war was a time, fantastic in retrospect, of innumerable international writers' conferences. They were summoned to prepare a plan for a new international encyclopædia, to proclaim the solidarity of the world's writers against fascism, or with their exiled German, Austrian and Czech colleagues, or in favour of the Spanish Republicans; conferences full of dust and fury, of remorseless quarrels behind the scenes as well as upon the rostrum, which gave the opportunity to pour out a vast flood of rhetoric to those who had a fancy for making exhibitions of themselves in that way, and to weave the most elaborate and entangled intrigues behind the scenes to those who had suddenly found an outlet in them for long-suppressed political ambitions.    How few of all the hundreds of thousands of words that the over-worked multi-lingual stenographers recorded can have any validity or interest today—how devoutly many must hope that those records are lost for ever.    These conferences, exciting to some, painfully boring to others who nevertheless felt it was their duty to attend and associate themselves with the declared aims, effectively kept creative writers from creating; I never heard of a good poem or story inspired by any one of them; but they did nevertheless give heart to those who were suffering and fighting, and often collected money for them; they some-times resulted in surprising attacks on the pro-Communist line to which their organizers, or the political wire-pullers behind them, tried to keep them attached; and above all they gave writers a wonderful opportunity, in more intimate gatherings outside the conference-room, to meet interesting writers from other countries.    I treated them, I must confess, from a purely practical point of view: they made excellent opportunities for me to intensify my search for contributors to *New Writing*, and, keeping my mouth shut during the speeches and the squabbles, feeling rather ignoble and unheroically inarticulate, would mark my prey down and stalk him (or her) through the jungles of recrimination that followed among the cafés and restaurants. Wystan and Christopher managed to keep away from most of these orgies, but Stephen was an ardent and popular figure, always commanding respect by his illuminated Shelleyan look: he had the gift of taking the whole thing extremely seriously, and at the same time seeing, and exposing the comic or pretentious side with a ruthless sudden perspicacity that astonished and confused the targets of his laughter.

One of the earliest of these conferences took place in London, rather too hastily organized to be a success, and abstained from by most of the Distinguished Literary Figures of England (someone had trodden heavily on their toes), except H. G. Wells, who arrived at the end, hailed as a prize acquisition by the unsuspecting organizers: he proceeded to dynamite the whole affair with an angry, contemptuous speech. The international secretary, Etiemble, a brilliant authority on Chinese civilization, whirled in and out like a distraught wraith endeavouring to calm the gnashing of teeth for which he had not been responsible; on a distant bench I caught a glimpse of Cecil Day Lewis, stonily watching; but I remember it chiefly for my first sight of André Malraux, his pale, tense, unsmiling face with long nose and pointed chin, the downward droop to the lips, holding all eyes as he delivered his scorpion-like attacks on fuddled thinking and muddled personalities; and of British-hating Ilya Ehrenburg in action, a large, untidy figure with scowling features who made a biting speech in his characteristically humourless, sardonic vein. Ehrenburg had lived many years among the cafés of Paris in the early years of the Revolution, and seemed to me to have the crudest Frenchman's idea of English life combined with the narrowest Communist loathing of the arch-capitalist land. He was, however, prepared to modify this hatred when a new political line demanded it during the war; one must indeed take off one's hat to the skill this Kremlin lackey (or hyena?), whipper-in of the intelligentsia for his Politburo masters, has shown all these years in changing his views with every change in the Party ideology—even before the outside world knew of the change—a tight-rope act that he still survives.

Paris, as the centre not only of French intellectual life but also of the *émigré* activity of all the exiled writers from Italy, Germany, Austria, Poland, Hungary and later from Czecho-slovakia as well, was the scene of many more of these confer-ences; and in Paris I would always make a stop of a week or so on my way to and from Vienna, in order to gather material from books and magazines and look up my *copains* and *chers collègues* on *Monde* and *Vendredi* for news of new writers and new literary projects. I made great friends with André Chamson, whose watchdog pugnacity, ever ready to defend 1789 Revolu-tionary ideals, had been aroused by the fascist riots of 1934, to make him a leading spirit among the intellectual supporters of the Front Populaire and the editor-who-mattered on *Vendredi*. ' *On les aura!* ' was the dominant motive of his thought and action at the time, and by *them* he meant all the rats gnawing

away behind the arras, all the death-watch beetles at work in
the great rafters of the Republic, financial swindlers, fascist
plotters, the sly and secret friends of Hitler and Mussolini who
invisibly made their influence felt through social and political
contacts in the army, the police and the ' two hundred families '.
His pale, narrow, penknife face with its jutting, forceful chin
seemed to grow tense with passion as he talked of the dangers
that threatened his beloved France; his eyes gleamed danger-
ously under the high, intelligent forehead as he clenched his
fist and broke into a grin: ' *On les aura!* ', leaving one with a
vivid picture in one's imagination of what he would do to *them*
if they fell into his hands.   A warm Anglophile, he loved to
hear about English life and English letters, but I think he was
rather baffled by the Auden generation (like so many other
Frenchmen at the time); some esoteric complexity in their
attitude towards the crises of the age, the Freud–Groddeck
element, perhaps, mixed up with the unpredictably eccentric
English idea of a joke, was alien to a personality that had
evolved on such straightforward lines as Chamson's, with its
roots deep in the simplicities of French peasant life.   His own
writing has always drawn its strength from the directness of
his response to the simple virtues, loyalty, courage, adventurous-
ness, and the vividness with which he can convey horror or
disgust at cruelty, meanness and injustice; his stories of peasant
life and those based on the evocation of his childhood in the
*massif central* have, I believe, a touch of genius; but his handling
of themes which demanded a more complex psychological and
social interpretation has never been so sure.

Nothing, at first sight, seemed more unlikely than the friendship that united him with André Malraux, nothing more
opposed to his own extrovert nature than Malraux's brooding,
introspective obsession with destiny and spiritual fulfilment.
And yet, in spite of these fundamental differences, and beyond
a common love of art, they have always shared a profound
feeling for the importance of what St. Exupéry called, in his
famous *Letter to a Hostage*, ' the most precious fruit of our
civilization—human respect ' and the need to champion that
cause not merely by words but by action when the occasion
arose.   I felt powerfully drawn towards Malraux, and though

problems of timing and other technical obstacles always prevented me from using in the volumes of *New Writing* any
advance portion of *Le Temps du Mépris* or *L'Espoir* which he
freely offered me, I had many long talks with him during these
visits to Paris, fascinated by the flow of his political and
philosophical disquisitions, the mythopœic power with which
contemporary events were transformed in his passionate
words.

Malraux seems to me one of the key writers of our time, and
a man to whom, when one considers his activities as a whole,
one cannot refuse the title of genius. And yet I was aware,
almost from the first, that if one was to judge him strictly as a
novelist, there was something dissatisfying, some flaw or limita-
tion the importance of which I could not easily assess. I had
long debates with myself, which ran something like this:

*Prosecution:* Can you really call a novelist great, who appears to
have no sense of humour? Isn't Malraux a glaring example of
the tendency Lytton Strachey observed in so many modern
French writers—their loss of the classic French virtues of clarity
and wit, their acquisition of the worst Teutonic faults of turgidity
and inflated pseudo-philosophizing?

*Defence:* I am not sure that Dostoevsky shows very much sense
of humour in his major novels, either; but he is made great by
other qualities that outbalance that particular lack. Malraux
has irony: his sense of tragic irony is one of his most impressive
gifts. No one can really be found guilty of solemn word-flummery
who has this rare sense so powerfully developed.

*P.:* But isn't your taste offended by the constant use of such
words as Destiny, Fate, Death and Man, all (in effect) with
capital first letters?

*D.:* I must admit that I find it rather overpowering sometimes;
but I suspect that's because I am reacting from too careless a use
of these words by second-rate writers. Malraux never uses them
carelessly or shallowly: he gives them their full content. He is
not an armchair philosopher, he has tested the meaning of thought
in action, in the successive labours of his own legend.

*P.:* That may make him an interesting philosopher, but not a
good novelist. His power of creating character seems fatally
limited; the main characters in *L'Espoir*, for instance, are simply
various aspects of Malraux's own thought, of his own endless
debate with himself. They don't begin to wear that illusory

garment of flesh-and-blood reality that makes us feel that we know Mr. Micawber, or Natasha, or Raskolnikov personally.

*D.:* I am not sure that Malraux *is* a good novelist, pure and simple. He is perhaps something less—but he is also something more. And a great imaginative creator does not always show his genius through his characters. What one remembers first from Malraux's novels are certain supreme scenes of crucial significance: the prison hall scene at the end of *La Condition Humaine*, the scene in the San Carlos hospital in *L'Espoir*, the gas attack in *Les Noyers de l'Altenburg*.

*P.:* All the scenes you have mentioned are moments of great terror and physical agony. Isn't that another proof of Malraux's limitations? Wouldn't we think Shakespeare a lesser artist if we had not got Falstaff in his cups and Romeo in his ecstasy of happy love as well as Lear in his agony?

*D.:* I am not suggesting that Malraux has Shakespeare's stature. There are great geniuses and lesser geniuses. I think Malraux a genius partly because he is a writer who has imposed his own legend upon his age, as Byron and Rimbaud did—as Malraux's own favourite Lawrence of Arabia did in another way. And partly because of a belief which is inextricably involved with the scenes I chose. Malraux believes profoundly in individualism, in the individual's value and right to develop his own potentialities. But he also believes in the meaning that is given to life by the experience of human comradeship in the supreme tests—against the worst that circumstances can do.

*P.:* I'm not sure that those two faiths aren't mutually exclusive.

*D.:* On the contrary, I believe they are one of the few real hopes for our age, if they exist together: belief in individualism alone is as destructive as the belief that nothing matters except the shared experience of the mass. Malraux sees, as Wilfred Owen saw, that men realize their common human destiny, their brotherhood through suffering and endurance; but he wants that sense of brotherhood to result in a kind of society in which every man has his human dignity. And there, to my mind, is the basis of a faith, the only dynamic with which the West can challenge the East in the transformations of the twentieth century. And what writer in our time has searched more profoundly and more illuminatingly into the roots of art and its meaning for civilization? His belief that art is a means of man possessing his own destiny says so much more for me than the old classical idea of art, drama being a ' catharsis ', which has always seemed to me rather coldly clinical. . . .

Always, as this debate went on in my mind, I could see Malraux before me, his greenish, sea-creature's eyes fixed upon me under the falling lock of black hair, while a nervous twitch and sniff punctuated the electric outpouring of argument. Malraux shares with Silone, we see now that the cycle has been completed, the distinction of being one of the few European writers of the first class who acted in their own person the whole drama of modern Communist faith, and whose final disillusionment and rejection of that faith are all the more impressive and significant for the fullness of their experience. Thinking over their work in the perspective of a quarter of a century, one is, indeed, drawn to the conclusion that the experience of that cycle may have been *necessary* to make the greatest writers of our age (as a similar cycle made Wordsworth in a previous age), for it has been in the centre of the whole human and social dynamic of a generation.

Silone's perception of something being wrong, fundamentally, with Communist idealism in practice, was already evident in *Bread and Wine*. In fact, Silone had been much more closely identified with the Communist movement than Malraux, and from earliest youth, and his disillusionment antedated Malraux's. In *Bread and Wine*, Spina's realization that the Party line has nothing to do with the realities of peasant life and his growing fear that the end is being lost sight of in the pursuit of the means, are at the heart of the action. But before *Bread and Wine* appeared, I had accepted his incomparable short story, *The Fox*, brought to my notice by Gwenda David and Eric Mosbacher, the translators of *Fontamara*, and *The Journey to Paris*, less satisfactorily realized as a work of art but full of extraordinary flashes of imagination. It is an odd quirk of fate that has cheated Silone of the recognition he deserved in his own country. As he was living in exile in Switzerland, *Bread and Wine* was published in translation in the Anglo-Saxon countries before the Italians could read it in Italian, and after the war he seems to have reminded his compatriots too much of something they wanted to forget to receive his due honour. But who, apart from Malraux, is his peer among European philosopher-artists today? He has not, perhaps, the extraordinary power of

Malraux's vision of human destiny, but he has humour and also a deep sense of the continual, living reality of the Christian passion that marks him out from all other novelists. I have always regretted that I did not meet him in those days.

In Paris I also used to see Louis Aragon, whose great gifts seem to me to have remained unfulfilled because he failed to go through the spiritual evolution of Malraux and Silone. Perhaps the itch for political intrigue and combination was always too strong in him: he certainly had a remarkable flair for it, and seemed, when one visited him in his newspaper office, to be the spider controlling all the lines of the web of anti-fascist and Popular Front activity among the intellectuals. A spider of the utmost charm, sensibility and intelligence: a smile of great delicacy would illuminate his sensitive features as he talked of modern English literature, which he appeared to know as well as he spoke the English language. He had an immense admiration for Rosamond and her works, and used his subtlest powers of persuasion upon me to bring her into his web, to become a member of the Presidium of the anti-fascist writers' association, and to speak at one of the congresses in Paris. ' You must give the lie ', he would say again and again, ' to the legend that has such a hold on continental writers, that English writers are too individualist to act with their colleagues in defence of all we care about. It's nonsense—I know it to be a lie—but you must help me to prove it to the doubters.' The keen but gentle face, the beautiful grey eyes, the fine artistic hands gave little inkling of the demon of energy that drove him, that plunged him into the immense, complex and exhausting political labours of the movement, that made articles flow from his pen, rhetoric pour from his lips without cease while he was at the same time writing his gigantic novels. His cleverness was phenomenal: observing his myriad activities, reading his Communist poems of the time, one could not doubt that; and yet the poems were little more than poster-stuff, and one felt that he was too lacking in that essential artist's inner repose, repose at a deeper level, ever to create anything of the first order. When repose came, during the war, he produced at last, in his beautiful *Crève-Cœur* volume, something worthy of his gifts; while the demon, for all too brief a space of time, was in chains.

The *trahison des clercs* can act both ways; and a poet can be a traitor to his social responsibilities by neglecting poetry for politics and the vanity of the limelight of topical importance. Malraux has performed the miracle of being a politician and a creative writer at the same time, because his political action issued out of the same deeply reflected philosophical vision as his art, and because he has always possessed the artist's inmost repose and integrity.   It was impossible not to contrast Aragon with him; and with the so very different Louis Guilloux, a miniature, wiry figure with Roman nose and wide-open sailor's eyes, puffing his pipe and pushing his hand continually through his tousled black hair, as firmly convinced an anti-fascist as either but as strongly rooted in his calling as a novelist as in his Breton homeland.   Louis Guilloux was always there at the congresses and conferences, but never, it seemed to me, with the destructive urge to shine or dominate; and I remember many happy hours with him, walking up and down the Champs-Élysées, while he talked amusingly of his fellow-writers, and, with the fiery rhetoric of the politicos among them still ringing in our ears, asked me, as a question of the utmost importance and bearing, whether I thought Frenchwomen more beautiful than English; and whether I could explain the oddities of the English character—especially the English public-school character.

# 9

IT was only a few months after the first volume of *New Writing* had appeared, that the Spanish Civil War broke out; and everything, all our fears, our confused hopes and beliefs, our half-formulated theories and imaginings, veered and converged towards its testing and its opportunity, like steel filings that slide towards a magnet suddenly put near them.   For, as Stephen Spender wrote in the introduction to the anthology of *Poems for Spain* which we produced together two years later, what all felt was that ' the long, crushing, and confused process of defeat, which the democratic process has been undergoing, has been challenged in Spain, and this challenge has aroused hope all over the world '.   It is almost impossible to convey the strength of this feeling to anyone who was not subjected to the pressures that preceded the summer of 1936, the mixture of relief and apocalyptic hope that flared up as the struggle began, and made one poet, Rex Warner, write that ' Spain has torn the veil of Europe ', and another, Wystan Auden, in the most famous poem of the period :

> On that tableland scored by rivers,
> Our thoughts have bodies, the menacing shapes of our fever
> Are precise and alive. . . .

I was in Paris when the first news came through of the officers' revolt against the Republic.   I knew nothing of Iberian politics, and did not see any cause for special alarm.   But I happened, the next day, to go and see a Spanish writer then living in Paris, and found him in a state of the utmost agitation, with tears in his eyes.   ' Surely everything's going to be all right? ' I said, fumbling to offer comfort.   ' The Government'll have this under control in a few days—the news is already better.'   ' O no, no ! ' he cried.   ' You're making a great mistake.   It's extremely serious.   And it's going to be serious for everyone, for the whole of Europe.   You'll see, you'll see.'   Very soon after, this young poet returned home to fight.   He was captured by the fascists, and before the year was over I learnt that he had been shot.

When the full significance of what was happening in Spain gradually became apparent, and all the political parties, organizations, the unattached liberals, intellectuals and artists who had become aware that their own fate was deeply involved in the battles developing in front of Madrid and Barcelona, had banded themselves together to organize the International Brigade and the Spanish Medical Aid, I think every young writer began seriously to debate with himself how he could best be of use, by joining the Brigade, or driving an ambulance, or helping the active committees in England or France, or in some other way.   The pull was terrific : the pull of an international crusade to the ideals and aims of which all intellectuals (except those of strong Catholic attachment) who had been stirred by the fascist danger, felt they could, in that hour of apocalypse, whole-heartedly assent. It is strange, in retrospect, to see how the pattern of 1914 repeated itself, as it were in a different key. In 1914 the emotion had been the most idealistic patriotism identifying itself with a crusade against tyranny; which gradually succumbed to disillusionment as the war proceeded, as the realities of the carnage became known and doubts about the purity of the motives of the Allies mingled with the soldiers' feeling of fraternity with the soldiers in the opposite trenches. Rupert Brooke to Wilfred Owen: and the intellectuals, seeing the end lost sight of in the prosecution of the means, determined they would never be had in that way again. And yet when, in 1936, the emotion was anti-fascist idealism, identifying itself with an international crusade against tyranny, tyranny of class rather than race or nation, there was the same almost unquestioning, tragic acceptance of the purity of motive of ' our ' side. It was no question of defending ' the bad against the worse '— that more sombre, realistic mood was to come later, in 1939— and the problem of means and ends was again lost sight of while the necessity seemed, in the words of Garcia in Malraux's *Days of Hope*, ' to organize the apocalypse '; until the realities of the Communist struggle for power underneath the struggle of the Republic for its life became apparent, and people were ready to admit that the cruelties of one side had been matched by the cruelties and stupidities of the other. From Auden's *Spain* to George Orwell's *Homage to Catalonia*: the same parabola had been described.

Nearly all those who volunteered for Spain were either Communists (and it is doubtful if one can talk of volunteering in this case) or victims of this idealism; there were, however, exceptions; and one of them was Julian Bell. He had never been more than moderately sympathetic to the poetry of Auden, Spender and Day Lewis—a reservation that had been one of the causes of the friendly estrangement between us after I left the Hogarth Press. Believing as he did that poetry should be reasonable, masculine and public in the eighteenth-century manner, he disliked the esoteric jokes and the enthusiastic ' boy scout ' element in the poems they wrote during the early 'thirties. This temperamental hostility blinded him to the strength and originality of Wystan's work below the superficial topical flourishes. Cecil Day Lewis's work he found more to his liking, and to him he addressed a long Open Letter on ' The Proletariat and Poetry ' (reprinted in the memorial volume), criticizing the ' movement ' for disguising personal neurotic malaise under Marxist ideology, and for sentimentalizing the proletariat. ' The myth of the proletarian saviour is an inheritance from D. H. Lawrence and the early days of your movement ', he wrote. ' But the search for him is surely another symptom of softness and enthusiasm.' He also attacked them for pretending that what to Julian was an obvious good—the leisured cultured life with its ethos of freedom and tolerance that bourgeois conditions provided for intellectuals in the West— was bad in itself: ' The business of intelligence is to recognize that we are confronted by an essentially tragic situation. We have to abandon what is good, a free, tolerant, humane culture, and follow what is evil, violence, compulsion, cruelty.' He was making his criticisms, he declared, ' from the left-centre: from the position of a social-democrat '; but it was certainly a social democracy of an unusual sort, an essentially Bloomsbury sort. Julian would, I think, have laughed delightedly if he could have read Empson's *Just a Smack at Auden* :

> What was said by Marx, boys, what did he perpend?
> No good being sparks, boys, waiting for the end.
> Treason of the clerks, boys, curtains that descend,
> Lights becoming darks, boys, waiting for the end.

Underneath the surface, however, he was much more divided and distressed than the *Open Letter* revealed. He had always hated war, and yet something drew him towards it. He still, theoretically, disliked emotion in art, but the poetry he was writing had become strongly nostalgic, almost sentimental. He was restless in England, and jumped at the opportunity in 1935 to be appointed Professor of English in the University of Hankow. Before that, he had written to me:

I *can't, can't* get clear about politics. Again, there's an emotional contradiction, or set of contradictions. I'm Left by tradition, and

I'm an intellectual of the governing classes by tradition, and I can neither quite make up my mind to trying to get an economically intelligent Roosevelt ' Social Fascism ' nor give way to ' the Party ' with its fanatical war mentality. . . . I don't mind war as killing, nor as pain, nor utterly as destruction. But it means turning our minds and feelings downwards, growing hard (well, no harm, perhaps) but also savage and stupid and revengeful. You know, the Russians haven't escaped : spies and suspicion and tyranny, and no joke if your ' class origins ' aren't above suspicion. That's war—far more than the battlefields, even, tho' I think I shall live to see the people who talk about ' the masses ' in peace using those same masses like Haig and Wilson, until you've knocked the heart out of them. . . . As you'll see, I'm not yet clear, and pretty near despair either way. I believe one of the differences in our points of view comes from the circumstances of our private lives. I don't know at all, but I fancy you don't hit back when you're hurt. I do. When one has seen the extent of human beastliness and cruelty in oneself as well as outside one hesitates to let loose devils. There's nothing in the world fouler than enthusiasm, the enthusiasm of a fighting group, not even jealousy or suspicion, not even open-eyed causing of misery.

Julian saw pretty clearly, clearer than most of his generation, as this letter shows, the danger in any war, whether revolutionary or national, of ends being lost in means. In China, at first, his gloom and indecision deepened, though the mood may have arisen partly from a prostrating illness. In October, 1935, he wrote to me :

At times I get homesick for the secure familiar English background. I suppose I may harden and get able to do without it, but having been ill is very weakening. I want to have the untroubled bourgeois holiday again. I suppose I shan't get it for long, ever. You know, I'm not going to be really good at the new world.

As time went on, however, and he made more Chinese friends, this mood began to change. He made a long journey with one of his students, Yeh (who later came to England during the war), through some territory which had recently been held by the Chinese Red army. ' Their record is extremely formidable, and I suspect that at the moment they're the best-led army in the world,' he wrote at the end of September 1936. While he was away, the Spanish War had broken out.

> What a show, Gods, what a show [he wrote in the same letter]. Better, really, than Germany or Vienna, but still—Not even the satisfaction of seeing the facts prove that revolutions don't occur and civil wars do, as I've always held, really compensates, even at this distance. It all happened while we were away from news; in Chengtu we had a Chinese paper talking about some kind of revolt in Ma Shan, which we eventually concluded was a Riff rising in Morocco. Then we got back—I by air to Peking— after three weeks, and it was in full swing. The Press here is wildly reactionary, as you might suppose, and it's hard to know what is happening.

I think his journey, and the news from Spain, brought Julian's desire to be involved in action, if possible violent action, never very deeply buried in his psychology, up to the surface again. He seemed more self-confident and settled; but he did not go further than saying he had made up his mind to get a job in politics on his return. When he did get home, however, in 1937, he decided almost at once to join the Spanish Medical Aid, and went out to Cordoba as a driver with an ambulance unit. We had missed one another, by ill chance, before he left for China, and we were to miss one another again on this occasion. To my everlasting regret; for only a month later, on July 18th, he was killed by a bomb from one of Franco's aeroplanes on the Brunete front. I can never read Wogan Philipps's poignantly vivid sketch *An Ambulance Man in Spain* without thinking of Julian in his last battle. His letters from Spain gave the impression that he was amazingly happy and fulfilled in what he had undertaken; and in spite of his high intellectual ambitions, he had once written to his mother, Vanessa, that he would rather be killed violently than die any other way.

For me, it is as hard to forgive the killing of Julian as the killing of Lorca, wanton and deliberate as the murder of the young Spanish genius was compared with Julian's death; and I have been unable to find it in my heart to visit Spain as long as Franco's régime lasts.

The Spanish war presented *New Writing* with an opportunity that appeared at the same time as an imperative. I wanted, I felt it absolutely necessary, to make *New Writing* mirror this latest, crucial phase of ' a new life breathing through the old ', and become the place where whatever imaginative writing came out of the Spanish experience should naturally be published; the poems and stories from writers of our class appearing side by side with poems and stories I believed would come from new, inexperienced writers thrown up by the popular upheaval out of the darkness of the masses. I soon began to hear not only of what famous authors such as Sender, Alberti and Bergamin were writing, but also of the *Romances of the Civil War*, that extraordinary outburst of lyrics on themes of the day, which poets all over Republican Spain were writing. I wanted to get the best of these translated as soon as possible, but in this case it was rather a question of choosing between a host of eager volunteer translators: almost every English writer whose sympathies were engaged on the Republican side seemed to be burning to tackle them. Not knowing Spanish myself, I was presented even more urgently with the problem that had already become familiar in connection with Russian translations: to discover, when a poem, or draft of a poem in its English version appeared to me weak or trite, how much was due to the translator and how much to the original poet. My files of the time are full of letters about translations, selecting, checking, suggesting emendations and polishing: V. S. Pritchett, Stephen Spender, Inez Pern, Pablo Neruda, Nancy Cunard, A. L. Lloyd all came to my help, and by the time the third volume of *New Writing* had to go to press I had managed to include some of the ' Romances ', as well as contributions by Alberti and Arconada, and the first personal story of an English volunteer to the International Brigade, John Sommerfield's *To Madrid*.

Ironically, however, in this volume, which was dedicated to Ralph Fox, who had been killed in action a few months before, and in which it seems to me now I rather lost my judgement in the enthusiasm of the hour and included too much for ' political ' reasons and too little for literary merit, the outstanding contributions, those which have best stood the test of time, had

nothing whatever to do with the war and little enough with
political events: Wystan's *Lay your sleeping head, my love*,
Christopher's *A Berlin Diary*, William Plomer's *A Letter from
the Seaside*, Tom Hopkinson's *I have been Drowned* and Jean
Giono's *The Corn Dies*; all but one of which have since been
star items in the post-war *New Writing* anthologies. And
yet Jose Herrera Petere's *Against the Cold in the Mountains* and
Gonzalez Tunon's *Long live the Revolution*, both from the
' Romances ', have, like many similar poems that were
written during the French Resistance in the next decade, a
poignancy that can still be felt though their worth as poetry
can scarcely be said to survive.   For, as Stephen justly wrote
in the Introduction to our *Poems for Spain*, which I have already
quoted :

> The fact that these poems should have been written at all has a
> literary significance parallel to the existence of the International
> Brigade.   For some of these poems, and many more which we
> have not been able to publish, were written by men for whom
> poetry scarcely existed before the Spanish War.   Some of these
> writers, first awakened to poetry by Spain, died before they had
> the opportunity to cultivate their talent.

Some of them, I believe, did achieve something greater than
topical significance.   In *Poems for Spain* we published two poems
by Miguel Hernandez, who, like Ilo Masashvili, whose work
had so struck me in Soviet Georgia, was the son of a goat-
herd and had spent his life tending goats and working as a
peasant labourer until he joined the Republican army at the
outbreak of the civil war.   Poetry then seemed suddenly to
pour out of him as if a rock had been struck and a spring
leapt out of it: *Hear this voice* and *The Winds of the People* are
poems that rise free of Dr. Johnson's judgement about occasional
poetry and occasional praise.   They are portents of what still
might happen if the Spanish people were to win the freedom
that was torn away from them by Franco, Mussolini and Hitler.
I have always had an affection for such spontaneous, untaught
writings, when, by a lucky chance, they escape the laboured
struggle with what their authors fondly imagine to be correct
and cultured diction; and to me one of the most moving

poems that came out of the Spanish war are the eight lines that were found scribbled, anonymously, on the leaf of a notebook by a soldier in the International Brigade:

> Eyes of men running, falling, screaming
> Eyes of men shouting, sweating, bleeding
> The eyes of the fearful, those of the sad
> The eyes of exhaustion, and those of the mad.
>
> Eyes of men thinking, hoping, waiting
> Eyes of men loving, cursing, hating
> The eyes of the wounded sodden in red
> The eyes of the dying and those of the dead.

The Spanish war also demonstrated that there are occasions when poetry concerned entirely with a political creed and the action resulting from it can have an enduring poetic power: warmly applauded in the political surge of the moment, rejected when disillusionment sets in, they are later found to have some uranium content that still makes them impressive and valid as poetry. In the fourth volume of *New Writing* we published a group of poems by John Cornford (son of Frances Cornford) a Cambridge undergraduate of only twenty-one, who had been killed fighting with the International Brigade. Though I now entirely reject the specific creed that inspired them, I still find them, for all their faults, among the most remarkable poems that came out of the Spanish war: untainted even by the suspicion of rhetoric that clings to Auden's *Spain*, more directly moving than that magnificent virtuoso piece in the Newbolt vein, Cecil Day Lewis's *The Nabara*, they are a rare example of closely packed thought in verse that is yet entirely clear, without private riddles, and transformed into a hard-muscled poetry in which often brutally realistic images are used—not always, for Cornford was still finding his way, but surprisingly frequently—without destroying the harmony of the whole. They gain enormously from being written as part of the experience of action: Cornford seems sometimes to write of the battle for Communism as Donne wrote of love; and though the deeply touching love-lyric *Heart of the heartless world* is the one that has had the widest appeal, I do not think it as important as the longer poems *Full Moon at*

*Tierz* or *As Our Might Lessens,* in which the movement and tension
come from the struggle against the fear of pain, the brooding
about pain in the poet's mind :

> Now the same night falls over Germany
> And the impartial beauty of the stars
> Lights from the unfeeling sky
> Oranienburg and freedom's crooked scars.
> We can do nothing to ease that pain
> But prove the agony was not in vain. . . .

I do not know whether John Cornford would have seen the
other side of the moon, the corruption of Stalinism, if he had
lived; but I believe, on the evidence of the power of the few
poems he left, in spite of their obvious moments of immaturity,
that if he had written about El Alamein or the storming of
Normandy as he wrote about the storming of Huesca, no other
poet of action in the Second World War could have touched
him: his name would be a household word today, with the
more literary-minded statesmen quoting him in their speeches
for solemn occasions.

In mood, as well as in the ' feel ' of the verse, nothing less like
Cornford's work could be imagined than the poems Stephen
Spender wrote during the Spanish war; but they have always
deeply moved me because they were not written from the side-
lines, but—like nearly all his best poems—they came freshly
out of personal experience. In his autobiography Stephen has
told the story of how he became involved in the human realities
behind the rhetoric through the misfortunes of a friend; with
the result that the poems were not the musical romantic
apostrophes that might have been expected from the author
of *O young men, O young comrades,* but troubled, disturbing
and anti-heroic. Stephen's quick, imaginative perception had
once more spotted a falsehood, and poems like *Regum Ultima
Ratio,* with their echo of Wilfred Owen, were a reply which
did not endear him to the Communists. His description of
André Chamson at the International Writers' Congress in
Madrid in the summer of 1937 (of which he wrote a personal
account for *New Writing*) has stayed in my mind for the same
reason :

Every morning I would go up to Chamson to enquire how he was
and he would reply, ' *Mal, mal, MAL!* ' He would go on to say
that the intellectual level of our Congress was appallingly low,
that we were irresponsible, light-hearted, we did not *feel.* . . .
Along paths which I can scarcely follow, Chamson had arrived
at a truth which few of the Congress—fêted, banqueted, received
enthusiastically, the women bridling with excitement at Ralph
Bates's or Ludwig Renn's uniform—had even glimpsed, that
the war is terrible, that the mind of Madrid, if it is sublime, like
Shakespeare's, is also terrible, like Shakespeare's. I myself had
learnt this through painful experiences some months before, not
at the Congress. I applaud Chamson.

I did not attend this Congress, or go to Spain on any other
delegation or weighty mission, like so many of my colleagues,
nor as a reporter, nor as an ambulance driver. Christopher,
with his insatiable passion for directing the destinies of his
friends as if he were allotting the parts in a play (mock-serious
melodrama generally), had immediately begun to invent
rôles for us; but I had already chosen mine. I had made
up my mind that I was going to see the Austrian drama
through to the end: I had created a home in Vienna, I had
many friends who were deeply involved, and I believed that
in a crisis I might be of help—of far more help than in a country
I knew almost nothing about, where so many international
experts of every sort had already gathered. But I realized, as
we all realized in Vienna, that the fate of Austria depended not
a little on the fate of Spain. Sometimes, as I sat at my desk
by the big window and the hubbub of the city seemed for a few
minutes to be stilled, the wind dropping as the clatter of trams
and horses' hooves died out, it was as if all Vienna was listening
for the echo of the guns in the far-away peninsula. . . . Every
Franco victory sent Nazi hopes soaring, every Republican
victory was secretly celebrated by the left-wing sympathizers
meeting in cafés or private houses unsuspected by the police. A
kind of underground railway was organized to get would-be
volunteers for the International Brigade out of the country to
the West, over the high mountain passes that could never be
completely patrolled by the frontier guards. Absorbed as I
was in the Central European scene, these movements in the

darkness had an endless fascination for me; nevertheless, as the fortunes of the long-drawn-out war moved gradually against the Republicans, as news came of the deaths of Ralph Fox, and Julian, and John Cornford, I could not help feeling the pull of Spain more and more, and a sense of release when I travelled home every few months through Paris and London, a sense of returning to the centre of desperately urgent activities. The wall of civilization was falling, and I was doing so little, posted at one remote corner, to shore it up.

It was not particularly easy to pursue the editorial work for *New Writing* under these conditions, and yet the very fact that I was in Vienna, and not in Paris or Madrid, helped me, I believe, to maintain a balance against the encroachments of politics into literature. Curiously enough, the close censorship on foreign mail that Schuschnigg's Government kept up under the cloak of *devisenkontrolle* did not ever prevent me receiving the packets of MSS. from my assistants in London—Elizabeth Bone in the tentative early days, then Beatrix, Willy Goldman and Stephen if he was on the spot—nor corresponding about them, nor correcting the proofs of many stories and poems that were concerned with the war. This work made me feel that, even at long range, I had some small if not particularly glorious part to play in the movement which was absorbing the energies of so many of my friends. Letters began to come in from contributors and fans of *New Writing* in Spain, which damped down the ever-smouldering fires of my guilt. Alfred Kantorowicz wrote from Madrid :

> An English friend showed me here *New Writing* No. 4 containing my Madrid Diary. . . . We stormed together with the 15e Brigade Villanueva de la Canada and Romanillos in the Brunete battle, always side by side with the English and American comrades; I had always to work with Major Nathan, the English hero of the 15e Brigade. Two days before his death I was wounded. . . .

Rosamond, whose husband Wogan Philipps had been wounded while working with his ambulance unit, kept up a long correspondence with me describing, with a sense of the phantasmagoric comedy as well as the tragic seriousness of the situation, what was going on in England and what it felt like to be the grass-widow of a volunteer hero in Spain. Right to the bitter end, when only the forlornest hopes remained, English intellectuals maintained their agitation for arms to be sent to the Republican Government, more I believe out of an unassuaged indignation at the farce of the Non-Intervention Committee and a still ineffacable horror at the wiping out of Guernica by Nazi bombers (with all it promised for ourselves), than with any idea that the agitation could be effective. In January of 1939 Rosamond wrote me a description of what must have been the last of the official demonstrations:

> Yesterday I took part in a deputation to the P.M., Attlee, Sinclair, Alfred Barnes. Attlee . . . spoke of ' exploring every avenue ' etc. etc. This roused a Welsh delegate to a fine frenzy of vituperation—and we all felt worse than ever. Sinclair, not having a party to lead, exhibited exceptional qualities of leadership. To my pained surprise I found myself committed to walking in a procession down Whitehall, holding a placard, with Dame Adelaide Livingstone in a fur toque and eyeveil in front of me, Amabel (Williams-Ellis) beside me, and various T.U.C. delegates at the back and before. 200 strong! We were stopped at No. 10, delivered a protest by letter to a flunkey, and were bidden to stand on the corner and shout ' Arms for Spain! '—when I escaped, and jumped into a taxi and came home. The policeman on duty gently suggested we should all go home quietly, which no doubt we did.

In the same letter she revealed more of her true feelings when she added: ' It's snowing here, and I await the fall of Barcelona with feelings to match the leaden skies.'

# 10

WE were extremely anxious at the beginning not only that we should publish translations of Russian stories, but also that our aims should evoke sympathy and understanding in Moscow intellectual circles. This was to prove a much more complex business than in our political unlicked-ness we guessed at the outset, even though cultural contacts between Russia and the outside world were far easier then—easier than anyone could imagine who judged from the Tibetan conditions of the years following the war. I had already written a rather naïvely semi-Marxist study of modern English literature for the Russian magazine *Internationalnaya Literatura*, and had introduced myself to its editors during a visit to Moscow. When I finally had the contracts for *New Writing* in my pocket, I wrote eagerly off to *Internationalnaya Literatura* and asked for their help in getting Russian authors. The editors promptly made the most interested and sympathetic gestures; but somehow or other we never got much beyond that, and practically all the Soviet material—apart from what I later collected myself in Georgia—came from *New Writing* enthusiasts in England who could read Russian and had a good collection of modern Russian books. From time to time I would send an urgent, pleading letter to Moscow, reminding them of their promises to assemble stories for me. After a long, long interval, during which at least one more number of *New Writing* had been prepared and sent to press, a telegram would suddenly arrive: MATERIAL ON ITS WAY FRATERNAL GREETINGS. Keyed up by this, I would wait a few more weeks, until a letter from one of the chief editors' secretaries appeared, announcing, ' I have to disappoint you, but I think truth is always better. The material was not and is not as yet being sent. . . .' What grim ideological battles lay behind this reversal I could not fathom then—indeed, I did not think to put it down to anything but Russian *schlamperei* (and I may well have been right). However, I tried again, with an obstinate refusal to admit defeat. The weeks passed, and no answer came. Suddenly the silence was broken by a telegram: EXTREMELY INTERESTED LATEST MOVEMENTS PEN CLUB PLEASE SEND FULL INFORMATION URGENT. After this stunning blow, I gave up and turned to my own English advisers and translators for Russian work, though I occasionally made a special search for Russian stories in French or German versions which I could read myself. And yet every now and then sudden signs were vouchsafed that *New Writing* was being closely watched in some mysterious Kremlin office. Our pathetic eagerness to win

Russian sympathy and Russian readers had been shown by the discussion that went on over the title of Christopher's first story. Originally he wanted it called *The Kulaks*.  Soon after the MS. reached me, however, he wrote:

> About The Kulaks: it occurs to me that maybe, if the book is to be read at all in Russia, the title conveys quite a wrong impression. Do you think I should change the family name?  I could do this, of course, in proof: or maybe it could be done before the MS. goes to press.  What about Nowack?  ' The  Nowacks '— Nowak, perhaps, is better?  Yes: ' The Nowaks '. . . .

Christopher's instinct was sound, for one day a Russian girl, emissary of Moscow, suddenly arrived in my office, and carried off copies of No. 1 proofs, and any other material lying about, and a few months later a little Russian booklet appeared on my desk with the picture of a youthful down-and-out on the cover, and the superscription in cyrillic characters: HOBAKN. But I never heard what the Soviet public made of Otto and his ambiguous adventures.

When I eventually set out again for Russia, on a hunting expedition from which I was determined to bring back a few rare specimens of new writing from Transcaucasia at least—for my imagination had been fired by the Caucasus, and I wanted to explore it with a book mistily in view—I was armed with all sorts of introductions to Russians, Georgians and *émigré* German writers who I hoped might put me on the right scent.  I felt that if I actually appeared on the spot, I might be able to circumvent the mysterious obstacles that had prevented me so far from ringing any bell in the Soviet Union.  I also had an introduction to Ivy Low, the English wife of Foreign Minister Litvinov; and tried to get in touch with her by telephone from my hotel in Moscow.  I rang up again and again, I enlisted the aid of my Intourist interpreter, of the handsome and efficient manageress, a former aristocrat who had ' gone over ' to the Bolsheviks, and various other friends; but always fruitlessly. The noise that came through the receiver reminded me of the confused humming, muttering and crackling that K., in Kafka's novel, hears when he tries to ring up the Castle.

Occasionally a sombre voice broke in with a few angry but unintelligible words of Russian before cutting me off. I very much doubt if I got anywhere near Litvinov's office or home; the line was probably tapped half a dozen times between the hotel and him; and I very much doubt also whether my Russian helpers rang up the right number, in spite of all the screaming and shouting they were obliged to indulge in by the antiquity of the instrument and the state of the lines—it was probably extremely unwise for them to do more than make a show for my benefit. Once or twice they assured me that Mme Litvinov was out but they had left messages. Then suddenly, an hour or two later, I would be called on the telephone, and an extraordinary thing would happen: through the confusion of sound a voice speaking broken American would suddenly emerge, and ask whether I would like to *see a circus*. . . . This happened several times, and each time the demand was more urgent. It reduced me to a state of panic: ' to see a circus ', I felt sure, was a code phrase which meant entering into contact with a counter-revolutionary group, and either someone in the group had been detailed to watch me or the secret police were testing me; I pictured a nice little ' circus ' in one of the interrogation rooms of the Lubyanka prison, way underground, with myself as performing elephant.

It was the time of the Moscow Trials, and the look of confidence and optimism which I had thought to observe on the faces of people I passed in the streets during my first visit seemed to have gone. Strange things were happening under the surface, people were jumpy and preoccupied, and much less willing to talk in public than they had been a couple of years before: I was forced to admit this to myself, in spite of my wish to see everything through rose-coloured spectacles. One day, in Rostov, I found myself being tracked by a tall, hawk-faced man of middle age, who finally cornered me and began to speak to me in halting French. Visions of the circus rose before me again: I tried to throw him off, but in vain. He wanted to talk to me, he said; there were many things he could show me in Rostov I wouldn't otherwise see. He wormed the name of my hotel out of me, and the next day emerged from a clump of trees further up the avenue as I came out. He pressed his company upon me, and insisted that as I was interested in modern Russian writing there were many books he could show me if I would come to his flat. In a sort of hypnotized trance, dreading to offend rather than impelled by curiosity—for he had a formidable personality—I allowed myself to be taken up to his small abode, where vodka was offered me. Then, gradually, the talk came round to the point. . . . There was much dissatisfaction in the Soviet Union, particularly in the Ukraine. . . . Secret opposition groups were at work. . . . He himself planned to escape, and had already collected some English pound notes. . . . Panic gripped me again, I was even more convinced than I had been in Moscow that the secret police were testing me, and I desperately tried to keep my answers as colourlessly polite as possible. Finally he saw he was not getting anywhere, and with a sigh abandoned his attempt to interest me further. When I got back to the hotel I looked under the bed and into the cupboards with anxious care; but my innocent papers did not seem to have been disturbed, not one of my letters read.

My actual experience of two hours in the hands of the Ogpu, when it came, was rather an anti-climax. I was strolling alone round the Batum water-front with my camera. Up the avenue, in the distance, a detachment of Soviet marines was approaching: the scene suddenly composed into an excellent picture, I lifted my Leica and pressed the shutter. Three minutes later, as I was wandering down to the sea's edge, I heard angry shouts behind me, and on turning round saw to my dismay that a naval lieutenant with drawn sword, accompanied by two of the marines hurriedly fixing their bayonets, was rushing towards me. I was placed under arrest in an instant, my stumbling expostulations in bad Russian were ignored by the lieutenant, who seemed beside himself with rage at the sight of my British passport, and I was marched off to Naval Headquarters down the road. I felt lucky not to have been put up against a wall and shot on the spot; but my constant repetition of the word ' Intourist ' had in the end the desired effect, my guide arrived half an hour later at the Headquarters, out of breath and very nervous, and persuaded the officers that I was harmless. Meanwhile, however, an Ogpu agent had also arrived, a little weasel-faced man in a cloth cap who grinned at me affably and explained that there was still one trifling formality before I could be freed: I must accompany him to a photographer in the town, where my film would be developed. My guide disappeared, and I found myself trying to explain to the Ogpu agent that the film was Panatomic and not even red light must be used in the developing room. Unfortunately, in the stress of the moment I could not remember the Russian word for light, and kept on saying ' *Ne krasne, ne krasne!* ' I noticed that the Ogpu man seemed to grow decidedly less affable at this, and refused to listen to me any longer. It was only too clear that he had mistaken my intention, when the film emerged from the developing room: one long roll entirely black, without a sign of a picture on it. Evidently some diabolical trick of the British Intelligence Service, to manage to obliterate all pictures at the moment of unmasking. . . . He released me rather reluctantly.

My hunt for new Soviet authors during the seven weeks of my visit was assiduous and single-minded, but not particularly rewarding. There were, however, other occasions of misunderstanding, less awkward for me personally, which have remained in memory as comic relief. I was taken one evening to the House of Writers in Moscow, where a celebration was being held to honour Berthold Brecht. After the speeches of welcome, a young Russian poet got up, to read a translation he had made of one of Brecht's famous longer poems: it was a fiery declamation, the young Russian lashed himself into a passion, gesticulating dramatically and turning purple in the face with the effort, and then sank back to his seat with bowed head. There were storms of applause. Then Brecht himself was asked to recite the same poem in his original German. He read it sitting down, with dead-pan face, in the totally flat, anti-rhetorical manner he had intended it. A look of bewilderment came into the young Russian poet's eyes; and embarrassed glances were exchanged among the other Russian writers there. At the end the applause was respectful rather than enthusiastic. I had a suspicion that Brecht was secretly deriving immense enjoyment from the episode.

I was told of another episode, in Tiflis, which amusingly

spotlighted not only the ignorance and lack of sophistication of the younger Soviet officials and literary world, bemused by years of solemn Marxist distortion of reality, but also the absurdities that constantly arose from sudden changes in the Party line about friends and enemies abroad. It was the time when André Gide was the great hero, Exhibit Number One of the triumph of Soviet sympathies among the intellectuals of the West. A tremendous celebration was arranged for him when he visited Tiflis, including a banquet in which local writers poured forth eulogies of his work. When it was all over and Gide had departed, someone casually mentioned *Corydon*. The speechmakers had never heard of it; and on being told what it contained and what Gide's frankly avowed sexual preferences were, they were utterly appalled. Violent quarrels broke out and raged for weeks. Someone may even have been sent to Siberia.

The person who told me this was a leading Georgian writer of a slightly older generation, with a great sense of humour, who could hardly reach the end of the story for silent laughter. He must have got a good deal of amusement out of me as well. He was extremely curious to know what was going on in the English literary world. I tried to describe the scene in terms of the current Soviet cant about Marxist realism and bourgeois writers who were ' coming over to the proletariat '. Naïvely I imagined this was what he wanted from me. As gently as possible he interrupted me: ' No, don't bother about Marxist interpretations. Tell me what's *really* going on. . . .'

I spent several evenings with him translating Georgian poetry for *New Writing*: he would give me a literal translation in English, or German when that failed him, and I would then try to make it into poetry, keeping as far as possible to the rhyme-schemes and rhythm of the originals as I listened to him repeating them. I was agreeably surprised to find that by no means all the outstanding poets felt it necessary at that time to write Odes to Stalin or the Five-Year Plan, but could still produce poems about the pleasures of love, and wine and nature that had an authentic Georgian ring—and were not just another piece of Marxist spam out of the Moscow tin. They seemed roughly to divide into three groups: those who had looked to

Paris before the Revolution, and were keeping up the Symbolist tradition; those who followed Mayakovsky's Futurism, and those who were trying to revive the old ballad and folk-song tradition of Georgia. There—perhaps only there, or rather where that native tradition fused with Symbolist influences—I felt there was some originality. I had the impression that in literature and in the theatre—where Kouchitashvili, the brilliant young Georgian producer who had worked in Paris for some years and had then decided to accept the Soviet invitation to return home, had a dominant influence—the Georgians, with their love of fun and the colour of life and their long romantic history, a tradition so entirely different from the Russian, did not take the earnest strivings of the Marxist purists very seriously, though they paid lip-service to the Party line and the necessity of Socialist optimism.

In painting, too, this saving grace still seemed to me happily apparent. As I wandered round the rooms of an exhibition of modern Georgian painting, every now and then I received an authentic shock of æsthetic pleasure—even if not of a very high voltage. Impossible in Moscow, where the official doctrines had extinguished life in the plastic arts as swiftly and completely as an old-fashioned snuffer clapped over a candle-flame: an obliteration only too painfully evident to one's hopeful gaze in the Soviet pavilion at the Paris Exhibition, even if one had not made the journey to Russia. Of this pavilion, and the monstrous twin figures of a Soviet worker and his lass which stood in front of it, E. M. Forster wrote, in the sad and witty description of the Exhibition he contributed to the number of *New Writing* which contained my first gathering of Georgian poems and stories:

> Passing beneath their sealed up petticoats and trousers we enter a realm which is earnest cheerful instructive constructive and consistent, but which has had to blunt some of the vagrant sensibilities of mankind and is consequently not wholly alive. Statistics, maps and graphs preach a numerical triumph, but the art-stuff on the walls might just as well hang on the walls of the German pavilion opposite: the incidents and the uniforms in pictures are different, but the mentality of the artists is the the same, and as tame.

He went on to say that the Soviet pavilion was nevertheless 'a nudge to the blind', meaning those who could not see the corrupting effect of money values. It might also have been a nudge to the blind of another sort. . . . But André Gide's eyes had already been opened, and the waves of rage and indignation were lashing round his famous little book *Au Retour de l'U.R.S.S.*

What happened to my Georgian friends later, when the screw was put on to art and literature all over the Soviet Union, turning them into little more than rubbishy propaganda, I have never known. Perhaps they were skilful enough to adapt themselves to the new line without losing their integrity, unlike so many of their Russian colleagues. My harvest, in prose as well as poetry, was lean enough, though I combed through many books that were sent after me. It was the last chance, though I did not know it at the time.

In my Moscow hotel I used sometimes after dinner (which means round about midnight) to meet Prince Mirski, whom I had known slightly in London before he made his gesture of returning to Russia. In spite of his conversion to Bolshevism, he could not rid himself entirely of the Old Adam: he used to give huge tips to the waiters (many of whom were themselves weary relics of the *ancien régime*) with an aristocratic disdain for the change, and conversed freely about literature in Bloomsbury terms. I remember talking with him one night about Zoschenko, Olyesha, and other Soviet writers who seemed not to care overmuch for the fatuous dictates of Socialist Realism. 'Yes, it still goes on,' he said in a rather gloomy undertone. 'But I wouldn't like to say how long our political leaders will stand for it.' When the wind changed to the north, Prince Mirski himself was one of those who vanished without trace: an ironic epilogue to his not uncourageous—and for the Bolsheviks politically useful—action.

# I I

IT was natural for me to have great expectations of finding writers from the working-class and from the anti-fascist underground in Vienna as well. I asked all my friends, in all the circles I knew; but to my surprise and chagrin, they had nothing, no one to suggest. My final, one and only discovery came by chance. The story of this young writer stands for me as an epitome of all the dignity and tragedy of the time of fascist triumph and threatening war.

After my early travels in Russia, I had made up my mind for future travels to get beyond the ' *Da* ' and ' *Spasebo* ' stage of Russian and learn it well enough to converse (when the Intourist guide wasn't looking) with chance encounters, and to get the drift of the newspapers. I looked round for a teacher in Vienna, and was recommended a young poet of Russian parentage who was eking out a living by giving lessons and by writing sketches for one of the many little café-cabarets which existed at that time in Vienna.

Yura Soyfer was a delicate-looking man, of just under average height, in his middle twenties. He had a soft voice, a gentle expression and great charm of manner; but under this mild exterior he concealed, as I was later to realize, not only a subtle understanding of his fellow-men but also a strong will and cool courage. His family was poor, and he earned far too little himself to live even an averagely comfortable life; but I never once heard him complain about it. His work as a poet and the pursuit of his political ideals absorbed him entirely.

I did learn some Russian from Yura; enough to understand the headlines in the newspapers and converse haltingly when I made my trips to the Caucasus; but I learnt far more about the literature of Austria and the secret political movements at my door. Yura, who had been a small child when his parents fled from the Bolshevik Revolution, had completely acclimatized himself to Viennese writing and art, and his great admirations were the three famous Austrian dramatists, Raimund, Nestroy

and Grillparzer, particularly the first two, so difficult to translate and interpret for anyone without an intimate knowledge
of the Viennese background. He would talk for hours about
these three and the history of the Austrian theatre; and I
believe that if he had lived he might have made some notable
contributions to it himself. Some of his cabaret plays have
survived and have been published since the war in Vienna:
they are clever, full of playful topical wit against the police-
rulers of the country, but above all remarkable—to me—for
their human warmth and the tenderness of their idealism.
Yura was the poet of a ruined and dispossessed generation, the
young men and women whose childhood had been the inflation
and revolutionary aftermath of the war in Central Europe, and
who had grown up to unemployment as a permanent condition
of the life around them. He expressed their half-despairing
longings, the gentleness that remained in the midst of the bitterness, the sense of civilized values so essentially Viennese (which
penetrated right down through the educated working classes),
with such truth of feeling that I have only to read the opening
lines of one of his sketches for the whole atmosphere of that
melancholy time to come back to me.

In politics, Yura's case was typical of the younger Austrian
intellectuals of those years. He began by being a fervent
Socialist, full of the idealism of the Viennese movement that
had accomplished such an extraordinary work of education and
welfare during the decade and a half of its control of the city's
government. But he belonged to that wing of it which believed
that the movement needed to be armed and prepared to fight
against the counter-revolutionary forces that were being
organized on the one side by Starhemberg and on the other by
the pan-German Nazis. I think Yura already belonged, before
1934, to the Schutzbund, and he certainly took part in some
capacity in the final stand, the despairing all-too-late gesture
of the out-manœuvred party. The disillusionment and bewilderment that followed it are not easy to describe now, when
we have become accustomed to far greater destruction and
horror and have learnt disenchantment with so many ideologies
that still had their appeal in those days. For Yura and his
friends the answer seemed clear: war, with fascism as its

driving force, was approaching fast, the Socialist parties of
Europe were going to put up only a half-hearted fight against a
movement that was entirely ruthless—they had seen what had
happened in Germany the year before and knew that Austria,
once Hitler and Mussolini came to terms, would be wide open
to the Nazis—and more extreme solutions were called for.
What remained in these circumstances but the Communists,
now pointing with I-told-you-so contempt at the leaders of a
party they had always despised, and offering a programme not
only of militant counter-action but also the true and only interpretation of Socialism, the gospel according to St. Lenin and
St. Stalin, which would, when the party was ready to seize
power, avoid all such errors as had made the February *débâcle*
possible?

I did not learn that Yura had joined the Communist underground at once, but only gradually as I gained his confidence
and he saw that my devouring interest in what was going on in
Vienna under the surface could be put to good use. He became
one of my chief sources of information, and also of supply of the
illegal pamphlets and diminutive newspapers, printed in eye-
teasing type on the flimsiest paper or duplicated, with crude but
amusing cartoons. I had had a secret cupboard built into the
new furniture of my flat, and there the copies of these extraordinary little productions, prepared with such devotion in
conditions of considerable danger or smuggled across the
frontier from Prague, were hidden until I could get them out
of the country myself or send a digest of them with my own
annotations to the papers which were interested.

When I told Yura about the *New Writing* project, he was
immensely interested, and wanted to know all about the English
writers who were contributing; most of the French, German
and Russian authors in the first number he already knew of.
He was excited by the idea of an international magazine that
planned to reflect the revolutionary ferment of the time, and
promised to see if he could find any suitable poems or stories
by unknown writers among his acquaintances in Vienna.
Looking over the first volume when it arrived in its bright
colours, exclaiming with delight about some of the contributions
(' the whole development of nineteenth-century philosophy is in

this!' he cried of Upward's *The Border Line*), he shook his head dolefully and told me he didn't think there was anyone of his generation who cared enough about writing to qualify; almost all Austrian talent had been drained off to Germany in the days of the Weimar Republic, as soon as it had shown itself; and now, well, who could begin a literary career under the hopeless political conditions in which they had been living ever since Hitler came to power across the frontier? Then I remembered that a little time before he had, very diffidently, mentioned a book on which he himself was working, a novel in which he wanted to give the whole inner story of the Socialists and the Schutzbund in the last months before they were crushed. From the way he had talked about it I had formed the impression that it would be a work of art and not a crude propaganda effort or a disguised piece of journalist's reportage. Not without difficulty, I at last managed to persuade him to let me look at some chapters which he considered were in a sufficiently finished state to be seen by a critical eye.

As soon as I had read them, I felt certain that I had found the real thing. With my keen Schutzbund sympathies of the time, I was fascinated by the theme: but I was particularly struck by the sensitive skill Yura had shown in creating atmosphere and in conveying the erratic, psychological weather of a group of characters waiting for a battle to begin, waiting in a state of nervy tension for their leaders to tell them when skirmishes and patrols in force by the enemy—which little by little were robbing them of all their advantages—could be answered by a real offensive. Much to Yura's surprise and delight, I told him that I would publish a section of what he had showed me as soon as I could get it translated; and in the second number of *New Writing* it appeared as *In the Corner* under the pseudonym of Georg Anders.

Publication, impossible in his own country, gave Yura a much-needed spur, and he set to work on the novel with renewed faith. I was convinced of its importance, and of the promise of Yura's gifts. I kept on urging him to greater speed as time went on, for like everyone else I felt the threat of a curtain falling, not merely on Yura's own illegal political activities in Austria but on the whole pattern of our lives.

Yura, however, was a slow worker, he was writing under
extremely difficult conditions, and he had to earn some kind of
a living by his cabaret sketches and the lessons he gave. What
was more, he had planned the novel on a large scale, and with
his passion for the smallest significant details the further he
worked into it the longer it seemed to him it would have to be.
I wanted to publish more in *New Writing*—it was only after his
death and after the outbreak of war, at Christmas 1939, that
another section appeared—but Yura realized as well as I did
that, pleasant as it might be to have fragments published in
translation abroad, he must find a publisher for the novel in
German. He was actually in contact with one in Prague,
when the first blow fell.

Schuschnigg's secret police did not lack efficiency, even
though a strange paralysis often seemed to come over them
when dealing with the Nazi underground, and in demoralized
Vienna there were plenty of informers to be blackmailed or
bought among the unemployed intellectuals and the working
population. I took many precautions to conceal my activities
as a collector of information about the hidden Socialist and
Communist organizations; but I suppose that the privileged
position any resident foreigner even of moderate means enjoyed
in those days made me careless in the end; though I think it
extremely unlikely that the first clue that brought the police
on to the trail of myself and several of those who kept me in
touch came from a slip of my own. I was remarkably foolish
not to have reflected more about the fact that for some weeks
there had always seemed to be a car starting up behind my own
when I went out in the evenings; if I had not been so happy at
that time in Vienna—it was, I think, the early summer of 1937
—I would have paid more attention to the fact that when I
went out to dine in an open-air restaurant in Grinzing or in the
Prater, a nearby table was so frequently occupied by two or
three men who did not quite appear to fit the place or the
occasion.

One morning, just after Frau Chval had arrived, there was a
ring at the door. A moment later she parted the curtains of
my bed-recess and hissed: '*Die Polizei!*' A glance at her
horrified face, and I leapt out of bed, to find myself confronted

by a youngish man of pleasant countenance and extremely courteous manner, who produced his secret-police badge and suggested that it was his regrettable duty to search the flat and put some tiresome questions to myself. He was accompanied by a decidedly less courteous acolyte.

I am, I believe, a person who is easily confused by the unexpected, but my good angel assuredly stood by my side that morning. In spite of my embarrassment, I decided in a flash to reveal all—or, to be strictly accurate, nearly all. I explained that I was a foreign journalist engaged in collecting every piece of information that might help to elucidate the real situation in Austria, and that I therefore kept as close contact as possible with the underground organizations. I opened the drawer of my desk for them to examine, pulled out several of the illegal pamphlets I happened to have been working on the day before, and invited them to explore further. Having got their assent to a quick shave and wash, I left them at their nosey work, and on my way to the shower-bath told Frau Chval in a whisper that the moment I was taken away by the detectives she was to ring up one or two of my friends among the Anglo-American journalists who might be able to pull strings for me. Feeling herself in passionate league with me against the hated police, she performed this mission with the utmost efficiency. Times have changed, but even so I would scruple to reveal this—governments come and go, but the police remain and have long memories—were it not that dear, brave, loyal, kind-hearted, hard-working Frau Chval, who burst into tears when, without warning, I knocked at her door one day after the war, is now dead and beyond all petty revenge or suspicion.

Having concluded their examination of the flat, without lighting on the secret cupboard, the detectives invited me down to their car, which was standing discreetly on the other side of the block, and suggested that the most agreeable place for us to continue our civilized conversation was the Police Headquarters. I soon found myself in that sombre fortress of seedy (but all-too-powerful) bureaucracy, and was ushered in to the presence of a high officer, who greeted me with politeness but without enthusiasm, and proceeded to fire some shrewd and pertinent questions at me, which showed how carefully my

movements had been watched for some weeks. The odd
pattern of the detectives who arrested me was repeated here:
behind the comparatively urbane officer was standing another
hefty individual of sinister aspect, who uttered his own commentary on the proceedings in furious hisses of indignation and
disbelief. How this second act of the uncomfortable comedy
would have concluded if it had run its course as the police
intended, I do not know; for in the middle of it another detective hurried into the room and whispered something to the
examining officer, the drift of which I was not slow to gather:
Frau Chval had done her job, and my friends had begun to
make inquiries. Reluctantly, but with a look that said 'Don't
worry, I'll get you in the end,' the officer released me. Reflecting with nervous relief on the curious fact that I must be one of
the few people in Europe at that time to have been arrested
(and released) by both fascist and Communist police, I walked
out into the free air of heaven.

It was all right for me; but very soon after—and here is my
reason for the interpolation of my own story at this point—I
heard that my arrest had been only part of a much wider swoop
the police had organized that morning against the left-wing
underground, and that several of my friends, including Yura,
had fallen into their net. That was the beginning of the end for
him. I cannot be sure of the detail of what happened to him
during the next two years, because I have lost all contact with
those mutual friends who might be able to refresh my memory;
as far as I can recollect, however, and as far as I was able to
piece the story together from fragmentary reports that reached
me during a time of dispersal and confusion, Yura was released
by the Austrians just before the *Anschluss* in 1938, but promptly
seized again by the Nazis when they overthrew Schuschnigg's
Government. A former Schutzbundler, a convicted illegal
worker for the Communists, and a Jew, he stood little chance:
the way led to Dachau.

The epilogue was told me one day in my office at the Hogarth
Press in Mecklenburgh Square, just after the outbreak of war.
An unknown young Austrian came to see me, who informed
me that he had known Yura in Buchenwald, whither he was
transferred from Dachau. So far from being crushed by this

disaster, the assassination of all his own hopes, and by all the horrors he had to witness, Yura, the gentle, smiling, fragile intellectual, had developed into a tower of physical strength and spiritual endurance. He worked miracles, his friend said, in keeping up the morale of his fellow-Austrians who were imprisoned with him, he even wrote—what must appear weirdest of all literary activities—cabaret pieces to be acted by the inmates of the concentration camp, and gained a grudging respect from the thugs who ruled it. They made him a sick-bay attendant; and then, in carrying out his duties during an epidemic of typhus, just as a visa for the United States reached him—the long-dreamed-of visa we had been working so hard for, that promised him a new start in a new country—he succumbed to the epidemic himself, and died.

Copies of Yura's Viennese cabaret sketches had been carried into the free world by friends before the war, and were published a few years ago in Austria in a memorial volume. Nothing remained of the novel, except the fragments I had preserved. Nearly all his poems were also, I believe, destroyed, except his beautiful *Lied der Einfachen Menschen*, and another deeply moving song which he wrote in Dachau and which the friend who came to see me had memorized. Later I translated it and published it in *Folios of New Writing* under the title of *Song of the Austrians in Dachau*. It had as its ironic theme the words that stood over the entrance to the concentration camp, *ARBEIT MACHT FREI*:

> Pitiless the barbed wire dealing
> Death that round our prison runs,
> And a sky that knows no feeling
> Sends us ice and burning suns;
> Lost to us the world of laughter,
> Lost our homes, our loves, our all;
> Through the dawns our thousands muster,
> To their work in silence fall.

> *But the slogan of Dachau is burnt on our brains*
> *And unyielding as steel we shall be;*
> *Are we men, brother? Then we'll be men when they've done,*
> *Work on, we'll go through with the task we've begun,*
> *For work, brother, work makes us free.*

Haunted by the gun-mouths turning
All our days and nights are spent;
Toil is ours—the way we're learning
Harder than we ever dreamt;
Weeks and months we cease to reckon
Pass, and some forget the years,
And so many men are broken
And their faces changed with fears.
> *But the slogan of Dachau is burnt on our brains*, etc.

Heave the stone and drag the truck,
Let no load's oppression show,
In your days of youth and luck
You thought lightly: now you know.
Plunge your spade in earth and shovel
Pity where heart cannot feel,
Purged in your own sweat and trouble
Be yourself like stone and steel.
> *But the slogan of Dachau is burnt on our brains*, etc.

One day sirens will be shrieking
One more roll-call, but the last.
And the stations we'll be seeking—
Outside, brother, prison past!
Bright the eyes of freedom burning,
Worlds to build with joy and zest
And the work begun that morning,
Yes, that work will be our best!
> *But the slogan of Dachau is burnt on our brains*, etc.

# I 2

EVERY new movement or impetus in literature sooner or later, if it has strength and direction, attempts to invade the theatre (if it is not born there).   This still seems to remain true as a general rule even nowadays, when, paradoxically, literature itself, in the novel, has been so deeply influenced by the tempo, cutting, and visual primacy of the cinema.   Christopher Isherwood's Berlin stories are one outstanding example (though very far from the only one) of this revolutionary influence; and Christopher, significantly, was one of those who led the way in the new theatrical movement of the 'thirties.

The lively, infuriating Unity Theatre was founded to present avowedly left-wing propagandist drama, such as was already being successfully played in little theatres in America, and specialized in witty, topical cabaret and revue sketches on political themes. Unity Theatre, like the Gate, was a *place*; you could find it in the back streets of North London and enjoy a totally different kind of evening there if you were bored with the West End theatre. The Group Theatre, however, which was launched in the autumn of 1935 under the fanatically single-minded direction of Rupert Doone, former Diaghilev dancer and choreographer, was a producing organization and used whatever theatre it could get.

Doone's first production was the first Auden–Isherwood play, *The Dog Beneath the Skin.* I was too much abroad to be in the swim of this adventure in experimental theatre, missed Dog-Skin (as Christopher always called it), but saw the next child of the famous and all-too-brief collaboration, *The Ascent of F6*, and Stephen Spender's *Trial of a Judge;* and shared in the excitement that steadily rose as the Group Theatre established itself as *the avant-garde* theatre movement of the time. It even seemed possible that the everlasting, conventionally tailored West End play with its neat three acts and superficial realism was at last doomed. First the Gate; now the Group. . . . But the walls of Shaftesbury Avenue did not fall at this blast of trumpets; and it is melancholy now to reflect for how brief a spring the new poetic drama ruled. There have been poetic plays in plenty during the last ten years, in fact a revival in poetic drama has been much talked of; T. S. Eliot, doyen still far in the van, has pursued his own remarkable way (which might be thought, after *The Confidential Clerk*, to be leading straight back to the prison of the conventional West End play); but the particular path explored by the Group Theatre has been abandoned and weeds have grown over it. *The Dog Beneath the Skin* and *The Ascent of F6* were genuine attempts to break entirely new ground, and began an experimental movement behind which one could feel the youthful pressure of new ideas and new notions of form; a movement that, in spite of a certain debt in its origins to German Expressionism, was original to England, taking an entirely different direction from either continental or American *avant-garde* theatre, as much in its mixture of the styles of cabaret-sketch and charade with elements of Greek drama, as in its philosophical content, its peculiarly Audenesque message, part Marx, part Groddeck and Freud, on the sickness of civilization. The plays have been criticized for the often slapdash schoolboy impertinence of the satire and a lack of subtlety in the drawing of the characters; but these objections seem to me irrelevant to what they were trying to do in a genre which deliberately aimed at preserving the speed and lightness of cabaret ' attack '. Christopher has told us that he had to keep a sharp eye on Auden to prevent the characters flopping down on their knees on the slightest pretext. . . . One would like to know more about the way the collaboration worked. Who invented Destructive Desmond, epitome of a philistine-fascist mentality not confined to totalitarian states? Who named Frustrax Abominum, that sinister Freudian plant that had evidently strayed from Mortmere to the slopes of F6?

By the time Stephen's *Trial of a Judge* was put on, the fame of the Group Theatre had spread far beyond the original circle of enthusiasts. Even Cabinet Ministers, it was reported, had been observed in the audience, had looked shaken as they went back to their desks and the Munich Agreement. Whatever statesmen might think, the drawing of imaginary statesmen in these plays was scornfully judged in some quarters. Soon after *On the Frontier* was put on, I encountered Guy Burgess one evening in the Athenæum, and with characteristic boisterousness he exclaimed: ' The trouble about Wystan, Christopher and Stephen is that they haven't got the foggiest notion what politicians are really like! ' They certainly hadn't got a clue to what Guy was really like.

Christopher had always been interested in the theatre, and it was inevitable that his close association with Auden should lead to the theatre. But, as he has described in *Lions and Shadows*, his interest in films had started even earlier, with a childhood passion for Westerns, and it was no surprising revolution that led him, just before the outbreak of war, to California and the studios of M.G.M. To that new life Berthold Viertel, the Viennese poet and producer, had obtained him entry. A close alliance, founded on a common love of theatre and cinema, had grown up between Berthold, Christopher and my sister Beatrix. Berthold had made a distinguished name for himself in Central Europe with his theatrical productions, and had come over to England as a film director: his best-known (though perhaps not best) production was *Rhodes of Africa*, with Oscar Homolka as Kruger. Physically he was small and stockily built, a small shaggy bear of a man, of enormous energy, much persuasive charm and finely perceptive intellect, capable of talking with brilliant wit and imagination for hours as he paced up and down his working-room in his dressing-gown, in and out of the huge piles of half-read books that always littered the floor; equally capable of changing his mood with the speed of lightning and growling with rage at some slight he detected, or imagined he detected, in the way he himself or one of his friends had been treated by the obtuser film-bosses with whom he had to work. A man of quite unusual, unshakeable integrity and loyalty; but not, I fancy, the easiest person, with his inflammable temperament, to be associated with professionally.

Christopher was an enthusiastic fan of Beatrix's art and a devoted admirer of Berthold, who believed in the genius of them both. When they were together, they were the most amusing and stimulating company imaginable: they struck sparks off one another and encouraged one another to the most grotesque imitations of famous actors and actresses and the most hilarious fantasies in film and play projects. But their ideas were, at bottom, serious enough: if Christopher and Berthold had stayed in Europe, if the war had not come, I believe that the alliance might have made theatrical—or film—history. As it was, Christopher worked with Berthold on the film of *Little Friend*, in which they 'discovered' Jimmy Hanley, and Berthold directed Beatrix in *The Passing of the Third Floor Back*. He also directed her in Rosamond's play *No More Music*, which had more than a *succès d'estime* when it was put on as a Sunday play early in 1938, but no luck in being taken on by a commercial management.

Beatrix was at a peak of her acting career at that time (though only a little while before she had been ill and in a mood of profoundest depression about getting work), and had just scored her greatest triumph of all as Electra in Eugene O'Neill's *Mourning becomes Electra*. No one who saw her performance will, I believe, ever be able to forget it. It had such an overwhelming effect on my mother when I took her to see it, that she fainted in the middle and had to be carried out of the theatre. I was away for the first night, but Berthold wrote me a long appreciation of it, as interesting as a revelation of his profound understanding of dramatic art as of Beatrix's performance. He had seen Beatrix for the first time as Hilda Wangel in *The Master Builder* four years before, and ever since had been convinced that London had in her ' without being fully aware of it ' (as he put it) ' an actress of the highest degree. The soundness, the definition and purpose in every word and gesture were as extraordinary as the spiritualization, the transformation which happened at the end of the play.' He had seen the Broadway production of *Mourning becomes Electra*, and had thought it failed to make the supreme last change of character which gives the play its meaning. What he called the ' uncontrolled exhibitionism ' of the usual kind of star performance could never pass that test:

How Beatrix spans the inner space for the later development of the character, how she spans an enormous arch in order to reach the sphere of humanity in her ultimate renunciation (this last scene belonging to the few most beautiful scenes in art I ever saw); the inexorableness of her characterization, how she is not afraid to be antipathetic and even repulsive in order to complete her task: all that is admirable and of course is being admired. But I admire even more what she omits, what she skips, understatement as a dramatic means. It is a new kind of acting altogether in which every small gesture is of the greatest importance and where one has to follow the thought, the thinking process becoming transparent. In a play like this one, in which neurotic complexes, not individuals, are the heroes, only this kind of acting can do any good, so she makes the play. And London, taken by surprise, makes the partly bewildered, partly enthusiastic audience.

Beatrix was to make almost as powerful an impression later in *Desire under the Elms*, and to confound the managers and producers—without, alas, their ever properly grasping it—who believed that she could only play the macabre and the sinister-tragic. That winter, however, Christopher, driven by the demon of restlessness that had been at his back ever since Hitler's triumph in Germany, left for China with Wystan, with the idea of writing a book about the Japanese invasion; and the many schemes that he had hatched with Beatrix and Berthold had to be postponed—as it turned out, fatally postponed—once more.

It was a strange irony that led two more of my friends to China, about which they knew nothing, so soon after Julian, who knew so much more and might have played so effective a part in the war that had broken out, had left it to die in Spain, about which he knew so little. On 24 February Christopher wrote to me from Hongkong, describing their plans for making their way by slow river-boat to Canton, which the Japanese were bombarding every afternoon at that time (though apparently doing their best to stick to military objectives, especially the railway):

We plan to stay in Canton two or three days. Then we meet a rather sinister Colonel Lawrence sort of man, who drives a lorry backwards and forwards between Canton and Hankow for a cigarette firm. The road is rather problematical, floods, broken bridges etc., and the journey may take as much as ten days. Once at Hankow, we'll be in the middle of things. Most of the government is there, and we can get the necessary passes and introductions for a visit to one or other of the fronts. Also, we hope to see the new British Ambassador, whom we met for a few minutes while he was passing through here. He is a very live wire, and ready to be helpful. Also, he reads Auden and enjoyed Sally Bowles. . . . Hongkong is the ugliest town in the loveliest harbour I have ever seen. A cross between Manchester and Buxton. The view from the peak of the island is a real Chinese painting, with junks and little rock-garden crags embedded in a green plate-glass sea. Yesterday evening, we dined with the Governor, and Sir Victor Sassoon showed us a coloured film he had taken himself of the Governor's arrival in Hongkong. Wystan, who is having a Proust fit, enjoyed himself hugely. I was slightly more acid, as I am suffering from a mild local variety of dysentery known as ' Hongkong Dog '. Most of the big nobs here are inclined to be pro-Chinese; and you can talk about the Communist troops in even the most polite society without a shudder. So much for the ideology of Business when its interests are really threatened!

The British Ambassador who enjoyed *Sally Bowles* was Sir Archibald Clark Kerr (afterwards Lord Inverchapel), whom I was to get to know very well some years later during the war, while he was occupying the key-post of Ambassador at Moscow. He was a staunch supporter of *New Writing* and all the young authors associated with it, but when I met him in London under bombardment he was very much disappointed that the two whose company he had enjoyed so much in China, and for whom he had done so much, had opted for America. It was on their return journey from China that Christopher and Wystan travelled west–east through America, and took the decision, so totally unexpected by their friends (and to me so sad and discouraging at a time when I had hoped for their close collaboration), that the United States was the country of the future and the country for them.

In the same letter Christopher had written of our mutual projects with a touch of unexpected nostalgia:

> Am longing to see *New Writing*. Could not a copy come out here? This address holds certainly till the end of May, if not later. And thank you so much for collating the typescripts of the ' Lost ' stories. I still don't know if America has taken the book; only that Harper's Bazaar has offered to make Sally Bowles into a serial. Do keep me posted on all the latest Hogarth Press and Daylight developments. If I am killed in China, I'd like my name on the notepaper just the same, with a cute little black cross against it. . . .

The remark about ' Hogarth Press developments ' referred to something which had just taken place, of some importance for myself and my *New Writing* plans.

# 13

ONE of the great hopes I had entertained when *New Writing* was transferred from John Lane to Lawrence & Wishart was that my new sponsors would be willing to publish a 'New Writing Library' of novels, autobiographies and books of poems by the authors I had come across in my explorations for the magazine. So many opportunities had already come my way in the first eighteen months, so many books or projects for books had been there for the taking if I had been a publisher as well as an editor, that it was becoming unbearable to me to be unable to do anything about them. Some of them, I feared, might never find a publisher to believe in them as I did; and I also saw the issuing of books as a completion of the work the magazine had started.

I managed to persuade Lawrence & Wishart to be interested in the idea; Edward Upward's *Journey to the Border*, Christopher's *North-West Passage* (which eventually came out as *Lions and Shadows*) and books by James Stern, Willy Goldman, John Sommerfield, B. L. Coombes, André Chamson, Jean Giono and Jean-Paul Sartre were among those I had first in mind. Prospects looked so rosy at one moment in 1937 that I actually got to the point of writing to several of the authors that the project was on. Hardly had I done so when Lawrence & Wishart began to change their minds and even lost interest in *New Writing* itself, the contract for which was coming to an end. It was a bitter set-back at the time, though I realize now that a publishing house with the political ties that bound Lawrence & Wishart could never have carried the project through, or have continued to give me a free hand indefinitely.

Once more I had to take my child by the hand, and find a new home for us both. When they got wind of it, several intelligent publishers showed the liveliest interest; and I was actually on the point of signing an agreement with one of them —I am still grateful to Michael Joseph for the appreciation and enterprise he showed at that difficult moment—when an extraordinary thing happened. I almost believe that it was some sixth sense that led me to call on Leonard and Virginia, whom I had not seen for some years. Any ill-feelings that were generated by my abrupt departure five years earlier had blown away, and I found them not only full of friendliness but also very much interested in the fate of *New Writing*. It was not long before they showed their hand: they were both tired of the drudgery of the Hogarth Press and wanted to sell it; and in spite of all that had happened, they still felt that I was the person they would most like to take it over. They offered me, in fact, not only a home for *New Writing* but also a resumption of my publishing career in which I should at last be able (or so it appeared) to fulfil my dream of a ' New Writing Library '.

The first scheme was that, after a two-year ' trial ' period, I should buy them both out. When I looked into the financial side of it, however, I realized that it was going to be rather difficult to find the money without embarrassing obligations; and in the end it was decided that I should buy only half of the Press—Virginia's half—and become after two years Leonard's full and equal partner as well as general manager. This seemed to me at the time almost incredible good luck; and I was particularly happy that I should again be working with Virginia. The agreement came into force in April, 1938, and on the 22nd Virginia wrote to me:

I am ashamed not to have answered your very nice kind and by all means welcome letter before. Nor can I write suitably now, because I am being badgered . . . to write an obituary of Otto-line. I'm full of sanguinity about the future; and thankful to lift the burden on to your back. Nor can I see myself any reason why we should quarrel; or why we should drink the Toast in cold water. What about a good dinner (not English) at Boulestin or some such place? You are hereby invited to be the guest of Virginia Woolf's ghost—the Hogarth ghost: who rises let us hope elsewhere.

Let's arrange it. We come back on Sunday: and then there'll be the usual uproar.

Much warmth of feeling in the bitter evening (sitting over the fire) from us both. And Lord! When I die don't ask anyone to write a few words about me in *The Times*.

Yours ever
V. W.

This decision, of course, as I could see, involved the gradual liquidation of my life abroad; but the sorrow had already been, for only six weeks earlier Hitler had marched into Austria, and I knew that I could no longer continue to live my happy life in the flat in the Invalidenstrasse.

# 14

SATURDAY morning, 12 March 1938. The early express from Prague to Vienna slowly drew out of the shadows of the terminus, and I sat back in my compartment, trying to order my chaotic thoughts and emotions.

A few days before, I had left Vienna to spend a fortnight in Czechoslovakia and find out what the Czechs were thinking and doing about the sudden turn for the worse that the Austrian situation had taken since Schuschnigg's journey to Berchtesgaden. But I had hardly been there long enough to establish contact with my harassed and excited friends, when the news came through that Schuschnigg had made his move, a lightning last moment move: there was to be a plebiscite at once, on Sunday. I decided that, after all the years I had lived in Vienna and so passionately followed the underground struggle, the tight-rope walk for independence, I could not miss the supreme trial of strength that the plebiscite was likely to be. I quickly cancelled the arrangements I had already made in Prague, and settled to return on Saturday afternoon. As a farewell fling, a group of Czech artists and poets asked me to come out with them on the Friday evening.

Our party must have started a little before seven. We were in high spirits, argued a lot, laughed a lot, drank a lot, wandered about the old town to explore out-of-the-way 'dives' where there was reputed to be good music or good wine. We bought no papers and listened to no wireless. About midnight we were still discussing what chances Austria had of remaining independent, when a boy came into the bar with the first editions of the morning papers. There was an immediate commotion, and the music broke off. I grabbed a copy as the boy passed me, and read: Schuschnigg had thrown in his hand, and Germany's armed forces were already over the frontier. . . . The whole of a pattern of life collapsed. .. ..

I do not think there were many passengers on that train actually destined for Vienna. Only a few foreigners on business or completing already planned tours and one or two Austrians who for some vitally urgent reason wanted to go *in* after the night's events. In my compartment there was an Egyptian who kept on praising the British Empire to me, a strange Englishwoman looking rather bewildered and desperate and not at all sure what she was meant to be doing entering German Austria that day, and a Czech business man hurrying down to get his daughter out of a Viennese school. The conversation consisted of each one of us in turn suddenly breaking out of a spell of anxious brooding and asking the others whether they thought we were going to be allowed in. The Englishwoman did not catch on at first; but when she realized that there was a real danger of our being turned back, she was thrown into a state of violently alternating indignation and panic. But all the time I was thinking of the Vienna I had left behind me a week before, the mood of hope that had suddenly swept the country at the last moment when Schuschnigg seemed to be coming out of his state of paralyzed apathy. I had been told by intellectuals in his circle that for days after Berchtesgaden he had been practically unapproachable, sitting with his head in his hands, refusing or incapable of action. And a picture came back to my mind of a year or so before: I had taken Violet Hammersley to visit the exquisite little Lustschloss in the Prater, when suddenly out of the trees Schuschnigg had appeared on horseback, with his equerry mounted beside him. He looked, I had thought then, the perfect type of civilized upper-class Austrian, dignified, intelligent, gentle, and not in the least like that Prince of Stendhal's Parma, whom in his actions he so closely resembled, master of tortuous intrigue and repressive cruelty. . . . I also thought of a brief discussion I had had not long before with an intelligent official in the Austrian Foreign Office, who, while admitting to me that things were very critical and that Schuschnigg's Berchtesgaden interview 'had not been at all a nice one ', still put his faith in Mussolini and discounted the evidence from Italy that he was quite wrong as the work of a brash young ' set ' who would soon be called to order. . . . As the train rattled through Moravia, I wondered what had happened to that Foreign Office official. And I wondered whether Frau Chval, Toni and his friends had been swept up into the flood. . . . whether my Jewish friends were still in their homes.

The frontier came at last. It looked extraordinarily quiet. When the passport official entered our compartment, the Czech business man hurried to ask him if we were going to be allowed in. ' Everything is just as before,' he replied with tight lips, putting his stamp into the purple inkpad, ' only a slight change in the regulation about those who want to *leave* the country. . . .'

The Austrian countryside looked as peaceful and deserted as any day. Could there be some mistake? Had the Czech papers blundered? There were flags hanging here and there from farmhouses, but there were more Austrian red-and-white flags than swastikas, and nobody seemed in a hurry to pull them down. Perhaps there had been some intervention from London or Paris at the last moment that had compelled the German troops to halt?

It was at the Vienna terminus that we encountered the first real evidence of what had happened. As we got out of the train, we had to pass through two lines of young Nazis with swastika armlets and rifles, and police behind them. The newly revealed Nazis looked slightly comic with their callow excited faces, in yesterday's knickerbockers with steel helmets on their heads; but they watched our progress as if we had pockets bursting with bombs.

Out in the streets there was still little or nothing to see. But only an hour or two later the transformation began that was to wipe out the Vienna I had known as if with one sweep of a sponge. Soon after I got back to my flat, to my relief Frau Chval and Toni appeared, unharmed, dismayed but obviously infected by the excitement, and we watched from my window the arrival of the German bombers, roaring in from the north-west in ever-increasing numbers and circling low and repeatedly over all districts of the city.   They were greeted with frenzied delight by the Nazi supporters who began to appear on the streets in jostling crowds; but it was easy to imagine that in many factories and apartment houses of the populous districts they provoked a different thought, precisely the thought they were there to provoke—that even the slightest resistance was useless.   Later, Toni told me that when the workers had arrived in their factories that morning, they found that armed guards were already installed, and their leaders of the previous day, the day of false dawn for democratic hopes, had vanished. The confusion of the night before in proletarian Vienna must have been fantastic.   As I walked through the streets in the afternoon a young garage-hand I knew ran up to me and told me one of the strangest stories of all.   On Thursday evening the *Internationale* was being openly sung in hundreds of workers' meetings, and the old greeting of *Freiheit* was heard even on the Kaerntnerstrasse.   Social-Democrat stalwarts who had lain low for years, he told me, suddenly began to draw people around them at the street corners and to harangue crowded tables in the beer and wine shops.   Late on Friday afternoon he had gone with his friends to an appointed meeting-place where all the workers were to collect and demonstrate for the promised plebiscite and the independence of Austria.   Just as Schuschnigg was making his broken farewell speech over the wireless, they formed up into a procession and set off for the main streets: they knew nothing of the speech.   As they turned a corner they saw a mass of police facing them at the top of the road.   The previous day such demonstrations had received police protection, and they imagined that they were there to clear a way for them.   But before they could advance any further, the policemen were making a savage charge at their ranks, and only too late my friend saw the swastika armlets they were carrying—already, though Schuschnigg's speech had only gone over the air a few minutes earlier.

The bombers thickened like a plague of locusts all Saturday, and all Sunday and Monday their droning roar continued. The noise acted as a form of third degree peculiarly crushing to the impressionable and pacifist-minded Viennese.   And soon another noise was added to it, the rumble of the Reichswehr lorries, the gun-carriages, the field-kitchens, the tanks that began to roll through all the main streets, advance guard of the weary-faced infantry and cavalry who grinned sheepishly or stared slightly bewildered at the cheering Nazi crowds. All Sunday this movement went on, and with the troops came busload after busload of German *Schupos* and German Frontier Police and German gendarmes and German S.S. By Sunday night all the biggest hotels had been cleared of their normal guests and were filled with German officers and their staffs. All except the Imperial, for which a higher honour was reserved, that of receiving Adolf Hitler himself. It was almost impossible to find a place in the restaurants of the Inner Town. I went to my favourite restaurant, and found it crowded out with German uniforms, the waiters, with an absolutely blank look on their faces, rushing to and fro and gasping *Heil Hitler* whenever a word was spoken to them. In the residential districts housemaids and shop-girls were already swooning on the arms of their blond deliverers from the north, but I saw no scenes of demonstrative fraternization or enthusiasm outside the centre of the town; and plenty of Viennese were already beginning to feel a little uncomfortable about the nature of the liberation that had taken place. Walking down the Ring, one saw every evidence that the Germans considered themselves the masters of a conquered country. The Reichswehr flag waved over the sentry-guarded Grand Hotel, where the German General Staff was quartered, and still troops were thundering by in their camouflaged lorries and vans. Placed there suddenly without any knowledge of what had actually happened, one could only have imagined that war was already raging, with the front only a few score miles away. And if one did know, a single thought was in one's mind all the time: when will it begin? All during those days I walked and drove about Vienna half in a daze of confusion and misery, half determined to see as much as I could as long as I could; wondering how long I had to get out, whether a bigger international explosion would follow, what would happen to my friends and my home, whether I should ever see them again.

Among the non-political masses, so deep had been the misery

through which they had gone for years, unemployment and shooting and repression, that the general feeling at the beginning, it seemed to me, in the dazed moment of the change-over, was that things couldn't be worse than they had been, that they must give the Nazis a chance and 'see if Hitler gives us work'. During the holidays that were celebrated directly after the *Anschluss* was formally proclaimed, the streets presented a weird caricature of what I had seen in the streets of Moscow on May Day. Students and workers were being whirled round in lorries, waving flags and cheering, while contingents of workers, ordered out from the factories, marched round carrying huge placards: WIR DANKEN DEM FUEHRER, and EIN VOLK—EIN REICH —EIN FUEHRER. At night there were torchlight processions : what struck me was that they were almost entirely composed of boys and girls under twenty, and a large proportion of them seemed scarcely older than sixteen. The culmination of the celebration was the long-delayed arrival in Vienna of Hitler himself. Young Nazis explained, when one asked why he was so slow in coming, that he wanted to see the joy of all the villages *en route*, that the crowds would not let him through, and so on ; only afterwards did the truth trickle through, that the great German Army had broken down. Tanks and motorized columns were stranded all over the roads from the frontier to Vienna, and Hitler was in a rage with his Generals. But at last he came, at last he made his triumphal entry into the Hotel Imperial, from which everyone had been bundled out at a moment's notice and without ceremony.

That evening I managed to get through to the Schwarzen-bergplatz, and from there, as twilight fell, worm my way slowly through the congealing crowds to a place where I could see the front of the Imperial. There was a steady hum of loud and excited conversation, but above this every few minutes or seconds the frenzied Nazi chants would break out : 'SIEG HEIL! SIEG HEIL! SIEG HEIL!' and in between 'HITLER!—HITLER!— HITLER!' All eyes were turned towards the first-floor balcony, behind which the rooms were brilliantly lit. After some time, the brown-uniformed figure that I had never actually set eyes on before, but whose myth-magnified demon image had haunted me with intimations of violence and evil ever since I had seen the candles burning before it in frozen Berlin five years earlier, Adolf Hitler emerged; and immediately a battery of arc-lamps, mounted on a moving trolley in the road, was turned upon him. He came to the front of the balcony and raised his hand in Nazi salute. Then, very slowly, with the perfect instinct of an actor, he marched toward one end of the balcony and raised his arm again. His face was sombre and appeared, in the glare of the lights, to be tense with emotion. Then he marched to the other end of the balcony, and saluted again there. All the time the chanting and yelling went on, and the crowd swayed and struggled. At last he went in again, and after some more cheering, people began slowly to disperse.

That week in Vienna completed, I think, a decisive change in my thinking about the way the political movements of our time worked: the final turn came with a sudden imaginative illumination. For I became overwhelmingly aware of the strength of the non-rational impulse in National-Socialism. I had for a time had growing doubts about the adequacy of the rational left-wing interpretation of the fascist phenomenon as the popular mask worn by finance-capitalism to organize the peoples of Western Europe for war against the Soviet Union, with behind it the cool, calculating head of the cynical profit-grabber. What I had seen in the streets, what I had heard in the tales of extraordinary incidents passed from mouth to mouth, made it clear to me that the head was not so cool after all, the cynicism—if that was still the right word—not so calculated. Rational people were looking for rational villainy: but what I had witnessed, sensed, was much more like the outburst of some tremendous force from irrational depths. These were people who could not be fitted into any conventional diplomatic calculation of a balance of power and the satisfaction of ' just aspirations ': they were possessed, and much more frightening for that reason than for all the guns and tanks by themselves. I suddenly realized that not only the callow youths, but probably also the leaders themselves, the Himmlers and Streichers and their underlings, *believed* the fantastic nonsense they preached. That the Jews were not merely scapegoats in their eyes, to be sacrificed to the discontent of the masses, but really and truly

authors of all evil and frustration that had befallen the noble
Aryans. . . .

Now in Austria the Terror was on. With the Jews, all the
enemies of National Socialism, the Communists, the Monarchists, the politically active Catholics, were caught like rats in a
trap: the impossible mirage of the plebiscite had held them from
making their get-away in time. There were undoubtedly
Austrians among the pace-makers, but I know that some of the
young Viennese who had joined the S.A. or S.S. were so revolted
by what they saw that they would have backed out if they had
dared. The scenes of agonized farewell at the Vienna stations
were followed by ghastlier scenes of arrest, indignity and plunder
at the frontiers. Night after night in all districts the visitations
went on. Hundreds, thousands were hauled off to prison, and
were not heard of for weeks, some never again alive. Jewish
shops were rifled, windows smashed, cars simply stolen from their
owners and taken off for a drunken party with the proceeds of
the raid. An eye-witness told me that in his district some
boys dragged an old Jew out on to the streets, and, urging him
on with plentiful kicks, forced him to wash out slogans painted
on the cobbles. A crowd gathered, some in an hysteria of
senseless hate, but others quite evidently revolted. The old
man was trembling, and finally fainted and had to be dragged
away. One Jew ran into a café near the Central Telegraph
office, screaming ' Heil Hitler! ' and brandishing a knife with
which he slashed at several people before cutting his own
throat. Hundreds of others among Vienna's enormous Jewish
population in those first days made a less spectacular end to a
life grown intolerable and meaningless. Many foreigners who
were present commented with bewilderment on the change
that seemed to have come over the Austrians, whom they had
always known as a peaceable and civilized people; but to be
in a smart café—swept of its former Jewish guests—and see the
fanaticism with which people jumped to their feet and sang
when *Deutschland Über Alles* blared from the loudspeaker, was
to catch a glimpse of what it had meant to be the impoverished
citizen of a small, defeated and defenceless country for so long.
The rumours and chatter that one heard in the shops and on
the trams were fantastic. The return of South Tirol was being

openly celebrated at one moment. I overheard one man
explaining to another, after a jubilant description of how two
Jewish stands in the big Market Hall had been sacked, that
Slovenia would be the next addition to Greater Germany
(' They're all Germans there! '), and that the Yugoslavs anyway had got hold of the country only because the priests had
supplied them with rifles to shoot from the church towers.
There was no limit to credulity or hate in those days, even
though, before a week was out, many were frightened, bewildered in the midst of the excitement. ' It can't last '—
' This is the beginning of a war '—' It's all over with us Austrians now, and for good '—these remarks were to be heard,
and not from Jews, nor Marxists, nor Monarchists, but ordinary
business and working people. And Vienna's large Czech
population kept their dark thoughts to themselves.

The plight that the Jews and other enemies of the régime
found themselves in, was brought home to me personally almost
immediately. An English friend of mine who was teaching
at the university happened to have in his possession some
incriminating documents. They had been given to him, while
he was in Berlin five years before at the time of Hitler's triumph,
by another friend who had had to flee the Third Reich at once.
He had brought them down with him to Vienna, and had forgotten to take them back on one of his vacation visits to England.
On the morning of the *Anschluss* he woke up to find the house
where he was staying surrounded by S.S. men. Being one of
those who suffer chronically from guilt feelings, he immediately
assumed that his secret was known and the cordon had been
drawn for him. He suffered twenty minutes of indescribable
panic; then, gradually pulling himself together, and reflecting
that his documents were hardly of all that importance, remembered that his landlord was a Jew and had been prominent in
various anti-Nazi campaigns in the Republic. The unfortunate man was lying ill in bed; but so determined were the
Nazis to get him that they had decided to put a watch round his
house until he was well enough to be dragged off. My friend,
however, saw that it was likely the house would be searched at
any moment and that, whether of first or trifling importance to

the Nazis, the documents must be got rid of.  There was no stove in his room, which was centrally heated.  He therefore went out to the telephone, beside which an extremely ugly customer of an S.S. man was standing, and said that he had to ring up an English friend, on business to do with his teaching, at once.  The S.S. man was extremely suspicious and pressed his ear as close as he could to the twin receiver while my friend was telephoning . . . which explained why the voice I heard at the other end sounded so extraordinary: it was as if somebody were undergoing torture and trying to make jokes about the weather at the same time. . . . Having obtained my promise to wait in for him, he put the documents with trembling fingers in his teacher's satchel, and assuming an air as truculently English and as solemnly donnish as the state of his nerves allowed, advanced upon the cordon.  The S.S. men were impressed, fingered the satchel—but did not open it;  and half an hour later he reached my flat with a look of almost hysterical relief on his face, and plunged the precious pages into the stove, which had already been lit to consume a number of documents of my own.

Fires were roaring all over Vienna that morning and the smoke from innumerable compromising letters, reports and records was pouring out of the chimneys of politicians, journalists and secret agents.  Soon after I reached Vienna five years before, I had made friends with G. E. R. Gedye, the brilliant journalist who had worked for the *Daily Telegraph* (and later for the *Daily Herald*) and the *New York Times*, and who eventually described the events of that week so graphically in *Fallen Bastions*.  His personal sympathies had been strongly with the Social-Democrats, and in his despatches after the February rising he had made little effort to conceal either his contempt for the clerical-fascist régime or his hatred of the Nazis.  Gedye's truculent wit and sanguine temperament were a tonic in the darkest days of foreboding and dismay.  He took to a fight with the zest of a street-urchin, and had a terrier's nose for any dirty secret smooth politicians were trying to conceal.  He was probably the best informed of all the members of the Anglo-American Press Association in Vienna about the underground activities of the Social-Democrat partisans.  Dollfuss and

Schuschnigg had handled foreign journalists with considerable caution, and left him alone, though they knew perfectly well where his sympathies lay. He had no reason to expect such respect from the Nazis, and that morning his stove was roaring more furiously than any other in Vienna: his face emerged from dense smoke as he cautiously opened a few inches of door in response to my ring at his bell. He was able to get his Jewish secretary, as attractive as she was efficient, out of Austria when he left for Czechoslovakia, only to meet another Nazi invasion there; but by that time she had married my own secretary, John Lepper, and had an English passport.

I think that every Englishman or American living in Vienna had at least one Jewish friend towards whom he felt he had a special responsibility, and for whom he tried to obtain an exit visa and a permit to enter his own country. It was an anxious business, a race against time as the process of despoiling and making outlaws or prisoners of the Jews went forward with relentless thoroughness. Yura was already beyond the reach of any help I could give him (or seemed to be at that time), and my own special care became Frau Schweiger, a plump, animated, amusing, violently Anglophile widow of considerable literary and musical accomplishments, to whose salon I had been introduced some years before, and who had given me inestimable help in getting to know the artistic life of Vienna. I kept in touch with her during those first few days of Nazi rule: she was putting up a very brave show, even forcing herself to believe (incredibly, like so many of her fellow Jews in Austria) that Austrian National-Socialism would be more tolerant and humane than the German version. These illusions did not last very long, and I remember that what eventually broke her nerve was a series of anonymous telephone calls she began to receive: day after day an unknown voice would threaten her, gloating over what it promised would be her end, and mixing the foulest obscenities with the threats. Her beaming, kindly face had always reminded me of a large, red flower, perhaps a double begonia, full-blown to the sun, and supported on a stalk too short for it. To see that face now so transformed by appre-hension and pain was tragic indeed. These telephone calls, which were being received by Jews all over Vienna, were of

unspeakable cruelty: I do not believe they were systematic,
but the work of local Nazis, raw youths or disappointed wretches
of the shop-keeper class who were working off the long-accumu-
lated envy of their mean souls.   Eventually we did manage to
obtain the necessary papers for Clothilde Schweiger and her
daughter Hertha, and after staying with us at Fieldhead for
some months, in a state of euphoria induced by all things
English, she sailed for America a little time before the
war.

About ten days after the *Anschluss*, I left Vienna for Yugoslavia with a friend.   I had written as detailed notes as possible
of everything I had seen and heard, and collected eye-witness
accounts of friends and acquaintances.   I planned to work all
this up into one or two articles for the English press, but
obviously could not send it all out from Vienna itself: censorship of letters had been spasmodic and erratic under the former
régime, but under the Nazis it was rigorous.   I therefore concealed my notes within the uncut folds of a large French novel,
having cut the first fifty pages or so.   When we reached the
frontier, I planned to be reading the cut pages of the novel, and
to hope for the best.   At the last station before the border a
horde of young S.A. men and frontier police sent down from
Germany invaded the train, and proceeded to conduct an even
more meticulous examination of everything and everybody
than I had expected.   A Yugoslav couple, with a suspiciously
Jewish name, had all their suitcases emptied on to the floor of
the carriage, the linings ripped up and the coats they contained
cut open as well: the Nazis were ostensibly looking for jewels
and valuables being smuggled out, but I had the feeling they
did it from wanton spite.   While this was going on, one of the
green-uniformed frontier police came in, looked at our passports,
and then—to my horror—took the books and magazines that
my fellow-passengers were reading, and shook them to see if
they contained thousand-schilling or other currency notes . . .
the French novel was likewise seized and shaken.   Nothing,
miraculously, fell out. . . . ' What was the matter with you? '
said my friend, who had been standing in the corridor, as the
train steamed into sunny and carefree Yugoslavia; ' I thought
you were going to be sick, you looked so green in the face.'   I

assured him that I was completely restored, bursting with health in fact, and invited him to explore the French novel himself.

# 15

LITERARY critics are sometimes accused of being disappointed authors, wreaking their spite on more creative poets and novelists for the poems and novels they themselves have failed to write. But why should they not once have written themselves? The spite is sometimes all too evident, the acid of disappointment running corrosively through everything a critic writes about his contemporaries; but these are rare cases, and in general I have always thought it a good thing that critics should also be creators, in however small a way. A reviewer who has written novels himself is likely to understand from the inside the problems a novelist faces, and write of his struggles with his material with imaginative sympathy: a sympathy that will save him from that far greater bane of academic classification mania, in which a critic treats authors as an entomologist treats dead butterflies.

An editor, too, may hide a frustrated author in his soul; and in his case I do not see why the secret influences should not act altogether beneficially. Nearly all my life I have harboured a straws-in-the-hair babbler in a corner of my brain, distracting me on walks and at concerts and keeping me awake at night with his impossible imaginings and inordinate ambitions for epics, song-cycles, sonnet-sequences, poetic dramas and novel series of modern life as long as the *Comédie Humaine*. Every new country I have visited, every new experience I have been involved in, every discovery I have made in human relationships, not to mention plays and films of genius I have seen, has set this babbler to his importunate demands on me. I could not carry out more than the tiniest fraction of his dizzy schemes: but he has made me look for their achievement in others, and know an excited satisfaction when I have come across authors whom I saw at once to be engaged on realizing in their art the new arrangement of life, the new music I had dreamed of myself, but knew to be beyond my powers.

It was this, I think, above all that made me find such pleasure in my work of editing *New Writing*. I enjoyed the arranging of every volume, grouping and contrasting contributions so that what was significant in them might be more effectively brought out and the reader's attention continually stimulated; and trying, by the mixture of different kinds of poetry and prose in a certain order to give the volume as a whole a vitality that might carry the weaker pieces along with it and add another dimension to the stronger. This of course was only an ideal, never to be realized entirely to my satisfaction; but as time went on I learnt not to try to impose an intention too rigidly or hastily, but to let the material that came to hand suggest its modification; and I learnt, too, to accept the disappointments, when promised contributions that I had thought essential failed to turn up, as a challenge to make my bricks with other straws, to create other combinations. And at the back of my mind was always the belief that the way I presented the contributions might not only stimulate readers but also the authors themselves. Nor could I have done any of this effectively if I had not endlessly enjoyed corresponding and talking with authors and making them think aloud for me about their projected work.

Nevertheless, during these years of building up *New Writing*, while part of my energies were absorbed in political journalism and in preparing my travel books *Prometheus and the Bolsheviks* and *Down River*, I was determined to keep my hand in as an imaginative writer, in however small a way. I wrote my (one and only) novel, *Evil Was Abroad*, and from time to time went on with my experiments in prose poems. Poetry itself took a back place, but I did not altogether abandon it. The problem of writing poems that should express the overwhelming interest that I had acquired in the political struggle seemed to me more and more difficult as time went on. I could see plenty of examples around me, especially among the manuscripts that came in to *New Writing*, of how *not* to write it; I realized that some of the things I wanted to do were being done by *New Writing* poets with a skill that made me unwilling to compete;

and I could also see that certain solutions which the more ingenious of my contemporaries had discovered, could never be my solutions. There was a kind of silent refusal to co-operate of some power in the inmost poetic chamber of my imagination; and as nearly all the pieces I began showed only too clearly the absence of this secret influence before I had gone very far, I tore them up. In fact, it was not until several years later, in the middle of the war, when I had abandoned the belief that topical passions and apocalyptic enthusiasms could ever be the stuff of *my* poetry, that the mysterious agency began to co-operate freely again.

In spite of this, some themes that haunted me continually entered deeply enough into my mind for me to feel that the poetry that arose from them had some authenticity, and made an original, if small, contribution to the poetic expression of the time. Chief of them, most persistent, was the feeling that war was approaching more certainly with every month that passed, while something in human nature refused to accept or be disturbed by the foreboding:

> Howling about the towers April comes
> Swirling the rain-clouds over sun-washed hills,
> Where roaming couples lift their laugh-flushed faces
>   Making unreal the thought that kills. . . .

Yet all the signs were gradually piling up in the years between Dollfuss and Hitler, they were too obvious to be missed by anyone who *wanted* to look as he walked about the streets and parks of Vienna in all their spring loveliness, bringing nearer step by step what still seemed incredible in its monstrosity, in contrast to the roaming couples and the chestnut blossoms and the carefree contentment of life with life that showed itself everywhere:

> Not these alone the evidence of Spring:
> Under the light green mist that veils the trees
> Soldiers parade in pride of tank and gun,
>   By High Command dolled-up to please;
>
> Policemen, too, put off their winter coats
> Eyeing the hungry with superb disdain,
> Flaunt bulwark torsos to the food-puffed features,
>   Glimpsed through the bar's class-conscious pane.

> Tanks and police-cars throw from year to year
> A huger shadow over branch and bloom,
> And spring-bathed eyes lose suddenly their light
> Appalled by still fantastic doom. . . .

The sense of something in human life indifferent to its great secular dramas and disasters, that crept into the irony of this poem, was classically expressed by Auden in his poem on Brueghel's Crucifixion, which we published as *Palais des Beaux Arts* in the spring 1939 issue of *New Writing*. But I was also continually coming back in my mind, and trying to make sense of the indifference of *Nature*; of the smallness of the tremendous happenings, that hang the tattered banners in our chapels, in the scheme of the universe. This feeling came to me very strongly one day when I made an expedition in my car with some friends to those foothills of the Alps between the Semmering pass and Vienna, with my thoughts continually returning to some phase of the international crisis that had filled the papers the day before:

> These night-green masses in their scented air,
> The frail snow-roses, clustering as they climb
>   The cold slope's bouldered stair,
>
> All this expanse of noiseless growth, and rock,
> Would hardly stir or change, though just beyond
>   World reeled in war's first shock;
>
> Only perhaps the bombing planes would cross
> Startling the eagles as they roared for towns,
>   Vanish, like bees from moss. . . .

I remember hearing, during the war, how, after a bomb explosion in one of the parks in London, the birds would gather round the crater, with a calm eye to the main chance, looking for worms exposed by the upheaval; and what an extraordinary lift of the heart this gave me. I find it difficult to believe that, even in the atomic wars of the future, nature would not soon reassert itself—even over the ruins of Moscow or New York.

When I wrote these few poems, I had a strong feeling that I was coming back to poetry, that there were many more coming to birth in their vein; but then the *Anschluss* burst over it, and my return to the Hogarth Press absorbed my energies once more in a different direction.

# 16

WHEN Leonard and Virginia had first suggested to me that I should buy them both out of the Hogarth Press, I had been fired with the idea that I could make of it a publishing centre for all the *New Writing* authors, with Christopher, Wystan and Stephen as my fellow-directors and literary advisers; but when it became clear that to buy a fifty-per-cent partnership was as much as I could reasonably manage, the idea had, to my great regret, to lapse. It would probably have lapsed anyway, because I was beginning to realize that Christopher's restlessness was too deep-seated for me ever to be able to count on him being at hand in London for any long period. In fact, he had scarcely returned from China before he left for Europe again. Nevertheless, he and Stephen agreed to appear as my advisory fellow-editors on the title-page of the 'New Series' of *New Writing* that the Hogarth Press now began to publish; this was as much a recognition of all the advice they had given and suggestions they had made in the past as an ideal blue-print for the future.

It did not work out very well, because, as I had foreseen, editorial discussions conducted at long range by post are bound to be unsatisfactory, even if one is prepared to take the risk of sending precious manuscripts to and fro across frontiers. Stephen was more easily available; he had been especially helpful over Spanish contributors and Spanish translations, and continued to help in this direction; but even he was liable to disappear at five minutes' notice on some mysterious and urgent journey aboard. As neither Christopher nor Stephen had any stake in the new set-up, I had no right to expect them, individualists both and following obdurate lines of destiny on their own palms, to feel any particular obligations beyond those of friendship and general identity of literary interests. There were times, however, during the early months of the new phase at the Hogarth Press, when I bitterly wished it could have been otherwise. Adjustment was not easy at first: when I originally joined Leonard and Virginia in 1931, I was too young, too grateful and too enthusiastic to wish to do anything but take the lead from them; but I returned with a reputation of my own made by the success of *New Writing*, and a much clearer (and more obstinately held) idea of the kind of writers I wanted to encourage. There were inevitable checks and clashes. Leonard and I sometimes seemed to be skirmishing in a wood of incomprehension in the shadows of which I perhaps appeared to him like a bearded anarchist with a smouldering, black, European bomb I was scheming to lay at the foundations of the Hogarth Press, and he to me like an implacable Abraham with knife raised over Isaac, the promising young writer of my choice; though Virginia's presence helped to cool our fevers and bring us back to the understanding that really underlay our differences. I wrote rather dismally to Christopher in Brussels about these starting troubles and the burden of work in Mecklenburgh Square—whither the Press now emigrated.

> I do think you could lighten your work, [Christopher wrote back] and incidentally rub several people up the right way, if you threw the weight of more decisions on the shoulders of the advisory board. After all, we have our uses, if only as an alibi. For instance, you could send Wystan more poetry. And you could send me more novels. . . . You know we are only too glad to co-operate, and I sometimes feel that you wouldn't feel yourself so isolated . . . if you appealed to the board more often. Stephen, I'm sure, would respond to this policy very warmly. What he really wants is to feel that he's being useful.

Touched as I was by this offer, I felt a certain irritation too; Christopher was dreaming and pretending to me about the possibilities of us all working together. Ever since the return from China, he had seemed withdrawn into obscure preoccupations, which he shared only with Wystan. What were they hatching together, out there in Brussels, with their vague hints of another trip to America so soon after the first? I answered rather tartly:

> How, may I ask, are you to lighten my work of reading at the Press, if you use England rather as I use my Club? A few weeks a year you seem to be available, and then off on the great trek again. But would-be Hogarth authors know no close season, nor

do their beaters, the agents. . . . Of course I'd like you and Wystan and all to read and advise more, and you mustn't imagine for a moment it's because I don't trust you. Stephen, for instance, can do really brilliant poetry reports. The simple fact is, not merely that you're rarely to be found, but that people must (and most certainly should) be rewarded for reading work, and the H.P. just can't afford a heavy overhead on this item.

Nevertheless, manuscripts did from time to time go across the Channel. Poems were sent over to Wystan, and came back with shrewd comments. ' I sometimes think that Hopkins ought to be kept on a special shelf like a dirty book, and only allowed to readers who won't be ruined by him,' he wrote about one young poet's work. ' I believe I've found a really first-class novel. I long for you to read it,' I wrote to Christopher in December 1938, ' L. hasn't pronounced yet.' This was the manuscript of Henry Green's *Party Going*, which Rosamond and Goronwy Rees had persuaded the author to show me : discouraged by the failure of that youthful work of genius, *Living*, to obtain more than a moderate *succès d'estime*, he had let it lie in a drawer for some years without attempting to send it round the publishers after the first refusals. The story of Christopher and *The Memorial* was repeating itself; and I had not been so excited by any book by an author of my generation since then. ' I'm longing to hear what you have to say about Henry Green's MS.,' I wrote to Christopher a few weeks later, ' which I have just sent you. I—and many others—think it is an amazing bit of work.' Christopher was favourable; and after some hesitations by Leonard and Virginia it was accepted by the Press and published in 1939.

The arrival of Henry Green as a Hogarth author was really the beginning of a new phase. Henry had not been a *New Writing* author, he had not been connected with us before, in spite of the fact that *Living* was the solution to many of the problems that had exercised us about ' proletarian ' writing. His arrival gave me confidence in the future, I felt that a new momentum was gathering, forcing me to turn my lingering gaze from the backward scene to the discoveries that were to come.

By the time it came out Christopher and Wystan had already

left on the second trip to America, though I was still unaware
that they were going in on the ' quota ' and not merely as
tourists.    Perhaps Christopher feared too many reproachful
looks from me, and plangent letters about the betrayal of all we
had plotted together.    He had, in fact, as I came to know later,
already left Europe in spirit long before, rejecting at last the
categories of its conflicts and dimly discerning that California
might reveal itself as the home he had looked for in vain since
the break-up of his Berlin life and German circle of friends.    As
I read the letter he sent to me at the beginning of May, I felt
that our troubles were already taking on a far away, wrong-
end-of-the-telescope look :

> As soon as I'm in Hollywood, I plan to write a piece for you, about
> New York.    I have quite a lot to say about it.    Oh God, what a
> city !    The nervous breakdown expressed in terms of architecture.
> The skyscrapers are all Father-fixations.    The police-cars are
> fitted with air-raid sirens, specially designed to promote paranoia.
> The elevated railway is the circular madness.    The height of the
> buildings produces visions similar to those experienced by Ransom
> in F6.    Which reminds me that F6 is being done, quite grandly,
> some time in August.    We have written a new ending, and, alto-
> gether, I hope it may be a real success.

In the same letter, he made a startling confession :

> I myself am in the most Goddamawful mess.    I have discovered,
> what I didn't realize before, or what I wasn't till now, that I am a
> pacifist.    That's one reason why I am going out to Hollywood, to
> talk to Gerald Heard and Huxley.    Maybe I'll flatly disagree
> with them, but I have to hear their case, stated as expertly as
> possible. . . . What are you feeling?    What are your plans?
> You sound so very unperturbed, amidst all the screaming we hear
> from the distant European shores.

That letter, that confession, I saw quite clearly and sadly,
wrote the epitaph to our friendship as we had known it, as I
had imagined it continuing into the future, a friendship that
had been the pivot of my life as a writer and editor-publisher
for nearly seven years.    I remembered that in the late summer
of the year before we had spent some days together in the Isle
of Wight, territory almost as sacred to him as to the Lehmanns.
On the way down in the car he had described chapter after

chapter of a sequence of fantastic ' Mortmere ' novels to me, novels that never had been set down on paper nor, for their Rabelaisian eccentricity, ever could be : it was not so much a description as an actual reading aloud from a text that seemed clear in his mind to the last detail.  The performance was repeated during the next forty-eight hours as we walked over the heather downs towards Alum Bay or up the chalk to the Tennyson monument, but this time it was a description of a trilogy of novels, sequels to *The Lost*, the general theme of which was the fate of all the odd characters thrown out of Germany by the arrival of the Nazis and living a rootless, restless life, forever struggling with the passport and permit nightmare, from one European capital to another.  He talked them aloud to me so vividly, that I could almost have taken them down for a finished copy on the spot : all the plots, all the incidents seemed completely worked out in his mind, and they struck me as far more entertaining, more dramatic and more moving than *Sally Bowles* and *The Landauers*.  It was a continuous perform-ance, broken only when one of us pointed out a pier or a tree-clump or a lodging-house famous in the annals of my childhood or his early days with Wystan on the island ; but this trilogy was never actually written either, not one chapter or paragraph. Christopher was changing too fast ; and so was the world.  It was not long before Munich, and a feeling of doom and menace hung over the island.  The old forts were re-occupied by young soldiers, and the guns were pointing seawards again.  We knew in our hearts that it was all over, the dream that the world could be transformed before it went down into war, and all our private dreams with it.

# I 7

Times change ; and the needs, conscious and unconscious, of another age demand a different remedy, another emphasis.  It may be difficult for anyone who was too young to experience the stresses of the generation that came to manhood just at the time when the Depression of the 'thirties spread over the world, to understand how urgent our need was amongst us to break out of what we felt to be an artistic impasse, a suffocating air, and in some way in all we wrote and did help to voice the anguish of a world caught in the cogs of a pitiless economic machine, a world that demanded a drastic remedy for mass unemployment and a virile attempt to halt the forces that were making for war. We may have been wrong in many of our judgements, absurd in many of our actions; but it was impossible, if one was not to be numbered among the dullards of whom Wilfred Owen, in an even more terrible context, had said: ' By choice they made themselves immune to pity ', to escape the urgency. When D. H. Lawrence wrote: ' The whole industrial system will undergo a change. Work will be different. Class will be different. . . . I know a change is coming—and I know we must have a more generous, more human system based on the life values and not on the money values ', he was speaking prophetically for the generation of the 'thirties. Would we had all, and all the time, had the sure instinct to follow him when he cried:

> O !   Start a revolution, somebody ! . . .
> Not to install the working classes,
> But to abolish the working classes forever
> And have a world of men.

In the very year that *New Writing* was born the Spanish Civil War had broken out, and dragged us all deeper into the morass of ideological conflict, putting to the sharpest test the idealism that the advance of fascism in Central Europe had awakened in us. Long before the Nazi–Soviet pact, the last stages of that war had seen the turning of the tide: volunteers and political workers home from Spain told stories of Communist ruthlessness, cynicism and intolerance towards minorities and minority opinion, or any opinion that did not square with the Party line, that we found it difficult to credit at first, but less and less easy to excuse as they accumulated. Very soon—within a year or two—the outstanding ' political ' novels were to be those which illuminated, not the cruelties of fascism and the perversions of fascist thinking, but the equally menacing evils that fanatical left-wing idealism could lead to: Graham Greene's *The Power and the Glory*, which so brilliantly reversed the usual rôles, making the outlawed whisky-priest the hero and the police-officer, sincere and selfless guardian of the Socialist revolution, the villain; Rex Warner's *The Aerodrome*, and Arthur Koestler's *Darkness at Noon*, which were also both illustrations, in their different ways of the same theme, of how impure means can corrupt good ends and produce more suffering than the wrongs they are intended to redress. Already, however, the hang-over had begun. George Orwell was not the only disillusioned revolutionary, but the most clear-sighted and the most articulate; and his account of what happened in Catalonia and of the fate of the P.O.U.M. broke the last resistance of many who had been desperately holding out against the shock of truth. But though truth might be unpleasant, it was better than the twisted logic that condoned crimes in the name of progress and freedom; it was better late than never to realize that we had been walking beside someone whose features we had never clearly discovered until then; to see after all that we had to choose between D. H. Lawrence's change of heart and a revolution engineered by forces that did not, would never speak the language we recognized as our own.

# 18

EVERYONE who has been deeply attached to a home, a local habitation, in his early life, learns, sooner or later, that he has to find another home: not the separate home that he makes for his own family or friends apart from his parents, but a home that is independent of the four walls of a house, the apple-trees in an orchard, a particular river, seascape or woodland scene on which his early affections had fastened. This discovery is, for most of us, made painfully, especially painfully by those who are unable to dig some kind of channel for their spiritual energies *inside* the work by which they have to earn their bread and butter. There are modern philosophers who have suggested that the pain, the sense of despair caused by this homelessness is the origin (though often unconscious) of all the irrational or material fanaticisms that have bedevilled our time. The more I thought about the experience of fascism of my generation, the more truth I was ready to admit in this analysis; though it was not till rather later that I began to see its equal relevance to the experience of Communism. Until machine civilization is transformed, in some still inconceivable way, these prison break-aways of the human spirit will, one imagines, go on recurring, though always in different disguises. Lucky, in such an age, is the artist; for his art is the other home he is looking for, there beside him all the time if he has the wit to open his eyes and recognize it. But the artists are few, and many who start off with an exalted hope that they will find their home in poetry, painting, sculpture or music, are obliged, at a crucial moment when it may seem almost too late to look elsewhere, to admit that they have been mistaken. This is the moment when painters wish they had become art teachers, composers the interpreters of other people's music, and poets editors or publishers; for out of these secondary pursuits also a home can be built; not so splendid, perhaps, but potential shelter at least against the destroying winds.

When I was very young, someone brushing my hair told me that I had a double crown, and that it meant I should eat my bread in two countries. I have eaten my bread in many countries, but I like to think that the true interpretation concerned my other home. How ambiguous the road signs were: was I to go to the left, to a poet's life, or to the right, to an editor's and publisher's life? The uprooting from Vienna was a reminder of the necessity of finding that other home, of accepting the fact that I was never likely to have the fortune (that still comes to some people) of combining my spiritual and physical homes. And, very soon after, the war, dissolving bricks and stones into a puff of dust and obliterating long cherished landmarks in a blinding second, was to rub in the lesson even more ruthlessly; though it was not to deprive me of my fertile dilemma, my double crown.

# INDEX